A Pocketful of Plays

Vintage Drama Volume II

David Madden

Louisiana State University

THOMSON
™
WADSWORTH

Australia • Canada • Mexico • Singapore • Spain
United Kingdom • United States

THOMSON

™

WADSWORTH

Pocketful of Plays: Vintage Drama, Volume II
David Madden

Publisher: *Michael Rosenberg*
Acquisitions Editor: *Aron Keesbury*
Development Editor: *Marita Sermolins*
Editorial Assistant: *Cheryl Forman*
Marketing Manager: *Carrie Brandon*
Marketing Assistant: *Dawn Giovanniello*
Associate Marketing Communications
 Manager: *Patrick Rooney*
Production Assistant: *Jen Kostka*

Associate Production Project Manager:
 Karen Stocz
Manufacturing Manager: *Marcia Locke*
Permissions Editor: *Stephanie Lee*
Compositor: *Cadmus Professional
 Communications*
Text Designer: *Jeanne Calabrese*
Cover Designer: *Paula Goldstein*
Printer: *West Group*

Thomson Higher Education
25 Thomson Place
Boston, MA 02210-1202
USA

Asia (including India)
Thomson Learning
5 Shenton Way
#01-01 UIC Building
Singapore 068808

Australia/New Zealand
Thomson Learning Australia
102 Dodds Street
Southbank, Victoria 3006
Australia

Canada
Thomson Nelson
1120 Birchmount Road
Toronto, Ontario M1K 5G4
Canada

UK/Europe/Middle East/Africa
Thomson Learning
High Holborn House
50–51 Bedford Road
London WC1R 4LR
United Kingdom

Latin America
Thomson Learning
Seneca, 53
Colonia Polanco
11560 Mexico
D.F. Mexico

Student Edition: ISBN 1-4130-1133-0
Instructor's Edition: ISBN 1-4130-1914-5

Credits appear on pages 355–357, which
constitute a continuation of the copyright page.

Spain (including Portugal)
Thomson Paraninfo
Calle Magallanes, 25
28015 Madrid, Spain

Contents

A Word from the Editor to Students and Teachers

COMPARED WITH $50 FOR EACH Broadway production, admission to the theater in your mind is pleasantly affordable. Compared with huge, floppy play anthologies, the one you hold in your hand is, I hope, companionable. And you can afford it.

As with the first Vintage anthology in the Pocketful series, this selection of some of the most commonly taught plays is aimed at satisfying the need for a concise, quality collection that students will find inexpensive and that instructors will enjoy teaching.

The reception of this series has supported our original assumption that students and teachers would welcome an innovative alternative to huge anthologies, which are rarely used entirely, tend to be too bulky to carry and to handle in class, and are, above all, expensive.

A Pocketful of Plays: Vintage Drama, Volume 2 contains nine plays that research reveals to be currently among the most commonly studied in classes around the country. Four one-act plays have been included to give instructors and students the opportunity to examine the one-act play and also gives the option of teaching multiple drama selections without the time it takes to examine a longer play. Arranged chronologically, the plays give a progression of drama through history.

At Wadsworth, my Acquisitions Editor, Aron Keesbury, and my Assistant Editor, Marita Sermolins, shared my vision of this text and supported my desire to try new approaches to the creation of textbooks. They helped shape the collection from start to finish. Thanks also to Production Project Manager, Karen Stocz, whose talents made it possible to meet the design and production challenges of the text.

At Wadsworth, my Publisher, Michael Rosenberg, my Acquisitions Editor, Aron Keesbury, and my Development Editor, Marita Sermolins, shared my vision of this text and supported my desire to see this collection in the classroom. They helped shape the final collection and spent many hours reading so they could challenge me on every story included. Thanks also to my Production Project Manager, Karen Stocz, and my Designer, Jeanne Calabrese, who were instrumental in the quality production of the text. All of us are proud to introduce these authors and their stories to the classroom and hope that your discussions will be lively and insightful. We believe this text serves as evidence of the quality and promise of new writers and new fiction.

We hope that students will find the cost refreshing and that the enhancement material and annotations will help broaden their experience with the plays.

David Madden
Louisiana State University

About the Editor

Professor of Creative Writing at Louisiana State University since 1968, David Madden is a well-known writer in all the genres in the Pocketful Series. Two of his ten novels have been nominated for the Pulitzer Prize, one of which, *The Suicide's Wife,* was made into a movie. His short stories, poems, and essays have appeared in magazines ranging from *Redbook* and *Playboy* to *The Kenyon Review* and *The New Republic.* His plays have had many productions throughout the country. He is the author of many books of criticism on major American, British, and French writers and on Civil War history.

Questions That Suggest How to See and Hear a Printed Play in the Theater of Your Mind

Four one act plays and five longer plays appear in this anthology to provide you with good examples for each of the following questions.

1. Have you imagined *a theater in your* head—auditorium (place to listen) and a stage (place to see) filled with an audience—with yourself as director? [Arch or arena stage]

2. Do you have in mind the *playwright's other plays* and *the times* in which this play was first produced?

3. Have you imagined the literal and implied significance of the *title?*

4. Have you noted the ages and relationships of the *characters?*

5. What is the time and place *setting* of the play?

6. What are the most important features of the playwright's description of the *set?*

7. Have you imagined the *design of the set?*

8. Have you become confused because you did not read the playwright's *stage directions* carefully?

9. Do you see clearly where the *entrances* onto the set are located?

10. Do you imagine the effects upon the audience of the *entrances* and *exits of* the characters?

11. As director *of* the theater in your head, have *you cast the play* with actors and actresses you have seen on stage or screen?

12. As director, have you imagined the *costumes* and their significance?

13. What given *situation is* revealed early in the play?

14. How does that *situation change* as the play progresses?

15. Why do the *characters do and say* what they do and say?

16. With what *attributes or characteristics* does the playwright endow each character?

17. Who is the *protagonist* and what are his or her motivations and problem?

18. Have you traced *a series of causes and effects* throughout the play?

19. In what *conflict is* the protagonist caught up?

20. What *revelations* does the protagonist experience?

21. How does the *protagonist change* as the action progresses?

22. What is the *plot* of the play and how is it structured?

23. At what point was your *interest* most aroused?

24. Where in the *structure* of the play does the first major *turning point occur?*

25. What *action* are you watching?

26. What are the causes of *tension and suspense?*

27. What are the stages *of* the development of the *dialog you* are listening to?

28. What is the function of *exposition* in dialog of previous action?

29. What *types of characters* are being presented?

30. What *types of functions* do the characters have in the play?

31. How do the *minor characters* parallel or enhance facets of the major characters?

32. What *comparisons and contrasts* do you see and hear about the characters?

33. Which *actions* most effectively *reveal character?*

34. Which *speeches* most effectively *reveal character?*

35. What is the function of *props* (objects used by the characters), from moment to moment, in the play?

36. What is the function of *on-stage* or *offstage sound effects?*

37. What is the function of *characters who never appear* but about whom the other characters speak?

38. How does an action on stage relate dramatically to an *action offstage?*

39. What makes the *openings of scenes and acts* effective?

40. Have you imagined the effect upon the audience of the way the scenes or the *acts climax?*

41. In what sense does *a new scene* begin every time any character enters or exits?

42. Does the playwright employ the device of *foreshadowing?*

43. What effects does the playwright achieve by employing the device of *repetition?*

44. Does the playwright create a pattern of *motifs or symbols* throughout the play?

45. Does the playwright create *irony* (verbal or dramatic)?

46. What effect does the *external context* (created by events occurring before or referred to during the action of the play) have upon the various elements in the play?

47. How does the *internal context* (created cumulatively as the play develops) enable the playwright to create implications that the audience catches even though the characters may not?

48. How does the *immediate context* (at any given moment) enable the playwright to create implications that the audience catches even though the characters may not?

49. What *type of play is* the one you are reading?

50. In what ways does one *play differ* from another?

51. Have you noted any *changes in the set* from scene to scene or act to act?

52. Have you noticed any special *lighting directions* and imagined their effects?

53. What overall *theatrical image* are you looking at?

54. What are the stages in the *development of* that *theatrical image?*

55. What *overall conception* holds this play together as an experience in theater?

56. What is the play about (what is the *theme*)?

57. What *meaning* may be derived from what the play is about?

58. Does the playwright deliberately create *ambiguities* in the play?

59. Now that you have watched and listened to the play in your head, why do you want to see and hear it in a real theater?

Your responses to these questions may prove, on first reading, difficult or bewildering. On second reading, at least on reviewing your highlighting and notes, answers may come quite readily and surprisingly clearly.

Sophocles, c. 496–406 B.C.

Antigonê c. 441 B.C.

Translated by Dudley Fitts and Robert Fitzgerald

CHARACTERS

Antigonê

Ismenê

Eurydicê

Creon

Haimon

Teiresias

A Sentry

A Messenger

Chorus

SCENE.

Before the palace of Creon, king of Thebes. A Central double door, and two lateral doors. A platforms extends the length of the façade, and from this platform three steps lead down into the "orchestra," or chorus-ground.

TIME.

Dawn of the day after the repulse of the Argive army from the assault on Thebes.

PROLOGUE

(Antigonê and Ismenê enter from the central door of the palace.)

ANTIGONÊ: Ismenê, dear sister,
    You would think that we had already suffered enough
    For the curse on Oedipus.[1]
    I cannot imagine any grief
5   That you and I have not gone through. And now—
    Have they told you of the new decree of our King Creon?
ISMENÊ: I have head nothing: I know
    That two sisters lost two brothers, a double death
    In a single hour; and I know that the Argive army
10   Fled in the night; but beyond this, nothing.
ANTIGONÊ: I thought so. And this is why I wanted you
    To come out here with me. There is something we must do.
ISMENÊ: Why do you speak so strangely?
ANTIGONÊ: Listen, Ismenê:
15   Creon buried our brother Eteoclês
    With military honors, gave him a soldier's funeral,
    And it was right that he should; but Polyneicês,
    Who fought as bravely and died as miserably,—
    They say that Creon has sworn
20   No one shall bury him, no one mourn for him,
    But his body must lie in the fields, a sweet treasure
    For carrion birds to find as they search for food.
    That is what they say, and our good Creon is coming here
    To announce it publicly; and the penalty—
25   Stoning to death in the public square!
                                    There it is,
    And now you can prove what you are:
    A true sister, or a traitor to your family.

---

[1] *Oedipus:* Once King of Thebes, was the father of Antigonê and Ismenê, and of
their brothers Polyneicês and Eteoclês. Oedipus unwittingly killed his father,
Laïos, and married his own mother, Iocastê. When he learned what he had
done, he blinded himself and Thebes. Eteoclês and Polyneicês quarreled;
Polyneicês was driven out but returned to assault Thebes. In the battle each
brother killed the other; Creon became king and ordered that Polyneicês be
left to rot unburied on the battlefield as a traitor.

ISMENÊ: Antigonê, you are mad! What could I possibly do?

ANTIGONÊ: You must decide whether you will help me or not.

30   ISMENÊ: I do not understand you. Help you in what?

ANTIGONÊ: Ismenê. I am going to bury him. Will you come?

ISMENÊ: Bury him! You have just said the new law forbids it.

ANTIGONÊ: He is my brother. And he is your brother, too.

ISMENÊ: But think of the danger! Think what Creon will do!

35   ANTIGONÊ: Creon is not strong enough to stand in my way.

ISMENÊ: Ah sister!

> Oedipus died, everyone hating him
> For what his own search brought to light, his eyes
> Ripped out by his own hand; and Jocastê died,
40   His mother and wife at once: she twisted the cords
> That strangled her life, and our two brothers died,
> Each killed by the other's sword. And we are left:
> But oh, Antigonê,
> Think how much more terrible than these
45   Our own death would be if we should go against Creon
> And do what he has forbidden! We are only women,
> We cannot fight with men, Antigonê!
> The law is strong, we must give in to the law
> In this thing, and in worse. I beg the Dead
50   To forgive me, but I am helpless: I must yield
> To those in authority. And I think it is dangerous business
> To be always meddling.

ANTIGONÊ: If that is what you think,
> I should not want you, even if you asked to come.
> You have made your choice, you can be what you want to be.
55   But I will bury him; and if I must die,
> I say that this crime is holy: I shall lie down
> With him in death, and I shall be as dear
> To him as he to me.
>   It is the dead,
> Not the living, who make the longest demands:
60   We die for ever. . . .
>   You may do as you like.
> Since apparently the laws of the gods mean nothing to you.

ISMENÊ: They mean a great deal to me; but I have no strength

To break laws that were made for the public good.

ANTIGONÊ: That must be your excuse, I suppose. But as for me,

65   I will bury the brother I love.

ISMENÊ: Antigonê,

I am so afraid for you!

ANTIGONÊ: You need not be:

You have yourself to consider, after all.

ISMENÊ: But no one must hear of this, you must tell no one!

70   I will keep it a secret, I promise!

ANTIGONÊ: O tell it! Tell everyone!

Think how they'll hate you when it all comes out

If they learn that you knew about it all the time!

ISMENÊ: So fiery! You should be cold with fear.

ANTIGONÊ: Perhaps. But I am doing only what I must.

75   ISMENÊ: But can you do it? I say that you cannot.

ANTIGONÊ: Very well: when my strength gives out,

      I shall do no more.

ISMENÊ: Impossible things should not be tried at all.

ANTIGONÊ: Go away, Ismenê:

80   I shall be hating you soon, and the dead will too,

For your words are hateful. Leave me my foolish plan:

I am not afraid of the danger; if it means death,

It will not be the worst of deaths—death without honor.

ISMENÊ: Go then, if you feel that you must.

85   You are unwise,

But a loyal friend indeed to those who love you.

(Exit into the palace. Antigonê goes off, left. Enter the Chorus.)

PÁRODOS

Strophe I

CHORUS: Now the long blade of the sun, lying

      Level east to west, touches with glory

      Thebes of the Seven Gates. Open, unlidded

90   Eye of golden day! O marching light

      Across the eddy and rush of Dircê's stream,[2]

---

[2] *Dircê's stream:* A stream west of Thebes.

Striking the white shields of the enemy
Thrown headlong backward from the blaze of morning!

CHORAGOS:[3] Polyneicês their commander
95   Roused them with windy phrases,
He the wild eagle screaming
Insults above our land,
His wings their shields of snow,
His crest their marshalled helms.

Antistrophe 1

100   CHORAGOS: Against our seven gates in a yawning ring
The famished spears came onward in the night:
But before his jaws were sated with our blood,
Or pinefire took the garland of our towers,
He was thrown back; and as he turned, great Thebes—
105   No tender victim for his noisy power—
Rose like a dragon behind him, shouting war.

CHORAGOS: For God hates utterly
The bray of bragging tongues;
And when he beheld their smiling,
110   Their swagger of golden helms,
The frown of his thunder blasted
Their first man from our walls.

Strophe 2

CHORUS: We heard his shout of triumph high in the air
Turn to a scream; far out in a flaming arc
115   He fell with his windy torch, and the earth struck him.
And other storming in fury no less than his
Found shock of death in the dusty joy of battle.

CHORAGOS: Seven captains at seven gates
Yielded their clanging arms to the god
120   That bends the battle-line and breaks it.
These two only, brothers in blood,
Face to face in matchless rage.

[3] *Choragos:* Leader of the Chorus.

Mirroring each the other's death,
Clashed in long combat.

Antistrophe 2

125 CHORUS: But now in the beautiful morning of victory
Let Thebes of the many chariots sing for joy!
With hearts for dancing we'll take leave of war:
Our temples shall be sweet with hymns of praise,
And the long nights shall echo with our chorus.

SCENE I

CHORAGOS: But now at last our new King is coming:
Creon of Thebes, Menoikeus' son
In this auspicious dawn of his reign
What are the new complexities

5   That shifting Fate has woven for him?
What is his counsel? Why has he summoned
The old men to hear him?

(*Enter Creon from the palace, center. He addresses the Chorus from the top step.*)

CREON: Gentlemen: I have the honor to inform you that our
Ship of State, which recent storms have threatened to

10   destroy, has come safely to harbor at last, guided by the
merciful wisdom of Heaven. I have summoned you here
this morning because I know that I can depend upon you:
your devotion to King Laïos was absolute; you never hesi-
tated in your duty to our late ruler Oedipus; and when

15   Oedipus died, your loyalty was transferred to his children. Unfortunately, as you know, his two sons, the
princes Eteoclês and Polyneicês, have killed each other in
battle; and I, as the next in blood, have succeeded to the
full power of the throne.

20   I am aware, of course, that no Ruler can expect complete
loyalty from his subjects until he has been tested in office.
Nevertheless, I say to you at the very outset that I have nothing but contempt for the kind of Governor who is afraid,

for whatever reason, to follow the course that he knows is
25   best for the State; and as for the man who sets private
friendship above the public welfare,—I have no use for him,
either. I call God to witness that if I saw my country headed
for ruin, I should not be afraid to speak out plainly; and I
need hardly remind you that I would never have any dealings
30   with an enemy of the people. No one values friendship more
highly than I: but we must remember that friends made at
the risk of wrecking our Ship are not real friends at all.

These are my principles, at any rate, and that is why I
have made the following decision concerning the sons of
35   Oedipus: Eteoclês, who died as a man should die, fighting for his country, is to be buried with full military honors, with all the ceremony that is usual when the greatest
heroes die; but his brother Polyneicês, who broke his
exile to come back with fire and sword against his native
40   city and the shrines of his fathers' gods, whose one idea
was to spill the blood of his blood and sell his own people
into slavery—Polyneicês, I say, is to have no burial: no
man is to touch him or say the least prayer for him; he
shall lie on the plain, unburied; and the birds and the
45   scavenging dogs can do with him whatever they like.

This is my command, and you can see the wisdom behind
it. As long as I am King, no traitor is going to be honored
with the loyal man. But whoever shows by word and deed
that he is on the side of the State—he shall have my respect
50   while he is living and my reverence when he is dead.
CHORAGOS: If that is your will, Creon son of Menoikeus,
You have the right to enforce it: we are yours.
CREON: That is my will. Take care that you do your part.
CHORAGOS: We are old men: let the younger ones carry it out.
55   CREON: I do not mean that: the sentries have been appointed.
CHORAGOS: Then what is it that you would have us do?
CREON: You will give no support to whoever breaks this law.
CHORAGOS: Only a crazy man is in love with death!
CREON: And death it is; yet money talks, and the wisest
60   Have sometimes been known to count a few coins too many.

Enter Sentry from left.

SENTRY: I'll not say that I'm out of breath from running,
    King, because, every time I stopped to think about what I
    have to tell you, I felt like going back. And all the time a
    voice kept saying, "You fool, don't you know you're walk-
65   ing straight into trouble?"; and then another voice: "Yes,
    but if you let somebody else get the news to Creon first, it
    will be even worse than that for you!" But good sense won
    out, at lest I hope it was good sense, and here I am with a
    story that makes no sense at all; but I'll tell it anyhow,
70   because, as they say, what's going to happen's going to
    happen and—
CREON: Come to the point. What have you to say?
SENTRY: I did not do it. I did not see who did it. You must not
    punish me for what someone else has done.
75 CREON: A comprehensive defense! More effective, perhaps, if I
    knew its purpose. Come: what is it?
SENTRY: A dreadful thing . . . I don't know how to put it—
CREON: Out with it!
SENTRY: Well, then;
    The dead man—

         Polyneicês—

(Pause: The Sentry is overcome, fumbles for words. Creon waits impassively.)

           Out there—

              someone,—

80   New dust on the slimy flesh!

(Pause. No sign from Creon.)

    Someone has given it burial that way, and Gone. . . .

(Long pause. Creon finally speaks with deadly control.)

CREON: And the man who dared do this?
SENTRY: I swear I
    Do not know! You must believe me!

                 Listen:
    The ground was dry, not a sign of digging, no,
85   Not a wheeltrack in the dust, no trace of anyone.

It was when they relieved us this morning: and one of them,
The corporal, pointed to it.

                     There it was,

The strangest—

             Look:

The body, just mounded over with light dust: you see?

90   Not buried really, but as if they'd covered it
Just enough for the ghost's peace. And no sign
Of dogs or any wild animal that had been there.

And then what a scene there was! Every man of us
Accusing the other: we all proved the other man did it,

95   We all had proof that we could not have done it.
We were ready to take hot iron in our hands,
Walk through fire, swear by all the gods,
It was not I!
I do not know who it was, but it was not I!

(Creon's rage has been mounting steadily, but the Sentry is too intent upon his story to notice it.)

100   And then, when this came to nothing, someone said
A thing that silenced us and made us stare
Down at the ground: you had to be told the news,
And one of us had to do it! We threw the dice,
And the bad luck fell to me. So here I am,

105   No happier to be here than you are to have me:
Nobody likes the man who brings bad news.

CHORAGOS: I have been wondering, King: can it be that the
    gods have done this?

CREON: (*Furiously*) Stop!

110   Must you doddering wrecks
Go out of your heads entirely? "The gods"!
Intolerable!
The gods favor this corpse? Why? How had he served them?
Tried to loot their temples, burn their images,

110   Yes, and the whole State, and its laws with it!
Is it your senile opinion that the gods love to honor bad men?
A pious thought!—

                No, from the very beginning

There have been those who have whispered together,
Stiff-necked anarchists, putting their head together,
120   Scheming against me in alleys. These are the men
And they have bribed my own guard to do this thing.
(*Sententiously.*) Money!
There's nothing in the world so demoralizing as money.
Down go your cities,
125   Homes gone, men gone, honest hearts corrupted.
Crookedness of all kinds, and all for money!
(*To Sentry*)   But you—
I swear by God and by the throne of God,
The man who has done this thing shall pay for it!
130   Find that man, bring him here to me, or your death
Will be the least of your problems: I'll string you up
Alive, and there will be certain ways to make you
Discover your employer before you die;
And the process may teach you a lesson you seem to have
    missed:
135   The dearest profit is sometimes all too dear:
That depends on the source. Do you understand me?
A fortune won is often misfortune.
SENTRY: King, may I speak?
CREON: Your very voice distresses me.
140   SENTRY: Are you sure that it is my voice, and not your conscience?
CREON: By God, he wants to analyze me now!
SENTRY: It is not what I say, but what has been done, that hurts
    you.
CREON: You talk too much.
SENTRY: Maybe; but I've done nothing.
145   CREON: Sold your soul for some silver: that's all you've done.
SENTRY: How dreadful it is when the right judge judges wrong!
CREON: Your figures of speech
May entertain you now; but unless you bring me the man,
You will get little profit from them in the end.

(*Exit Creon into the palace.*)

150   SENTRY: "Bring me the man"—!
I'd like nothing better than bringing him the man!

But bring him or not, you have seen the last of me here.
At any rate, I am safe!

(*Exit Sentry.*)

ODE I

Strophe 1

CHORUS: Numberless are the world's wonders, but not
155   More wonderful than man; the stormgray sea
        Yields to his prows, the huge crests bear him high;
        Earth, holy and inexhaustible, is graven
        With shining furrows where his plows have gone
        Year after year, the timeless labor of stallions.

Antistrophe 1

160   The lightboned birds and beasts that cling to cover,
        The lithe fish lighting their reaches of dim water,
        All are taken, tamed in the net of his mind;
        The lion on the hill, the wild horse windy-maned,
        Resign to him; and his blunt yoke has broken
165   The sultry shoulders of the mountain bull.

Strophe 2

        Words also, and thought as rapid as air,
        He fashions to his good use; statecraft is his,
        And his the skill that deflects the arrows of snow,
        The spears of winter rain: from every wind
170   He has made himself secure—from all but one:
        In the late wind of death he cannot stand.

Antistrophe 2

        O clear intelligence, force beyond all measure!
        O fate of man, working both good and evil!
        When the laws are kept, how proudly his city stands!
175   When the laws are broken, what of his city then?
        Never may the anārchic man find rest at my hearth,
        Never be it said that my thoughts are his thoughts.

SCENE II

(*Reenter Sentry leading Antigonê.*)

CHORAGOS: What does this mean? Surely this captive woman
    Is the Princess, Antigonê. Why should she be taken?
SENTRY: Here is the one who did it! We caught her
    In the very act of burying him.—Where is Creon?
5 CHORAGOS: Just coming from the house.

(*Enter Creon, center.*)

CREON: What has happened?
    Why have you come back so soon?
SENTRY: (*Expansively*)   O King,
    A man should never be too sure of anything:
10   I would have sworn
    That you'd not see me here again: your anger
    Frightened me so, and the things you threatened me with;
    But how could I tell then
    That I'd be able to solve the case so soon?
15   No dice-throwing this time: I was only too glad to come!
    Here is this woman. She is the guilty one:
    We found her trying to bury him.
    Take her, then; question her; judge her as you will.
    I am through with the whole thing now, and glad of it.
20 CREON: But this is Antigonê! Why have you brought her here?
SENTRY: She was burying him, I tell you!
CREON: (*Severely*)   Is this the truth?
SENTRY: I saw her with my own eyes. Can I say more?
CREON: The details: come, tell me quickly!
25 SENTRY: It was like this:
    After those terrible threats of yours, King,
    We went back and brushed the dust away from the body.
    The flesh was soft by now, and stinking,
    So we sat on a hill to windward and kept guard.
30   No napping this time! We kept each other awake.
    But nothing happened until the white round sun
    Whirled in the center of the round sky over us;
    Then, suddenly,

A storm of dust roared up from the earth, and the sky
Went out, the plain vanished with all its trees
In the stinging dark. We closed our eyes and endured it.
The whirlwind lasted a long time, but it passed;
And then we looked, and there was Antigonê!
I have seen
A mother bird come back to a stripped nest, heard
Her crying bitterly a broken note or two
For the young ones stolen. Just so, when this girl
Found the bare corpse, and all her love's work wasted,
She wept, and cried on heaven to damn the hands
That had done this thing.

       And then she brought more dust
And sprinkled wine three times for her brother's ghost.
We ran and took her at once. She was not afraid,
Not even when we charged her with what she had done.
She denied nothing.

        And this was a comfort to me,

50 And some uneasiness: for it is a good thing
To escape from death, but it is no great pleasure
To bring death to a friend.

         Yet I always say
There is nothing so comfortable as your own safe skin!
CREON: (*Slowly, dangerously*) And you, Antigonê,

55 You with your head hanging, —do you confess this thing?
ANTIGONÊ: I do. I deny nothing.
CREON: (*To Sentry*)   You may go.

(*Exit Sentry.*)

  (*To Antigonê*) Tell me, tell me briefly:
Had you heard my proclamation touching this matter?

60 ANTIGONÊ: It was public. Could I help hearing it?
CREON: And yet you dared defy the law.
ANTIGONÊ: I dared.
It was not God's proclamation. That final Justice
That rules the world below makes no such laws.

65 Your edict, King, was strong.

But all your strength is weakness itself against
The immortal unrecorded laws of God:
They are not merely now: they were, and shall be,
Operative for ever, beyond man utterly.

70   I knew I must die, even without your decree:
I am only mortal. And if I must die
Now, before it is my time to die,
Surely this is no hardship: can anyone
Living, as I live, with evil all about me,

75   Think Death less than a friend? This death of mine
Is of no importance; but if I had left my brother
Lying in death unburied, I should have suffered.
Now I do not.
               You smile at me. Ah Creon,
Think me a fool, if you like; but it may well be

80   That a fool convicts me of folly.

CHORAGOS: Like father, like daughter: both headstrong, deaf
    to reason!
She has never learned to yield.

CREON: She has much to learn.
The inflexible heart breaks first, the toughest iron

85   Cracks first, and the wildest horses bend their necks
At the pull of the smallest curb.
                    Pride? In a slave?
This girl is guilty of a double insolence,
Breaking the given laws and boasting of it.
Who is the man here,

90   She or I, if this crime goes unpunished?
Sister's child, or more than sister's child,
Or closer yet in blood—she and her sister
Win bitter death for this!
(*To servants*)   Go, some of you,

95   Arrest Ismenê: I accuse her equally.
Bring her: you will find her sniffling in the house there.
Her mind's a traitor: crimes kept in the dark
Cry for light, and the guardian brain shudders;
But how much worse than this

100   Is brazen boasting of barefaced anarchy!

ANTIGONÊ: Creon, what more do you want than my death?

CREON: Nothing.

      That gives me everything.

ANTIGONÊ: Then I beg you: kill me

      This talking is a great weariness: your words

105   Are distasteful to me, and I am sure that mine

      Seem so to you. And yet they should not seem so:

      I should have praise and honor for what I have done.

      All these men here would praise me

      Were their lips not frozen shut with fear of you.

110   (*Bitterly*) Ah the good fortune of kings,

      Licensed to say and do whatever they please!

CREON: You are alone here in that opinion.

ANTIGONÊ: No, they are with me. But they keep their tongues
      in leash.

CREON: Maybe. But you are guilty, and they are not.

115 ANTIGONÊ: There is no guilt in reverence for the dead.

CREON: But Eteoclês—was he not your brother too?

ANTIGONÊ: My brother too.

CREON: And you insult his memory?

ANTIGONÊ: (*Softly*) The dead man would not say that I insult it.

120 CREON: He would: for you honor a traitor as much as him.

ANTIGONÊ: His own brother, traitor or not, and equal in blood.

CREON: He made war on his country. Eteoclês defended it.

ANTIGONÊ: Nevertheless, there are honors due all the dead.

CREON: But not the same for the wicked as for the just.

125 ANTIGONÊ: Ah Creon, Creon,

      Which of us can say what the gods hold wicked?

CREON: An enemy is an enemy, even dead.

ANTIGONÊ: Its is my nature to join in love, not hate.

CREON: (*Finally losing patience*) Go join them then; if you must
      have your love,

      Find it in hell!

CHORAGOS: But see, Ismenê comes:

(*Enter Ismenê, guarded.*)

130   Those tears are sisterly, the cloud

That shadows her eyes rains down gentle sorrow.

CREON: You too, Ismenê,

Snake in my ordered house, sucking my blood
Stealthily—and all the time I never knew

135 That these two sisters were aiming at my throne!

Ismenê,

Do you confess your share in this crime, or deny it?
Answer me.

ISMENÊ: Yes, if she will let me say so. I am guilty.

ANTIGONÊ: (Coldly) No, Ismenê. You have no right to say so.

140 You would not help me; and I will not have you help me.

ISMENÊ: But now I know what you meant: and I am here
To join you, to take my share of punishment.

ANTIGONÊ: The dead man and the gods who rule the dead
Know whose act this was. Words are not friends.

145 ISMENÊ: Do you refuse me, Antigonê? I want to die with you:
I too have a duty that I must discharge to the dead.

ANTIGONÊ: You shall not lessen my death by sharing it.

ISMENÊ: What do I care for life when you are dead?

ANTIGONÊ: Ask Creon. You're always hanging on his opinions.

150 ISMENÊ: You are laughing at me. Why, Antigonê?

ANTIGONÊ: It's a joyless laughter, Ismenê.

ISMENÊ: But can I do nothing?

ANTIGONÊ: Yes. Save yourself. I shall not envy you.
There are those who will praise you; I shall have honor, too.

155 ISMENÊ: But we are equally guilty!

ANTIGONÊ: No more, Ismenê.
You are alive, but I belong to Death.

CREON: (To the Chorus) Gentlemen, I beg you to observe these girls:
One has just now lost her mind; the other,

160 It seems, has never had a mind at all.

ISMENÊ: Grief teaches the steadiest minds to waver, King.

CREON: Yours certainly did, when you assumed guilt with the guilty!

ISMENÊ: But how could I go on living without her?

CREON: You are.
She is already dead.

165 ISMENÊ: But your own son's bride!

CREON: There are places enough for him to push his plow.

I want no wicked women for my sons!

ISMENÊ: O dearest Haimon, how your father wrongs you!

CREON: I've had enough of your childish talk of marriage!

170 CHORAGOS: Do you really intend to steal this girl from your son?

CREON: No; Death will do that for me.

CHORAGOS: Then she must die?

CREON: (*Ironically*) You dazzle me.

                    —But enough of this talk!

(*To Guards*) You, there, take them away and guard them well:

175 For they are but women, and even brave men run

When they see Death coming.

(*Exeunt Ismenê, Antigonê, and Guards.*)

ODE II

Strophe 1

CHORUS: Fortunate is the man who has never tasted

God's vengeance!

Where once the anger of heaven has struck, that house is

shaken

For ever: damnation rises behind each child

5 Like a wave cresting out of the black northeast,

When the long darkness under sea roars up

And bursts drumming death upon the windwhipped sand.

Antistrophe 1

I have seen this gathering sorrow from time long past

Loom upon Oedipus' children: generation from generation

10 Takes the compulsive rage of the enemy god.

So lately this last flower of Oedipus' line

Drank the sunlight! But now a passionate word

And a handful of dust have closed up all its beauty.

Strophe 2

What mortal arrogance

15 Transcends the wrath of Zeus?

Sleep cannot lull him nor the effortless long months

Of the timeless gods: but he is young for ever,

And his house is the shining day of his Olympos.

All that is and shall be,
20   And all the past, is his.
No pride on earth is free of the curse of heaven.

Antistrophe 2

The straying dreams of men
        May bring them ghosts of joy:
But as they drowse, the waking embers burn them;
25   Or they walk with fixed eyes, as blind men walk.
But the ancient wisdom speaks for our own times:
        Fate works most for woe
        With Folly's fairest show
Man's little pleasure is the spring of sorrow.

SCENE III

CHORAGOS: But there is Haimon, King, the last of all your sons.
    It is grief for Antigonê that brings him here,
    And bitterness at being robbed of his bride?

(*Enter Haimon.*)

CREON: We shall soon see, and no need of diviners.
                                                —Son,
5   You have heard my final judgment on that girl:
    Have you come here hating me, or have you come
    With deference and with love, whatever I do?
HAIMON: I am your son, father. You are my guide.
    You make things clear for me, and I obey you.
    No marriage means more to me than your continuing
10   wisdom.
CREON: Good. That is the way to behave: subordinate
    Everything else, my son, to your father's will.
    This is what a man prays for, that he may get
    Sons attentive and dutiful in his house,
15   Each one hating his father's enemies,
    Honoring his father's friends. But if his sons
    Fail him, if they turn out unprofitably,
    What has be fathered but trouble for himself

And amusement for the malicious?

So you are right

20 Not to lose your head over this woman.

Your pleasure with her would soon grow cold, Haimon,

And then you'd have a hellcat in bed and elsewhere.

Let her find her husband in Hell!

Of all the people in this city, only she

25 Has had contempt for my law and broken it.

Do you want me to show myself weak before the people?

Or to break my sworn word? No, and I will not.

The woman dies.

I suppose she'll plead "family ties." Well, let her

30 If I permit my own family to rebel,

How shall I earn the world's obedience?

Show me the man who keeps his house in hand.

He's fit for public authority.

I'll have no dealings.

With lawbreakers, critics of the government:

35 Whoever is chosen to govern should be obeyed—

Must be obeyed, in all things, great and small,

Just and unjust! O Haimon,

The man who knows how to obey, and that man only,

Knows how to give commands when the time comes.

40 You can depend on him, no matter how fast

The spears come: he's a good soldier, he'll stick it out.

Anarchy, anarchy! Show me a greater evil!

This is why cities tumble and the great houses rain down,

This is what scatters armies!

45 No, no: good lives are made so by discipline

We keep the laws then, and the lawmakers,

And no woman shall seduce us. If we must lose,

Let's lose to a man, at least! Is a woman stronger than we?

CHORAGOS: Unless time has rusted my wits,

50 What you say, King, is said with point and dignity.

HAIMON: (*Boyishly earnest*) Father:

Reason is God's crowning gift to man, and you are right

To warn me against losing mine. I cannot say—

I hope that I shall never want to say!—that you

55 Have reasoned badly. Yet there are other men
Who can reason, too; as their opinions might be helpful.
You are not in a position to know everything
That people say or do, or what they feel:
Your temper terrifies—everyone
60 Will tell you only what you like to hear.
But I, at any rate, can listen; and I have heard them
Muttering and whispering in the dark about this girl.
They say no woman has ever, so unreasonably,
Died so shameful a death for a generous act:
65 "She covered her brother's body. Is this indecent?
She kept him from dogs and vultures. Is this a crime?
Death?—she should have all the honor that we can give her!"

This is the way they talk out there in the city.

You must believe me:
Nothing is closer to me than your happiness.
70 What could be closer? Must not any son
Value his father's fortune as his father does his?
I beg you, do not be unchangeable:
Do not believe that you alone can be right.
The man who thinks that,
75 The man who maintains that only he has the power
To reason correctly, the gift to speak, the soul—
A man like that, when you know him, turns out empty.
It is not reason never to yield to reason!

In flood time you can see how some trees bend,
80 And because they bend, even their twigs are safe,
While stubborn trees are torn up, roots and all
And the same thing happens in sailing:
Make you sheet fast, never slacken,—and over you go,
Head over heels and under: and there's your voyage.
85 Forget you are angry! Let yourself be moved!
I know I am young; but please let me say this:
The ideal condition
Would be, I admit, that men should be right by instinct;

But since we are all too likely to go astray,

90   The reasonable thing is to learn from those who can teach.

CHORAGOS: You will do well to listen to him, King,

If what he says is sensible. And you, Haimon,

Must listen to your father.—Both speak well.

CREON: You consider it right for a man of my years and
experience

95   To go to school to a boy?

HAIMON: It is not right

If I am wrong. But if I am young, and right,

What does my age matter?

CREON: You think it right to stand up for an anarchist?

HAIMON: Not at all. I pay no respect to criminals.

100   CREON: Then she is not a criminal?

HAIMON: The City would deny it, to a man.

CREON: And the City proposes to teach me how to rule?

HAIMON: Ah. Who is it that's talking like a boy now?

CREON: My voice is the one voice giving orders in this City!

105   HAIMON: It is no City if it takes orders from one voice.

CREON: The state is the King!

HAINON: Yes, if the State is a desert.

(*Pause.*)

CREON: This boy, it seems, had sold out to a woman.

HAIMON: If you are a woman: my concern is only for you.

110   CREON: So? Your "concern"! In a public brawl with your father!

HAIMON: How about you, in a public brawl with justice?

CREON: With justice, when all that I do is within my rights?

HAIMON: You have no right to trample on God's right.

CREON: (*Completely out of control*)

Fool, adolescent fool! Taken in by a woman!

115   HAIMON: You'll never see me taken in by anything vile.

CREON: Every word you say is for her!

HAIMON: (*Quietly, darkly*)   And for you.

And for me. And for the gods under the earth.

CREON: You'll never marry her while she lives.

HAIMON: Then she must die.— But her death will cause

120   another.

CREON: Another?

Have you lost your senses? Is this an open threat?

HAIMON: There is no threat is speaking to emptiness.

CREON: I swear you'll regret this superior tone of yours!

125   You are the empty one!

HAIMON: If you were not my father.

I'd say you were perverse.

CREON: You girl-struck fool, don't play at words with me!

HAIMON: I am sorry. You prefer silence.

CREON: Now, by God—

I swear, by all the gods in heaven above us,

130   You'll watch it, I swear you shall!

(*To the servants.*)   Bring her out!

Bring the woman out! Let her die before his eyes!

Here, this instant, with her bridegroom beside her!

HAIMON: Not here, no; she will not die here, King.

135   And you will never see my face again.

Go on raving as long as you've a friend to endure you.

(*Exit Haimon.*)

CHORAGOS: Gone, gone.

Creon, a young man in a rage is dangerous!

CREON: Let him do, or dream to do; more than a man can.

140   He shall not save these girls from death.

CHORAGOS: These girls?

You have sentenced them both?

CREON: No, you are right.

I will not kill the one whose hands are clean.

CHORAGOS: But Antigonê?

CREON: (*Somberly*)   I will carry her far away

Out there in the wilderness, and lock her

145   Living in a vault of stone. She shall have food,

As the custom is, to absolve the State of her death.

And there let her pray to the gods of hell:

They are her only gods:

Perhaps they will show her an escape from death,

150 Or she may learn,
                    though late,
      That piety shown the dead is piety in vain.

(*Exit Creon.*)

ODE III

Strophe

CHORUS: Love unconquerable
      Waster of rich men, keeper
      Of warm lights and all-night vigil
      In the soft face of a girl:
5   Sea-wanderer, forest-visitor!
      Even the pure Immortals cannot escape you,
      And the mortal man, in his one day's dusk,
      Trembles before your glory.

Antistrophe

      Surely you swerve upon ruin
10   The just man's consenting heart,
      As here you have made bright anger
      Strike between father and son—
      And none has conquered but Love!
      A girl's glance working the will of heaven:
15   Pleasure to her alone who mocks us,
      Merciless Aphroditê.[4]

SCENE IV

CHORAGOS: (*As Antigonê enters guarded*) But I can no longer stand
      in awe of this,
      Nor, seeing what I see, keep back my tears.
      Here is Antigonê, passing to that chamber
      Where all find sleep at last.

[4] *Aphrodite:* Goddess of love.

Strophe 1

5 ANTIGONÊ: Look upon me, friends, and pity me
      Turning back at the night's edge to say
      Good-by to the sun that shines for me no longer;
      Now sleepy Death
      Summons me down to Acheron,[5] that cold shore:
10   There is no bridesong there, nor any music.
    CHORUS: Yet not unpraised, not without a kind of honor,
      You walk at last into the underworld;
      Untouched by sickness, broken by no sword.
      What woman has ever found your way to death?

Antistrophe 1

15 ANTIGONÊ: How often I have heard the story of Niobê,[6]
      Tantalos' wretched daughter, how the stone
      Clung fast about her, ivy-close: and they say
      The rain falls endlessly
      And sifting soft snow; her tears are never done.
20   I feel the loneliness of her death in mine.
    CHORUS: But she was born of heaven, and you
      Are woman, woman-born. If her death is yours,
      A mortal woman's, is this not for you
      Glory in our world and in the world beyond?

Strophe 2

25 ANTIGONÊ: You laugh at me. Ah, friends, friends
      Can you not wait until I am dead? O Thebes,
      O men many-charioted, in love with Fortune,
      Dear springs of Dircê, sacred Theban grove,
      Be witnesses for me, denied all pity,
30   Unjustly judged! and think a word of love
      For her whose path turns
      Under dark earth, where there are no more tears.

[5] *Acheron:* A river of the underworld, which was ruled by Hades.
[6] *Niobê:* Niobê boasted of her numerous children, provoking Leto, the mother of Apollo, to destroy them. Niobê wept profusely, and finally was turned to stone on Mount Sipylus, whose streams are her tears.

CHORUS: You have passed beyond human daring and come at last
Into a place of stone where Justice sits.
35   I cannot tell
What shape of your father's guilt appears in this.

Antistrophe 2

ANTIGONÊ: You have touched it as last: that bridal bed
Unspeakable, horror of son and mother mingling:
Their crime, infection of all our family!
40   O Oedipus, father and brother!
Your marriage strikes from the grave to murder mine.
I have been a stranger here in my own land:
All my life
The blasphemy of my birth has followed me.
45 CHORUS: Reverence is a virtue, but strength
Lives in established law: that must prevail.
You have made your choice,
Your death is the doing of your conscious hand.

Epode

ANTIGONÊ: Then let me go, since all your words are bitter,
50   And the very light of the sun is cold to me.
Lead me to my vigil, where I must have
Neither love nor lamentation; no song, but silence.
(*Creon interrupts impatiently.*)
CREON: If dirges and planned lamentations could put off death,
Men would be singing for ever.
55   (*To the servants*)   Take her, go!
You know your orders: take her to the vault
And leave her alone there. And if she lives or dies,
That's her affair, not ours: our hands are clean.
ANTIGONÊ: O tomb, vaulted bride-bed in eternal rock,
60   Soon I shall be with my own again
Where Persephonê[7] welcomes the thin ghosts underground:
And I shall see my father again, and you, mother,

---

[7] *Persephonê:* Queen of the underworld.

And dearest Polyneicês—

                dearest indeed

To me, since it was my hand

65 That washed him clean and poured and ritual wine:

And my reward is death before my time!

And yet, as men's hearts know, I have done no wrong,

I have not sinned before God. Or if I have,

I shall know the truth in death. But if the guilt

70 Lies upon Creon who judged me, then, I pray,

May his punishment equal my own.

CHORAGOS: O passionate heart,

Unyielding, tormented still by the same winds!

CREON: Her guards shall have good cause to regret their delaying.

ANTIGONÊ: Ah! That voice is like the voice of death!

75 CREON: I can give you no reason to think you are mistaken.

ANTIGONÊ: Thebes, and you my fathers' gods,

And rulers of Thebes, you see me now, the last

Unhappy daughter of a line of kings,

Your kings, led away to death. You will remember

80 What things I suffer, and at what men's hands,

Because I would not transgress the laws of heaven.

(*To the Guards, simply*) Come: let us wait no longer.

(*Exit Antigonê, left, guarded.*)

ODE IV

Strophe I

CHORUS: All Danaê's beauty was locked away

In a brazen cell where the sunlight could not come:

A small room, still as any grave, enclosed her.

Yet she was a princess too,

5 And Zeus in a rain of gold poured love upon her.

O child, child,

No power in wealth or war

Or tough sea-blackened ships

Can prevail against untiring Destiny!

Antigonê | 27

Antistrophe I

10   And Dryas' son [8] also, that furious king,
      Bore the god's prisoning anger for his pride:
      Sealed up by Dionysos in deaf stone,
      His madness died among echoes.
      So at the last he learned what dreadful power
15   His tongue had mocked:
      For he had profaned the revels,
      And fired the wrath of the nine
      Implacable Sisters[9] that love the sound of the flute.

Strophe 2

      And old men tell a half-remembered tale
20   Of horror where a dark ledge splits the sea
      And a double surf beats on the grāy shōres:
      How a king's new woman,[10] sick
      With hatred for the queen he had imprisoned,
      Ripped out his two sons' eyes with her bloody hands
25   While grinning Arês[11] watched the shuttle plunge
      Four times: four blind wounds crying for revenge,

Antistrophe 2

      Crying, tears and blood mingled.—Piteously born,
      Those sons whose mother was of heavenly birth!
      Her father was the god of the North Wind
30   And she was cradled by gales,
      She raced with young colts on the glittering hills
      And walked untrammeled in the open light:
      But in her marriage deathless Fate found means
      To build a tomb like yours for all her joy.

---

[8] *Dryas' son:* Lycurgus, King of Thrace.
[9] *Sisters:* The Muses.
[10] *King's new woman:* Eidothea, second wife of King Phineus, blinded her step-sons. Their mother, Cleopatra, had been imprisoned in a cave. Phineus was the son of a king, and Cleopatra, his first wife, was the daughter of Boreas, the North Wind, but this illustrious ancestry could not protect his sons from violence and darkness.
[11] *Arês:* God of war.

SCENE V

(Enter blind Teiresias, led by a boy. The opening speeches of Teiresias should be in singsong contrast to the realistic lines of Creon.)

TEIRESIAS: This is the way the blind man comes, Princes, Princes,
    Lock-step, two heads lit by the eyes of one.
CREON: What new thing have you to tell us, old Teiresias?
TEIRESIAS: I have much to tell you: listen to the prophet,
    Creon.
5   **CREON:** I am not aware that I have ever failed to listen.
TEIRESIAS: Then you have done wisely, King, and ruled well.
CREON: I admit my debt to you. But what have you to say?
TEIRESIAS: This, Creon: you stand once more on the edge of fate.
CREON: What do you mean? Your words are a kind of dread.
10   **TEIRESIAS:** Listen, Creon:
    I was sitting in my chair of augury, at the place
    Where the birds gather about me. They were all a-chatter,
    As is their habit, when suddenly I heard
    A strange note in their jangling, a scream, a
15   Whirring fury; I knew that they were fighting,
    Tearing each other, dying
    In a whirlwind of wings clashing. And I was afraid.
    I began the rites of burnt-offering at the altar.
    But Hephaistos[12] failed me: instead of bright flame,
20   There was only the sputtering slime of the fat thigh-flesh
    Melting: the entrails dissolved in gray smoke,
    The bare bone burst from the welter. And no blaze!

    This was a sign from heaven. My boy described it,
    Seeing for me as I see for others.

25   I tell you, Creon, you yourself have brought
    This new calamity upon us. Our hearths and altars
    Are stained with the corruption of dogs and carrion birds
    That glut themselves on the corpse of Oedipus' son.
    The gods are deaf when we pray to them, their fire

---

[12] *Hephaistos:* God of fire.

30   Recoils from our offering, their birds of omen
       Have no cry of comfort, for they are gorged
       With the thick blood of the dead.

                             O my son,
       These are no trifles! Think: all men make mistakes,
       But a good man yields when he knows his course is wrong,
35   And repairs the evil. The only crime is pride.
       Give in to the dead man, then: do not fight with a corpse—
       What glory is it to kill a man who is dead?
       Think, I beg you:
       It is for your own good that I speak as I do.
40   You should be able to yield for your own good.
    CREON: It seems that prophets have made me their especial
         province.
       All my life long
       I have been a kind of butt for the dull arrows
       Of doddering fortune-tellers!
45   No, Teiresias:
       If your birds—if the great eagles of God himself
       Should carry him stinking bit by bit to heaven,
       I would not yield. I am not afraid of pollution:
       No man can defile the gods.

                       Do what you will,
50   Go into business, make money, speculate
       An India gold or that synthetic gold from Sardis,
       Get rich otherwise than by my consent to bury him.
       Teiresias, it is a sorry thing when a wise man
       Sells his wisdom, lets out his words for hire!
55 TEIRESIAS: Ah Creon! Is there no man left in the world—
    CREON: To do what?—Come, let's have the aphorism!
    TEIRESIAS: No man who knows that wisdom outweighs any wealth?
    CREON: As surely as bribes are baser than any baseness.
    TEIRESIAS: You are sick, Creon! You are deathly sick!
60 CREON: As you say: it is not my place to challenge a prophet.
    TEIRESIAS: Yet you have said my prophecy is for sale.
    CREON: The generation of prophets has always loved gold.
    TEIRESIAS: The generation of kings has always loved brass.
    CREON: You forget yourself! You are speaking to your King.

65 **TEIRESIAS**: I know it. You are a king because of me.

CREON: You have a certain skill; but you have sold out.

TEIRESIAS: King, you will drive me to words that—

CREON: Say them, say them!

Only remember: I will not pay you for them.

70 **TEIRESIAS**: No, you will find them too costly.

CREON: No doubt. Speak:

Whatever you say, you will not change, my will.

TEIRESIAS: Then take this, and take it to heart!

The time is not far off when you shall pay back

Corpse for corpse, flesh of your own flesh.

75 You have thrust the child of this world into living night,

You have kept from the gods below the child that is theirs:

The one in a grave before her death, the other,

Dead, denied the grave. This is your crime:

And the Furies and the dark gods of Hell

80 Are swift with terrible punishment for you.

Do you want to buy me now, Creon?

Not many days,

And your house will be full of men and women weeping,

And curses will be hurled at you from far

Cities grieving for sons unburied, left to rot

85 Before the walls of Thebes.

These are my arrows, Creon: they are all for you.

(*To Boy.*) But come, child: lead me home.

Let him waste his fine anger upon younger men.

Maybe he will learn at last

90 To control a wiser tongue in a better head.

(*Exit Teiresias.*)

CHORAGOS: The old man has gone, King, but his words

Remain to plague us. I am old, too,

But I cannot remember that he was ever false.

CREON: That is true. . . . It troubles me.

95 Oh it is hard to give in! but it is worse

To risk everything for stubborn pride.

CHORAGOS: Creon: take my advice.

CREON: What shall I do?

CHORAGOS: Go quickly: free Antigonê from her vault
100   And build a tomb for the body of Polyneicês.
CREON:. You would have me do this!
CHORAGOS: Creon, yes!
        And it must be done at once: God moves
        Swiftly to cancel the folly of stubborn men.
105 CREON: It is hard to deny the heart! But I
        Will do it: I will not fight with destiny.
CHORAGOS: You must go yourself, you cannot leave it to others.
CREON: I will go.
                —Bring axes, servants:
        Come with me to the tomb. I buried her, I
        Will set her free.
                    Oh quickly!
        My mind misgives—
110   The laws of the gods are mighty, and a man must serve them
        To the last day of his life!

(*Exit Creon.*)

Paean[13]

Strophe I

CHORAGOS: God of many names
CREON: O Iacchos
                                son
        of Kadmeian Sémelê
                    O born of the Thunder!
        Guardian of the West
                    Regent
        of Eleusis' plain
                    O Prince of maenad Thebes
        and the Dragon Field by rippling Ismenós:[14]

---

[13] *Paean:* A hymn (here dedicated to Iacchos, also called Dionysos. His
father was Zeus, his mother was Sémelê, daughter of Kadmos. Iacchos's
worshipers were the Maenads, whose cry was "*Evohé evohé*").
[14] *Ismenós:* A river east of Thebes (from a dragon's teeth, sown near the river,
there sprang men who became the ancestors of the Theban nobility).

Antistrophe I

CHORAGOS: God of many names
CHORUS: the flame of torches
   flares on our hills
                  the nymphs of Iacchos
   dance at the spring of Castalia:[15]
   from the vine-close mountain
                           come ah come in ivy:
   Evohé evohé! sings through the streets of Thebes

Strophe 2

5 **CHORAGOS:** God of many names
   CHORUS: Iacchos of Thebes
      heavenly Child
                  of Sémelê bride of the Thunderer!
      The shadow of plague is upon us:
                              come
      with clement feet
                  oh come from Parnassos
      down the long slopes
                     across the lamenting water

Antistrophe 2

CHORAGOS: Iô Fire! Chorister of the throbbing stars!
   O purest among the voices of the night!
   Thou son of God, blaze for us!
10 **CHORUS:** Come, with choric rapture of circling Maenads
   Who cry *Iô Iacche!*

                God of many names!

---

[15] *Paean Castalia:* A spring on Mount Parnassos.

EXODOS

Enter Messenger from left.

MESSENGER: Men of the line of Kadmos,[16] you who live
   Near Amphion's citadel,[17]
                              I cannot say
   Of any condition of human life "This is fixed,
   This is clearly good, or bad." Fate raises up,
15   And Fate casts down the happy and unhappy alike:
   No man can foretell his Fate.
                              Take the case of Creon:
   Creon was happy once, as I count happiness:
   Victorious in battle, sole governor of the land,
   Fortunate father of children nobly born.
20   And now it has all gone from him! Who can say
   That a man is still alive when his life's joy fails?
   He is a walking dead man. Grant him rich,
   Let him live like a king in his great house:
   If his pleasure is gone, I would not give
25   So much as the shadow of smoke for all he owns.

CHORAGOS: Your words hint at sorrow: what is your news for us?

MESSENGER: They are dead. The living are guilty of their death.

CHORAGOS: Who is guilty? Who is dead? Speak!

MESSENGER: Haimon.
   Haimon is dead; and the hand that killed him
30   Is his own hand.

CHORAGOS: His father's? or his own?

MESSENGER: His own, driven mad by the murder his father
   had done.

CHORAGOS: Teiresias, Teiresias, how clearly you saw it all!

35   MESSENGER: This is my news: you must draw what conclusions
   you can from it.

CHORAGOS: But look: Eurydicê, our Queen:
   Has she overheard us?

---

[16] *Kadmos:* Who sowed the dragon teeth, was founder of Thebes.

[17] *Amphion's citadel:* Amphion played so sweetly on his lyre that he charmed
   stones to form a wall around Thebes.

(*Enter Eurydicê from the palace, center.*)

EURYDICE: I have head something, friends:
40   As I was unlocking the gate of Pallas'[18] shrine,
For I needed her help today, I heard a voice
Telling of some new sorrow. And I fainted
There at the temple with all my maidens about me.
But speak again: whatever it is, I can bear it:
45   Grief and I are no strangers.

MESSENGER: Dearest Lady,
I will tell you plainly all that I have seen.
I shall not try to comfort you: what is the use,
Since comfort could lie only in what is not true?
The truth is always best.

                      I went with Creon
50   To the outer plain where Polyneicês was lying,
No friend to pity him, his body shredded by dogs.
We made our prayers in the place to Hecatê
And Pluto,[19] that they would be merciful. And we bathed
The corpse with holy water, and we brought
55   Fresh-broken branches to burn what was left of it,
And upon the urn we heaped up a towering barrow
Of the earth of his own land.

                    When we were done, we ran
To the vault where Antigonê lay on her couch of stone.
One of the servants had gone ahead,
60   And while he was yet far off he heard a voice
Grieving within the chamber, and he came back
And told Creon. And as the King went closer,
The air was full of wailing, the words lost,
And he begged us to make all haste. "Am I a prophet?"
65   He said, weeping, "And must I walk this road,
The saddest of all that I have gone before?
My son's voice calls me on. Oh quickly, quickly!
Look through the crevice there, and tell me
If it is Haimon, or some deception of the gods!"

[18] *Pallas*: Pallas Athene, goddess of wisdom.
[19] *Hecatê / And Pluto*: Hecatê and Pluto (also known as Hades) were deities of the underworld.

70 We obeyed; and in the cavern's farthest corner
    We saw her lying:
    She had made a noose of her fine linen veil.
    And hanged herself. Haimon lay beside her,
    His arms about her waist, lamenting her,
75 His love lost under ground, crying out
    That his father had stolen her away from him.
    When Creon saw him the tears rushed to his eyes
    And he called to him: "What have you done, child?
      Speak to me.
80 What are you thinking that makes your eyes so strange?
    O my son, my son, I come to you on my knees!"
    But Haimon spat in his face. He said not a word,
    Staring—
              And suddenly drew his sword
    And lunged. Creon shrank back, the blade missed; and the
      boy,
    Desperate against himself, drove it half its length
85 Into his own side, and fell. And as he died
    He gathered Antigonê close in his arms again,
    Choking, his blood bright red on her white cheek.
    And now he lies dead with the dead, and she is his
    At last, his bride in the house of the dead.

(*Exit Eurydice into the palace.*)

90 CHORAGOS: She has left us without a word. What can this mean?
    MESSENGER: It troubles me, too; yet she knows what is best,
        Her grief is too great for public lamentation,
        And doubtless she has gone to her chamber to weep
        For her dead son, leading her maidens in his dirge.

(*Pause.*)

95 CHORAGOS: It may be so: but I fear this deep silence.
    MESSENGER: I will see what she is doing. I will go in.

(*Exit Messenger into the palace.*)

(*Enter Creon with attendants, bearing Haimon's body.*)

    CHORAGOS: But here is the king himself: oh look at him,
        Bearing his own damnation in his arms.

CREON: Nothing you say can touch me any more.
100　My own blind heart has brought me
　　From darkness to final darkness. Here you see
　　The father murdering, the murdered son—
　　And all my civic wisdom!
　　Haimon my son, so young, so young to die,
105　I was the fool, not you; and you died for me.
CHORAGOS: That is the truth; but you were late in learning it.
CREON: This truth is hard to bear. Surely a god
　　Has crushed me beneath the hugest weight of heaven,
　　And driven me headlong a barbaric way
110　To trample out the thing I held most dear.
　　The pains that men will take to come to pain!

(*Enter Messenger from the palace.*)

MESSENGER: The burden you carry in your hands is heavy,
　　But it is not all: you will find more in your house.
CREON: What burden worse than this shall I find there?
115　MESSENGER: The Queen is dead.
CREON: O port of death, deaf world,
　　Is there no pity for me? And you, Angel of evil,
　　I was dead, and your words are death again.
　　Is it true, boy? Can it be true?
　　Is my wife dead? Has death bred death?
120　MESSENGER: You can see for yourself.

(*The doors are opened and the body of Eurydicê is disclosed within.*)

CREON: Oh pity!
　　All true, all true, and more than I can bear!
　　O my wife, my son!
125　MESSENGER: She stood before the altar, and her heart
　　Welcomed the knife her own hand guided,
　　And a great cry burst from her lips for Megareus[20] dead,
　　And for Haimon dead, her sons; and her last breath
　　Was a curse for their father, the murderer of her sons.

---

[20] *Megareus:* Megareus, brother of Haimon, had died in the assault on Thebes.

130   And she fell, and the dark flowed in through her closing eyes.
          CREON: O God, I am sick with fear.

              Are there no swords here? Has no one a blow for me?
          MESSENGER: Her curse is upon you for the deaths of both.
          CREON: It is right that it should be. I alone am guilty.
135   I know it, and I say it. Lead me in,
              Quickly, friends.
              I have neither life nor substance. Lead me in.
          CHORAGOS: You are right, if there can be right in so much
              wrong.
              The briefest way is best in a world of sorrow.
140   CREON: Let it come,
              Let death come quickly, and be kind to me.
              I would not ever see the sun again.
          CHORAGOS: All that will come when it will; but we, meanwhile,
              Have much to do. Leave the future to itself.
145   CREON: All my heart was in that prayer!
          CHORAGOS: Then do not pray any more: the sky is deaf.
          CREON: Lead me away. I have been rash and foolish.
              I have killed my son and my wife.
              I look for comfort; my comfort lies here dead.
150   Whatever my hands have touched has come to nothing.
              Fate has brought all my pride to a thought of dust.

          (*As Creon is being led into the house, the Choragos advances and speaks directly to
          the audience.*)

          CHORAGOS: There is no happiness where there is no wisdom;
              No wisdom but in submission to the gods.
              Big words are always punished,
155   And proud men in old age learn to be wise.

William Shakespeare 1564–1616

The Tragedy of Othello, The Moor of Venice *1604*

CHARACTERS

Othello, *the Moor*

Brabantio, *father to Desdemona*

Cassio, *an honorable lieutenant*

Iago, *a villain*

Roderigo, *a gulled gentleman*

Duke of Venice

Senators

Montano, *Governor of Cyprus*

Gentlemen of Cyprus

Lodovico and Gratiano, *two noble Venetians*

Sailors

Clown

Desdemona, *wife to Othello*

Emilia, *wife to Iago*

Bianca, *a courtesan*

(Messenger, Herald, Officers, Gentlemen, Musicians, Attendants

Scene: Venice and Cyprus)

ACT I

Scene I. (Venice. A street.)

(*Enter Roderigo and Iago.*)

RODERIGO: Tush! Never tell me? I take it much unkindly
    That thou, Iago, who hast had my purse
    As if the strings were thine, shouldst know of this.
IAGO: 'Sblood,[1] but you'll not hear me!
5   If ever I did dream of such a matter,
    abhor me.
RODERIGO: Thou told'st me
    Thou didst hold him in thy hate.
IAGO: Despise me
    If I do not. Three great ones of the city,
10   In personal suit to make me his lieutenant,
    Off-capped [2] to him; and by the faith of man,
    I know my price; I am worth no worse a place.
    But he, as loving his own pride and purposes,
    Evades them with a bombast circumstance,[3]
15   Horribly stuffed with epithets of wars;
    And, in conclusion,
    Nonsuits[4] my mediators. For, "Certes," says he,
    "I have already chose my officer."
    And what was he?
20   Forsooth, a great arithmetician,[5]
    One Michael Cassio, a Florentine,
    (A fellow almost dammed in a fair wife)[6]
    That never set a squadron in the field,
    Nor the division of a battle knows
25   More than a spinster; unless the bookish theoric,

---

[1] *'Sblood:* By God's blood.   [2] *Off-capped:* Doffed their cups—as a mark of respect.   [3] *bombast circumstance:* Stuffed, roundabout speech.   [4] *nonsuits:* Rejects. [5] *arithmetician:* Theorist (rather than practical).   [6] *A . . . wife:* A much-disputed passage, which is probably best taken as a general sneer at Cassio as a dandy and a ladies' man. But in the story from which Shakespeare took his plot the counterpart of Cassio is married, and it may be that at the beginning of the play. Shakespeare had decided to keep him married but later changed his mind.

Wherein the tongued[7] consuls can propose
As masterly as he. Mere prattle without practice
Is all his soldiership. But he, sir had th' election;
And I, of whom his eyes had seen the proof
30   At Rhodes, at Cyprus, and on other grounds
Christened and heathen, must be belee'd and calmed
By debitor and creditor. This counter-caster,[8]
He, in good time, must his lieutenant be,
And I—God bless the mark!—his Moorship's ancient.[9]

35 **RODERIGO:** By heaven, I rather would have been his hangman.

IAGO: Why, there's no remedy. 'Tis the curse of service:
Preferment goes by letter and affection,[10]
And not by old gradation,[11] where each second
Stood heir to th' first. Now, sir, be judge yourself,
40   Whether I in any just term am affined[12]
To love the Moor.

RODERIGO: I would not follow him then.

IAGO: O, sir, content you,
I follow him to serve my turn upon him.
45   We cannot all be masters, nor all masters
Cannot be truly followed. You shall mark
Many a duteous and knee-crooking[13] knave
That, doting on his own obsequious bondage,
Wears out his time, much like his master's ass,
50   For naught but provender; and when he's old, cashiered.
Whip me such honest knaves! Others there are
Who trimmed in forms and visages of duty,
Keep yet their hearts attending on themselves,
And, throwing but shows of service on their lords,
55   Do well thrive by them, and when they have lined their coats,
Do themselves homage. These fellows have some soul;
And such a one do I profess myself. For, sir,
It is as sure as you are Roderigo,
Were I the Moor, I would not be Iago.

---

[7] *tongued:* Eloquent.   [8] *counter-caster:* I.e., a bookkeeper who *casts* (reckons up) figures on a *counter* (abacus).   [9] *ancient:* Standard-bearer; an underofficer.   [10] *letter and affection:* Recommendations (from men of power) and personal preference.   [11] *old gradation:* Seniority.   [12] *affined:* Bound.   [13] *knee-crooking:* Bowing.

60   In following him, I follow but myself.
     Heaven is my judge, not I for love and duty,
     But seeming so, for my peculiar[14] end;
     For when my outward action doth demonstrate
     The native[15] act and figure of my heart
65   In compliment extern,[16] tis not long after
     But I will wear my heart upon my sleeve
     For daws to peck at; I am not what I am.
     RODERIGO: What a full fortune does the thick-lips owe[17]
     If he can carry't thus!
70   **IAGO:**   Call up her father,
     Rouse him. Make after him, poison his delight,
     Proclaim him in the streets, incense her kinsmen,
     And though he in a fertile climate dwell,
     Plague him with flies; though that his joy be joy,
75   Yet throw such chances of vexation on't
     As it may lose some color.
     RODERIGO: Here is her father's house. I'll call aloud.
     IAGO: Do, with like timorous[18] accent and dire yell
     As when, by night and negligence, the fire
80   Is spied in populous cities.
     RODERIGO: What, ho, Brabantio! Signor Brabantio, ho!
     IAGO: Awake! What, ho, Brabantio! Thieves! Thieves!
       Look to your house, your daughter, and your bags!
       Thieves! Thieves!

(*Brabantio above*[19] *[at a window].*)

85   **BRABANTIO:** What is the reason of this terrible summons?
       What is the matter there?
     RODERIGO: Signior, is all your family within?
     IAGO: Are your doors locked?
     BRABANTIO: Why, wherefore ask you this?
90   IAGO: Zounds, sir, y're robbed! For shame. Put on your gown!
       Your heart is burst, you have lost half your soul.

---

[14] *peculiar:* Personal.   [15] *native:* Natural, innate.   [16] *complement extern:* Outward
appearances.   [17] *owe:* Own.   [18] *timorous:* Frightening.   [19] *above:* I.e., on the
small upper stage above and to the rear of the main platform stage, which re-
sembled the projecting upper story of an Elizabethan house.

Even now, now, very now, an old black ram
Is tupping your white ewe. Arise, arise!
Awake the snorting citizens with the bell,
95   Or else the devil will make a grandsire of you.
Arise, I say!

BRABANTIO: What, have you lost your wits?

RODERIGO: Most reverend signior, do you know my voice?

BRABANTIO: Not I. What are you?

100 **RODERIGO**: My name is Roderigo.

BRABANTIO: The worser welcome!
I have charged thee not to haunt about my doors.
In honest plainness thou hast heard me say
My daughter is not for thee; and now, in madness,
105   Being full of supper and distemp'ring draughts,[20]
Upon malicious knavery dost thou come
To start[21] my quiet

RODERIGO: Sir, sir, sir——

BRABANTIO: But thou must needs be sure
110   My spirits and my place[22] have in their power
To make this bitter to thee.

RODERIGO: Patience, good sir.

BRABANTIO: What tell'st thou me of robbing? This is Venice;
My house is not a grange.[23]

115 **RODERIGO**:   Most grave Brabantio,
In simple and pure soul I come to you.

IAGO: Zounds, sir, you are one of those that will not
serve God if the devil bid you. Because we come to do you
service and you think we are ruffians, you'll have your
120   daughter covered with a Barbary[24] horse, you'll have your
nephews[25] neigh to you, you'll have coursers
for cousins,[26] and gennets for germans.[27]

BRABANTIO: What profane wretch art thou?

IAGO: I am one, sir that comes to tell you your daughter and
125   the Moor are making the beast with two backs.

---

[20] *distemp'ring draughts:* Unsetling drinks.   [21] *start:* Disrupt.   [22] *place:* Rank, I.e.,
of senator.   [23] *grange:* Isolated house.   [24] *Barbary:* Arabian, i.e., Moorish.
[25] *nephews:* I.e., grandsons.   [26] *cousins:* Relations.   [27] *gennets for germans:* Spanish
horses for blood relatives.

BRABANTIO: Thou art a villain.

IAGO: You are—a senator,

BRABANTIO: This thou shalt answer. I know thee, Roderigo.

ROBERIGA: Sir I will answer anything. But I beseech you,

130   If't be your pleasure and most wise consent,

As partly I find it is, that your fair daughter,

At this odd-even[28] and dull watch o' th' night,

Transported, with no worse nor better guard

But with a knave of common hire, a gondolier,

135   To the gross clasps of a lascivious Moor—

If this be known to you, and your allowance,

We then have done you bold and saucy wrongs;

But if you know not this, my manners tell me

We have your wrong rebuke. Do not believe

140   That form the sense of all civility[29]

I thus would play and trifle with your reverence.

Your daughter, if you have not given her leave,

I say again, hath made a gross revolt,

Tying her duty, beauty, wit, and fortunes

145   In an extravagant[30] and wheeling stranger

Of here and everywhere. Straight satisfy yourself.

If she be in her chamber, or your house,

Let loose on me the justice of the state

For thus deluding you.

150   **BRABANTIO**:   Strike on the tinder, ho!

Give me a taper! Call up all my people!

This accident[31] is not unlike my dream.

Belief of it oppresses me already.

Light, I say! Light!

(*Exit [above].*)

155   **IAGO**:   Farewell, for I must leave you.

It seems not meet, nor wholesome to my place,

To be produced—as, if I stay, I shall—

---

[28] *odd-even*: Between night and morning.   [29] *sense of all civility*: Feeling of what is proper.   [30] *extravagant*: Vagrant, wandering (Othello is not Venetian and thus may be considered a wandering soldier of fortune).   [31] *accident*: Happening.

Against the Moor. For I do know the State,
However this may gall him with some check,[32]
160   Cannot with safety cast[33] him; for he's embarked
With such loud reason to the Cyprus wars,
Which even now stands in act,[34] that for their souls
Another of his fathom[35] they have none
To lead their business; in which regard,
165   Though I do hate him as I do hell-pains,
Yet, for necessity of present life,
I must show out a flag and sign of love,
Which is indeed but sign. That you shall surely find him,
Lead to the Sagittary[36] the raised search;
170   And there will I be with him. So farewell.

(*Exit.*)

(*Enter Brabantio [in his nightgown,] with Servants and torches.*)

BRABANTIO: It is too true an evil. Gone she is;
And what's to come of my despisèd time
Is naught but bitterness. Now, Roderigo,
Where didst thou see her? —O unhappy girl!—
175   With the Moor, Say'st thou?—Who would be a father?—
How dist thou know 'twas she?—O, she deceives me
Past thought!—What said she to you? Get moe[37] tapers!
Raise all my kindred!—Are they married,think you?
ROBERIGO: Truly I think they are.
180   **BRABANTIO:** O heaven! How got she out? O treason of the blood!
Fathers from hence trust not your daughters' minds
By what you see them act[38]. Is there not charms
By which the property[39] of youth and maidhood
May be abused? Have you not read, Roderigo,
185   Of some such thing?
ROBERIGO: Yes, sir I have indeed.
BRABANTIO: Call up my brother.—O, would you had had her!—
Some one way, some another.—Do you know

---

[32] *check:* Restraint.   [33] *cast:* Dismiss.   [34] *stands in act:* Takes place.   [35] *fathom:* Ability.   [36] *Sagittary:* Probably the name of an inn.   [37] *moe:* More.   [38] *act:* Do.   [39] *property:* True nature.

Where we may apprehend her and the Moor?

190 **ROBERIGO:** I think I can discover him, if you please
　　To get good guard and go along with me.
　　BRABANTIO: Pray you lead on. At every house I'll call;
　　I may command at most.—Get weapons, ho!
　　And raise some special officers of might.—
195　　On, good Roderigo; I will deserve your pains.[40]

(*Exeunt.*)

SCENE 2. (*A street.*)

(*Enter Othello, Iago, Attendants with torches.*)

IAGO: Though in the trade of war I have slain men,
　　Yet do I hold it very stuff[1] o' th' conscience
　　To do no contrived murder. I lack iniquity.
　　Sometimes to do me service. Nine or ten times
5　　I had thought t' have yerked[2] him here, under the ribs.
　　OTHELLO: 'Tis better as it is.
　　IAGO:　　　　　　　　　Nay, but he prated,
　　And spoke such scurvy and provoking terms
　　Against your honor
　　　　that with the little godliness I have,
10　　I did full hard forbear him. But, I pray you, sir,
　　Are you fast married? Be assured of this,
　　That the magnifico[3] is much beloved,
　　And hath in his effect a voice potential
　　As double as the Duke's.[4] He will divorce you,
15　　Or put upon you what restraint or grievance
　　The law, with all his might to enforce it on,
　　Will give him cable.[5]
　　OTHELLO:　　　　　　Let him do his spite.
　　My services which I have done the Signiory[6]

---

[40] *deserve your pains:* Be worthy of (and reward) your efforts.　[1] *stuff:* Essence.
[2] *yerked:* Stabbed.　[3] *magnifico:* Nobleman.　[4] *hath . . . Duke's:* I.e., can be as
effective as the Duke.　[5] *cable:* Range, scope.　[6] *Signiory:* The rulers of Venice.
[7] *yet to know:* Unknown as yet.

20 Shall out-tongue his complaints. 'Tis yet to know[7]—
Which when I know that boasting is an honor
I shall promulgate—I fetch my life and being
From men of royal siege;[8] And my demerits[9]
May speak unbonneted to as proud a fortune
25 As this that I have reached.[10] For know, Iago,
But that I love the gentle Desdemona,
I would not my unhousèd[11] free condition
Put into circumscription and confine
For the seas' worth. But look, what lights come yond?

(*Enter Cassio, with [Officers and] torches.*)

30 IAGO: Those are the raisèd father and his friends.
You were best go in.
OTHELLO: Not I. I must be found.
My parts, my title, any my perfect soul[12]
Shall manifest me rightly. Is it they?
35 IAGO: By Janus, I think no.
OTHELLO: The servants of the Duke? And my lieutenant?
The goodness of the night upon you, friends.
What is the news?
CASSIO: The Duke does greet you, general;
40 And he requires your haste-posthaste appearance
Even on the instant.
OTHELLO: What is the matter, think you?
CASSSIO: Something from Cyprus, as I may divine.
It is a business of some heat. The galleys
45 Have sent a dozen sequent[13] messengers,
This very night at one another's heels,
And many of the consuls, raised and met,
Are at the Duke's already. You have been hotly called for.
When, being not at your lodging to be found,
50 The Senate hath sent about three several[14] quests
To search you out.

---

[8] *siege:* Rank.   [9] *demerits:* Deserts.   [10] *May . . . reached:* I.e., are the equal of the family I have married into.   [11] *unhoused:* Unconfined.   [12] *perfect soul:* Clear, unflawed conscience.   [13] *sequent:* Successive.   [14] *several:* Separate.

OTHELLO: 'Tis well I am found by you.
I will but spend a word here in the house,
And go with you.

(*Exit.*)

55 CASSIO: Ancient, what makes he here?
IAGO: Faith, he tonight hath boarded a land carack.[15]
    If it prove lawful prize, he's made forever.
CASSIO: I do not understand.
IAGO: He's married.
60 CASSIO: To who?

(*Enter Othello.*)

IAGO: Marry,[16] to—Come, captain, will you go?
OTHELLO: Have with you.
CASSIO: Here comes another troop to seek for you.

(*Enter Brabantio, Roderigo, with Officers and torches.*)

IAGO: It is Brabantio. General, be advised.
65   He comes to bad intent.
OTHELLO: Holla! Stand there!
RODERIGO: Signor, it is the Moor.
BRABANTIO: Down with him, thief!

(*They draw swords.*)

IAGO: You, Roderigo? Come, sir, I am for you.
70 OTHELLO: Keep up your bright swords, for the dew will
        rust them.
    Good signor, you shall more command with years
    Than with your weapons.
BRABANTIO: O thou foul thief, where hast thou stowed my
        daughter?
    Damned as thou art, thou has enchanted her!
75   For I'll refer me to all things of sense,[17]
    If she in chains of magic were not bound,
    Whether a maid so tender, fair, and happy,

---

[15] *carack:* Treasure ship.   [16] *Marry:* By Mary (an interjection).   [17] *refer . . . sense:* I.e., base (my argument) on all ordinary understanding of nature.

So opposite to marriage that she shunned
The wealthy, curlèd darlings of our nation,
80 Would ever have, t' incur a general mock,[18]
Run from her guardage to the sooty bosom
Of such a thing as thou—to fear, not to delight.
Judge me the world if 'tis not gross in sense[19]
That thou has practiced[20] on her with foul charms,
85 Abused her delicate youth with drugs or minerals
That weaken motion.[21] I'll have't disputed on;
'Tis probable, and palpable to thinking.
I therefore apprehend and do attach[22] thee
For an abuser of the world, a practicer
90 Of arts inhibited and out of warrant.[23]
Lay hold upon him. If he do resist,
Subdue him at his peril.

OTHELLO: Hold your hands,
Both you of my inclining and the rest.
95 Were it my cue to fight, I should have known it
Without a prompter. Whither will you that I go
To answer this your charge?

BRABANTIO: To prison, till fit time
Of law and course of direct session
100 Call thee to answer.

OTHELLO: What if I do obey?
How may the Duke be therewith satisfied,
Whose messengers are here about my side
Upon some present[24] business of the state
105 To bring me to him?

OFFICER: 'Tis true, most worthy signor.
The Duke's in council, and your noble self
I am sure is sent for.

BRABANTIO: How? The Duke in council?
110 In this time of the night? Bring him away.
Mine's not an idle cause. The Duke himself,

---

[18] *general mock:* Public shame.   [19] *gross in sense:* Obvious.   [20] *practiced:* Used tricks.
[21] *motion:* though, I.e., reason.   [22] *attach:* Arrest.   [23] *inhibited . . . warrant:* Prohibited and illegal (black magic).   [24] *present:* Immediate.

Or any of my brothers[25] of the state,
Cannot but feel this wrong as 'twere their own;
For if such actions may have passage free,
115   Bondslaves and pagans shall our statesmen be.

(*Exeunt.*)

SCENE 3. (*A council chamber.*)

(*Enter Duke, Senators, and Officers [set at a table, with lights and Attendants].*)

DUKE: There's no composition[1] in this news
    That gives them credit.[2]
FIRST SENATOR: Indeed, they are disproportioned.
    My letters say a hundred and seven galleys.
5 DUKE: And mine a hundred forty.
SECOND SENATOR: And mine two hundred.
    But though they jump[3] not on a just account[4]—
    As in these cases where the aim[5] reports
    'Tis oft with difference—yet do they all confirm
10   A Turkish fleet, and bearing up to Cyprus.
DUKE. Nay, it is possible enough to judgment.[6]
    I do not so secure me in the error,
    But the main article I do approve.
    In fearful sense.[7]
15 SAILOR: (*Within*) What, ho! What, ho! What, ho!

(*Enter Sailor.*)

OFFICER: A messenger from the galleys.
DUKE: Now? What's the business?
SAILOR: The Turkish preparation make for Rhodes.
    So was I bid report here to the State
20   By Signor Angelo.

---

[25] *brothers*: I.e., the other senators. [1] *composition*: Agreement. [2] *gives them credit*: Makes them believable. [3] *jump*: Agree. [4] *just Account*: Exact counting. [5] *aim*: Approximation. [6] *to judgment*: When carefully considered. [7] *I do . . . sense*: I.e., Just because the numbers disagree in the reports, I do not doubt that the principal information (that the Turkish fleet is out) is fearfully true.

DUKE: How say you by this change?

FIRST SENATOR: This cannot be
By no assay of reason. 'Tis a pageant[8]
To keep us in false gaze.[9] When we consider
25   Th' importancy of Cyprus to the Turk,
And let ourselves again but understand
That, as it more concerns the Turk than Rhodes,
So may he with more facile question[10] bear it,
For that it stands not in such warlike brace,[11]
30   But altogether lacks th' abilities
That Rhodes is dressed in. If we make thought of this,
We must not think the Turk is so unskillful
To leave that latest which concerns him first,
Neglecting an attempt of ease and gain
35   To wake and wage a danger profitless.

DUKE: Nay, in all confidence he's not for Rhodes.

OFFICER: Here is more news.

(Enter a Messenger.)

MESSENGER: The Ottomites, reverend and gracious,
Steering with the due course toward the isle of Rhodes,
Have there injointed them with an after[12] fleet.

FIRST SENATOR: Ay, so I thought. How many, as you guess?

40   MESSENGER: Of thirty sail; and now they do restem
Their backward course, bearing with frank appearance
Their purposes toward Cyprus. Signior Montano,
Your trusty and most valiant servitor,
With his free duty[13] recommends[14] you thus,
45   And prays you to believe him.

DUKE: 'Tis certain then for Cyprus.
Marcus Luccicos, is not he in town?

FIRST SENATOR: He's now in Florence.

DUKE: Write from us to him; post-post-haste dispatch.

50   FIRST SENATOR: Here comes Brabantio and the valiant Moor.

---

[8] *pageant:* Show, pretense.   [9] *in false gaze:* Looking the wrong way.   [10] *facile question:* Easy struggle.   [11] *warlike brace:* "Military posture."   [12] *after:* Following.   [13] *free duty:* Unlimited respect.   [14] *recommends:* Informs.

(*Enter Brabantio, Othello, Cassio, Iago, Roderigo, and Officers.*)

DUKE: Valiant Othello, we must straight[15] employ you
    Against the general[16] enemy Ottoman.
    (*To Brabantio*) I did not see you. Welcome, gentle signor.
    We lacked your counsel and your help tonight.

BRABANTIO: So did I yours. Good your grace, pardon me.
55   Neither my place, nor aught I heard of business,
    Hath raised me from my bed; nor doth the general care
    Take hold on me; for my particular grief
    Is of so floodgate and o'erbearing nature
    That it engluts and swallows other sorrows,
60   And it is still itself.

DUKE.   Why, what's the matter?

BRABANTIO: My daughter! O, my daughter!

SENATORS: Dead?

BRABANTIO: Ay, to me.
65   She is abused, stol'n from me, and corrupted
    By spells and medicines brought of mountebanks;
    For nature so prepost'rously to err,
    Being not deficient, blind, or lame of sense,
    Sans[17] witchcraft could not.

70 **DUKE**: Whoe'er he be that in this foul proceeding
    Hath thus beguiled your daughter of herself,
    And you of her, the bloody book of law
    You shall yourself read in the bitter letter
    After your own sense; yea, though our proper[18] son
75   Stood in your action.[19]

BRABANTIO: Humbly I thank your Grace.
    Here is the man—this Moor, whom now, it seems,
    Your special mandate for the state affairs
    Hath hither brought.

80 **ALL**:   We are very sorry for't.

DUKE: (*To Othello*) What in your own part can you say to this?

BRABANTIO: Nothing, but this is so.

OTHELLO: Most potent, grave, and reverend signors,

---

[15] *straight*: At once.   [16] *general*: Universal.   [17] *Sans*: Without.   [18] *proper*: Own.
[19] *Stood in your action*: Were the accused in your suit.

My very noble and approved[20] good master,

85 That I have ta'en away this old man's daughter,

It is most true; true I have married her.

The very head and front[21] of my offending

Hath this extent, no more. Rude am I in my speech,

And little blessed with the soft phrase of peace,

90 For since these arms of mine had seven years' pith[22]

Till now some nine moons wasted,[23] they have used

Their dearest[24] action in the tented field;

And little of this great world can I speak

More than pertains to feats of broils and battle;

95 And therefore little shall I grace my cause

In speaking for myself. Yet, by your gracious patience,

I will a round[25] unvarnished tale deliver

Of my whole course of love—what drugs, what charms,

What conjuration, and what mighty magic,

100 For such proceeding I am charged withal,

I won his daughter—

BRABANTIO: A maiden never bold,

Of spirit so still and quiet that her motion

Blushed at herself;[26] and she, in spite of nature,

105 Of years, of country, credit, everything,

To fall in love with what she feared to look on!

It is a judgment maimed and most imperfect

That will confess perfection so could err

Against all rules of nature, and must be driven

110 To find out practices of cunning hell

Why this should be. I therefore vouch again

That with some mixtures pow'rful o'er the blood,

Or with some dram, conjured to this effect,

He wrought upon her.

115 **DUKE:**   To vouch this is no proof,

Without more wider and more overt test

---

[20] *approved:* Tested, proven by past performance.   [21] *head and front:* Extreme form (*front* = forehead).   [22] *pith:* Strength.   [23] *wasted:* Past.   [24] *dearest:* Most important.   [25] *round:* Blunt.   [26] *her motion/Blushed at herself:* I.e., she was so modest that she blushed at every thought (and movement).

Than these thin habits[27] and poor likelihoods
Of modern[28] seeming do prefer against him.

FIRST SENATOR: But, Othello, speak.

120   Did you by indirect and forcèd courses
Subdue and poison this young maid's affections?
Or came it by request, and such fair question[29]
As soul to soul affordeth?

OTHELLO: I do beseech you,

125   Send for the lady to the Sagittary
And let her speak of me before her father.
I you do find me foul in her report,
The trust, the office, I do hold of you
Not only take away, but let your sentence

130   Even fall upon my life.

DUKE.   Fetch Desdemona hither.

OTHELLO. Ancient, conduct them; you best know the place.

(*Exit Iago, with two or three Attendants.*)

And till she come, as truly as to heaven
I do confess the vices of my blood,

135   So justly to your grave ears I'll present
How I did thrive in this fair lady's love,
And she in mine.

DUKE.   Say it, Othello.

OTHELLO. Her father loved me; oft invited me;

140   Still[30] questioned me the story of my life
From year to year, the battle, sieges, fortune
That I have passed.
I ran it through, even from my boyish days
To th' very moment that he bade me tell it.

145   Wherein I spoke of most disastrous chances,
Of moving accidents by flood and field,
Of hairbreadth scapes i' th' imminent[31] deadly breach.
Of being taken by the insolent foe
And sold to slavery, of my redemption thence

---

[27] *habits:* Clothing.   [28] *modern:* Trivial.   [29] *question:* Discussion.   [30] *Still:* Regularly.   [31] *imminent:* Threatening.

150   And portance[32] in my travel's history,

Wherein of antres[33] vast and deserts idle,[34]

Rough quarries, rocks, and hills whose heads touch heaven,

It was my hint to speak. Such was my process.

And of the Cannibals that each other eat,

155   The Anthropophagi,[35] and men whose heads

Grew beneath their shoulders. These things to hear

Would Desdemona seriously incline,

But still the house affairs would draw her thence;

Which ever as she could with haste dispatch,

160   She'd come again, and with a greedy ear

Devour up my discourse. Which I observing,

Took once a pliant hour, and found good means

To draw from her a prayer of earnest heart

That I would all my pilgrimage dilate,[36]

165   Whereof by parcels she had something heard,

But not intentively.[37] I did consent,

And often did beguile her of her tears

When I did speak of some distressful stroke

That my youth suffered. My story being done,

170   She gave me for my pains a world of kisses.

She swore in faith 'twas strange, 'twas passing[38] strange;

'Twas pitiful, 'twas wondrous pitiful.

She wished she had not heard it; yet she wished

That heaven had made her such a man. She thanked me,

175   And bade me, if I had a friend that loved her,

I should but teach him how to tell my story,

And that would woo her. Upon this hint I spake.

She loved me for the dangers I had passed,

And I loved her that she did pity them.

180   This only is the witchcraft I have used.

Here comes the lady. Let her witness it.

(Enter Desdemona, Iago, Attendants.)

---

[32] *portance:* Manner of acting.   [33] *antres:* Caves.   [34] *idle:* Empty, sterile.
[35] *Anthropophagi:* Man-eaters.   [36] *dilate:* Relate in full.   [37] *intentively:* At length
and in sequence.   [38] *passing:* Surpassing.

DUKE. I think this tale would win my daughter too.

    Good Brabantio, take up this mangled matter at the best.[39]

    Men do their broken weapons rather use

185   Than their bare hands.

BRABANTIO: I pray you hear her speak.

    If she confess that she was half the wooer,

    Destruction on my head if my bad blame

    Light on the man. Come hither, gentle mistress,

190   Do you perceive in all this noble company

    Where most you owe obedience?

DESDEMONA: My noble father,

I do perceive here a divided duty.

To you I am bound for life and education;

195   My life and education both do learn me

    How to respect you. You are the lord of duty,

    I am hitherto your daughter. But here's my husband,

    And so much duty as my mother showed

    To you, preferring you before her father,

200   So much I challenge[40] that I may profess

    Due to the Moor my lord.

BRABANTIO: God be with you. I have done.

    Please it your Grace, on to the state affairs.

    I had rather to adopt a child than get[41] it.

205   Come hither, Moor.

    I here do give thee that will all my heart

    Which, but thou has already, with all my heart

    I would keep from thee. For your sake,[42] jewel,

    I am glad at soul I have no other child,

210   For thy escape would teach me tyranny,

    To hang clogs on them. I have done, my lord.

DUKE: Let me speak like yourself and lay a sentence[43]

    Which, as a grise[44] or step, may help these lovers.

    When remedies are past, the griefs are ended

---

[39] take . . . best: I.e., make the best of this disaster.   [40] challenge: Claim as right.

[41] get: Beget.   [42] For your sake: Because of you.   [43] lay a sentence: Provide a maxim.

[44] grise: Step.

215 By seeing the worst, which late on hopes depended.[45]
To mourn a mischief that is past and gone
Is the next[46] way to draw new mischief on.
What cannot be preserved when fortune takes,
Patience her injury a mock'ry makes.
220 The robbed that smiles, steals something from the thief;
He robs himself that spends a bootless[47] grief.

BRABANTIO: So let the Turk of Cyprus us beguile:
We lose it not so long as we can smile.
He bears the sentence well that nothing bears
225 But the free comfort which from thence he hears;
But he bears both the sentence and the sorrow
That to pay grief must of poor patience borrow.
These sentences, to sugar, or to gall,
Being strong on both sides, are equivocal.
230 But words are words. I never yet did hear
That the bruisèd heart was piercèd[48] through the ear.
I humbly beseech you, proceed to th' affairs of state.

DUKE: The Turk with a most mighty preparation makes for
Cyprus. Othello, the fortitude[49] of the place is best
known to you; and though we have there a substitute[50] of
most allowed sufficiency,[51] yet opinion, a more sovereign
mistress of effects, throws a more safer voice on you.[52]
You must therefore be content to slubber[53] the gloss of
your new fortunes with this more stubborn and boisterous[54] expedition.

OTHELLO: The tyrant Custom, most grave senators;
235 Hath made the flinty and steel couch of war

---

[45] *late on hopes depended:* Was supported by hope (of a better outcome) until lately.
[46] *next:* Closest, surest. [47] *bootless:* Valueless [48] *pierced:* Some editors emend to
pieced, i.e., healed. But *pierced* makes good sense: Brabantio is saying in effect
that his heart cannot be further hurt [pierced] by the indignity of the useless,
conventional advice the Duke offers him. *Pierced* can also mean, however,
"lanced" in the medical sense, and would then mean "treated." [49] *fortitude:*
Fortification. [50] *substitute:* Viceroy. [51] *most allowed sufficiency:* Generally
acknowledged capability. [52] *opinion . . . you:* I.e., the general opinion, which
finally controls affairs, is that you would be the best man in this situation.
[53] *slubber:* Besmear. [54] *stubborn and boisterous:* Rough and violent.

My thrice-driven[55] bed of down. I do agnize[56]
A natural and prompt alacrity
I find in hardness and do undertake
This present wars against the Ottomites.
240   Most humbly, therefore, bending to your state,
I crave fit disposition for my wife,
Due reference of place, and exhibition,[57]
With such accommodation and besort
As levels with[58] her breeding.

245   **DUKE:**   Why, at her father's.
BRABANTIO: I will not have it so.
OTHELLO: Nor I.
DESDEMONA: Nor would I there reside,
To put my father in impatient thoughts
250   By being in his eye. Most gracious duke,
To my unfolding[59] lend your prosperous[60] ear,
And let me find a charter[61] in your voice,
T' assist my simpleness.

DUKE: What would you, Desdemona?
255   **DESDEMONA:** That I love the Moor to live with him,
My downright violence, and storm of fortunes,
May trumpet to the world. My heart's subdued
Even to the very quality of my lord.[62]
I saw Othello's visage in his mind,
260   And to his honors and his valiant parts
Did I my soul and fortunes consecrate.
So that, dear lords, if I be left behind,
A moth of peace, and he go to the war,
The rites[63] for why I love him are bereft me,
265   And I a heavy interim shall support
By his dear absence. Let me go with him.

---

[55] *thrice-driven:* I.e., softest.   [56] *agnize:* Know in myself.   [57] *exhibition:* Grant of
funds.   [58] *levels with:* Is suitable to.   [59] *unfolding:* Explanation.   [60] *prosperous:*
Favoring.   [61] *charter:* Permission.   [62] *My . . . lord:* I.e., I have become one in
nature and being with the man I married (therefore, I too would go to the wars
like a soldier).   [63] *rites:* May refer either to the marriage rites or to the rites,
formalities, of war.

OTHELLO: Let her have your voice.[64]

    Vouch with me, heaven, I therefore beg it not

    To please the palate of my appetite,

270   Nor to comply with heat[65]—the young affects[66]

    In me defunct—and proper satisfaction;[67]

    But to be free and bounteous to her mind;

    And heaven defend[68] your good souls that you think

    I will your serious and great business scant

275   When she is with me. No, when light-winged toys

    Of feathered Cupid seel[69] with wanton[70] dullness

    My speculative and officed instrument,[71]

    That my disports corrupt and taint my business,

    Let housewives make a skillet of my helm,

280   And all indign[72] and base adversities

    Make head[73] against my estimation[74]—

DUKE: Be it as you shall privately determine,

    Either for her stay or going. Th' affair cries haste,

    And speed must answer it.

285 **FIRST SENATOR:**   You must away tonight.

OTHELLO: With all my heart.

DUKE: At nine i' th' morning here we'll meet again

    Othello, leave some officer behind,

    And he shall our commission bring to you,

290   And such things else of quality and respect

    As doth import you.

OTHELLO: So please your Grace, my ancient;

    A man he is of honesty and trust.

    To his conveyance I assign my wife,

295   With what else needful your good grace shall think

    To be sent after me.

DUKES: Let it be so.

    Good night to every ones. (*To Brabantio*) And, noble signor,

---

[64] *voice:* Consent. [65] *heat:* Lust [66] *affects:* Passions. [67] *proper satisfaction:* I.e., consummation of the marriage. [68] *defend:* Forbid. [69] *seel:* Sew up. [70] *wanton:* Lascivious. [71] *speculative . . . instrument:* I.e., sight (and, by extension, the mind). [72] *indign:* Unworthy. [73] *make head:* From an army, i.e., attack. [74] *estimation:* Reputation.

If virtue no delighted[75] beauty lack,

300   Your son-in-law is far more fair than black.

FIRST SENATOR. Adieu, brave Moor. Use Desdemona well.

BRABANITO: Look to her, Moor, if thou hast eyes to see:

She has deceived her father, and may thee.

(*Exeunt Duke, Senators, Officers, & c.*)

OTHELLO: My life upon her faith! Honest Iago,

305   My Desdemona must I leave to thee.

I prithee let thy wife attend on her,

And bring them after in the best advantage.[76]

Come, Desdemona. I have but an hour

Of love, of worldly matter, and direction

310   To spend with thee. We must obey the time.

(*Exit [Moor with Desdemona].*)

RODERIGO: Iago?

IAGO: What say'st thou, noble heart?

RODERIGO: What will I do, think'st thou?

IAGO: Why, go to bed and sleep.

315   **RODERIGO:** I will incontinently[77] drown myself.

IAGO: If thou dost, I shall never love thee after. Why, thou silly gentleman?

RODERIGO: It is silliness to live when to live is torment; and then have we a prescription to die when death is our physician.

IAGO: O villainous! I have looked upon the world for four times seven years, and since I could distinguish betwixt a benefit and an injury, I never found man that knew how to love himself. Ere I would say I would drown myself for the love of a guinea hen, I would change my humanity with a baboon.

RODERIGO: What should I do? I confess it is my shame to be so fond, but it is not in my virtue[78] to amend it.

---

[75] *delighted:* Delightful.   [76] *advantage:* Opportunity.   [77] *incontinently:* At once.

[78] *virtue:* Strength (Roderigo is saying that his nature controls him).

320   **IAGO:** Virtue? A fig! 'Tis in ourselves that we are thus, or thus.
Our bodies are our gardens, to the which our wills are
gardeners; so that if we will plant nettles or sow lettuce,
set hyssop and weed up thyme, supply it with one gender
of herbs or distract[79] it with many—either to have it sterile
325   with idleness or manured with industry—why, the power
and corrigible[80] authority of this lies in our wills. If the
balance of our lives had not one scale of reason to poise
another of sensuality, the blood and baseness of our
natures would conduct us to most prepost'rous conclu-
330   sions.[81] But we have reason to cool our raging motions,
our carnal stings or unbitted[82] lusts, whereof I take this
that you call love to be a sect or scion.[83]

   RODERIGO: It cannot be.

   IAGO: It is merely a lust of the blood and a permission of the
335   will. Come, be a man! Drown thyself? Drown cats and
blind puppies! I have professed me thy friend, and I
confess me knit of thy deserving with cables of perdurable
toughness. I could never better stead[84] thee than now.
Put money in thy purse. Follow thou the wars; defeat thy
340   favor[85] with an usurped[86] beard. I say, put money in thy
purse. It cannot be long that Desdemona should continue
her love to the Moor. Put money in thy purse. Nor he his
to her. It was a violent commencement in her and thou
shalt see an answerable[87] sequestration— put but money in
345   thy purse. These Moors are changeable in their wills—fill
thy purse with money. The food that to him now is as lus-
cious as locusts[88] shall be to him shortly as bitter as coloquintida.[89] She must change for youth; when she is sated
with his body, she will find the errors of her choice.
350   Therefore, put money in thy purse. If thou wilt needs
damn thyself, do it a more delicate way than drowning.

---

[79] *distract:* Vary.   [80] *corrigible:* Corrective.   [81] *conclusions:* Ends.   [82] *unbitted:* I.e.,
uncontrolled   [83] *sect or scion:* Offshoot.   [84] *stead:* Serve.   [85] *defeat thy favor:*
Disguise your face.   [86] *usurped:* Assumed.   [87] *answerable:* Similar.   [88] *locusts:*
A sweet fruit.   [89] *coloquintida:* A purgative derived from a bitter apple.

Make all the money thou canst. If sanctimony[90] and a
frail vow betwixt an erring[91] barbarian and supersubtle
Venetian be not too hard for my wits, and all the tribe of
hell, thou shalt enjoy her. Therefore, make money. A pox
355 of drowning thyself, it is clean out of the way. Seek thou
rather to be hanged in compassing[92] thy joy than to be
drowned and go without her.

RODERIGO: Wilt thou be fast to my hopes, if I depend on the
issue?

IAGO: Thou art sure of me. Go, make money. I have told thee
360 often, and I retell thee again and again, I hate the Moor.
My cause is hearted;[93] thine hath no less reason. Let us be
conjunctive[94] in our revenge against him. If thou canst
cuckold him, thou dost thyself a pleasure, me a sport.
There are many events in the womb of time, which will be
365 delivered. Traverse, go, provide thy money! We will have
more of this tomorrow. Adieu.

RODERIGO: Where shall we meet i' th' morning?

IAGO: At my lodging.

RODERIGO: I'll be with thee betimes.

370 IAGO: Go to, farewell. Do you hear, Roderigo?

RODERIGO: I'll sell all my land.

(*Exit.*)

IAGO: Thus do I ever make my fool my purse:
For I mine own gained knowledge[95] should profane
If I would time expend with such snipe
375 But for my sort and profit. I hate the Moor,
And it is thought abroad that 'twixt my sheets
H'as done my office. I know not if't be true,
But I, for mere suspicion in that kind,
Will do, as if for surety.[96] He holds me well;
380 The better shall my purpose work on him.

---

[90] *sanctimony:* Sacred bond (of marriage).   [91] *erring:* Wandering.
[92] *compassing:* Encompassing, achieving.   [93] *hearted:* Deep-seated in the heart.
[94] *conjunctive:* Joined.   [95] *gained knowledge:* I.e., practical, worldly wisdom.
[96] *surety:* Certainty.

Cassio's a proper[97] man. Let me see now:
To get his place, and to plume up my will[98]
In double knavery. How? How? Let's see.
After some time, to abuse Othello's ears
That he is too familiar with his wife.
385   He hath a person and a smooth dispose[99]
To be suspected—framed[100] to make women false.
The Moor is of a free and open nature
That thinks men honest that but seem to be so;
And will as tenderly be led by th' nose
390   As asses are.
I have't! It is engendered! Hell and night
Must bring this monstrous birth to the world's light.

(*Exit.*)

ACT 2

SCENE I. (*Cyprus.*)

(*Enter Montano and two Gentlemen.*)

MONTANO: What from the cape can you discern at sea?
FIRST GENTLEMAN: Nothing at all, it is a high-wrought flood.
   I cannot 'twixt the heaven and the main
   Descry a sail.
5   **MONTANO:** Methinks the wind hath spoke aloud at land;
   A fuller blast ne'er shook our battlements.
   If it hath ruffianed so upon the sea,
   What ribs of oak, when mountains melt on them,
   Can hold the mortise? What shall we hear of this?
10   **SECOND GENTLEMAN:** A segregation[1] of the Turkish fleet.
   For do but stand upon the foaming shore,

---

[97] *proper:* Handsome.   [98] *plume up my will:* Many explanations have been offered for this crucial line, which in Q1 reads "make up my will." The general sense is something like "to make more proud and gratify my ego." [99] *dispose:* Manner.   [100] *framed:* Designed.   [1] *segregation:* Separation.

The chidden billow seems to pelt the clouds;
The wind-shaked surge, with high and monstrous main.[2]
Seems to cast water on the burning Bear
15   And quench the guards of th' ever-fixed pole.[3]
I never did like molestation view
On the enchafed flood.
MONTANO: If that the Turkish fleet
Be not ensheltered and embayed, they are drowned;
20   It is impossible to bear it out.

(*Enter a [third] Gentleman.*)

THIRD GENTLEMAN: News, lads! Our wars are done.
The desperate tempest hath so banged the Turks
That their designment halts. A noble ship of Venice
Hath seen a grievous wrack and sufferance[4]
25   On most part of their fleet.
MONTANO: How? Is this true?
THIRD GENTLEMAN: The ship is here put in,
A Veronesa; Michael Cassio,
Lieutenant to the warlike Moor Othello,
30   Is come on shore; the Moor himself at sea,
And is in full commission here for Cyprus.
MONTANO: I am glad on't. 'Tis a worthy governor.
THIRD GENTLEMAN: But this same Cassio, though he speak of
   comfort.
Touching the Turkish loss, yet he looks sadly
35   And prays the Moor be safe, for they were parted
With foul and violent tempest.
MONTANO: Pray heavens he be;
For I have served him, and the man commands
Like a full soldier. Let's to the seaside, ho!
40   As well to see the vessel that's come in
As to throw out our eyes for brave Othello,

---

[2] *main*: Both "ocean" and "strength." [3] *Seems . . . pole*: The constellation Ursa Minor contains two stars which are the *guards*, or companions, of the *pole*, or North Star. [4] *sufferance*: Damage.

Even till we make the main and th' aerial blue
An indistinct regard.[5]

THIRD GENTLEMAN: Come, let's do so;

45 For every minute is expectancy
Of more arrivance.[6]

(*Enter Cassio.*)

CASSIO: Thanks, you the valiant of the warlike isle,
That so approve[7] the Moor. O, let the heavens
Give him defense against the elements,

50 For I have lost him on a dangerous sea.

MONTANO: Is he well shipped?

CASSIO: His bark is stoutly timbered, and his pilot
Of very expert and approved allowance;[8]
Therefore my hopes, not surfeited to death,[9]

55 Stand in bold cure.[10]

(*Within*) A sail, a sail, a sail!

CASSIO: What noise?

FIRST GENTLEMAN: The town is empty; on the brow o' th' sea
Stand ranks of people, and they cry, "A sail!"

CASSIO: My hopes do shape him for the governor.

(*A shot.*)

60 **SECOND GENTLEMAN:** They do discharge their shot of courtesy.
Our friends at least.

CASSIO: I pray you, sir, go forth
And give us truth who 'tis that is arrived.

SECOND GENTLEMAN: I shall.

(*Exit.*)

65 **MONTANO:** But, good lieutenant, is your general wived?

CASSIO: Most fortunately. He hath achieved a maid
That paragons[11] description and wild frame,[12]

---

[5] *the main . . . regard:* I.e., the sea and sky become indistinguishable. [6] *arrivance:* Arrivals. [7] *approve:* "Honor" or, perhaps, are as warlike and valiant as your governor." [8] *approved allowance:* Known and tested. [9] *not surfeited to death:* I.e., not so great as to be in danger. [10] *Stand in bold cure:* I.e., are likely to be restored. [11] *paragons:* Exceeds. [12] *wild fame:* Extravagant report.

One that excels the quirks of blazoning pens,[13]
And in th' essential vesture of creation[14]
70   Does tire the engineer.[15]

(*Enter [Second] Gentleman.*)

                    How now? Who has put in?
SECOND GENTLEMAN: 'Tis one Iago, ancient to the general.
CASSIO: H'as had most favorable and happy speed:
    Tempests themselves, high seas, and howling winds,
75   The guttered[16] rocks and congregated[17] sands,
    Traitors ensteeped[18] to enclog the guiltless keel,
    As having sense[19] of beauty, do omit
    Their mortal[20] natures, letting go safely by
    The divine Desdemona.
80 **MONTANO:**   What is she?
CASSIO: She that I spake of, our great captain's captain,
    Left in the conduct of the bold Iago,
    Whose footing[21] here anticipates our thoughts
    A sennight's[22] Great Jove, Othello guard,
85   And swell his sail with thin own pow'rful breath,
    That he may bless this bay with his tall[23] ship,
    Make love's quick pants in Desdemona's arms,
    Give renewed fire to our extincted spirits.

(*Enter Desdemona, Iago, Roderigo, and Emilia.*)

    O, behold! The riches of the ship is come on shore!
90   You men of Cyprus, let her have your knees.

(*Kneeling.*)

    Hail to thee, lady! and the grace of heaven,
    Before, behind thee, and on every hand,
    Enwheel thee round.

---

[13] *quirks of blazoning pens:* Ingenuities of praising pens.   [14] *essential vesture of creation:* I.e., essential human nature as given by the Creator.   [15] *tire the engineer:* A difficult line which probably means something like "outdo the human ability to imagine and picture."   [16] *guttered:* Jagged.   [17] *congregated:* Gathered.   [18] *ensteeped:* Submerged.   [19] *sense:* Awareness.   [20] *mortal:* Deadly.   [21] *footing:* Landing.   [22] *se'nnight's:* Week's.   [23] *tall:* Brave.

DESEMONA: I thank you, valiant Cassio.

95 What tidings can you tell of my lord?

CASSIO: He is not yet arrived, nor know I aught

  But that he's well and will be shortly here.

DESDEMONA: O but I fear. How lost you company?

CASSIO: The great contention of sea and skies

100 Parted our fellowship.

  (*Within*) A sail, a sail!

(*A shot.*)

       But hark. A sail!

SECOND GENTLEMAN: They give this greeting to the citadel.

  This likewise is a friend.

CASSIO: See for the news.

(*Exit Gentleman.*)

105 Good Ancient, you are welcome. (*To Emilia*) Welcome, mistress.

  Let it not gall your patience, good Iago,

  That I extend[24] my manners. 'Tis my breeding[25]

  That gives me this bold show of courtesy. (*Kisses Emilia.*)

IAGO: Sir, would she give you so much of her lips

110 As of her tongue she oft bestows on me,

  You would have enough.

DESDEMONA: Alas, she has no speech.

IAGO: In faith, too much.

  I find it still when I have leave to sleep[26]

115 Marry, before your ladyship,[27] I grant,

  She puts her tongue a little in her heart

  And chides with thinking.

EMILIA: You have little cause to say so.

IAGO: Come on, come on! You are pictures[28] out of door,

120 Bells in your parlors, wildcats in your kitchens,

  Saints in your injuries,[29] devils being offended,

---

[24] *extend*: Stretch. [25] *breeding*: Careful training in manners (Cassio is considerably, more the polished gentleman than Iago, and aware of it). [26] *still . . . sleep*: I.e., even when allows me to sleep she continues to scold. [27] *before your ladyship*: In your presence. [28] *pictures*: Models (of virtue). [29] *in your injuries*: When you injure others.

Players in your housewifery,[30] and housewives in your beds.

DESDEMONA: O, fie upon thee, slanderer!

IAGO: Nay, it is true, or else I am a Turk:

125　　　You rise to play, and go to bed to work

EMILIA: You shall not write my praise.

IAGO:　　　　　　　　　　　　No, let me not.

DESDEMONA: What wouldst write of me, if thou shouldst praise
　　　me?

IAGON: O gentle lady, do not put me to't,

130　　　For I am nothing if not critical.

DESDEMONA: Come on, assay. There's one gone to the harbor?

IAGO: Ay, madam.

DESDEMONA: (*Aside*) I am not merry; but I do beguile
　　　The thing I am by seeming otherwise.—

135　　　Come, how wouldst thou praise me?

IAGO: I am about it; but indeed my invention
　　　Comes from my pate as birdlime[31] does from frieze[32]—
　　　It plucks out brains and all. But my Muse labors,
　　　And thus she is delivered:

140　　　If she be fair[33] and wise: fairness and wit,
　　　The one's for use, the other useth it.

DESDEMONA: Well praised. How if she be black[34] and witty?

IAGO: If she be black, and thereto have a wit,
　　　She'll find a white that shall her blackness fit.

145　**DESDEMONA**: Worse and worse!

EMILIA: How if fair and foolish?

IAGO: She never yet was foolish that was fair,
　　　For even her folly helped her to an heir.

DESDEMONA: These are old fond[35] paradoxes to make fools

150　　　laugh i' th' alehouse. What miserable praise hast thou for
　　　her that's foul and foolish?

---

[30] *housewifery:* This word can mean "careful, economical household manage-
ment," and Iago would then be accusing women of only pretending to be good
housekeepers, while in bed they are either [1] economical of their
favors, or more likely [2] serious and dedicated workers.　[31] *birdlime:* A sticky
substance put on branches to catch birds.　[32] *frieze:* Rough cloth.　[33] *fair:* Light-
complexioned.　[34] *black:* Brunette.　[35] *fond:* Foolish.

IAGO: There's none so foul, and foolish thereunto,
But does foul pranks which fair and wise ones do.

DESDEMONA: O heavy ignorance. Thou praisest the worst best.

155 But what praise couldst thou bestow on a deserving
woman indeed—one that in the authority of her merit did
justly put on the vouch of very malice itself?[36]

IAGO: She that was ever fair, and never proud;
Had tongue at will, and yet was never loud;

160 Never lacked gold, and yet went never gay;
Fled from her wish, and yet said "Now I may";
She that being angered, her revenge being nigh,
Bade her wrong stay, and her displeasure fly;
She that in wisdom never was so frail

165 To change the cod's head for the salmon's tail;[37]
She that could think, and nev'r disclose her mind;
See suitors following, and not look behind:
She was wight[38] (if ever such wights were)—

DESDEMONA: To do what?

170 IAGO: To suckle fools and chronicle small beer.[39]

DESDEMONA: O most lame and impotent conclusion. Do not
learn of him, Emilia, though he be thy husband. How
say you, Cassio? Is he not a most profane and liberal[40]
counselor?

CASSIO: He speaks home[41] madam. You may relish him more
in[42] the soldier than in the scholar. (*Takes Desdemona's hand.*)

IAGO: (*Aside*) He takes her by the palm. Ay, well said,
whisper! With as little a web as this will I ensnare as great a
fly as Cassio. Ay, smile upon her, do! I will gyve[43] thee in
thine own courtship.—You say true; 'tis so, indeed!—If
such tricks as these strip you out of your lieutenantry, it
had been batter you had not kissed your three fingers so

---

[36] *one . . . itself:* I.e., a woman so honest and deserving that even malice would
be forced to approve of her.   [37] *To . . . tail:* I.e., to exchange something valuable for something useless.   [38] *wight:* Person.   [39] *chronicle small beer:* I.e., keep
household accounts (the most trivial of occupations in Iago's opinion).
[40] *liberal:* Licentious.   [41] *speaks home:* Thrusts deeply with his speech.   [42] *relish
him more:* In enjoy him more as.   [43] *gyve:* Bind.

oft—which now again you are most apt to play the sir?[44]
In. Very good! Well kissed! An excellent curtsy![45] 'Tis so,
indeed. Yet again your fingers to your lips? Would they
were clyster pipes[46] for your sake! (*Trumpets within.*) The
Moor! I know his trumpet.[47]

CASSIO: 'Tis truly so.

DESDEMONA: Let's meet him and receive him.

70 CASSIO: Lo, where he comes.

(*Enter Othello and Attendants.*)

OTHELLO: O my fair warrior!

DESDEMONA: My dear Othello.

OTHELLO: It gives me wonder great as my content
     To see you here before me. O my soul's joy!
75   If after every tempest come such calms,
     May the winds blow till they have wakened death,
     And let the laboring bark climb hills of seas
     Olympus-high, and duck again as low
     As hell's from heaven. If it were now to die,
80   'Twere now to be most happy; for I fear
     My soul hath her coritent so absolute
     That not another comfort like to this
     Succeeds in unknown fate.

DESDEMONA: The heavens forbid
85   But that our loves and comforts should increase
     Even as our days do grow.

OTHELLO: Amen to that, sweet powers!
     I cannot speak enough of this content;
     It stops me here (*touches his heart*); it is too much of joy.
90   And this, and this, the greatest discords be

(*They kiss.*)

     That e'er our hearts shall make!

IAGO: (*Aside*) O, you are well tuned now!

___

[44] *the sir:* The fashionable gentleman.   [45] *curtsy:* Courtesy, i.e., bow.   [46] *clyster pipes:* Enema tubes.   [47] *his trumpet:* Great men had their own distinctive calls.

But I'll set down the pegs[48] that make this music,
As honest as I am.

95 **OTHELLO:**   Come, let us to the castle.
News, friends! Our wars are done; the Turks are drowned.
How does my old acquaintance of this isle?
Honey, you shall be well desired in Cyprus;
I have found great love amongst them. O my sweet,

100 I prattle out of fashion, and I dote
In mine own comforts. I prithee, good Iago,
Go to the bay and disembark my coffers.
Bring thou the master to the citadel;
He is a good one, and his worthiness

105 Does challenge[49] much respect. Come, Desdemona,
Once more well met at Cyprus.

(Exit Othello and Desdemona [and all but Iago and Roderigo].)

IAGO: *(To an Attendant)* Do thou meet me presently at the harbor.
(To Roderigo) Come hither. If thou be'st valiant (as they say
base men being in love have then a nobility in their
natures more than is native to them), list me. The lieutenant tonight watches on the court of guard.[50] First, I
must tell thee this: Desdemona is directly in love with him.

RODERIGO: With him? Why, 'tis not possible.

IAGO: Lay thy finger thus *(puts his finger to his lips)*, and let thy soul
be instructed. Mark me with what violence she first loved
the Moor but for bragging and telling her fantastical lies.
To love him still for prating? Let not thy discreet heart
think it. Her eye must be fed. And what delight shall she
have to look on the devil? When the blood is made dull
with the act of sport, there should be a game[51] to inflame
it and to give satiety a fresh appetite, loveliness in favor,[52]
sympathy in years,[53] manners, and beauties; all which the
Moor is defective in. Now for want of these required

---

[48] *set down the pegs:* Loosen the strings (to produce discord).   [49] *challenge:*
Require, exact.   [50] *court of guard:* Guardhouse.   [51] *game:* Sport (with the added
sense of "gamey," "rank").   [52] *favor:* Countenance, appearance.   [53] *sympathy in
years:* Sameness of age.

conveniences,[54] her delicate tenderness will find itself
abused, begin to heave the gorge,[55] disrelish and abhor
the Moor. Very nature will instruct her in it and compel
her to some second choice. Now, sir, this granted—as it is
a most pregnant[56] and unforced position—who stands so
eminent in the degree of this fortune as Cassio does? A
knave very voluble; no further conscionable[57] than in
putting on the mere form of civil and humane[58] seeming
for the better compass of his salt[59] and most hidden
loose[60] affection. Why, none! Why, none! A slipper[61] and
subtle knave, a finder of occasion, that has an eye can
stamp and counterfeit advantages, though true advantage
never present itself. A devilish knave. Besides, the knave is
handsome, young, and hath all those requisites in him
that folly and green minds looks after. A pestilent complete knave, and the woman hath found him already.

110   RODERIGO: I cannot believe that in her; she's full of most
blessed condition.

IAGO: Blessed fig's-end! The wine she drinks is made of
grapes. If she had been blessed, she would never have
loved the Moor. Blessed pudding! Didst thou not see her
paddle with the palm of his hand? Didst not mark that?

RODERIGO: Yes, that I did; but that was but courtesy.

IAGO: Lechery, by this hand! (*Extends his index finger.*) An index[62]
and obscure prologue to the history of lust and foul
thoughts. They met so near with their lips that their
breaths embraced together. Villainous thoughts,
Roderigo. When these mutualities so marshal the way,
hard at hand comes the master and main exercise, th'
incorporate[63] conclusion: Pish! But, sir, be you ruled by
me. I have brought you from Venice. Watch you tonight;
for the command, I'll lay't upon you. Cassio knows you
not. I'll not be far from you. Do you find some occasion

---

[54] *conveniences*: Advantages.   [55] *have the gorge*: Vomit.   [56] *pregnant*: Likely.   [57] *no further conscionable*: Having no more conscience.   [58] *humane*: Polite.   [59] *salt*: Lech-erous.   [60] *loose*: Immoral.   [61] *slipper*: Slippery.   [62] *index*: Pointer.   [63] *incorporate*: Carnal.

to anger Cassio, either by speaking too loud, or tainting[64]
his discipline, or from what other course you please
which the time shall more favorably minister.

RODERIGO: Well.

115   **IAGO:** Sir, he's rash and very sudden in choler,[65] and haply
may strike at you. Provoke him that he may; for even
out of that will I cause these of Cyprus to mutiny, whose
qualification shall come into no true taste[66] again but by
the displanting of Cassio. So shall you have a shorter
journey to your desires by the means I shall then have to
prefer them; and the impediment most profitably
removed without the which there were no expectation of
our prosperity.

RODERIGO: I will do this if you can bring it to any opportunity.

IAGO: I warrant thee. Meet me by and by at the citadel.
I must fetch his necessaries ashore. Farewell.

RODERIGO: Adieu.

(*Exit.*)

IAGO: That Cassio loves her, I do well believe 't;
120   That she loves him, 'tis apt and of great credit.
      The Moor, howbeit that I endure him not,
      Is of a constant, loving, noble nature,
      And I dare think he'll prove o Desdemona
      A most dear[67] husband. Now I do love her too;
125   Not out of absolute[68] lust, though peradventure[69]
      I stand accountant for as great a sin,
      But partly led to diet[70] my revenge,
      For that I do suspect the lusty Moor
      Hath leaped into my seat; the thought whereof
130   Doth, like a poisonous mineral, gnaw my inwards;
      And nothing can or shall content my soul

---

[64] *tainting:* Discrediting.   [65] *choiler:* Anger.   [66] *qualification . . . taste:* I.e.,
appeasement will not be brought about (wine was "qualified" by adding water).
[67] *dear:* Expensive.   [68] *out of absolute:* Absolutely out of.   [69] *peradventure:* Perchance.   [70] *diet:* Feed.

Till I am evened with him, wife for wife,
Or failing so, yet that I put the Moor
At least into a jealousy so strong
135 That judgment cannot cure. Which thing to do,
If this poor trash of Venice, whom I trace[71]
For his quick hunting, stand the putting on,
I'll have our Michael Cassio on the hip,
Abuse him to the Moor in the right garb[72]
140 (For I fear Cassio with my nightcap too),
Make the Moor thank me, love me, and reward me
For making him egregiously an ass
And practicing upon[73] his peace and quiet,
Even to madness. 'Tis here, but yet confused:
145 Knavery's plain face is never seen till used.

(*Exit.*)

SCENE 2. (*A street.*)

(*Enter Othello's Herald, with a proclamation.*)

HERALD: It is Othello's pleasure, our noble and valiant general, that upon certain tidings now arrived importing the
mere perdition[1] of the Turkish fleet, every man put himself into triumph. Some to dance, some to make bon-
fires, each man to what sport and revels his addition[2]
leads him. For, besides these beneficial news, it is the cel-
ebration of his nuptial. So much was his pleasure should
be proclaimed. All offices[3] are open, and there is full liberty of feasting from this present hour of five till the bell
have told eleven. Bless the isle of Cyprus and our noble
general Othello!

(*Exit.*)

---

[71] *trace:* Most editors emend to "trash," meaning to hang weights on a dog to
slow his hunting; but "trace" clearly means something like "put on the trace"
or "set on the track." [72] *right garb:* "Proper fashion." [73] *practicing
upon:* Scheming to destroy. [1] *mere perdition:* Absolute destruction. [2] *addition:*
Rank. [3] *offices:* Kitchens and storerooms of food.

SCENE 3. (*The citadel of Cyprus.*)

(*Enter Othello, Desdemona, Cassio, and Attendants.*)

OTHELLO: Good Michael, look you to the guard tonight.
　　Let's teach ourselves that honorable stop,
　　Not to outsport discretion.
CASSIO: Iago hath direction what to do:
5　　But notwithstanding, with my personal eye
　　Will I look to't.
OTHELLO:　　　　　Iago is most honest.
　　Michael, good night. Tomorrow with your earliest
　　Let me have speech with you. [*To Desdemona*]
10　　　　　　　　　　　Come, my dear love,
　　The purchase made, the fruits are to ensue,
　　That profit's yet to come 'tween me and you.
　　Goodnight.

(*Exit [Othello with Desdemona and Attendants].*)

(*Enter Iago.*)

CASSIO: Welcome, Iago, We must to the watch.
15　IAGO: Not this hour, lieutenant; 'tis not yet ten o' th' clock.
　　Our general cast[1] us thus early for the love of his
　　Desdemona; who let us not therefore blame. He hath
　　not yet made wanton the night with her, and she is sport
　　for Jove.
CASSIO: She's a most exquisite lady.
20　IAGO: And, I'll warrant her, full of game.
CASSIO: Indeed, she's a most fresh and delicate creature.
IAGO: What an eye she has! Methinks it sounds a parley to
　　provocation.
CASSIO: An inviting eye; and yet methinks right modest.
IAGO: And when she speaks, is it not an alarum[2] to love?
25　CASSIO: She is indeed perfection.
IAGO: Well, happiness to their sheets! Come, lieutenant, I have
　　a stoup[3] of wine, and here without are a brace of Cyprus

---

[1] *cast:* Dismissed.　　[2] *alarum:* The call to action, "general quarters."　　[3] *stoup:*
Two-quart tankard.

gallants that would fain have a measure to the health of
black Othello.

CASSIO: Not tonight, good Iago. I have very poor and unhappy
brains for drinking; I could well wish courtesy would
invent some other custom of entertainment

IAGO: O, they are our friends. But one cup! I'll drink for you.

CASSIO: I have drunk but one cup tonight, and that was craftily
qualified[4] too; and behold what innovation it makes here.
I am unfortunate in the infirmity and dare not task my
weakness with any more.

30 IAGO: What, man! 'Tis a night of revels, the gallants desire it.

CASSIO: Where are they?

IAGO: Here, at the door. I pray you call them in.

CASSIO: I'll do't, but it dislikes me.

(*Exit.*)

IAGO: If I can fasten but one cup upon him
35   With that which he hath drunk tonight already,
        He'll be as full of quarrel and offense
        As my young mistress' dog. Now, my sick fool Roderigo,
        Whom love hath turned almost the wrong side out,
        To Desdemona hath tonight caroused
40   Potations pottle-deep;[5] and he's to watch
        Three else[6] of Cyprus, noble swelling spirits,
        That hold their honors in a wary distance,[7]
        The very elements of this warlike isle,
        Have I tonight flustered with flowing cups,
45   And they watch too. Now, 'mongst this flock of drunkards
        Am I to put our Cassio in some action
        That may offend the isle. But here they come.

(*Enter Cassio, Montano, and Gentlemen.*)

        If consequence do but approve my dream,
        My boat sails freely, both with wind and steam.
50 CASSIO: 'Fore God, they have given me a rouse[8] already.

---

[4] *qualified:* Diluted.   [5] *pottle-deep:* To the bottom of the cup.   [6] *else:* Others.
[7] *hold . . . distance:* Scrupulous in maintaining their honor.   [8] *rouse:* Drink.

MONTANO: Good faith, a little one; not past a pint, as I am
    a soldier.

IAGO: Some wine, ho! (*Sings*)

And let me the canakin clink, clink;

    "And let me the canakin clink.

55   A soldier's a man;

        O man's life's but a span,

        Why then, let a solider drink."

    Some wine, boys!

CASSIO: 'Fore God, an excellent song!

60 IAGO: I learned it in England, where indeed they are most
    potent in potting. Your Dane, your German, and your
    swag-bellied[9] Hollander—Drink, ho!—are nothing to your
    English.

CASSIO: Is your Englishman so exquisite[10] in his drinking?

IAGO: Why, he drinks you with facility your Dane dead drunk;
    he sweats not to overthrow your Almain; he gives your
    Hollander a vomit ere the next pottle can be filled.

CASSIO: To the health of our general!

MONTANO: I am for it, lieutenant, and I'll do you justice.

IAGO: O sweet England!

65 (*Sings*) "King Stephen was and a worthy peer;

        His breeches cost him but a crown;

        He held them sixpence all too dear,

        With that he called the tailor lown.[11]

70   He was a wight of high renown,

        And thou art but of low degree:

        'Tis pride that pulls the country down;

        And take thine auld cloak about thee."

    Some wine, ho!

75 CASSIO: 'For God, this is a more exquisite song than the other.

IAGO: Will you hear't again?

CASSIO: No, for I hold him to be unworthy of his place that
    does those things. Well, God's above all; and there be
    souls must be saved, and there be souls must not be saved.

---

9 *swag-bellied:* Hanging.   10 *exquisite:* Superb.   11 *lown:* Lout.

IAGO: It's true, good lieutenant.

CASSIO: For mine own part—no offense to the general, nor any man of quality—I hope to be saved.

80 IAGO: And so do I too, lieutenant.

CASSIO: Ay, but, by your leave, not before me. The lieutenant is to be saved before the ancient. Let's have no more of this; let's to our affairs.—God forgive us our sins!— Gentlemen, let's look to our business. Do not think, gentlemen, I am drunk. This is my ancient; this is my right hand, and this is my left. I am not drunk now. I can stand well enough, and I speak well enough.

GENTLEMEN: Excellent well!

CASSIO: Why, very well then. You must not think then that I am drunk.

(*Exit.*)

MONTANO: To th' platform, masters. Come, let's set the watch.

85 IAGO: You see this fellow that is gone before.

He's a soldier fit to stand by Caesar
And give direction; and do but see his vice.
'Tis to his virtue a just equinox,[12]
The one as long as th' other. 'Tis pity of him.

90 I fear the trust Othello puts him in,
On some odd time of his infirmity,
Will shake this island.

MONTANO: But is he often thus?

IAGO: 'Tis evermore his prologue to his sleep:

95 He'll watch the horologe a double set[13]
If drink rock not his cradle.

MONTANO: It were well
The general were put in mind of it.
Perhaps he sees it not, or his good nature

100 Prizes the virtue that appears in Cassio
And looks not on his evils. Is not this true?

(*Enter Roderigo.*)

---

[12] *just equinox:* Exact balance (of dark and light).   [13] *watch . . . set:* Stay awake twice around the clock.

IAGO: (*Aside*) How no, Roderigo?

I pray you after the lieutenant, go! (*Exit Roderigo.*)

MONTANO: And 'tis great pity that the noble Moor

105 Should hazard such a place as his own second

With one of an ingraft[14] infirmity.

It were an honest action to say so

To the Moor.

IAGO: Not I, for this fair island!

110 I do love Cassio well and would do much

To cure him of this evil. (*"Help! Help!" Within.*)

But hark? What noise?

(*Enter Cassio, pursuing Roderigo.*)

CASSIO: Zounds, you rogue! You rascal!

MONTANO: What's the matter, lieutenant?

115 CASSIO: A knave teach me my duty? I'll beat the knave into a

twiggen[15] bottle.

RODERIGO: Beat me?

CASSIO: Dost thou prate, rogue?

(*Strikes him.*)

MONTANO: Nay, good lieutenant! I pray you, sir, hold your hand.

(*Stays him.*)

CASSIO: Let me go, sir, or I'll knock you o'er the mazzard.[16]

120 MONTANO: Come, come, you're drunk!

CASSIO: Drunk?

(*They fight.*)

IAGO: (*Aside to Roderigo*) Away, I say! Go out and cry a mutiny!

(*Exit Roderigo.*)

Nay, good lieutenant. God's will, gentlemen!

Help, ho! Lieutenant. Sir. Montano.

125 Help, masters! Here's a goodly watch indeed!

(*A bell rings.*)

[14] *ingraft:* Ingrained. [15] *twiggen:* Wicker-covered. [16] *mazzard:* Head.

Who's that which rings the bell? Diablo, ho!
The town will rise. God's will, lieutenant,
You'll be ashamed forever.

(*Enter Othello and Attendants.*)

OTHELLO: What is the matter here?
130   **MONTANO**:   Zounds, I bleed still.
I am hurt to the death.
He dies!

(*He and Cassio fight again.*)

OTHELLO: Hold for your lives!
IAGO: Hold, ho! Lieutenant. Sir. Montano. Gentlemen!
135   Have you forgot all place of sense and duty?
Hold! The general speaks to you. Hold, for shame!
OTHELLO: Why, how now, ho? From whence ariseth this?
Are we turned Turks, and to ourselves do that
Which heaven hath forbid the Ottomites?[17]
140   For Christian shame put by this barbarous brawl!
He that stirs next to carve for his own rage
Holds his soul light;[18] he dies upon his motion.
Silence that dreadful bell! It frights the isle
From her propriety.[19] What is the matter, masters?
145   Honest Iago, that looks dead with grieving,
Speak. Who began this? On thy love, I charge thee.
IAGO: I do not know. Friends all, but now, even now,
In quarter[20] and in terms like bride and groom
Devesting them for bed; and then, but now—
150   As if some planet had unwitted men—
Swords out, and tilting one at other's breasts
In opposition bloody. I cannot speak
Any beginning to this peevish odds,[21]
And would in action glorious I had lost
155   Those legs that brought me to a part of it!

---

[17] *heaven . . . Ottomites*: I.e., by sending the storm which dispersed the Turks.
[18] *Holds his soul light*: Values his soul lightly.   [19] *propriety*: Proper order.   [20] *In quarter*: On duty.   [21] *odds*: Quarrel.

OTHELLO: How comes it, Michael, you are thus forgot?

CASSIO: I pray you pardon me; I cannot speak.

OTHELLO: Worthy Montano, you were wont to be civil;

    The gravity and stillness of your youth

160   The world hath noted, and your name is great

    In mouths of wisest censure.[22] What's the matter

    That you unlace[23] your reputation thus

    And spend your rich opinion[24] for the name

    Of a night-brawler? Give me answer to it.

165 MONTANO: Worthy Othello, I am hurt to danger.

    Your officer, Iago, can inform you,

    While I spare speech, which something now offends[25] me,

    Of all that I do know; nor know I aught

    By me that's said or done amiss this night,

170   Unless self-charity be sometimes a vice,

    And to defend ourselves it be a sin

    When violence assails us.

OTHELLO: Now, by heaven,

    My blood begins my safer guides to rule,

175   And Passion, having my best judgment collied,[26]

    Assay to lead the way. If I once stir

    Or do but lift this arm, the best of you

    Shall sink in my rebuke. Give me to know

    How this foul rout began, who set it on;

180   And he that is approved in this offense,

    Though he had twinned with me, both at a birth,

    Shall lose me. What? In a town of war

    Yet wild, the people's hearts brimful of fear,

    To manage[27] private and domestic quarrel?

185   In night, and on the court and guard of safety?

    'Tis monstrous. Iago, who began't?

MONTANO: If partially affined, or leagued in office,[28]

---

[22] *censure:* Judgment.   [23] *unlace:* Undo (the term refers specifically to the dressing of a wild boar killed in the hunt).   [24] *opinion:* reputation.   [25] *offends:* Harms, hurts.   [26] *collied:* Darkened.   [27] *manage:* Conduct.   [28] *If . . . office:* If you are partial because you are related ("affined") or the brother officer (of Cassio).

Thou dost deliver more or less than truth,
Thou art no soldier.

190 **IAGO:** Touch me not so near.
I had rather have this tongue cut from my mouth
Than it should do offense to Michael Cassio.
Yet I persuade myself to speak the truth
Shall nothing wrong him. This it is, general
195 Montano and myself being in speech,
There comes a fellow crying out for help,
And Cassio following him with determined sword
To execute upon him. Sir, this gentleman
Steps in to Cassio and entreats his pause.
200 Myself the crying fellow did pursue,
Lest by his clamor—as it so fell out—
The town might fall in fright. He, swift of foot,
Outran my purpose; and I returned then rather
For that I heard the clink and fall of swords,
205 And Cassio high in oath; which till tonight
I ne'er might say before. When I came back—
For this was brief—I found them close together
At blow and thrust, even as again they were
When you yourself did part them.
210 More of this matter cannot I report;
But men are men; the best sometimes forget,
Though Cassio did some little wrong to him,
As men in rage strike those that wish them best,
Yet surely Cassio I believe received
215 From him that fled some strange indignity,
Which patience could not pass.²⁹

OTHELLO: I know, Iago,
Thy honesty and love doth mince³⁰ this matter,
Making it light to Cassio. Cassio, I love thee;
220 But never more be officer of mine.

(*Enter Desdemona, attended.*)

²⁹ *pass:* Allow to pass. ³⁰ *mince:* Cut up (i.e., tell only part of).

Look if my gentle love be not raised up.

I'll make thee an example.

DESDEMONA: What is the matter, dear.

OTHELLO: All's well, sweeting;

225   Come away to bed.

(*To Montano*) Sir, for your hurts,

Myself will be your surgeon.

Lead him off.

(*Montano led off.*)

Iago, look with care about the town

230   And silence those whom this vile brawl distracted.

Come, Desdemona: 'tis the soldiers' life

To have their balmy slumbers waked with strife.

(*Exit [with all but Iago and Cassio].*)

IAGO: What, are you hurt, Lieutenant?

CASSIO: Ay, past all surgery.

235   **IAGO:** Marry, God forbid!

CASSIO: Reputation, reputation, reputation! O, I have lost my
    reputation! I have lost the immortal part of myself, and what
    remains is bestial. My reputation, Iago, my reputation.

IAGO: As I am an honest man, I had thought you had received
    some bodily wound. There is more sense[31] in that than in
    reputation. Reputation is an idle and most false imposi-
    tion[32] oft got without merit and lost without deserving.
    You have lost no reputation at all unless you repute your-
    self such a loser. What, man, there are more ways to
    recover the general again. You are but now cast in his
    mood[33]—a punishment more in policy[34] than in malice—
    even so as one would beat his offenseless dog to affright
    an imperious lion. Sue to him again, and he's yours.

CASSIO: I will rather sue to be despised than to deceive so good
    a commander with so slight, so drunken, and so indiscreet
    an officer. Drunk! And speak parrot![35] And squabble!

---

[31] *sense*: Physical feeling.   [32] *imposition*: External thing.   [33] *cast in his mood*: Dismissed because of his anger.   [34] *in policy*: Politically necessary.   [35] *speak
parrot*: Gabble without sense.

Swagger! Swear! and discourse fustian[36] with one's own shadow! O thou invisible spirit of wine, if thou hast no name to be known by, let us call thee devil!

IAGO: What was he that you followed with your sword? What had he done to you?

240 CASSIO: I know not.

IAGO: Is't possible?

CASSIO: I remember a mass of things, but nothing distinctly: a quarrel, but nothing wherefore. O God, that men should put an enemy in their mouths to steal away their brains! that we should with joy, pleasance, revel, and applause transform ourselves into beasts!

IAGO: Why but you are now well enough. How came you thus recovered?

CASSIO: It hath pleased the devil drunkenness to give place to the devil wrath. One unperfectness shows me another, to make me frankly despise myself.

245 IAGO: Come, you are too severe a moraler. As the time, the place, and the condition of this country stands, I could heartily wish this had not befall'n; but since it is as it is, mend it for your own good.

CASSIO: I will ask him for my place again: he shall tell me I am a drunkard. Had I as many months as Hydra, such an answer would stop them all. To be now a sensible man, by and by a fool, and presently a beast! O strange! Every inordinate cup is unblest, and the ingredient is a devil.

IAGO: Come, come, good wine is a good familiar creature if it be well used. Exclaim no more against it. And, good lieutenant, I think you think I love you.

CASSIO: I have well approved it, sir. I drunk!

IAGO: You or any man living may be drunk at a time, man. I tell you what you shall do. Our general's wife is now the general. I may say so in this respect, for that he hath devoted and given up himself to the contemplation, mark, and devotement of her parts[37] and graces. Confess

---

[36] *discourse fustian*: Speak nonsense ("fustian" was a coarse cotton cloth used for stuffing).   [37] *devotement of her parts*: Devotion to her qualities.

yourself freely to her; importune her help to put you in
your place again. She is of so free, so kind, so apt, so
blessed a disposition she holds it a vice in her goodness
not to do more than she is requested. This broken joint
between you and her husband entreat her to splinter;[38]
and my fortunes against any lay[39] worth naming, this
crack or your love shall grow stronger than it was before.

250   CASSIO: You advise me well.

IAGO: I protest, in the sincerity of love and honest kindness.

CASSIO: I think it freely; and betimes in the morning I will
beseech the virtuous Desdemona to undertake for me.
I am desperate of my fortunes if they check[40] me.

IAGO: You are in the right. Good night, lieutenant; I must to
the watch.

CASSIO: Good night, honest Iago.

(*Exit Cassio.*)

255   IAGO: And what's he then that says I play the Villain,
When this advice is free[41] I give, and honest,
Probal to[42] thinking, and indeed the course
To win the Moor again? For 'tis most easy
Th' inclining[43] Desdemona to subdue
260   In any honest suit; she's framed as fruitful[44]
As the free elements.[45] And then for her
To win the Moor—were't to renounce his baptism,
All seals and symbols of redeemèd sin—
His soul is so enfettered to her love
265   That she may make, unmake, do what she list,
Even as her appetite[46] shall play the god
With his weak function.[47] How am I then a villain
To counsel Cassio to this parallel course,
Directly to his good? Divinity of hell!
270   When devils will the blackest sins put on,[48]

---

[38] *splinter:* Splint. [39] *lay:* Wager. [40] *check:* Repulse. [41] *free:* Generous and
open. [42] *Probal to:* Provable by. [43] *inclining.* Inclined (to be helpful).
[44] *framed as fruitful:* Made as generous. [45] *elements:* I.e., basic nature. [46] *appetite:*
Liking. [47] *function:* Thought. [48] *put on:* Advance, further.

They do suggest at first with heavenly shows,[49]
As I do now. For whiles this honest fool
Plies Desdemona to repair his fortune,
And she for him pleads strongly to the Moor,
275   I'll pour this pestilence into his ear:
That she repeals him[50] for her body's lust;
And by how much she strives to do him good,
She shall undo her credit with the Moor.
So will I turn her virtue into pitch,
280   And out of her own goodness make the net
That shall enmesh them all. How now, Roderigo?

(*Enter Roderigo.*)

RODERIGO: I do follow here in the chase, not like a hound that
hunts, but one that fills up the cry.[51] My money is almost
spent; I have been tonight exceedingly well cudgeled; and
I think the issue will be, I shall have so much experience
for my pains; and so, with no money at all, and a little
more wit, return again to Venice.

IAGO: How poor are they that have not patience!
What wound did ever heal but by degrees?
285   Thou know'st we work by wit, and not by witchcraft;
And wit depends on dilatory time.
Does't not go well? Cassio hath beaten thee,
And thou by that small hurt hath cashiered Cassio,
Though other things grow fair against the sun,
290   Yet fruits that blossom first will first be ripe.
Content thyself awhile. By the mass, 'tis morning!
Pleasure and action make the hours seem short.
Retire thee; go where thou art billeted.
Away, I say! Thou shalt know more hereafter.
295   Nay, get thee gone!

(*Exit Roderigo.*)

---

[49] *shows:* Appearances.   [50] *repeals him:* Asks for (Cassio's reinstatement).
[51] *fills up the cry:* Makes up one of the hunting pack, adding to the noise but not
actually tracking.

Two things are to be done:
My wife must move[52] for Cassio to her mistress;
I'll set her on;
Myself awhile[53] to draw the Moor apart
And bring him jump[54] when he may Cassio find
300   Soliciting his wife. Ay, that's the way!
Dull not device by coldness and delay.

(*Exit.*)

ACT 3

SCENE I. (*A Street.*)

(*Enter Cassio [and] Musicians.*)

CASSIO: Masters, play here. I will content your pains.[1]
    Something that's brief; and bid "Good morrow, general."

(*They play.*)

(*Enter Clown.*[2])

CLOWN: Why, masters, have your instruments been in Naples[3]
    that they speak i' th' nose thus?
MUSICIAN: How, sir, how?
5   CLOWN: Are these, I pray you, wind instruments?
MUSICIAN: Ay, marry, are they, sir.
CLOWN: O, thereby hangs a tale.
MUSICIAN: Whereby hangs a tale, sir?
CLOWN: Marry, sir, by many a wind instrument that I know.
    But, masters, here's money for you; and the general so
    likes your music that he desires you, for love's sake, to
    make no more noise with it.
10   MUSICIAN: Well, sir, we will not.

---

[52] *move:* Petition.   [53] *awhile:* At the same time.   [54] *jump:* At the precise
moment and place.   [1] *content your pains:* Reward your efforts.   [2] *Clown:* Fool.
[3] *Naples:* This may refer either to the Neapolitan nasal tone, or to syphilis—rife
in Naples—which breaks down the nose.

CLOWN: If you have any music that may not be heard, to't
again. But, as they say, to hear music the general does not
greatly care.

MUSICIAN: We have none such, sir.

CLOWN: Then put up your pipes in your bag, for I'll away. Go,
vanish into air, away!

(*Exit Musicians.*)

CASSIO: Dost thou hear me, mine honest friend?

15 CLOWN: No. I hear not your honest friend. I hear you.

CASSIO: Prithee keep up thy quillets.[4] There's a poor piece
of gold for thee. If the gentlewoman that attends the
general's wife be stirring, tell her there's one Cassio
entreats her a little favor of speech. Wilt thou do this?

CLOWN: She is stirring, sir. If she will stir hither, I shall seem
to notify unto her.[5]

(*Exit Clown.*)

(*Enter Iago.*)

CASSIO: In happy time, Iago.

IAGO: You have not been abed then?

20 CASSIO: Why no, the day had broke before we parted.
I have made bold, Iago, to send in to your wife;
My suit to her is that she will to virtuous Desdemona
Procure me some access.

IAGO: I'll send her to you presently,

25   And I'll devise a mean to draw the Moor
Out of the way, that your converse and business
May be more free.

CASSIO: I humbly thank you for't.

(*Exit [Iago].*)

                    I never knew

30   A Florentine[6] more kind and honest.

---

[4] *quillets:* Puns.   [5] *seem . . . her:* The Clown is mocking Cassio's overly elegant
manner of speaking.   [6] *Florentine:* I.e., Iago is as king as if he were from Cassio's home town. Florence.

(*Enter Emilia.*)

EMILIA. Good morrow, good Lieutenant. I am sorry
 For your displeasure;[7] but all will sure be well.
 The general and his wife are talking of it,
 And she speaks for you stoutly. The Moor replies
35 That he you hurt is of great fame in Cyprus
 And great affinity,[8] and that in wholesome wisdom
 He might not but refuse you. But he protests he loves you,
 And needs no other suitor but his likings
 To bring you in again.
40 CASSIO: Yet I beseech you,
 If you think fit, or that it may be done,
 Give me advantage of some brief discourse
 With Desdemona alone.
EMILIA: Pray you come in.
45   I will bestow you where you shall have time
 To speak your bosom[9] freely.
CASSIO: I am much bound to you.

(*Exeunt.*)

SCENE 2. (*The citadel.*)

(*Enter Othello, Iago, and Gentlemen.*)

OTHELLO: These letters give, Iago, to the pilot
 And by him do my duties to the Senate.
 That done, I will be walking on the works;
 Repair[1] there to me.
5 IAGO: Well, my good lord, I'll do't.
OTHELLO: This fortification, gentlemen, shall we see't?
GENTLEMEN: We'll wait upon your lordship.

(*Exeunt.*)

---

[7] *displeasure:* Discomforting. [8] *affinity:* Family. [9] *bosom:* Inmost thoughts.
[1] *Repair:* Go.

SCENE 3 (*The citadel.*)

(*Enter Desdemona, Cassio, and Emilia.*)

DESDEMONA: Be thou assured, good Cassio, I will do
All my abilities in thy behalf.
EMILIA: Good madam, do. I warrant it grieves my husband
As if the cause were his.
DESDEMONA: O, that's an honest fellow. Do not doubt,
Cassio,
5   But I will have my lord and you again
As friendly as you were.
CASSIO: Bounteous madam,
Whatever shall become of Michael Cassio,
He's never anything but your true servant.
10   **DESDEMONA:** I know't; I thank you. You do love my lord.
You have known him long, and be you well assured
He shall in strangeness stand no father off
Than in a politic distance.[1]
CASSIO: Ay, but, lady,
20   That policy may either last so long,
Or feed upon such nice[2] and waterish diet,
Or breed itself so out of circumstances,[3]
That, I being absent, and my place supplied,[4]
My general will forget my love and service.
25   **DESDEMONA:** Do not doubt[5] that; before Emilia here
I give thee warrant of thy place. Assure thee,
If I do vow a friendship, I'll perform it
To the last article. My lord shall never rest;
I'll watch him tame[6] and talk him out of patience;
30   His bed shall seem a school, his board a shrift;[7]
I'll intermingle everything he does
With Cassio's suit. Therefore be merry, Cassio,

---

[1] *He . . . distance:* I.e., he shall act no more distant to you than is necessary for political reasons.   [2] *nice:* Trivial.   [3] *Or . . . circumstances:* I.e., or grow so on the basis of accidental happenings and political needs.   [4] *supplied:* Filled.   [5] *doubt:* Imagine.   [6] *watch him tame:* Animals were tamed by being kept awake.   [7] *board a shrift:* Table (seem) a confessional.

For they solicitor shall rather die
Than give thy cause away.

(*Enter Othello and Iago [at a distance].*)

35   **EMILIA:** Madam, here comes my lord.

CASSIO: Madam, I'll take my leave.

DESDEMONA: Why, stay, and hear me speak.

CASSIO: Madam, not now. I am very ill at ease,
    Unfit for mine own purposes.

40   **DESDEMONA:** Well, do you discretion.

(*Exit Cassio.*)

IAGO: Ha! I like not that.

OTHELLO: What dost thou say?

IAGO: Nothing, my lord; or if—I know not what.

OTHELLO: Was not that Cassio parted from my wife?

45   **IAGO:** Cassio, my lord? No, sure, I cannot think it
    That he would steal away so guilty-like,
    Seeing your coming.

OTHELLO: I do believe 'twas he.

DESDEMONA: (*Coming to them*) How now, my lord?

50   I have been talking with, a suitor here,
    A man that languishes in your displeasure.

OTHELLO: Who is't you mean?

DESDEMONA: Why, your lieutenant, Cassio. Good my lord,
    If I have any grace or power to move you,

55   His present[8] reconciliation take.
    For if he be not one that truly loves you,
    That errs in ignorance, and not in cunning,
    I have no judgment in an honest face.
    I prithee call him back.

60   **OTHELLO:**   Went he hence now?

DESDEMONA: I' sooth so humbled
    That he hath left part of his grief with me
    To suffer with him. Good love, call him back.

OTHELLO: Not now, sweet Desdemon: some other time.

---

[8] *present:* Immediate.

65 **DESDEMONA:** But shall't be shortly?

OTHELLO: The sooner, sweet, for you.

DESDEMONA: Shall't be tonight at supper?

OTHELLO: No, not tonight.

DESDEMONA: Tomorrow dinner then?

70 **OTHELLO:**   I shall not dine at home;

I meet the captains at the citadel.

DESDEMONA: Why then, tomorrow night, on Tuesday morn,

On Tuesday noon, or night, on Wednesday morn.

I prithee name the time, but let it not

75 Exceed three days. In faith, he's penitent;

And yet his trespass, in our common reason

(Save that, they say, the wars must make example

Out of her best), is not almost a fault

T' incur a private check.[9] When shall he come?

80 Tell me, Othello. I wonder in my soul

What you would ask me that I should deny

Or stand so mamm'ring[10] on. What? Michael Cassio,

That came awooing with you, and so many a time,

When I have spoke of you dispraisingly,

85 Hath ta'en your part—to have so much to do

To bring him in? By'r Lady, I could do much—

OTHELLO: Prithee no more. Let him come when he will!

I will deny thee nothing.

DESDEMONA: Why this is not a boon;

90 'Tis as I should entreat you wear your gloves,

Or feed on nourishing dishes, or keep you warm,

Or sue to you to do a peculiar profit[11]

To your own person. Nay, when I have a suit

Wherein I mean to touch your love indeed,

95 It shall be full of poise[12] and difficult weight,

And fearful to be granted.

OTHELLO: I will deny thee nothing!

Whereon I do beseech thee grant me this,

---

[9] *is . . . check:* Is almost not serious enough for a private rebuke (let alone a public disgrace).   [10] *mamm'ring:* Hesitating.   [11] *peculiar profit:* Particularly personal
good.   [12] *poise:* Weight.

To leave me but a little to myself.

100 DESDEMONA: Shall I deny you? No. Farewell, my lord.

OTHELLO: Farewell, my Desdemona: I'll come to thee
    straight.¹³

DESDEMONA: Emilia, come. Be as your fancies teach you;
    Whate'er you be, I am obedient.

(*Exit [with Emilia].*)

OTHELLO: Excellent wretch! Perdition catch my soul

105   But I do love thee! And when I love thee not,
    Chaos is come again.

IAGO: My noble lord——

OTHELLO: What dost thou say, Iago?

IAGO: Did Michael Cassio, when you wooed my lady,

110   Know of your love?

OTHELLO: He did, from first to last. Why dost thou ask?

IAGO: But for a satisfaction of my thought,
    No further harm.

OTHELLO: Why of they thought, Iago?

115 IAGO: I did not think he had been acquainted with her.

OTHELLO: O, yes, and went between us¹⁴ very oft.

IAGO: Indeed?

OTHELLO: Indeed? Ay, indeed! Discern'st thou aught in that?
    Is he not honest?

120 IAGO: Honest, my lord?

OTHELLO: Honest? Ay, honest.

IAGO: My lord, for aught I know.

OTHELLO: What dost thou think?

IAGO: Think, my lord?

125 OTHELLO: Think, my lord?
    By heaven, thou echoest me,
    As if there were some monster in thy thought
    Too hideous to be shown. Thou dost mean something.
    I heard thee say even now, thou lik'st not that,

130   When Cassio left my wife. What didst not like?

---

¹³ *straight:* At once.   ¹⁴ *between us:* I.e., as messenger.

And when I told thee he was of my counsel[15]
Of my whole course of wooing, thou cried'st "Indeed?"
And didst contract and purse thy brow together,
As if thou then hadst shut up in thy brain
135   Some horrible conceit.[16] If thou dost love me,
Show me thy thought.

IAGO: My lord, you know I love you.

OTHELLO: I think thou dost;
And, for I know thou'rt full of love and honesty
140   And weigh'st thy words before thou giv'st them breath,
Therefore these stops[17] of thine fright me the more;
For such things in a false disloyal knave
Are tricks of custom;[18] but in a man that's just
They're close dilations,[19] working from the heart
145   That passion cannot rule.

IAGO: For Michael Cassio,
I dare be sworn, I think that he is honest.

OTHELLO: I think so too.

IAGO: Men should be what they seem;
150   Or those that be not, would they might seem none!

OTHELLO: Certain, men should be what they seem.

IAGO: Why then, I think Cassio's an honest man.

OTHELLO: Nay, yet there's more in this?
I prithee speak to me as to thy thinkings,
155   As thou dost ruminate, and give thy worst of thoughts
The worst of words.

IAGO: Good my lord, pardon me:
Though I am bound to every act of duty,
I am not bound to that all slaves are free to.
160   Utter my thoughts? Why, say they are vile and false,
As where's that palace where into foul things
Sometimes intrude not? Who has that breast so pure
But some uncleanly apprehensions
Keep leets and law days,[20] and in sessions sit

---

[15] *of my counsel:* In my confidence.   [16] *conceit:* Thought.   [17] *stops:* Interruptions.
[18] *of custom:* Customary.   [19] *close dilations:* Expressions of hidden thoughts.
[20] *leets and law days:* Meeting of local courts.

165   With meditations lawful?

    OTHELLO: Thou dost conspire against thy friend, Iago,

        If thou but think'st him wronged, and mak'st his ear

        A stranger to thy thoughts.

    IAGO: I do beseech you—

170   Though I perchance am vicious in my guess

        (As I confess it is my nature's plague

        To spy into abuses, and of my jealousy

        Shape faults that are not), that your wisdom

        From one that so imperfectly conceits

175   Would take no notice, nor build yourself a trouble

        Out of his scattering and unsure observance.

        It were not for your quiet nor your good,

        Nor for my manhood, honesty, and wisdom,

        To let you know my thoughts.

180   OTHELLO: What dost thou mean?

    IAGO: Good name in man and woman, dear my lord,

        Is the immediate jewel of their souls.

        Who steals my purse steals trash; 'tis something, nothing;

        'Twas mine, 'tis his, and has been slave to thousands;

185   But he that filches from me my good name

        Robs me of that which not enriches him

        And makes me poor indeed.

    OTHELLO: By heaven, I'll know thy thoughts!

    IAGO: You cannot, if my heart were in your hand;

190   Nor shall not whilst 'tis in my custody.

    OTHELLO: Ha!

    IAGO: O, beware, my lord, of jealousy!

        It is the green-eyed monster, which doth mock

        The meat it feeds on. That cuckold lives in bliss

195   Who certain of his fate, loves not his wronger;

        But O, what damnèd minutes tells[21] he o'er

        Who dotes, yet doubts—suspects, yet fondly[22] loves!

    OTHELLO: O misery.

    IAGO: Poor and content is rich, and rich enough;

200   But riches fineless[23] is as poor as winter

---

[21] *tells:* Counts.   [22] *fondly:* Foolishly.   [23] *fineless:* Infinite.

To him that ever fears he shall be poor.
Good God the souls of all my tribe defend
From jealousy!

OTHELLO: Why? Why is this?

205   Think'st thou I'd make a life of jealousy,
To follow still[24] the changes of the moon
With fresh suspicions? No! To be once in doubt
Is to be resolved. Exchange me for a goat
When I shall turn the business of my soul

210   To such exsufflicate and blown[25] surmises,
Matching thy inference. 'Tis not to make me jealous
To say my wife is fair, feeds well, loves company,
Is free of speech, sings, plays, and dances;
Where virtue is, these are more virtuous.

215   Nor from mine own weak merits will I draw
The smallest fear or doubt of her revolt,
For she had eyes, and chose me. No, Iago;
I'll see before I doubt; when I doubt, prove;
And on the proof there is no more but this:

220   Away at once with love or jealousy!

IAGO: I am glad of this; for now I shall have reason
To show the love and duty that I bear you
With franker spirit. Therefore, as I am bound,
Receive it from me. I speak not yet of proof.

225   Look to your wife; observe her well with Cassio;
Wear your eyes thus: not jealous nor secure.
I would not have your free and noble nature
Out of self-bounty[26] be abused. Look to't.
I know our country disposition well:

230   In Venice they do let heaven see the pranks
They dare not show their husbands; their best conscience
Is not to leave't undone, but kept unknown.[27]

---

[24] *To follow still:* To change always (as the phases of the moon).   [25] *exsufflicate and blown:* Inflated and flyblown.   [26] *self-bounty:* Innate kindness (which attributes his own motives to others).   [27] *their . . . unknown:* I.e., their morality does not forbid adultery, but it does forbid being found out.

OTHELLO: Dost thou say so?

IAGO: She did deceive her father, marrying you;

235 And when she seemed to shake and fear your looks,

 She loved them most.

OTHELLO: And so she did.

IAGO: Why, go to, then!

 She that so young could give out such a seeming

240 To seel[28] her father's eyes up close as oak[29]—

 He thought 'twas witchcraft. But I am much to blame.

 I humbly do beseech you of your pardon

 For too much loving you.

OTHELLO: I am bound to thee forever.

245 IAGO: I see this hath a little dashed your spirits.

OTHELLO: Not a jot, not a jot.

IAGO: Trust me, I fear it has.

 I hope you will consider what is spoke

 Come from my love. But I do see y' are moved.

250 I am to pray you not to strain[30] my speech

 To grosser issues, nor to larger reach[31]

 Than to suspicion.

OTHELLO: I will not.

IAGO: Should you do so, my lord,

255 My speech should fall into such vile success

 Which my thoughts aimed not. Cassio's my worthy friend—

 My lord, I see y' are moved.

OTHELLO: No, not much moved.

 I do not think but Desdemona's honest.

260 IAGO: Long live she so. And long live you to think so.

OTHELLO: And yet, how nature erring from itself——

IAGO: Ay, there's the point, as (to be bold with you)

 Not to affect many proposed matches

 Of her own clime, complexion, and degree,[32]

265 Whereto we see in all things nature tends[33]—

 Foh! one may smell in such a will most rank,

---

[28] *seel*: Hoodwink. [29] *oak*: A close-grained wood. [30] *strain*: Enlarge the meaning of. [31] *reach*: Meaning. [32] *degree*: Social station. [33] *in . . . tends*: I.e., all things in nature seek out their own kind.

Foul disproportions, thoughts unnatural.
But, pardon me, I do not in position[34]
Distinctly[35] speak of her; though I may fear
270 Her will, recoiling to her better judgment,
May fall to match[36] you with her country forms,[37]
And happily[38] repent.

OTHELLO: Farewell, farewell!
If more thou dost perceive, let me know more.
275 Set on thy wife to observe. Leave me, Iago.

IAGO: My lord, I take my leave.

(Going.)

OTHELLO: Why did I marry? This honest creature doubtless
Sees and knows more, much more, than he unfolds.

IAGO: (Returns.) My lord, I would I might entreat your honor
280 To scan this thing no farther. Leave it to time.
Although 'tis fit that Cassio have his place,
For sure he fills it up with great ability,
Yet, if you please to hold him off awhile,
You shall by that perceive him and his means.
285 Note if your lady strain his entertainment[39]
With any strong or vehement importunity,
Much will be seen in that. In the meantime
Let me be thought too busy in my fears
(As worthy cause I have to fear I am)
290 And hold her free, I do beseech your honor.

OTHELLO: Fear not my government.[40]

IAGO: I once more take my leave.

(Exit.)

OTHELLO: This fellow's of exceeding honesty,
And knows all qualities,[41] with a learned spirit
295 Of human dealings. If I do prove her haggard.[42]

---

[34] position: General argument.   [35] Distinctly: Specifically.   [36] fall to match: Happen to compare.   [37] country forms: I.e., the familiar appearances of her countrymen.   [38] happily: By chance.   [39] strain his entertainment: Urge strongly that he be reinstated.   [40] government: Self-control.   [41] qualities: Natures, types of people.   [42] haggard: A partly trained hawk which has gone wild again.

Though that her jesses[43] were my dear heartstrings,
I'd whistle her off and let her down the wind[44]
To prey at fortune. Haply for[45] I am black
And have not those soft parts[46] of conversation
300   That chamberers[47] have, or for I am declined
Into the vale of years—yet that's not much—
She's gone. I am abused, and my relief
Must be to loathe her. O curse of marriage,
That we can call these delicate creatures ours,
305   And not their appetites! I had rather be a toad
And live upon the vapor of a dungeon
Than keep a corner in the thing I love
For others' uses. Yet 'tis the plague to great ones;
Prerogatived are they less than the base.
310   'Tis destiny unshunnable, like death.
Even then this forked[48] plague is fated to us
When we do quicken.[49] Look where she comes.

(Enter Desdemona and Emilia.)

If she be false, heaven mocked itself!
I'll not believe't.
315   **DESDEMONA:**   How now, my dear Othello?
Your dinner, and the generous islanders
By you invited, do attend[50] your presence.
OTIIELLO: I am to blame.
DESDEMONA: Why do you speak so faintly?
320   And you not well?
OTHELLO: I have a pain upon my forehead, here.[51]
DESDEMONA: Why, that's with watching; 'twill away again.
Let me but bind it hard, within this hour
It will be well.

---

[43] *Jesses:* Straps which held the hawk's legs to the trainer's wrist.   [44] *I'd . . . wind:*
I would release her (like an untamable hawk) and let her fly free.
[45] *Haply for:* It may be because.   [46] *soft parts:* Gentle qualities and manners.
[47] *chamberers:* Courtiers—or perhaps, accomplished seducers.   [48] *forkèd:* Horned
(the sign of the cuckold was horns).   [49] *do quicken:* Are born.   [50] *attend:* Wait.
[51] *here:* The points to his imaginary horns.

325   **OTHELLO:**   Your napkin[52] is too little;

(He pushes the handkerchief away, and it falls.)

      Let it[53] alone. Come, I'll go in with you.

DESDEMONA: I am very sorry that you are not well.

(Exit [with Othello].)

EMILIA: I am glad I have found this napkin;

      This was her first remembrance from the Moor.

330   My wayward husband hath a hundred times

      Wooed me to steal it; but she so loves the token

      (For he conjured her she should ever keep it)

      That she reserves it evermore about her

      To kiss and talk to. I'll have the work ta'en out[54]

335   And give't Iago. What he will do with it,

      Heaven knows, not I; I nothing[55] but to please his fantasy.[56]

(Enter Iago.)

IAGO: How now? What do you here alone?

EMILIA: Do not you chide; I have a thing for you.

IAGO: You have a thing for me? It is a common thing——

340   **EMILIA:** Ha?

IAGO: To have a foolish wife.

EMILIA: O, is that all? What will you give me now

      For that same handkerchief?

IAGO: What handkerchief?

345   **EMILIA:** What handkerchief?

      Why, that the Moor first gave to Desdemona,

      That which so often you did bid me steal.

IAGO: Hast stol'n it from her?

EMILIA: No, but she let it drop by negligence,

350   And to th' advantage,[57] I, being here, took't up.

      Look, here't is.

---

[52] *napkin:* Elaborately worked handkerchief.   [53] *it:* It makes a considerable difference in the interpretation of later events whether this "it" refers to Othello's forehead or to the handkerchief; nothing in the text makes the reference clear.   [54] *work ta'en out:* Needlework copied.   [55] *I nothing:* I wish nothing. [56] *fantasy:* Fancy, whim.   [57] *to th' advantage:* Being lucky.

IAGO: A good wench. Give it me.

EMILIA: What will you do with't, that you have been so earnest
To have me filch it?

355 **IAGO:** Why, what is that to you?

(*Takes it.*)

EMILIA: If it be not for some purpose of import,[58]
Give't me again. Poor lady, she'll run mad
When she shall lack[59] it.

IAGO: Be not acknown on't.[60]

360 I have use for it. Go, leave me.

(*Exit Emilia.*)

I will in Cassio's lodging lose this napkin
And let him find it. Trifles light as air
Are to the jealous confirmations strong
As proofs of Holy Writ. This may do something.

365 The Moor already changes with my poison:
Dangerous conceits are in their natures poisons,
Which at the first are scarce found to distaste,[61]
But, with a little,[62] act upon the blood,
Burn like the mines of sulfur. I did say so.

(*Enter Othello.*)

370 Look where he comes! Not poppy nor mandragora,[63]
Nor all the drowsy syrups of the world,
Shall ever medicine thee to that sweet sleep
Which thou owedst[64] yesterday.

OTHELLO: Ha! ha! False to me?

375 **IAGO:** Why, how now, general? No more of that.

OTHELLO: Avaunt! be gone! Thou hast set me on the rack.
I swear 'tis better to be much abused
Than but to know't a little.

IAGO: How now, my lord?

---

[58] *import:* Importance. [59] *lack:* Miss. [60] *Be not acknown on't:* Forget you ever
saw it. [61] *are scarce found to distaste:* Scarcely can be tasted. [62] *with a little:* In a
short time. [63] *poppy nor mandragora:* Soporincs. [64] *owedst:* Possessed.

375   OTHELLO: What sense had I of her stol'n hours of lust?
      I saw't not, thought it not, it harmed not me;
      I slept the next night well, fed well, was free and merry;
      I found not Cassio's kisses on her lips.
      He that is robbed, not wanting[65] What is stol'n,
380   Let him not know't, and he's not robbed at all.
  IAGO: I am sorry to hear this.
  OTHELLO: I had been happy if the general camp,
      Pioners[66] and all, had tasted her sweet body,
      So I had nothing known. O now, forever
385   Farewell the tranquil mind! Farewell content!
      Farewell the plumèd troops, and the big wars
      That makes ambition virtue! O, farewell!
      Farewell the neighing steed and the shrill trump,
      The spirit-stirring drum, th' ear-piercing fife,
390   The royal banner, and all quality,
      Pride, pomp, and circumstance[67] of glorious war!
      And O you mortal engines[68] whose rude throats
      Th' immortal Jove's dread clamors[69] counterfeit,
      Farewell! Othello's occupation's gone!
400   IAGO: Is't possible, my lord?
  OTHELLO: Villain, be sure thou prove my love a whore!
      Be sure of it; give me the ocular proof;
      Or, by the worth of mine eternal soul,
      Thou hadst been better have been born a dog
405   Than answer my waked wrath!
  IAGO: Is't come to this?
  OTHELLO: Make me to see't; or at the least so prove it
      That the probation[70] bear no hinge nor loop
      To hang a doubt on—or woe upon thy life!
410   IAGO: My noble lord——
  OTHELLO: If thou dost slander her and torture me,
      Never pray more; abandon all remorse;
      On horror's head horrors accumulate;

---

[65] *wanting:* Missing.   [66] *Pioners:* The basest manual laborers in the army, who dug trenches and mines.   [67] *circumstance:* Pageantry.   [68] *mortal engines:* Lethal weapons, i.e., cannon.   [69] *clamors:* I.e., thunder.   [70] *probation:* Proof.

Do deeds to make heaven weep, all earth amazed;
415   For nothing canst thou to damnation add
      Greater than that.

IAGO: O grace! O heaven forgive me!
      Are you a man? Have you a soul or sense?
      God b' wi' you! Take mine office. O wretched fool,
420   That lov'st to make thine honesty a vice!
      O monstrous world! Take note, take note, O world,
      To be direct and honest is not safe.
      I thank you for this profit, and from hence
      I'll love no friend, sith[71] love breeds such offense.

425   OTHELLO: Nay, stay. Thou shouldst be honest.

IAGO: I should be wise; for honesty's a fool
      And loses that it works for.

OTHELLO: By the world,
      I think my wife be honest, and think she is not;
430   I think that thou art just, and think thou art not.
      I'll have some proof. My name, that was as fresh
      As Dian's[72] visage, is now begrimed and black
      As mine own face. If there be cords, or knives,
      Poison, or fire, or suffocating streams,
435   I'll not endure it. Would I were satisfied!

IAGO: I see you are eaten up with passion.
      I do repent me that I put it to you.
      You would be satisfied?

OTHELLO: Would? Nay, and I will.

440   IAGO: And may; but how? How satisfied, my lord?
      Would you, the supervisor,[73] grossly gape on?
      Behold her topped?

OTHELLO: Death and damnation! O!

IAGO: It were a tedious[74] difficulty, I think,
445   To bring them to that prospect.[75] Damn them then,
      If ever mortal eyes do see them bolster[76]
      More than their own! What then? How then?

---

[71] *sith:* Since.   [72] *Dian's:* Diana's (goddess of the moon and of chastity).
[73] *supervisor:* Onlooker.   [74] *tedious:* Hard to arrange.   [75] *prospect:* Sight (where they can be seen).   [76] *bolster:* Go to bed.

What shall I say? Where's satisfaction?
It is impossible you should see this,
450 Were they as prime[77] as goats, as hot as monkeys,
As salt as wolves in pride,[78] and fools as gross
As ignorance made drunk. But yet, I say,
If imputation and strong circumstances
Which lead directly to the door of truth
455 Will give you satisfaction, you might have't.

OTHELLO: Give me a living reason she's disloyal.

IAGO: I do not like the office.[79]
But sith I am entered in this cause so far,
Pricked[80] to't by foolish honesty and love,
460 I will go on. I lay with Cassio lately.
And being troubled with a raging tooth,
I could not sleep.
There are a kind of men so loose of soul
That in their sleeps will mutter their affairs.
465 One of this kind is Cassio.
In sleep I heard him say, "Sweet Desdemona,
Let us be wary, let us hide our loves!"
And then, sir, would he gripe[81] and wring my hand,
Cry "O sweet creature!" Then kiss me hard,
470 As if he plucked up kisses by the roots
That grew upon my lips; laid his leg o'er my thigh,
And sigh, and kiss, and then cry, "Cursèd fate
That gave thee to the Moor!".

OTHELLO: O monstrous! monstrous!

475 IAGO: Nay, this was but his dream.

OTHELLO: But this denoted a foregone conclusion,[82]
'Tis a shrewd doubt,[83] though it be but a dream.

IAGO: And this may help to thicken other proofs
That do demonstrate[84] thinly.

480 OTHELLO: I'll tear her all to pieces!

IAGO: Nay, yet be wise. Yet we see nothing done;

---

[77] *prime, Salt:* Lustful.   [78] *pride:* Heat.   [79] *office:* Duty.   [80] *Pricked:* Spurred.
[81] *gripe:* Seize.   [82] *foregone conclusion:* Consummated fact.   [83] *shrewd doubt:* Penetrating guess.   [84] *demonstrate:* Show, appear.

She may be honest yet. Tell me but this:
Have you not sometimes seen a handkerchief
Spotted with strawberries in your wife's hand?

485 OTHELLO: I gave her such a one; 'twas my first gift.

IAGO: I know not that; but such a handkerchief—
I am sure it was your wife's—did I today
See Cassio wipe his beard with.

OTHELLO: If it be that——

490 IAGO: If it be that, or any that was hers,
It speaks against her with the other proofs.

OTHELLO: O, that the slave had forty thousand lives!
One is too poor, too weak for my revenge.
Now do I see 'tis true. Look here, Iago:

495 All my fond love thus do I blow to heaven.
'Tis gone.
Arise, black vengeance, from the hollow hell!
Yield up, O Love, thy crown and hearted[85] throne
To tyrannous hate! Swell, bosom, with thy fraught,[86]

500 For 'tis of aspics'[87] tongues.

IAGO: Yet be content.[88]

OTHELLO: O, Blood, blood, blood!

IAGO: Patience, I say. Your mind may change.

OTHELLO: Never, Iago. Like to the Pontic Sea,[89]

505 Whose icy current and compulsive course
Nev'r keeps retiring ebb, but keeps due on
To the Propontic and the Hellespont,
Even so my bloody thoughts, with violent pace,
Shall nev'r look back, nev'r ebb to humble love,

510 Till that a capable and wide[90] revenge
Swallow them up. (*He kneels.*) Now, by yond marble heaven,
In the due reverence of a sacred vow
I here engage my words.

IAGO: Do not rise yet.

---

[85] *hearted:* Seated in the heart.   [86] *fraught:* Burden.   [87] *aspics':* Asps'.   [88] *content:* Patient, quiet.   [89] *Pontic Sea:* The Black Sea (famous for the strong and constant current with which it flows through the Bosporus into the Mediterranean, where the water level is lower).   [90] *capable and wide:* Sufficient and far-reaching.

(Iago kneels.)

515　　Witness, you ever-burning light above,
　　　　You elements that clip[91] us round about,
　　　　Witness that here Iago doth give up
　　　　The execution[92] of his wit, hands, heart
　　　　To wronged Othello's service! Let him command,
520　　And to obey shall be in me remorse,[93]
　　　　What bloody business ever.[94]

(They rise.)

OTHELLO:　　　　　　　　I greet thy love,
　　　　Not with vain thanks but with acceptance bounteous,[95]
　　　　And will upon the instant put thee to't.[96]
525　　Within these three days let me hear thee say
　　　　That Cassio's not alive.
IAGO: My friend is dead. 'Tis done at your request.
　　　　But let her live.
OTHELLO:　　　　　　Damn her, lewd minx! O, damn her!
　　　　Damn her!
530　　Come, go with me apart. I will withdraw
　　　　To furnish me with some swift means of death
　　　　For the fair devil. Now art thou my lieutenant.
IAGO: I am your own forever.

(Exeunt.)

SCENE 4 *(A street.)*

(Enter Desdemona, Emilia, and Clown.)

DESDEMONA: Do you know, sirrah, where Lieutenant Cassio
　　　　lies?[1]
5　**CLOWN:** I dare not say he lies anywhere.
DESDEMONA: Why, man?

---

[91] *clip:* Enfold.　[92] *execution:* Workings, action.　[93] *remorse:* Pity.　[94] *ever:*
Soever.　[95] *bounteous:* Absolute.　[96] *to't:* I.e., to the work you have said you
are prepared to do.　[1] *lies:* Lodges.

CLOWN: He's a soldier, and for me to say a soldier lies, 'tis
    stabbing.

DESDEMONA: Go to. Where lodges he?

CLOWN: To tell you where he lodges is to tell you where I lie.

10 DESDEMONA: Can anything be made of this?

CLOWN: I know not where he lodges, and for me to devise a
    lodging, and say he lies here or he lies there, were to lie
    in mine own throat.[2]

DESDEMONA: Can you enquire him out, and be edified[3]
    by report?

CLOWN: I will catechize the world for him; that is, make ques-
    tions, and by them answer.

15 DESDEMONA: Seek him, bid him come hither. Tell him I have
    moved[4] my lord on his behalf and hope all will be well.

CLOWN: To do this is within the compass[5] of man's wit, and
    therefore I will attempt to doing it.

(*Exit Clown.*)

DESDEMONA: Where should[6] I lose the handkerchief. Emilia?

EMILIA: I know not, madam.

20 DESDEMONA: Believe me, I had rather have lost my purse
    Full of crusadoes.[7] And but my noble Moor
    Is true of mind, and made of no such baseness
    As jealous creatures are, it were enough
    To put him to ill thinking.

25 EMILIA: Is he not jealous?

DESDEMONA: Who? He? I think the sun where he was born
    Drew all such humors[8] from him.

EMILIA: Look where he comes.

(*Enter Othello.*)

DESDEMONA: I will not leave him now till Cassio

30   Be called to him. How is't with you, my lord?

---

[2] *lie in mine own throat:* To lie in the throat is to lie absolutely and completely.
[3] *edified:* Enlightened (Desdemona mocks the Clown's overly elaborate
diction).   [4] *moved:* Pleaded with.   [5] *compass:* Reach.   [6] *should:* Might.   [7] *crusa-
does:* Portuguese gold coins.   [8] *humors:* Characteristics.

OTHELLO: Well, my good lady. (*Aside*) O, hardness to
    dissemble[9]—

    How do you, Desdemona?

DESDEMONA: Well, my good lord.

OTHELLO: Give me your hand. This hand is moist,[10] my lady.

35 **DESDEMONA:** It hath felt no age nor known no sorrow.

OTHELLO: This argues[11] fruitfulness and liberal[12] heart.

    Hot, hot, and moist. This hand of yours requires

    A sequester[13] from liberty; fasting and prayer;

    Much castigation; exercise devout;

40   For here's a young and sweating devil here

    That commonly rebels. 'Tis a good hand,

    A frank one.

DESDEMONA: You may, indeed, say so;

    For 'twas that hand that gave away my heart.

45 **OTHELLO:** A liberal hand! The hearts of old gave hands,

    But our new heraldry[14] is hands, not hearts.

DESDEMONA: I cannot speak of this. Come now, your promise!

OTHELLO: What promise, chuck?

DESDEMONA: I have sent to bid Cassio come speak with you.

50 **OTHELLO:** I have a salt and sorry rheum[15] offends me.

    Lend me thy handkerchief.

DESDEMONA: Here, my lord.

OTHELLO: That which I gave you.

DESDEMONA: I have it not about me.

55 **OTHELLO:** Not?

DESDEMONA: No, indeed, my lord.

OTHELLO: That's a fault.

    That handkerchief

---

[9] *hardness to dissemble:* Othello may refer here either to the difficulty he has in maintaining his appearance of composure, or to what he believes to be Desdemona's hardened hypocrisy. [10] *moist:* A moist, hot hand was taken as a sign of a lustful nature. [11] *argues:* Suggests. [12] *liberal:* Free, open (but also with a suggestion of "licentious"; from here on this scene Othello's words bear a double meaning, seeming to be normal but accusing. Desdemona of being unfaithful). [13] *sequester:* Separation. [14] *heraldry:* Heraldio symbolism. [15] *a salt and sorry rheum:* A heavy, running head cold.

Did an Egyptian to my mother give.
60 She was a charmer,[16] and could almost read
The thoughts of people. She told her, while she kept it
'Twould make her amiable[17] and subdue my father
Entirely to her love, but if she lost it
Or made a gift of it, my father's eye
65 Should hold her loathèd, and his spirits should hunt
After new fancies. She, dying, gave it me,
And bid me, when my fate would have me wived,
To give it her. I did so; and take heed on't;
Make it a darling like your precious eye.
70 To lose't or give't away were such perdition
As nothing else could match.

DESDEMONA: Is't possible?

OTHELLO: 'Tis true. There's magic in the web[18] of it.
A sibyl that had numbered in the world
75 The sun to course two hundred compasses,
In her prophetic fury[19] sewed the work;
The worms were hallowed that did breed the silk,
And it was dyed in mummy[20] which the skillful
Conserved of maidens' hearts.

80 DESDEMONA: Indeed? Is't true?

OTHELLO: Most veritable. Therefore look to't well.

DESDEMONA: Then would to God that I had never seen't!

OTHELLO: Ha! Wherefore?

DESDEMONA: Why do you speak so startingly and rash

85 OTHELLO: Is't lost? Is't gone? Speak, is it out o' th' way?

DESDEMONA: Heaven bless us!

OTHELLO: Say you?

DESDEMONA: It is not lost. But what an if it were?

OTHELLO: How?

90 DESDEMONA: I say it is not lost.

OTHELLO: Fetch't, let me see't!

---

[16] *charmer*: Magician. [17] *amiable*: Desirable. [18] *web*: Weaving. [19] *prophetic fury*: Seized by the spirit and able to prophesy. [20] *mummy*: Liquid drained from embalmed bodies.

DESDEMONA: Why, so I can; but I will not now.
　　This is a trick to put me from my suit:
　　Pray you let Cassio be received again.
95　OTHELLO: Fetch me the handkerchief! My mind misgives.
DESDEMONA: Come, come!
　　You'll never meet a more sufficient[21] man——
OTHELLO: The handkerchief!
DESDEMONA:　　　　　　A man that all his time
100　Hath founded his good fortunes on your love,
　　Shared dangers with you——
OTHELLO: The handkerchief!
DESDEMONA: I'faith, you are to blame,
OTHELLO: Away!

(*Exit Othello.*)

105　EMILIA: Is not this man jealous?
DESDEMONA: I nev'r saw this before.
　　Sure there's some wonder in this handkerchief;
　　I am most unhappy in the loss of it.
EMILIA: 'Tis not a year or two shows us a man.
110　They are all but stomachs, and we all but food;
　　They eat us hungerly, and when they are full,
　　They belch us.

(*Enter Iago and Cassio.*)

　　　　　　Look you, Cassio and my husband.
IAGO: There is no other way; 'tis she must do't.
115　And lo the happiness! Go and importune her.
DESDEMONA: How now, good Cassio? What's the news with you?
CASSIO: Madam, my former suit. I do beseech you
　　That by your virtuous means I may again
　　Exist, and be a member of his love
120　Whom I with all the office[22] of my heart
　　Entirely honor. I would not be delayed.
　　If my offense be of such mortal kind
　　That nor my service past, nor present sorrows,

---

[21] *sufficient:* Complete, with all proper qualities.　[22] *office:* Duty.

Nor purposed merit in futurity,
125 Can ransom me into his love again,
But to know so must be my benefit.²³
So shall I clothe me in a forced content,
And shut myself up in some other course
To fortune's alms.

130 **DESDEMONA:** Alas, thrice-gentle Cassio,
My advocation²⁴ is not now in tune.
My lord is not my lord; nor should I know him
Were he in favor²⁵ as in humor altered.
So help me every spirit sanctified
135 As I have spoken for you all my best
And stood within the blank²⁶ of his displeasure
For my free speech. You must awhile be patient.
What I can do I will; and more I will
Than for myself I dare. Let that suffice you.

140 **IAGO:** Is my lord angry?
EMILIA: He went hence but now,
And certainly in strange unquietness.

IAGO: Can he be angry? I have seen the cannon
When it hath blown his ranks into the air
145 And, like the devil, from his very arm
Puffed his own brother. And is he angry?
Something of moment²⁷ then. I will go meet him.
There's matter in't indeed if he be angry.

DESDEMONA: I prithee do so.

(Exit [Iago].)

150 Something sure of state²⁸
Either from Venice or some unhatched practice²⁹
Made demonstrable here in Cyprus to him,
Hath puddled³⁰ his clear spirit; and in such cases
Men's natures wrangle with inferior things,
155 Though great ones are their object. 'Tis even so.

---

²³ *benefit*: Good.   ²⁴ *advocation*: Advocacy.   ²⁵ *favor*: Countenance.   ²⁶ *blank*:
Bull's-eye of a target.   ²⁷ *moment*: Importance.   ²⁸ *of state*: State affair.
²⁹ *unhatched practice*: Undisclosed plot.   ³⁰ *puddled*: Muddied.

For let our finger ache, and it endues[31]
Our other, healthful members even to a sense
Of pain. Nay, we must think men are not gods,
Nor of them look for such observancy
160   As fits the bridal. Beshrew me much, Emilia,
I was, unhandsome warrior as I am,
Arraigning his unkindness with my soul;
But now I find I had suborned the witness,
And he's indicted falsely.

165 **EMILIA:**   Pray heaven it be
State matters, as you think, and no conception
Nor no jealous toy[32] concerning you.

DESDEMONA: Alas the day! I never gave him cause.

EMILIA: But jealous souls will not be answered so;
170   They are not ever jealous for the cause,
But jealous for they're jealous. It is a monster
Begot upon itself, born on itself.

DESDEMONA: Heaven keep the monster from Othello mind!

EMILIA: Lady, amen.

175 **DESDEMONA:** I will go seek him. Cassio, walk her about.
If I do find him fit,[33] I'll move your suit
And seek to effect it to my uttermost.

CASSIO: I humbly thank your ladyship.

(*Exit [Desdemona with Emilia].*)

(*Enter Bianca.*)

BIANCA: Save you, friend Cassio!

180 **CASSIO:**   What make you from home?
How is't with you, my most fair Bianca?
I' faith, sweet love, I was coming to your house.

BIANCA: And I was going to your lodging, Cassio.
What, keep a week away? Seven days and nights?
185   Eightscore eight hours? And lovers' absent hours
More tedious than the dial eightscore times?
O weary reck'ning.[34]

---

[31] *endues*: Leads.   [32] *toy*: Trifle.   [33] *fit*: Receptive.   [34] *reck'ning*: Addition.

CASSIO: Pardon me, Bianca.

     I have this while with leaden thoughts been pressed,

190   But I shall in a more continuate[35] time

     Strike off this score[36] of absence. Sweet Bianco,

(Gives her Desdemona's handkerchief.)

     Take me this work out.

BIANCA: O Cassio, whence came this?

     This is some token from a newer friend.

195   To the left absence now I feel a cause.

     Is't come to this? Well, well.

CASSIO: Go to, woman!

     Throw your vile guesses in the devil's teeth,

     From whence you have them. You are jealous now

200   That this is from some mistress, some remembrance.

     No, by my faith, Bianca.

BIANCA: Why, whose is it?

CASSIO: I know not neither, I found it in my chamber.

     I like the work well; ere it be demanded,[37]

205   As like enough it will, I will, I would have it copied.

     Take it and do't and leave me for this time.

BIANCA: Leave you? Wherefore?

CASSIO: I do attend here on the general

     And think it no addition, nor my wish,

210   To have him see me womaned.

BIANCA: Why, I pray you?

CASSIO: Not that I love you not.

BIANCA: But that you not love me!

     I pray you bring[38] me on the way a little,

215   And say if I shall see you soon at night.

CASSIO: 'Tis but a little way that I can bring you,

     For I attend here; but I'll see you soon.

BIANCA: 'Tis very good. I must be circumstanced.[39]

(Exeunt omnes.)

---

[35] *continuate:* Uninterrupted. [36] *Strike off this score:* I.e., pay this bill (the *score* being the account of drinks kept in a tavern). [37] *demanded:* Asked for (by the person who lost it). [38] *bring:* Accompany. [39] *circumstanced:* Accept things as they are.

ACT 4

SCENE I. (*A street.*)

(*Enter Othello and Iago.*)

IAGO: Will you think so?
OTHELLO: Think so, Iago?
IAGO: What,
    To kiss in private?
5   OTHELLO: An unauthorized[1] kiss?
IAGO: Or to be naked with her friend in bed
    An hour or more, not meaning any harm?
OTHELLO: Naked in bed, Iago, and not mean harm?
    It is hypocrisy against the devil.
10   They that mean virtuously, and yet do so,
    The devil their virtue tempts, and they tempt heaven.
IAGO: If they do nothing, 'tis a venial slip.
    But if I give my wife a handkerchief——
OTHELLO: What then?
15   IAGO: Why, then 'tis hers, my lord; and being hers,
    She may, I think, bestow't on any man.
OTHELLO: She is protectress of her honor too.
    May she give that?
IAGO: Her honor is an essence that's not seen;
20   They have it very oft that have it not.
    But for the handkerchief——
OTHELLO: By heaven, I would most gladly have forgot it!
    Thou said'st—O, it comes o'er my memory
    As doth the raven[2] o'er the infected house,
25   Boding to all—he had my handkerchief.
IAGO: Ay, what of that?
OTHELLO: That's not so good now.
IAGO: What if I had said I had seen him do you wrong?
    Or heard him say—as knaves be such abroad[3]
30   Who having, by their own importunate suit,

---

[1] *unauthorized:* Illicit.   [2] *raven:* A harbinger of death.   [3] *abroad:* I.e., in the world.

Or voluntary dotage[4] of some mistress,

Convincèd or supplied[5] them, cannot choose

But they must blab——

OTHELLO: Hath he said anything?

35   IAGO: He hath, my lord; but be you well assured,

No more than he'll unswear.

OTHELLO: What hath he said?

IAGO: Why, that he did—I know not what he did.

OTHELLO: What? what?

40   IAGO: Lie——

OTHELLO: With her?

IAGO: With her, on her; what you will.

OTHELLO: Lie with her? Lie on her?—We say lie on her when
they belie her.—Lie with her! Zounds, that's fulsome.[6]—
Handkerchief—confessions—handkerchief!—To confess,
and be hanged for his labor—first to be hanged, and then
to confess! I tremble at it. Nature would not invest herself
in such shadowing passion without some instruction.[7] It
is not words that shakes me thus.—Pish! Noses, ears, and
lips? Is't possible?—Confess?—Handkerchief?—O devil!

(*Falls in a trance.*)

IAGO: Work on.

45   My med'cine works! Thus credulous fools are caught,

And many worthy and chaste dames even thus,

All guiltless, meet reproach.[8] What, ho! My lord!

My lord, I say! Othello!

(*Enter Cassio.*)

How now, Cassio?

50   CASSIO: What's the matter?

IAGO: My lord is fall'n into an epilepsy.

This is his second fit; he had one yesterday.

---

[4] *voluntary dotage:* Weakness of the will.   [5] *Convincèd or supplied:* Persuaded or grati-
fied (the mistress).   [6] *fulsome:* Foul, repulsive.   [7] *Nature . . . instruction:* I.e.,
my mind would not become so darkened (with anger) unless there were something in this (accusation); (it should be remembered that Othello
believes in the workings of magic and supernatural forces).   [8] *reproach:* Shame.

CASSIO: Rub him about the temples.

IAGO: The lethargy[9] must have his quiet course.

55   If not, he foams at mouth, and by and by
    Breaks out to savage madness. Look, he stirs.
    Do you withdraw yourself a little while.
    He will recover straight. When he is gone.
    I would on great occasion[10] speak with you.

(*Exit Cassio.*)

60   How is it, general? Have you not hurt your head?

OTHELLO: Dost thou mock[11] me?

IAGO: I mock you not, by heaven.
    Would you would bear your fortune like a man.

OTHELLO: A hornèd man's a monster and a beast.

65 **IAGO:** There's many a beast then in a populous city,
    And many a civil[12] monster.

OTHELLO: Did he confess it?

IAGO: Good, sir, be a man.
    Think every bearded fellow that's but yoked
70   May draw[13] with you. There's millions now alive
    The nightly lie in those unproper[14] beds
    Which they dare swear peculiar.[15] You case is better.
    O, 'tis the spite of hell, the fiend's arch-mock,
    To lip a wanton in a secure couch,
75   And to suppose her chaste. No, let me know;
    And knowing what I am, I know what she shall be.

OTHELLO: O, thou art wise! 'Tis certain.

IAGO: Stand you awhile apart;
    Confine yourself but in a patient list.[16]
80   Whilst you were here, o'erwhelmèd with your grief—
    A passion most unsuiting such a man—
    Cassio came hither. I shifted him away[17]

---

[9] *lethargy:* Coma.   [10] *great occasion:* Very important matter.   [11] *mock:* Othello takes Iago's comment as a reference to his horns—which it is.   [12] *civil:* City-dwelling. [13] *draw:* I.e., like the horned ox.   [14] *unproper:* I.e., not exclusively the husband's. [15] *peculiar:* Their own alone.   [16] *a patient list:* The bounds of patience.   [17] *shifted him away:* Got rid of him by a stratagem.

And laid good 'scuses upon your ecstasy;[18]
Bade him anon return, and here speak with me;

85 The which he promised. Do but encave[19] yourself
And mark the fleers,[20] the gibes, and notable[21] scorns
That dwell in every region of his face.
For I will make him tell the tale anew:
Where, how, how oft, how long ago, and when

90 He hath, and is again to cope your wife.
I say, but mark his gesture. Marry patience,
Or I shall say you're all in all in spleen,[22]
And nothing of a man.

OTHELLO: Dost thou hear, Iago?

95 I will be found most cunning in my patience;
But—dost thou hear?—most bloody.

IAGO: That's not amiss;
But yet keep time in all. Will you withdraw?

(*Othello moves to one side, where his remarks are not audible to Cassio and Iago.*)

Now will I question Cassio of Bianca,

100 A huswife[23] that by selling her desires
Buys herself bread and cloth. It is a creature
That dotes on Cassio, as 'tis the strumpet's plague
To beguile many and be beguiled by one.
He, when he hears of her, cannot restrain

105 From the excess of laughter. Here he comes.

(*Enter Cassio.*)

As he shall smile, Othello shall go mad;
And his unbookish[24] jealousy must conster[25]
Poor Cassio's smiles, gestures, and light behaviors
Quite in the wrong. How do you, lieutenant?

110 **CASSIO:** The worser that you give me the addition[26]
Whose want even kills me.

---

[18] *ecstasy:* Trance (the literal meaning, "outside one-self," bears on the meaning of the change Othello is undergoing).   [19] *encave:* Hide.   [20] *fleers:* Mocking looks or speeches.   [21] *notable:* Obvious.   [22] *spleen:* Passion, particularly anger.   [23] *huswife:* Housewife (but with the special meaning here of "prostitute").   [24] *unbookish:* Ignorant.   [25] *conster:* Construe.   [26] *addition:* Title.

IAGO: Ply Desdemona well, and you are sure on't.

    Now, if this suit lay in Bianca's power,

    How quickly should you speed!

115 CASSIO: Alas, poor caitiff![27]

OTHELLO: Look how he laughs already!

IAGO: I never knew woman love man so.

CASSIO: Alas, poor rogue! I think, i' faith, she loves me.

OTHELLO: Now he denies it faintly, and laughs it out.

120 IAGO: Do you hear, Cassio?

OTHELLO: Now he importunes him

    To tell it o'er. Go to! Well said, well said!

IAGO: She gives it out that you shall marry her.

    Do you intend it?

125 CASSIO: Ha, ha, ha!

OTHELLO: Do ye triumph, Roman? Do you triumph?

CASSIO: I marry? What, a customer?[28] Prithee bear some

    charity to my wit; do not think it so unwholesome. Ha,

    ha, ha!

OTHELLO: So, so, so, so. They laugh that win.

IAGO: Why, the cry goes that you marry her.

130 CASSIO: Prithee, say true.

IAGO: I am a very villain else.

OTHELLO: Have you scored[29] me? Well.

CASSIO: This is the monkey's own giving out. She is persuaded

    I will marry her out of her own love and flattery, not out

    of my promise.

OTHELLO: Iago beckons me; now he begins the story.

(Othello moves close enough to hear.)

135 CASSIO: She was here even now; she haunts me in every place.

    I was the other day talking on the sea bank with certain

    Venetians, and thither comes the bauble,[30] and falls me

    thus about my neck—

OTHELLO: Crying "O dear Cassio!" as it were. His gesture

    imports it.

---

[27] *caitiff:* Wretch.   [28] *customer:* One who sells, a merchant (here, a prostitute).
[29] *scored:* Marked, defaced.   [30] *bauble:* Plaything.

CASSIO: So hangs, and lolls, and weeps upon me; so shakes and
pulls me! Ha, ha, ha!

OTHELLO: Now he tells how she plucked him to my chamber.
O, I see that nose of yours, but not that dog I shall throw
it to.

CASSIO: Well, I must leave her company.

140 IAGO: Before me!³¹ Look where she comes.

(*Enter Bianca.*)

CASSIO: 'Tis such another fitchew!³² Marry a perfumed one?
What do you mean by this haunting of me?

BIANCA: Let the devil and his dam haunt you! What did you
mean by that same handkerchief you gave me even now? I
was a fine fool to take it. I must take out the work? A
likely piece of work that you should find it in your chamber and know not who left it there! This is some minx's
token, and I must take out the work? There! (*She throws
down the handkerchief.*) Give it your hobbyhorse.³³
Wheresoever you had it, I'll take out no work on't.

CASSIO: How now, my sweet Bianca? how now? how now?

OTHELLO: By heaven, that should be my handkerchief!

145 BIANCA: If you'll come to supper tonight, you may; if you will
not, come when you are next prepared for.³⁴

(*Exit.*)

IAGO: After her, after her!

CASSIO: Faith, I must; she'll rail in the streets else.

IAGO: Will you sup there?

CASSIO: Yes, I intend so.

150 IAGO: Well, I may chance to see you, for I would very fain speak
with you.

CASSIO: Prithee come. Will you?

IAGO: Go to, say no more.

(*Exit Cassio.*)

---

³¹ *Before me!:* An exclamation of surprise.   ³² *fitchew:* Polecat, i.e., strong-
smelling creature.   ³³ *hobbyhorse:* Prostitute.   ³⁴ *next prepared for:* Next expected—
i.e., never.

OTHELLO: (*Comes forward.*) How shall I murder him, Iago?

IAGO: Did you perceive how he laughed at his vice?

155 **OTHELLO:** O Iago!

IAGO: And did you see the handkerchief?

OTHELLO: Was that mine?

IAGO: Yours, by this hand! And to see how he prizes the foolish
woman your wife! She gave it him, and he hath giv'n it his
whore.

OTHELLO: I would have him nine years a-killing!—A fine
woman, a fair woman, a sweet woman?

160 **IAGO:** Nay, you must forget that.

OTHELLO: Ay, let her rot, and perish, and be damned tonight;
for she shall not live. No, my heart is turned to stone; I
strike it, and it hurts my hand. O, the world hath not a
sweeter creature! She might lie by an emperor's side and
command him tasks.

IAGO: Nay, that's not your way.[35]

OTHELLO: Hang her! I do but say what she is. So delicate with
her needle. An admirable musician. O, she will sing the
savageness out of a bear! Of so high and plenteous wit
and invention[36]—

IAGO: She's the worse for all this.

165 **OTHELLO:** O, a thousand, a thousand times. And then, of so
gentle a condition?[37]

IAGO: Ay, too gentle.

OTHELLO: Nay, that's certain. But yet the pity of it, Iago. O
Iago, the pity of it, Iago.

IAGO: If you are so fond over her iniquity, give her patent
to offend; for if it touch[38] not you, it comes near
nobody.

OTHELLO: I will chop her into messes![39] Cuckold me!

170 **IAGO:** O, 'tis foul in her.

OTHELLO: With mine officer!

IAGO: That's fouler.

---

35 *way:* Proper course. 36 *invention:* Imagination. 37 *gentle a condition:* (1) well
born (2) of a gentle nature. 38 *touch:* Affects. 39 *messes:* Bits.

OTHELLO: Get me some poison, Iago, this night. I'll not
   expostulate with her, lest her body and beauty unprovide
   my mind[40] again. This night, Iago!

IAGO: Do it not with poison. Strangle her in her bed, even the
   bed she hath contaminated.

170 OTHELLO: Good, good! The justice of it pleases. Very good!

IAGO: And for Cassio, let me be his undertaker.[41] You shall
   hear more by midnight.

OTHELLO: Excellent good!

(*A trumpet.*)

                              What trumpet is that same?

IAGO: I warrant something from Venice.

(*Enter Lodovico, Desdemona, and Attendants.*)

175   'Tis Lodovico.
   This comes from the Duke. See, your wife's with him.

LODOVICO: God save you, worthy general.

OTHELLO: With[42] all my heart, sir.

LODOVICO: The Duke and the senators of Venice greet you.

(*Gives him a letter.*)

180 OTHELLO: I kiss the instrument of their pleasures.

(*Opens the letter and reads.*)

DESDEMONA: And what's the news, good cousin Lodovico?

IAGO: I am very glad to see you, signior.
   Welcome to Cyprus.

LODOVICO: I thank you. How does Lieutenant Cassio?

185 IAGO: Lives, sir.

DESDEMONA: cousin, there's fall'n between him and my lord
   An unkind[43] breach; but you shall make all well.

OTHELLO: Are you sure of that?

DESDEMONA: My lord?

---

[40] *unprovide my mind:* Undo my resolution.   [41] *undertaker:* Not "burier" but "one who undertakes to do something".   [42] *With:* I.e., I greet you with.   [43] *unkind:* Unnatural.

190 OTHELLO: (*Reads*) "This fail you not to do, as you will——"

LODOVICO: He did not call; he's busy in the paper.

Is there division 'twixt my lord and Cassio?

DESDEMONA: A most unhappy one. I would do much

I' atone[44] them, for the love I bear to Cassio.

195 OTHELLO: Fire and brimstone!

DESDEMONA: My lord?

OTHELLO: Are you wise?

DESDEMONA: What, is he angry?

LODOVICO: May be th' letter moved him;

200 For, as I think, they do command him home,

Deputing Cassio in his government.[45]

DESDEMONA: Trust me, I am glad on't.

OTHELLO: Indeed?

DESDEMONA: My lord?

205 OTHELLO: I am glad to see you mad.

DESDEMONA: Why, sweet Othello—

OTHELLO: Devil!

(*Strikes her.*)

DESDEMONA: I have not deserved this.

LODOVICO: My lord, this would not be believed in Venice,

210 Though I should swear I saw't. 'Tis very much.

Make her amends; she weeps.

OTHELLO: O devil, devil!

If that the earth could teem[46] with woman's tears,

Each drop she falls[47] would prove a crocodile[48].

215 Out of my sight!

DESDEMONA: I will not stay to offend you. (*Going.*)

LODOVICO: Truly, an obedient lady.

I do beseech your lordship call her back.

OTHELLO: Mistress!

220 DESDEMONA: My lord?

OTHELLO: What would you with her, sir?

LODOVICO: Who? I, my lord?

---

[44] *atone*: Reconcile.   [45] *government*: Office.   [46] *teem*: Conceive.   [47] *falls*: Drops.

[48] *crocodile*: The crocodile was supposed to shed false tears to lure its victims.

OTHELLO: Ay! You did wish that I would make her turn.
    Sir, she can turn, and turn, and yet go on
225   And turn again; and she can weep, sir, weep;
    And she's obedient; as you say, obedient.
    Very obedient. Proceed you in your tears.
    Concerning this, sir—O well-painted passion!
    I am commanded home.—Get you away;
230   I'll send for you anon.—Sir, I obey the mandate
    And will return to Venice.—Hence, avaunt!

(*Exit Desdemona.*)

    Cassio shall have my place. And, sir, tonight
    I do entreat that we may sup together.
    You are welcome, sir, to Cyprus.—Goats and monkeys!

(*Exit.*)

235 LODOVICO: Is this the noble Moor whom our full Senate
    Call all in all sufficient? Is this the nature
    Whom passion could not shake? Whose solid virtue
    The shot of accident nor dart of chance
    Could neither graze nor pierce?
240 IAGO: He is much changed.
LODOVICO: Are his wits safe? Is he not light of brain?
IAGO: He's that he is; I may not breathe my censure.
    What he might be (if, what he might, he is not)
    I would to heaven he were!
245 LODOVICO: What, strike his wife?
IAGO: Faith, that was not so well; yet would I knew
    That stroke would prove the worst.
LODOVICO: Is it his use?[49]
    Or did the letters work upon his blood[50]
250   And new-create his fault?
IAGO: Alas, alas!
    It is not honesty in me to speak
    What I have seen and known. You shall observe him.
    And his own courses[51] will denote him so

[49] *use:* Habit.   [50] *blood:* Passion.   [51] *courses:* Actions.

255   That I may save my speech. Do but go after
        And mark how he continues.

LODOVICO: I am sorry that I am deceived in him.

(*Exeunt.*)

SCENE 2 (*The citadel.*)

(*Enter Othello and Emilia.*)

OTHELLO: You have seen nothing then?

EMILIA: Nor ever heard, nor ever did suspect.

OTHELLO: Yes, you have seen Cassio and she together.

EMILIA: But then I saw no harm, and then I heard

5   Each syllable that breath made up[1] between them.

OTHELLO: What, did they never whisper?

EMILIA: Never, my lord.

OTHELLO: Nor send you out o' th' way?

EMILIA: Never.

10 **OTHELLO:** To fetch her fan, her gloves, her mask, nor
        nothing?

EMILIA: Never, my lord.

OTHELLO: That's strange.

EMILIA: I durst, my lord, to wager she is honest.
      Lay down my soul at stake.[2] If you think other,

15   Remove your thought. It doth abuse your bosom.
      If any wretch have put this in your head,
      Let heaven requite it with the serpent's curse,[3]
      For if she be not honest,[4] chaste, and true,
      There's no man happy. The purest of their wives

20   Is foul as slander.

OTHELLO: Bid her come hither. Go.

(*Exit Emilia.*)

      She says enough; yet she's a simple bawd[5]
      That cannot say as much. This is a subtle whore,

---

[1] *that breath made up:* Spoken.   [2] *at stake:* As the wager.   [3] *serpent's curse:* God's curse
on the serpent after the fall in Eden.   [4] *honest:* Chaste.   [5] *bawd:* Procuress.

A closet lock and key of villainous secrets,

20   And yet she'll kneel and pray; I have seen her do't.

(*Enter Desdemona and Emilia.*)

DESDEMONA: My lord, what is your will?

OTHELLO: Pray you, chuck, come hither.

DESDEMONA: What is your pleasure?

OTHELLO: Let me see your eyes.

25   Look in my face.

DESDEMONA: What horrible fancy's this?

OTHELLO: (*To Emilia*) Some of your function,[6] mistress:

Leave procreants alone and shut the door;

Cough or cry hem if anybody come.

30   Your mystery,[7] your mystery! Nay, dispatch!

(*Exit Emilia.*)

DESDEMONA: Upon my knee, what doth your speech import?

I understand a fury in your words.[8]

OTHELLO: Why, what art thou?

DESDEMONA: Your wife, my lord; your true

35   And loyal wife.

OTHELLO: Come, swear it, damn thyself;

Lest, being like one of heaven, the devils themselves

Should fear to seize thee. Therefore be double-damned:

Swear thou art honest.

40 **DESDEMONA:**   Heaven doth truly know it.

OTHELLO: Heaven truly knows that thou art false as hell.

DESDEMONA: To whom, my lord? With whom? How am I false?

OTHELLO: Ah, Desdemon! Away! Away! Away!

DESDEMONA: Alas the heavy day! Why do you weep?

45   Am I the motive[9] of these tears, my lord?

If haply[10] you my father do suspect

An instrument of this your calling back,

Lay not your blame on me. If you have lost him,

I have lost him too.

---

[6] *Some of your function:* Do your proper work (as the operator of a brothel).
[7] *mystery:* Trade. [8] *words:* Q1 adds to this line, "But not the words". [9] *motive:*
Cause. [10] *haply:* By chance.

45 **OTHELLO:**   Had it pleased heaven
       To try me with affliction, had they rained
       All kinds of sores and shames on my bare head,
       Steeped[11] me in poverty to the very lips,
       Given to captivity me and my utmost hopes,
50   I should have found in some place of my soul
       A drop of patience. But, alas, to make me
       The fixèd figure for the time of scorn[12]
       To point his slow and moving finger at.
       Yet could I bear that too, well, very well.
55   But there where I have garnered up my heart,
       Where either I must live or bear no life,
       The fountain from the which my current runs
       Or else dries up—to be discarded thence,
       Or keep it as a cistern for foul toads
60   To knot and gender[13] in—turn thy complexion there,
       Patience, thou young and rose-lipped cherubin!
       I here look grim as hell![14]
DESDEMONA: I hope my noble lord esteems me honest.
OTHELLO: O, ay, as summer flies are in the shambles,[15]
65   That quicken even with blowing.[16] O thou weed,
       Who art so lovely fair, and smell'st so sweet,
       That the sense aches at thee, would thou hadst never been
         born!
DESDEMONA: Alas, what ignorant[17] sin have I committed?
OTHELLO: Was this fair paper, this most goodly book,
70   Made to write "whore" upon? What committed?
       Committed? O thou public commoner,[18]
       I should make very forges of my cheeks
       That would to cinders burn up modesty,
       Did I but speak thy deeds. What committed?

---

[11] *Steeped:* Submerged.   [12] *The . . . scorn:* The very image of scorn in our time.
[13] *knot and gender:* Twist in bunches and procreate.   [14] *turn . . . hell:* The rough
sense would seem to be, "even Patience would grow pale, turn complexion, at
Desdemona's perfidy, but that Othello looks grimly on".   [15] *shambles:* Abat-
toirs.   [16] *quicken even with blowing:* Become impregnated as soon as they lay their
eggs.   [17] *ignorant:* Unknowing.   [18] *commoner:* Prostitute.

70   Heaven stops the nose at it, and the moon winks;[19]

    The bawdy wind that kisses all it meets

    Is hushed within the hollow mine of earth

    And will not hear't. What committed?

DESDEMONA: By heaven you do me wrong!

75   OTHELLO: Are not you a strumpet?

DESDEMONA: No, as I am a Christian!

    If to preserve this vessel for my lord

    From any other foul unlawful touch

    Be not to be a strumpet, I am none.

80   OTHELLO: What, not a whore?

DESDEMONA: No, as I shall be saved!

OTHELLO: Is't possible?

DESDEMONA: O, heaven forgive us!

OTHELLO: I cry you mercy[20] then.

85   I took you for that cunning whore of Venice

    That married with Othello. (*Calling*) You, mistress,

(*Enter Emilia.*)

    That have the office opposite to Saint Peter

    And keep the gate of hell! You, you, ay, you!

    We have done our course; there's money for your pains.

(*Throws her some coins.*)

90   I pray you turn the key and keep your counsel.

(*Exit.*)

EMILIA: Alas, what does this gentleman conceive?

    How do you, madam? How do you, my good lady?

DESDEMONA: Faith, half asleep.

EMILIA: Good madam, what's the matter with my lord?

95   DESDEMONA: With who?

EMILIA: Why, with my lord, madam.

DESDEMONA: Who is thy lord?

EMILIA: He that is yours, sweet lady.

---

[19] *winks:* Closes its eyes (the moon was the symbol of chastity).   [20] *cry you mercy:* Ask your pardon.

DESDEMONA: I have none. Do not talk to me, Emilia.
100   I cannot weep, nor answers have I none
       But what should go by water.[21] Prithee tonight
       Lay on my bed my wedding sheets, remember;
       And call thy husband hither.
EMILIA: Here's a change indeed!

(*Exit.*)

105   **DESDEMONA:** 'Tis meet I should be used so, very meet.
       How have I been behaved, that he might stick
       The small'st opinion on my least misuse?[22]

(*Enter Iago and Emilia.*)

IAGO: What is your pleasure, madam? How is't with you?
DESDEMONA: I cannot tell. Those that do teach young babes
110   Do it with gentle means and easy tasks.
       He might have child me so; for, in good faith,
       I am a child to chiding.
IAGO: What is the matter, lady?
EMILIA: Alas, Iago, my lord hath so bewhored her,
115   Thrown such despite[23] and heavy terms upon her
       That true hearts cannot bear it.
DESDEMONA: Am I that name, Iago?
IAGO: What name, fair lady?
DESDEMONA: Such as she said my lord did say I was.
120   **EMILIA:** He called her whore. A beggar in his drink
       Could not have laid such terms upon his callet.[24]
IAGO: Why did he so?
DESDEMONA: I do not know; I am sure I am none such.
IAGO: Do not weep, do not weep. Alas the day.
125   **EMILIA:** Hath she forsook so many noble matches,
       Her father and her country, and her friends,
       To be called whore? Would it not make one weep?
DESDEMONA: It is my wretched fortune.
IAGO: Beshrew[25] him for't!
130   How comes this trick upon him?

---

[21] *water:* Tears.   [22] *stick ... misuse:* Base any doubt on my smallest fault.
[23] *despite:* Abuse.   [24] *callet:* Slut.   [25] *Beshrew:* Curse.

DESChIMONA: Nay, heaven doth know.

EMILIA: I will be hanged if some eternal villain,

     Some busy and insinuating rogue,

     Some cogging,[26] cozening slave, to get some office,

135   Have not devised this slander. I will be hanged else.

IAGO: Fie, there is no such man! It is impossible.

DESDEMONA: If any such there be, heaven pardon him.

EMILIA: A halter pardon him! And hell gnaw his bones!

     Why should he call her whore? Who keeps her company?

140   What place? What time? What form? What likelihood?

     The Moor's abused by some most villainous knave,

     Some base notorious knave, some scurvy fellow.

     O heavens, that such companions[27] thou'dst unfold,[28]

     And put in every honest hand a whip

145   To lash the rascals naked through the world

     Even from the east to th' west!

IAGO: Speak within door.[29]

EMILIA: O, fie upon them! Some such squire[30] he was

     That turned your wit the seamy side without

150   And made you to suspect me with the Moor.

IAGO: You are a fool. Go to.

DESDEMONA: Alas, Iago,

     What shall I do to win my lord again?

     Good friend, go to him, for, by this light of heaven,

155   I know not how I lost him. Here I kneel:

     If e'er my will did trespass' gainst his love

     Either in discourse of thought[31] or actual deed,

     Or that mine eyes, mine ears, or any sense

     Delighted them in any other form;

160   Or that I do not yet, and ever did,

     And ever will (though he do shake me off

     To beggarly divorcement) love him dearly,

     Comfort forswear me. Unkindness may do much.

     And his unkindness may defeat[32] my life,

---

[26] *cogging:* Cheating.   [27] *companions:* Fellows rogues.   [28] *unfold:* Disclose.
[29] *within door:* More quietly and moderately.   [30] *squire:* A term of contempt.
[31] *discourse of thought:* Thinking.   [32] *defeat:* Destroy.

165   But never taint my love. I cannot say "whore."
        It does abhor me now I speak the word;
        To do the act that might the addition earn
        Not the world's mass of vanity could make me.
IAGO: I pray you be content. 'Tis but his humor.[33]
170   The business of the state does him offense.
DESDEMONA: If 'twere no other.
IAGO: It is but so; I warrant.

(*Trumpets within.*)

        Hark how these instruments summon to supper.
        The messengers of Venice stay the meat.[34]
170   Go in, and weep not. All things shall be well.

(*Exeunt Desdemona and Emilia.*)
(*Enter Roderigo.*)

        How now, Roderigo?
RODERIGO: I do not find that thou deal'st justly with me.
IAGO: What in the contrary?
RODERIGO: Every day thou daff'st[35] me with some device,[36]
        Iago, and rather, as it seems to me now, keep'st from me
        all conveniency[37] than suppliest me with the least advan-
        tage of hope. I will indeed no longer endure it; nor am
        I yet persuaded to put up[38] in peace what already I have
        foolishly suffered.
170 IAGO: Will you hear me, Roderigo?
RODERIGO: I have heard too much, and your words and per-
        formances are no kin together.
IAGO: You charge me most unjustly.
RODERIGO: With naught but truth. I have wasted myself out of
        my means. The jewels you have had from me to deliver
        Desdemona would half have corrupted a votarist.[39] You
        have told me she hath received them, and returned me
        expectations and comforts of sudden respect[40] and
        acquaintance; but I find none.

---

[33] *humor:* Mood.   [34] *stay the meat:* Await the meal.   [35] *daff'st:* Put off.   [36] *device:*
Scheme.   [37] *conveniency:* What is needful.   [38] *put up:* Accept.   [39] *votarist:* Nun.
[40] *sudden respect:* Immediate consideration.

170   IAGO: Well, go to; very well.

RODERIGO: Very well? Go to? I cannot go to, man; nor 'tis not very well. Nay, I think it is scurvy, and begin to find myself fopped[41] in it.

IAGO: Very well.

RODERIGO: I tell you 'tis not very well. I will make myself known to Desdemona. If she will return me my jewels, I will give over my suit and repent my unlawful solicitation. If not, assure yourself I will seek satisfaction of you.

IAGO: You have said now?

175   RODERIGO: Ay, and said nothing but what I protest[42] intendment of doing.

IAGO: Why, now I see there's mettle[43] in thee, and even from this instant do build on thee a better opinion than ever before. Give me thy hand, Roderigo. Thou hast taken against me a most just exception;[44] but yet I protest. I have dealt most directly[45] in thy affair.

RODERIGO: It hath not appeared.

IAGO: I grant indeed it hath not appeared, and your suspicion is not without wit and judgment. But, Roderigo, if thou hast that in thee indeed which I have greater reason to believe now than ever—I mean purpose, courage, and valor—this night show it. If thou the next night following enjoy not Desdemona, take me from this world with treachery and devise engines for[46] my life.

RODERIGO: Well, what is it? Is it within reason and compass?[47]

180   IAGO: Sir, there is especial commission come from Venice to depute Cassio in Othello's place.

RODERIGO: Is that true? Why, then Othello and Desdemona return again to Venice.

IAGO: O, no; he goes into Mauritania and taketh away with him the fair Desdemona, unless his abode be lingered here by some accident; wherein none can be so determinate[48] as the removing of Cassio.

RODERIGO: How do you mean, removing him?

---

[41] *fopped:* Duped.   [42] *protest:* Aver.   [43] *mettle:* Spirit.   [44] *exception:* Objection.
[45] *directly:* Straightforwardly.   [46] *engines for:* Schemes against.   [47] *compass:* Possibility.   [48] *determinate:* Effective.

185   **IAGO:** Why, by making him uncapable of Othello's place—
       knocking out his brains.

      RODERIGO: And that you would have me to do?

      IAGO: Ay, if you dare do yourself a profit and a right.
       He sups tonight with a harlotry,[49] and thither will I go to
       him. He knows not yet of his honorable fortune. If you
       will watch his going thence, which I will fashion to fall
       out[50] between twelve and one, you may take him at your
       pleasure. I will be near to second[51] your attempt, ad he
       shall fall between us. Come, stand not amazed at it, but
       go along with me. I will show you such a necessity in his
       death that you shall think yourself bound to put it on
       him. It is now high supper time, and the night grows to
       waste. About it.

      RODERIGO: I will hear further reason for this.

190   **IAGO:** And you shall be satisfied.

      (*Exeunt.*)

SCENE 3 (*The citadel.*)

(*Enter Othello, Lodovico, Desdemona, Emilia, and Attendants.*)

      LODOVICO: I do beseech you, sir, trouble yourself no further.

      OTHELLO: O, pardon me; 'twill to me good to walk.

      LODOVICO: Madam, good night. I humbly thank your ladyship.

      DESDEMONA: Your honor is most welcome.

5   **OTHELLO:** Will you walk, sir? O, Desdemona.

      DESDEMONA: My lord?

      OTHELLO: Get you to bed on th' instant; I will be returned
       forthwith. Dismiss your attendant there.
       Look't be done.

      DESDEMONA: I will, my lord.

      (*Exit [Othello, with Lodovico and Attendants].*)

      EMILIA: How goes it now? He looks gentler than he did.

10   **DESDEMONA:** He says he will return incontinent[I]

---

[49] *harlotry:* Female.   [50] *fall out:* Occur.   [51] *second:* Support.   [I] *incontinent:* At once.

And hath commanded me to go to bed,

And bade me to dismiss you.

EMILIA: Dismiss me?

DESDEMONA: It was his bidding; therefore, good Emilia,

15   Give me my nightly wearing, and adieu.

We must not now displease him.

EMILIA: I would you had never seen him!

DESDEMONA: So would not I. My love doth so approve him

That even his stubbornness, his checks,[2] his frowns—

20   Prithee unpin me—have grace and favor.

EMILIA: I have laid these sheets you bade me on the bed.

DESDEMONA: All's one.[3] Good Father, how foolish are our minds!

If I do die before, prithee shroud me

In one of these same sheets.

25 **EMILIA:**   Come, come! You talk.

DESDEMONA: My mother had a maid called Barbary.

She was in love; and he she loved proved mad

And did forsake her. She had a song of "Willow';

And old thing 'twas, but it expressed her fortune,

30   And she died singing it. That song tonight

Will not go from my mind; I have much to do

But to go from my mind; I have much to do

But to go hang my head all at one side

And sing it like poor Barbary. Prithee dispatch.

35 **EMILIA:** Shall I go fetch your nightgown?

DESDEMONA: No, unpin me here.

This Lodovico is a proper man.

EMILIA: A very handsome man.

DESDEMONA: He speaks well.

40 **EMILIA:** I know a lady in Venice would have walked barefoot to

Palestine for a touch of his nether lip.

DESDEMONA: (*Sings*)

"The poor soul sat singing by a sycamore tree,

Sing all a green willow;

Her hand on her bosom, her head on her knee,

Sing willow, willow, willow.

---

[2] *checks:* Rebukes.   [3] *All's one:* No matter.

The fresh steams ran by her and murmured her moans;
    Sing willow, willow, willow;
45   Her sat tears fell from her, and soft'ned the stones—
    Sing willow, willow, willow—"
Lay by these.

(*Gives Emilia her clothes.*)

"Willow, Willow"—
Prithee hie[4] thee; he'll come anon.[5]
    "Sing all a green willow must be my garland.
50   Let nobody blame him; his scorn I approve"——
Nay, that's not next. Hark! Who is't that knocks?
EMILIA: It is the wind.
DESDEMONA: (*Sings*)
    "I called my love false love; but what said he then?
55   Sing willow, willow, willow:
    If I court moe[6] women, you'll couch with moe men."
So, get thee gone; good night. Mine eyes do itch.
Doth that bode weeping?
EMILIA: 'Tis neither here nor there.
60 **DESDEMONA**: I have heard it said so. O, these men, these men.
Dost thou is conscience think, tell me, Emilia,
That there be women do abuse their husbands
In such gross kind?
EMILIA: There be some such, no question
DESDEMONA: Wouldst thou do such a deed for all the world?
EMILIA: Why, would not you?
DESDEMONA: No, by this heavenly light!
65 **EMILIA**: Nor I neither by this heavenly light.
I might do't as well i' th' dark.
DESDEMONA: Wouldst thou do such a deed for all the world?
EMILIA: The world's a huge thing; it is a great price for a small
vice.
DESDEMONA: In troth, I think thou wouldst not.
70 **EMILIA**: In troth, I think, I should; and undo't when I had done.
Marry, I would not do such a thing for a joint-ring,[7] nor

---

[4] *hie*: Hurry.   [5] *anon*: At once.   [6] *moe*: More.   [7] *joint-ring*: A ring with two interlocking halves.

for measures of lawn,[8] nor for gowns, petticoats, nor caps,
nor any petty exhibition,[9] but for al the whole world? Why,
who would not make her husband a cuckold to make him a
monarch? I should venture purgatory for't.

DESDEMONA: Beshrew me if I would do such a wrong for the
whole world.

EMILIA: Why, the wrong is but a wrong i' th' world; and having
the world for your labor, 'tis a wrong in your own world,
and you might quickly make it right.

DESDEMONA: I do not think there is any such woman.

EMILIA: Yes, a dozen; and as many to th' vantage as would
store[10](the world they played for.

75   But I do think it is their husbands' faults
      If wives do fall. Say that they slack their duties
      And pout our treasures into foreigh[11] laps;
      Or else break out in peevish jealousies,
      Throwing restraint upon us; or say they strike us.
80   Or scant our former having in despite[12]—why, we have
      galls; and though we have some grace,
      Yet have we some revenge, Let husbands know
      Their wives have sense like them. They see, and smell,
      And have their palates both for sweet and sour,
      As husbands have. What is it that they do
85   When they change[13] us for others? Is it sport?
      I think it is. And doth affection[14] breed it?
      I think it doth. Is't frailty that thus errs?
      It is so too. And have not we affections?
      Desires for sport? And frailty? as men have?
90   Then let them use well; else let them know,
      The ills we do, their ills instruct us so.[15]

DESDEMONA: Good night, good night. Heaven me such uses[16]
    send,
    Not to pick bad from bad, but by bad mend.

(*Exeunt.*)

---

[8] *lawn:* Fine linen.   [9] *exhibition:* Payment.   [10] *to . . . store:* In addition as would
fill.   [11] *foreign:* Alien, i.e., other than the wife.   [12] *scant . . . despite:* Reduce, in
spite, our household allowance (?).   [13] *change:* Exchange.   [14] *affection:* Strong
feeling, desire.   [15] *instruct us so:* Teach us to do likewise.   [16] *uses:* Practices.

ACT 5

SCENE I. (*A street.*)

(*Enter Iago and Roderigo.*)

IAGO: Here, stand behind this bulk;[1] straight will he come.
    Wear thy good rapier bare, and put it home.
    Quick, quick! Fear nothing; I'll be at thy elbow.
    It makes us, or it mars us, think on that,
5   And fix most firm thy resolution.
RODERIGO: Be near at hand; I may miscarry in't.
IAGO: Here, at thy hand. Be bold, and take thy stand.

(*Moves to one side.*)

RODERIGO: I have no great devotion to the deed,
    And yet he hath given me satisfying reasons.
10   'Tis but a man gone. Forth my sword! He dies!
IGOA: I have rubbed this young quat[2] almost to the sense,[3]
    And he grows angry. Now, whether he kill Cassio,
    Or Cassio him, or each do kill the other,
    Every way makes my gain. Live Roderigo,
15   He calls me to a restitution large
    Of gold and jewels that I bobbed[4] from him
    As gifts to Desdemona.
    It must not be. If Cassio do remain,
    He hath a daily beauty in his life
20   That makes me ugly; and besides, the Moor
    May unfold me to him; there stand I in much peril.
    No, he must die. But so, I hear him coming.

(*Enter Cassio.*)

RODERIGO: I know his gait. 'Tis he. Villain, thou diest!

(*Thrusts at Cassio.*)

CASSIO: That trust had been mine enemy indeed
25   But that my coat[5] is better than thou know'st.

[1] *bulk:* Projecting stall of a shop.   [2] *quat:* Pimple.   [3] *to the sense:* Raw.   [4] *bobbed:* Swindled.   [5] *coat:* I.e., a mail or bulletproof vest.

I will make proof of thine.

(*Fights with Roderigo.*)

RODERIGO: O, I am slain![6]

CASSIO: I am maimed forever. Help, ho! Murder! Murder!

(*Enter Othello [to one side].*)

OTHELLO: The voice of Cassio. Iago keeps his word.

30   RODERIGO: O, villain that I am!

OTHELLO: It is even so.

CASSIO: O help, ho! Light! A surgeon!

OTHELLO: 'Tis he. O brave Iago, honest and just,

    That hast such noble sense of thy friend's wrong!

35   Thou teachest me. Minion,[7] your dear lies dead,

    And your unblest [8] fate hies.[9] Strumpet, I come.

    Forth of my heart those charms, thine eyes, are blotted.

    They bed, lust-stained, shall with lust's blood be spotted.

(*Exit Othello.*)

(*Enter Lodovico and Gratiano.*)

CASSIO: What ho? No watch? No passage?[10] Murder! Murder!

40   GRATIANO: 'Tis some mischance. The voice is very direful.

CASSIO: O, help!

LADOVICO: Hark!

RODERIGO. O wretched villain!

LODOVICO: Two or three groan. 'Tis heavy night.

45   These may be counterfeits. Let's think't unsafe

    To come into the cry without more help.

RODERIGO: Nobody come? The shall I bleed to death.

LADOVICO: Hark!

(*Enter Iago [with a light].*)

---

[6] *slain*: Most editors add here a stage direction which has Iago wounding Cassio in the leg from behind, but remaining unseen. However, nothing in the text requires this, and Cassio's wound can be given him in the fight with Roderigo, for presumably when Cassio attacks Roderigo the latter would not simply accept the thrust but would parry. Since Iago enters again at line 46, he must exit at some point after line.   [7] *Minion*: Hussy, i.e., Desdemona.   [8] *unblest*: Unsanctified.   [9] *hies*: Approaches swiftly.   [10] *passage*: Passersby.

GRATIANO: Here's one come in his shirt, with light and
    weapons.

50   IAGO: Who's there? Whose noise in this that cries on murder?

LODOVICO: We do not know.

IAGO: Do not you hear a cry?

CASSIO: Here, here! For heaven's sake, help me!

IAGO: What's the matter?

55   GRATIANO: This is Othello's ancient, as I take it.

LODOVICO: The same indeed, a very valiant fellow.

IAGO: What are you here that cry so grievously?

CASSIO: Iago? O, I am spoiled, undone by villains.
    Give me some help.

60   IAGO: O me, lieutenant! What villains have done this?

CASSIO: I think that one of them is hereabout
    And cannot make away.

IAGO: O treacherous villains!

(*To Lodovico and Gratiano*) what are you there? Come in, and give
some help.

RODERIGO: O, help me there!

65   CASSIO: That's one of them.

IAGO: O murd'rous slave! O villain!

(*Stabs Roderigo.*)

RODERIGO: O damned Iago! O inhuman dog!

IAGO: Kill men i' th' dark?—Where be these bloody thieves?—
    How silent is this town!—Ho! Murder! Murder!—

70   What may you be? Are you of good or evil?

LADOVICO: As you shall prove us, praise us.

IAGO: Signior Lodovico?

LADOVICO: He, sir.

IAGO: I cry you mercy. Here's Cassio hurt by villains.

75   GRATIANO: Cassio?

IAGO: How is't, brother?

CASSIO: My leg is cut in two.

IAGO: Marry, heaven forbid!
    Light, gentlemen, I'll bind it with my shirt.

(*Enter Bianca.*)

80   **BIANCA** : What is the matter, ho? Who is't that cried?

  IAGO: Who is't that cried?

  BIANCA: O my dear Cassio! My sweet Cassio!

    Cassio, Cassio, Cassio!

  IAGO: O notable strumpet!—Cassio, may you suspect

85   Who they should be that have thus mangled you?

  CASSIO: No.

  GRATIANO: I am sorry to find you thus. I have been to seek you.

  IAGO: Lend me a garter. So. O for a chair

    To bear him easily hence.

90   **BIANCA**: Alsa, he faints! Oh Cassio, Cassio, Cassio!

  IAGO: Gentleman all, I do suspect this trash

    To be a party in this injury.—

    Patience awhile, good Cassio.—Come, come.

    Lend me a light. Know we this face or no?

95   Alas, my friend and my dear countryman

    Roderigo? No.—Yes, Sure—Yes, 'tis Roderigo!

  GRATIANO: What, of Venice?

  IAGO: Even he, sir. Did you know him?

  GRATIANO: Know him? Ay.

100   **IAGO**: Signior Gratiano? I cry your gentle pardon.

    These bloody accidents must excuse my manners

    That so neglected you.

  GRATIANO: I am glad to see you.

  IAGO: How do you, Cassio?—O, a chair, a chair!

105   **GRATIANO**: Roderigo?

  IAGO: He, he, 'tis he! (*A chair brought in.*) O, that's well said;[11] the

    chair.

    Some good man bear him carefully from hence.

    I'll fetch the general's surgeon. (*To Bianca*) For you, mistress,

    Save you your labor. (*To Cassio*) He that lies slain here, Cassio,

110   Was my dear friend. What malice was between you?

  CASSIO: None in the world; nor do I know the man.

  IAGO: What, look you pale?—O, bear him out o' th' air.

(*Cassio is carried off.*)

---

[11] *well said*: Well done.

Stay you, good gentlemen.—Look you pale, mistress?
Do you perceive the gastness[12] of her eye?
115   Nay, if you stare, we shall hear more anon.
Behold her well; I pray you look upon her.
Do you see, gentlemen? Nay guiltiness will speak,
Though tongues were out of use.[13]

(*Enter Emilia.*)

EMILIA: Alsa, what is the matter? What is the matter, husband?
120 IAGO: Cassio hath here been set on in the dark
By Roderigo and fellows that are scaped.
He's almost slain, and Roderigo quite dead.
EMILIA: Alsa, good gentleman! Alas, good Cassio!
IAGO: This is the fruits of whoring. Prithee, Emilia,
125   Go know of Cassio where he supped tonight.
(*To Bianca*) What, do you shake at that?
BIANCA: He supped at my house; but I therefore shake not.
IAGO: O, did he so? I charge[14] you go with me.
EMILIA: Oh fie upon thee, strumpet!
130 BIANCIA: I am no strumpet, but of life as honest
As you that thus abuse me.
EMILIA: As I? Fie upon thee!
IAGO: Kind gentlemen, let's go see poor Cassio dressed.[15]
(*To Bianca*) Come, mistress, you must tell's another tale.
Emilia, run you to the citadel
And tell my lord and lady what hath happed.

(*Exit Emilia.*)

135   Will you go on afore?

(*Exeunt [all but Iago].*)

This is the night
That either makes me or fordoes me quite.[16]

(*Exit.*)

---

[12] *gastness:* Terror. [13] *tongues were out of use:* Men no longer spoke. [14] *charge:* Command. [15] *dressed:* Bandaged. [16] *fordoes me quite:* Completely ruins me.

SCENE 2. (*Desdemona's chamber.*)

(*Enter Othello [with a light]; and Desdemona in her bed.*)

OTHELLO: It is the cause, it is the cause, my soul.
　　Let me not name it to you, you chaste stars.
　　It is the cause. Yet I'll not shed her blood,
　　Nor scar that whiter skin of hers than snow,
5　　And smooth as monumental alabaster.
　　Yet she must die, else she'll betray more men.
　　Put out the light, and then put out the light.
　　If I quench thee, thou flaming minister,[1]
　　I can again thy former light restore,
10　　Should I report me; but once put out thy light,
　　Thou cunning'st[2] pattern of excelling nature,
　　I know not where is that Promethean heat[3]
　　That can thy light relume.[4] When I have plucked the rose.
　　I cannot give it vital[5] growth again;
15　　It needs must wither. I'll smell thee on the tree.

(*He kisses her.*)

　　O balmy breath, that dost almost persuade
　　Justice to break her sword. One more, one more!
　　Be thus when thou art dead, and I will kill thee,
　　And love thee after. One more, and that's the last!
20　　So sweet was ne'er so fatal. I must weep,
　　But they are cruel tears. This sorrow's heavenly;
　　It strikes where it doth love. She wakes.
DESDEMONA: Who's there? Othello?
OTHELLO: 　　　　　　　　　　　　Ay, Desdemona.
25　**DESDEMONA:** Will you come to bed, my lord?
OTHELLO: Have you prayed tonight, Desdemon?
DESDEMONA: 　　　　　　　　　　　　Ay, my lord.
OTHELLO: If you bethink yourself of any crime

---

[1] *minister:* Worker, servant.　　[2] *cunning'st:* Most intricate and skillfully wrought (by nature excelling itself).　　[3] *Promethean heat:* Divine fire (Prometheus is the Titan who stole fire from heaven and gave it to man).　　[4] *relume:* Relight.
[5] *vital:* Living.

Unreconciled as yet to heaven and grace,

30   Solicit for it straight.

DESDEMONA: Alack, my lord, what may you mean by that?

OTHELLO: Well, do it, and be brief; I will walk by.[6]

I would not kill thy unprepared spirit.

No, heavens forfend! I would not kill thy soul.

35   DESDEMONA: Talk you of killing?

OTHELLO: Ay, I do.

DESDEMONA: Then heaven

Have mercy on me!

OTHELLO: Amen, with all my heart.

40   DESDEMONA: If you say so, I hope you will not kill me.

OTHELLO: Humh.

DESDEMONA: And yet I fear you; for you're fatal then

When your eyes roll so. Why I should fear I know not.

Since guiltiness I know not; but yet I feel I fear.

45   OTHELLO: Think on thy sins.

DESDEMONA: They are loves I bear to you.

OTHELLO: Ay, and for that thou diest.

DESDEMONA: That death's unnatural that kills for loving.

Alas, why gnaw you so your nether lip?

50   Some bloody passion shakes your very frame.

These are portents; but yet I hope, I hope,

They do not point on me.

OTHELLO: Peace and be still.

DESDEMONA: I will so. What's the matter?

55   OTHELLO: That handkerchief which I so loved and gave thee.

Thou gav'st to Cassio.

DESDEMONA: No, by my life and soul!

Send for the man and ask him.

OTHELLO: Sweet soul, take heed,

60   Take heed of perjury; thou art on thy deathbed.

DESDEMONA: Ay, but not yet to die.

OTHELLO: Presently.[7]

Therefore confess thee freely of thy sin,

For to deny each article[8] with oath

---

[6] *by:* Nearby.   [7] *Presently:* Immediately.   [8] *article:* Item (of the charge of adultery. Othello makes, heavy use of legal terms in this scene).

65 Cannot remove nor choke the strong conception
That I do groan withal. Thou art to die.

DESDEMONA: Then Lord have mercy on me.

OTHELLO: I say, amen.

DESDEMONA: And have you mercy too. I never did

70 Offend you in my life; never loved Cassio
But with such general warranty⁹ of heaven
As I might love. I never gave him token.

OTHELLO: By heaven, I saw my handkerchief in's hand!
O perjured woman! thou dost stone¹⁰ my heart,

75 And mak'st me call what I intend to do
A murder, which I thought a sacrifice.
I saw the handkerchief.

DESDEMONA: He found it then.
I never gave it him. Send for him hither.

80 Let him confess a truth.

OTHELLO: He hath confessed.

DESDEMONA: What, my lord?

OTHELLO: That he hath used thee.

DESDEMONA: How? Unlawfully?

85 **OTHELLO:**   Ay.

DESDEMONA: He will not say so.

OTHELLO: No, his mouth is stopped.
Honest Iago hath ta'en order for't¹¹.

DESDEMONA: O, my fear interprets. What, is he dead?

90 **OTHELLO:** Had all his hairs been lives, my great revenge Had
    stomach¹² for them all.

DESDEMONA: Alas, he is betrayed, and I undone!

OTHELLO: Out, strumpet! Weep'st thou for him to my face?

DESDEMONA: O, banish me, my lord, but kill me not!

95 **OTHELLO:** Down, strumpet!

DESDEMONA: Kill me tomorrow; let me live tonight!

OTHELLO: Nay, if you strive——

DESDEMONA: But half an hour!

OTHELLO: Being done, there is no pause.

---

⁹ *warranty:* Allowance.   ¹⁰ *stone:* Turn to stone.   ¹¹ *ta'en order for't:* Make sure
of it.   ¹² *stomach:* Appetite.

100 **DESDEMONA**: But while I say one prayer!

OTHELLO: It is too late.

(*Smothers her.*)

(*Emilia at the door.*)

EMILIA: (*Calls within.*) My lord, my lord! What, ho, my lord, my
   lord!

OTHELLO: What noise is this? Not dead? Not yet quite dead?
   I that am cruel am yet merciful;
105   I would not have thee linger in thy pain.
   So, so.

EMILIA: (*Within*) What, ho! My lord, my lord!

OTHELLO: Who's there?

EMILIA: (*Within*) O, good speak a word with you.

110 **OTHELLO**: Yes, 'tis Emilia.—By and by.—She's dead.—
   'Tis like she comes to speak of Cassio's death.
   The noise was high.[13] Ha! No more moving?
   Still as the grave.—Shall she come in? Were't good?—
   I think she stirs again. No.—What's best to do?
115   If she come in, she'll sure speak to my wife.
   My wife! My wife! What wife? I have no wife.
   O, insupportable! O heavy hour!
   Methinks[14] it should be now a huge eclipse
   Of sun and moon, and that th' affrighted globe
120   Should yawn[15] at alteration.

EMILIA: (*Within*) I do beseech you
   That I may speak with you, O good my lord!

OTHELLO: I had forgot thee. O, come in Emilia.
   Soft, by and by.—Let me the curtains draw.—

(*Draws the bed hangings and then opens the door.*)

120   Where art thou?

(*Enter Emilia.*)

   What's the matter wit thee now?

[13] *high:* Loud (Q1 reads "here").   [14] *Methinks . . . alteration:* The Elizabethans believed that great changes in human affairs were reflected by disorders in nature.
[15] *yawn:* Gape open (as in an earthquake).

EMILIA: O my good lord, yonder's foul murders done!

OTHELLO: What? Now?

EMILIA: But now, my lord.

120 OTHELLO: It is the very error[16] of the moon.

She comes more nearer earth than she was wont

And makes men mad.

EMILIA: Cassio, my lord, hath killed a young Venetian

Called Roderigo.

OTHELLO: Roderigo killed?

125 And Cassio killed?

EMILIA: No, Cassio is not killed.

OTHELLO: Not Cassio killed? Then murder's out of tune,

And sweet revenge grows harsh.

DESDEMONA: O, falsely, falsely murdered!

130 EMILIA: O Lord! What cry is that?

OTHELLO: That? What?

EMILIA: Out and alas! that was my lady's voice.

Help! Help, ho! Help! O lady, speak again!

Sweet Desdemona! O sweet mistress, speak!

135 DESDEMONA: A guiltless death I die.

EMILIA: O, who hath done this deed?

DESDEMONA: Nobody—I myself. Farewell.

Commend me to my kind lord. O, farewell!

(*She dies.*)

OTHELLO: Why, how should she be murd'red?

140 EMILIA: Alas, who knows?

OTHELLO: You heard her say herself, it was not I.

EMILIA: She said so. I must needs report the truth.

OTHELLO: She's like a liar gone to burning hell!

'Twas I that killed her.

145 EMILIA: O, the more angel she,

And you the blacker devil!

OTHELLO: She turned to folly, and she was a whore.

EMILIA: Thou dost belie her, and thou art a devil.

---

[16] *error:* Wandering out of regular course (disorders in the heavens were believed by some to cause disorders on earth, as well as vice versa).

OTHELLO: She was false as water.

150 EMILIA: Thou art rash as fire to say
    That she was false. O, she was heavenly true!

OTHELLO: Cassio did top her. Ask thy husband else.
    O, I were damned beneath all depth in hell
    But that I did proceed upon just grounds
    To this extremity. Thy husband knew it all.

155 EMILIA: My husband?

OTHELLO: Thy husband.

EMILIA: That she was false to wedlock?

OTHELLO: Ay, with Cassio. Had she been true,
    If heaven would make me such another world

160   Of one entire and perfect chrysolite,[17]
    I'd not have sold her for it.

EMILIA: My husband?

OTHELLO: Ay, 'twas he that told me on her first.
    An honest man he is, and hates the slime

165   That sticks on filthy deeds.

EMILIA: My husband?

OTHELLO: What needs this iterance? Woman, I say thy husband.

EMILIA: O mistress, villainy hath made mocks with love!
    My husband say she was false?

170 OTHELLO: He, woman.
    I say, thy husband. Dost understand the word?
    My friend, thy husband; honest, honest Iago.

EMILIA: If he say so, may his pernicious soul
    Rot half a grain a day! He lies to th' heart.

175   She was too fond of her most filthy bargain.

OTHELLO: Hah?

EMILIA: Do thy worst.
    This deed of thine is no more worthy heaven
    Than thou wast worthy her.

180 OTHELLO: Peace, you were best.[18]

EMILIA: Thou hast not half that pow'r to do me harm
    As I have to be hurt. O gull! O dolt!
    As ignorant as dirt! Thou hast done a deed—

---

[17] *chrysolite:* Topaz.   [18] *Peace, you were best:* I.e., you had better be silent.

(Othello moves to draw his sword.)

> I care not for thy sword; I'll make thee known,
185 > Though I lost twenty lives. Help! Help! Ho! Help!
> The Moor hath killed my mistress! Murder! murder!

(Enter Montano, Grantiano, and Iago [and Others].)

MONTANO: What is the matter? How now, general?

EMILIA: O, are you come, Iago? You have done well,
> That men must lay their murders on your neck.

190 **GRATIANO:** What is the matter?

EMILIA: Disprove this villain, if thou be'st a man.
> He says thou told'st him that his wife was false.
> I know thou didst not; thou'rt not such a villain.
> Speak, for my heart is full.

195 **IAGO:** I told him what I thought, and told no more
> Than what he found himself was apt and true.

EMILIA: But did you ever tell him she was false?

IAGO: I did.

EMILIA: You told a lie, an odious damnèd lie!
200 > Upon my soul, a lie! A wicked lie!
> She false with Cassio? Did you say with Cassio?

IAGO: With Cassio, mistress. Go to, charm[19] your tongue.

EMILIA: I will not charm my tongue; I am bound to speak:
> My mistress here lies murdered in her bed.

205 **ALL:** O heavens forfend!

EMILIA: And your reports have set the murder on.

OTHELLO: Nay, stare not, masters. It is true indeed.

GRATIANO: 'Tis a strange truth.

MONTANO: O monstrous act!

210 **EMILIA:**   Villainy, villainy, villainy!
> I think upon't—I think I smell't!—O villainy!
> I thought so then.—I'll kill myself for grief.—
> O villainy, villainy!

IAGO: What, are you mad? I charge you get you home.

215 **EMILIA:** Good gentlemen, let me have leave to speak.

---

[19] *charm:* Control.

'Tis proper I obey him, but not now.
Perchance, Iago, I will ne'er go home.

OTHELLO: O! O! O!

(*Falls on the bed.*)

EMILIA: Nay, lay thee down and roar,
220   For thou has killed the sweetest innocent
That e'er did lift up eye.

OTHELLO: O, she was foul!

(*Rises.*)

I scarce did know you, uncle. There lies your niece
Whose breath, indeed, these hands have newly stopped.
225   I know this act shows horrible and grim.

GRATIANO: Poor Desdemon! I am glad thy father's dead
Thy match was mortal to him, and pure grief
Shore his old thread in twain. Did he live now,
This sight would make him do a desperate turn;
230   Yea curse his better angel from his side,
And fall to reprobation.[20]

OTHELLO: This pitiful; but yet Iago knows
That she with Cassio hath the act of shame
A thousand times committed. Cassio confessed it;
235   And she did gratify his amorous works
With that recognizance and pledge of love,
Which I first gave her. I saw it in his hand.
It was a handkerchief, and antique token
My father gave my mother.

240   **EMILIA:** O God! O heavenly God!

IAGO: Zounds, hold your peace!

EMILIA: 'Twill out, 'twill out! I peace?
No, I will speak as liberal as the north.[21]
Let heaven and men and devils, let them all,
245   All, all, cry shame against me, yet I'll speak.

IAGO: Be wise, and get you home.

EMILIA: I will not.

---

[20] *reprobation:* Damnation.   [21] *liberal as the north:* Freely (and bitingly) as the north wind blows.

(Iago draws and threatens Emilia.)

GRATIANO: Fie! Your sword upon a woman?

EMILIA: O thou dull Moor, that handkerchief thou speak'st of
250   I found by fortune, and did give my husband; ·
    For often with a solemn earnestness—
    More than indeed belonged to such a trifle—
    He begged of me to steal't.

IAGO: Villainous whore!

255 EMILIA: She give it Cassio? No, alas, I found it,
    And I did give't my husband.

IAGO: Filth, thou liest!

EMILIA: By heaven, I do not, I do not, gentlemen.
    O murd'rous coxcomb! What should such a fool
260   Do with so good a wife?

OTHELLO: Are there no stones[22] in heaven
    But what serves for the thunder? Precious villain!

(The Moor runs at Iago, but is disarmed by Montano Iago kills his wife.)

GRATIANO: The woman falls. Sure he hath killed his wife.

EMILIA: Ay, ay. O, lay me by my mistress' side.

(Exit Iago.)

265 GRATIANO: He's gone, but his wife's killed.

MONTANO: 'Tis a notorious[23] villain. Take you this weapon,
    Which I have recovered from the Moor.
    Come, guard the door without. Let him not pass,
    But kill him rather. I'll after that same villain,
270   For 'tis a damned slave.

(Exit [with all but Othello and Emilia].)

OTHELLO: I am not valiant neither;
    But every puny whipster[24] gets my sword.
    But why should honor outlive honesty?
    Let it go all.

275 EMILIA: What did thy song bode, lady?

---

[22] *stones:* Thunderbolts. [23] *notorious:* Out-and-out. [24] *puny whipster:* Small top-whipping boy (?).

Hark, canst thou hear me? I will play the swan,
And die in music. (*Sings*) "Willow, willow, willow.
Moor, she was chaste. She loved thee, cruel Moor,
So come my soul to bliss as I speak true.
275 So speaking as I think, alas, I die.

(*She dies.*)

OTHELLO: I have another weapon in this chamber;
It was a sword of Spain, the ice-brook's temper.
O, here it is.—uncle, I must come forth.
GRATIANO: (*Within*) If thou attempt it, it will cost thee dear.
280 Thou hast no weapon, and perforce must suffer.
OTHELLO: Look in upon me then and speak with me,
Of, naked as I am, I will assault thee.

(*Enter Gratiano.*)

GRATIANO: What is the matter?
OTHELLO: Behold, I have a weapon;
285 A better never did itself sustain
Upon a soldier's thing. I have seen the day
That with this little arm and this good sword
I have made my way through more impediments
Than twenty times your stop. But O vain boast!
290 Who can control his fate? 'Tis not so now.
Be not afraid, though you do see me weaponed
Here is my journey's end, here is my butt,[25]
And very seamark of my utmost sail.[26]
Do you go back dismayed? 'Tis a lost fear.
295 Man out a rush[27] against Othello's breast,
And he retires. Where should Othello go?
Now, how dost thou look now? O ill-starred wench!
Pale as thy smock! When we shall meet at compt,[28]
This look of thine will hurl my soul from heaven,
300 And fiends will snatch at it. Cold, cold, my girl?
Even like thy chastity.

---

[25] *butt:* Target, stopping place.   [26] *seamark of my utmost sail:* Marker of my farthest journey.   [27] *Man but a rush:* Attack with only a reed.   [28] *compt:* Judgment Day.

O cursèd, cursèd slave! Whip me, ye devils,
From the possession of[29] this heavenly sight!
Blow me about in winds! Roast me in sulfur!
305 Wash me instep-down gulfs of liquid fire!
O Desdemon! Dead Desdemon; dead. O! O!

(*Enter Lodovico, Cassio, Montano, and Iago [as prisoner,] with Officers.*)

LODOVICO: Where is this rash and most unfortunate man?
OTHELLO: That's he that was Othello; Here I am.
LODOVICO: Where is that viper? Bring the villain forth.
310 OTHELLO: I look down towards his feet[30]—but that's a fable
If that thou be'st a devil, I cannot kill thee.

(*Wounds Iago.*)

LODOVICO: Wrench his sword from him.

(*Othello is disarmed.*)

IAGO: I bleed, sir, but not killed.
OTHELLO: I am not sorry neither. I'd have thee live;
315 For in my sense, 'tis happiness to die.
LODOVICO: O thou Othello that was once so good,
Fall'n in the practice[31] of a cursèd slave,
What shall be said to thee?
OTHELLO: Why, anything
320 An honorable murderer, if you will;
For naught I did in hate, but all in honor.
LODOVICO: This wretch hath part confessed his villainy.
Did you and he consent in Cassio's death?
OTHELLO: Ay.
325 CASSIO: Dear general, I never gave you cause.
OTHELLO: I do believe it, and ask your pardon.
Will you, I pray, demand that demi-devil
Why he hath thus ensnared my soul and body?
IAGO: Demand me nothing. What you know, you know
330 From this time forth I never will speak word.

---

[29] *the possession of*: Being possessed by. [30] *towards his feet*: I.e., for is cloven hoofs.
[31] *practice*: Plotting.

LODOVICO: What, not to pray?

GRATIANO: Torments will ope your lips

OTHELLO: Well, thou dost best.

LODOVICO: Sir, you shall understand what hath befall'n

    Which, as I think, you know not. Here is a letter

335   Found in the pocket of the slain Roderigo;

    And here another. The one of them imports

    The death of Cassio to be undertook

    By Roderigo.

OTHELLO: O villain!

340 CASSIO: Most heathenish and most gross!

LODOVICO: Now here's another discontented paper

    Found in his pocket too; and this, it seems,

    Roderigo meant t' have sent this damnèd villain;

    But that, belike, Iago in the interim

345   Came in and satisfied him.

OTHELLO: O thou pernicious caitiff

    How came you, Cassio, by that handkerchief

    That was my wife's?

CASSIO: I found it in my chamber;

350   And he himself confessed it but even now

    That there he dropped it for a special purpose

    Which wrought to his desire.

OTHELLO: O fool! Fool! Fool!

CASSIO: There is besides in Roderigo's letter,

355   How he upbraids Iago that he made him

    Brave me upon the watch; whereon it came

    That I was cast; and even but now he spake,

    After long seeming dead—Iago hurt him,

    Iago set him on.

360 LODOVICO: Your must forsake this room and go with us.

    Your power and your command is taken off,

    And Cassio rules in Cyprus. For this slave,

    If there be any cunning cruelty

    That can torment him much and hold him long,

365   It shall be his. You shall close prisoner rest

    Till that the nature of your fault be known

    To the Venetian state. Come, bring away.

OTHELLO: Soft you , a word or two before you go.
I have done the state some service, and they know't.
370 No more of that. I pray you, in your letters,
When you shall these unlucky deeds relate,
Speak of me as I am. Nothing extenuate,
Nor set down aught in malice. Then must you speak
Of one that loved not wisely, but too well;
375 Of one not easily jealous, but, being wrought,
Perplexed in the extreme; of one whose hand,
Like the base Judean,[32] threw a pearl away
Richer than all his tribe; of one whose subdued eyes,
Albeit unusèd to the melting mood;
380 Drops tears as fast as the Arabian trees
Their med'cinable gum. Set you down this.
And say besides that in Aleppo once,
Where a malignant and a turbaned Turk
Beat a Venetian and traduced the state,
385 I took by th' throat the circumcisèd dog
And smote him—thus.

(*He stabs himself.*)

LODOVICO: O bloody period![33]
GRATIANO: All that is spoke is marred.
OTHELLO: I kissed thee ere I killed thee. No way but this,
390 Killing myself, to die upon a kiss.

(*He falls over Desdemona and dies.*)

CASSIO: This did I fear, but thought he had no weapon;
For he was great of heart.
LODOVICO: (*To Iago*) O Spartan dog,
More fell[34] than anguish, hunger, or the sea!
395 Look on the tragic loading of this bed.
This is thy work. The object poisons sight;
Let it be hid.

---

[32] *Judean:* Most editors use the Q1 reading, "Indian," here, but F is clear; both readings point toward the infidel, the unbeliever.   [33] *period:* End.   [34] *fell:* Cruel.

(Bed curtains drawn.)

>   Gratiano, keep[35] the house,
>   And seize upon the fortunes of the Moor,
> 400   For they succeed on you. To you, lord governor,
>   Remains the censure of this hellish villain,
>   The time, the place, the torture. O, enforce it!
>   Myself will straight aboard, and to the state
>   This heavy act with heavy heart relate.

(Exeunt.)

---

[35] *keep:* Remain in.

August Strindberg, 1849–1912

Miss Julie *1888*

Translated by Harry G. Carlson

CHARACTERS

Miss Julie, *25 years old*
Jean, *her father's valet, 30 years old*
Kristine, *her father's cook, 35 years old*

The action takes place in the count's kitchen on midsummer eve.

SETTING. *A large kitchen, the ceiling and side walls of which are hidden by draperies. The rear wall runs diagonally from down left to up right. On the wall down left are two shelves with copper, iron, and pewter utensils; the shelves are lined with scalloped paper. Visible to the right is most of a set of large, arched glass doors, through which can be seen a fountain with a statue of Cupid, lilac bushes in bloom, and the tops of some Lombardy poplars. At down left is the corner of a large tiled stove; a portion of its hood is showing. At right, one end of the servants' white pine dining table juts out; several chairs stand around it. The stove is decorated with birch branches; juniper twigs are strewn on the floor. On the end of the table stands a large Japanese spice jar, filled with lilac blossoms. An ice-box, a sink, and a washstand. Above the door is an old-fashioned bell on a spring; to the left of the door, the mouthpiece of a speaking tube is visible.*

Kristine is frying something on the stove. She is wearing a light-colored cotton dress and an apron. Jean enters. He is wearing livery and carries a pair of high riding-boots with spurs, which he puts down on the floor where they can be seen by the audience.

JEAN: Miss Julie's crazy again tonight; absolutely crazy!

KRISTINE: So you finally came back?

JEAN: I took the Count to the station and when I returned past the barn I stopped in for a dance. Who do I see but Miss Julie leading off the dance with the gamekeeper! But as soon as she saw me she rushed over to ask me for the next waltz. And she's been waltzing ever since—I've never seen anything like it. She's crazy!

KRISTINE: She always has been, but never as bad as the last two weeks since her engagement was broken off.

5 JEAN: Yes, I wonder what the real story was there. He was a gentleman, even if he wasn't rich. Ah! These people have such romantic ideas. (*Sits at the end of the table*) Still, it's strange, isn't it? I mean that she'd rather stay home with the servants on midsummer eve instead of going with her father to visit relatives?

KRISTINE: She's probably embarrassed after that row with her fiancé.

JEAN: Probably! He gave a good account of himself, though. Do you know how it happened, Kristine? I saw it, you know, though I didn't let on I had.

KRISTINE: No! You saw it?

JEAN: Yes, I did——That evening they were out near the stable, and she was "training" him—as she called it. Do you know what she did? She made him jump over her riding crop, the way you'd teach a dog to jump. He jumped twice and she hit him each time. But the third time he grabbed the crop out of her hand, hit her with it across the cheek, and broke it in pieces. Then he left.

10 KRISTINE: So, that's what happened! I can't believe it!

JEAN: Yes, that's the way it went!——What have you got for me that's tasty, Kristine?

KRISTINE: (*Serving him from the pan*) Oh, it's only a piece of kidney I cut from the veal roast.

JEAN: (*Smelling the food*) Beautiful! That's my favorite *délice*. (*Feeling the plate*) But you could have warmed the plate!

KRISTINE: You're fussier than the Count himself, once you start! (*She pulls his hair affectionately.*)

15   JEAN: (*Angry*) Stop it, leave my hair alone! You know I'm touchy about that.

KRISTINE: Now, now, it's only love, you know that. (*Jean eats. Kristine opens a bottle of beer.*)

JEAN: Beer? On midsummer eve? No thank you! I can do better than that. (*Opens a drawer in the table and takes out a bottle of red wine with yellow sealing wax*) See that? Yellow seal! Give me a glass! A wine glass! I'm drinking this *pur*.

KRISTINE: (*Returns to the stove and puts on a small saucepan*) God help the woman who gets you for a husband! What a fuss-budget.

JEAN: Nonsense! You'd be damned lucky to get a man like me. It certainly hasn't done you any harm to have people call me your sweetheart. (*Tastes the wine*) Good! Very good! Just needs a little warming. (*Warms the glass between his hands*) We bought this in Dijon. Four francs a liter, not counting the cost of the bottle, or the customs duty.——What are you cooking now? It stinks like hell!

20   KRISTINE: Oh, some slop Miss Julie wants to give her dog Diana.

JEAN: Watch your language, Kristine. But why should you have to cook for that damn mutt on midsummer eve? Is she sick?

KRISTINE: Yes, she's sick! She sneaked out with the gatekeeper's dog—and now there's hell to pay. Miss Julie won't have it!

JEAN: Miss Julie has too much pride about some things and not enough about others, just like her mother was. The Countess was most at home in the kitchen and the cowshed, but a *one*-horse carriage wasn't elegant enough for her. The cuffs of her blouse were dirty, but she had to have her coat of arms on her cufflinks.——And Miss Julie won't take proper care of herself either. If you ask me, she just isn't refined. Just now, when she was dancing in the barn, she pulled the gamekeeper away from Anna and made him dance with her. *We* wouldn't behave like that, but that's what happens when aristocrats pretend they're common people—they get *common*!——But she is quite a woman! Magnificent! What shoulders, and what—et cetera!

KRISTINE: Oh, don't overdo it! I've heard what Clara says, and she dresses her.

25 JEAN: Ha, Clara! You're all jealous of each other! I've been out riding with her . . . And the way she dances!

KRISTINE: Listen, Jean! You're going to dance with me, when I'm finished here, aren't you?

JEAN: Of course I will.

KRISTINE: Promise?

JEAN: Promise? When I say I'll do something, I do it! By the way, the kidney was very good. (*Corks the bottle*)

30 JULIE: (*In the doorway to someone outside*) I'll be right back! You go ahead for now! (*Jean sneaks the bottle back into the table drawer and gets up respectfully. Miss Julie enters and crosses to Kristine by the stove.*) Well? Is it ready? (*Kristine indicates that Jean is present.*)

JEAN: (*Gallantly*) Are you ladies up to something secret?

JULIE: (*Flicking her handkerchief in his face*) None of your business!

JEAN: Hmm! I like the smell of violets!

JULIE: (*Coquettishly*) Shame on you! So you know about perfumes, too? You certainly know how to dance. Ah ah! No peeking! Go away.

35 JEAN: (*Boldly but respectfully*) Are you brewing up a magic potion for midsummer eve? Something to prophesy by under a lucky star, so you'll catch a glimpse of your future husband!

JULIE: (*Caustically*) You'd need sharp eyes to see him! (*To Kristine*) Pour out half a bottle and cork it well.——Come and dance a schottische with me, Jean . . .

JEAN: (*Hesitating*) I don't want to be impolite to anyone, and I've already promised this dance to Kristine . . .

JULIE: Oh, she can have another one—can't you Kristine? Won't you lend me Jean?

KRISTINE: It's not up to me, ma'am (*To Jean*) If the mistress is so generous, it wouldn't do for you to say no. Go on, Jean, and thank her for the honor.

40 JEAN: To be honest, and no offense intended, I wonder whether it's wise for you to dance twice running with the same partner, especially since these people are quick to jump to conclusions.

JULIE: (*Flaring up*) What's that? What sort of conclusions? What do you mean?

JEAN: (*Submissively*) If you don't understand, ma'am, I must speak more plainly. It doesn't look good to play favorites with your servants . . .

JULIE: Play favorites! What an idea! I'm astonished! As mistress of the house, I honor your dance with my presence. And when I dance, I want to dance with someone who can lead, so I won't look ridiculous.

JEAN: As you order ma'am! I'm at your service!

45 JULIE: (*Gently*) Don't take it as an order! On a night like this we're all just ordinary people having fun, so we'll forget about rank. Now, take my arm!——Don't worry, Kristine! I won't steal your sweetheart! (*Jean offers his arm and leads Miss Julie out.*)

MIME: *The following should be played as if the actress playing Kristine were really alone. When she has to, she turns her back to the audience. She does not look toward them, nor does she hurry as if she were afraid they would grow impatient. Schottische music played on a fiddle sounds in the distance. Kristine hums along with the music. She clears the table, washes the dishes, dries them, and puts them away. She takes off her apron. From a table drawer she removes a small mirror and leans it against the bowl of lilacs on the table. She lights a candle, heats a hairpin over the flame, and uses it to set a curl on her forehead. She crosses to the door and listens, then returns to the table. She finds the handkerchief Miss Julie left behind, picks it up, and smells it. Then, preoccupied, she spreads it out, stretches it, smoothes out the wrinkles, and folds it into quarters, and so forth.*

JEAN: (*Enters alone*) God, she really *is* crazy! What a way to dance. Everybody's laughing at her behind her back. What do you make of it, Kristine?

KRISTINE: Ah! It's that time of the month for her, and she always gets peculiar like that. Are you going to dance with me now?

JEAN: You're not mad at me, are you, for leaving . . .?

KRISTINE: Of course not!——Why should I be, for a little thing like that? Besides, I know my place . . .

50 JEAN: (*Puts his arm around her waist*) You're a sensible girl Kristine, and you'd make a good wife . . .

JULIE: (*Entering; uncomfortably surprised; with forced good humor*) What a charming escort—running away from his partner.

JEAN: On the contrary, Miss Julie. Don't you see how I rushed back to the partner I abandoned!

JULIE: (*Changing her tone*) You know, you're a superb dancer!—— But why are you wearing livery on a holiday? Take it off at once!

JEAN: Then I must ask you to go outside for a moment. You see, my black coat is hanging over here . . . (*Gestures and crosses right*)

55 JULIE: Are you embarrassed about changing your coat in front of me? Well, go in your room then. Either that or stay and I'll turn my back.

JEAN: With your permission, ma'am! (*He crosses right. His arm is visible as he changes his jacket.*)

JULIE: (*To Kristine*) Tell me, Kristine—you two are so close—. Is Jean your fiancé?

KRISTINE: Fiancé? Yes, if you wish. We can call him that.

JULIE: What do you mean?

60 KRISTINE: You had a fiancé yourself, didn't you? So . . .

JULIE: Well, we were properly engaged . . .

KRISTINE: But nothing came of it, did it? (*Jean returns dressed in a frock coat and bowler hat.*)

JULIE: *Très gentil, monsieur Jean! Très gentil!*

JEAN: *Vous voulez plaisanter, madame!*

65 JULIE: *Et vous voulez parler français!* Where did you learn that?

JEAN: In Switzerland, when I was wine steward in one of the biggest hotels in Lucerne!

JULIE: You look like a real gentleman in that coat! *Charmant!* (*Sits at the table*)

JEAN: Oh, you're flattering me!

JULIE: (*Offended*) Flattering you?

70 JEAN: My natural modesty forbids me to believe that you would really compliment someone like me, and so I took the liberty of assuming that you were exaggerating, which polite people call flattering.

JULIE: Where did you learn to talk like that? You must have been to the theatre often.

JEAN: Of course. And I've done a lot of traveling.

JULIE: But you come from here, don't you?

JEAN: My father was a farm hand on the district attorney's estate nearby. I used to see you when you were little, but you never noticed me.

75 JULIE: No! really?

JEAN: Sure. I remember one time especially . . . but I can't talk about that.

JULIE: Oh, come now! Why not? Just this once!

JEAN: No, I really couldn't, not now. Some other time, perhaps.

JULIE: Why some other time? What's so dangerous about now?

80 JEAN: It's not dangerous, but there are obstacles.——Her, for example. (*Indicates Kristine, who has fallen asleep in a chair by the stove.*)

JULIE: What a pleasant wife she'll make! She probably snores, too.

JEAN: No, she doesn't, but she talks in her sleep.

JULIE: (*Cynically*) How do *you* know?

JEAN: (*Audaciously*) I've heard her! (*Pause, during which they stare at each other*)

85 JULIE: Why don't you sit down?

JEAN: I couldn't do that in your presence.

JULIE: But if I order you to?

JEAN: Then I'd obey.

JULIE: Sit down, then.——No, wait. Can you get me something to drink first?

90 JEAN: I don't know what we have in the ice box. I think there's only beer.

JULIE: Why do you say "only"? My tastes are so simple I prefer beer to wine. (*Jean takes a bottle of beer from the ice box and opens it. He looks for a glass and a plate in the cupboard and serves her.*)

JEAN: Here you are, ma'am.

JULIE: Thank you. Won't you have something yourself?

JEAN: I'm not partial to beer, but if it's an order . . .

95 JULIE: An order?——Surely a gentleman can keep his lady company.

JEAN: You're right, of course. (*Opens a bottle and gets a glass*)

JULIE: Now, drink to my health! (*He hesitates.*) What? A man of the world—and shy?

JEAN: (*In mock romantic fashion, he kneels and raises his glass.*) Skål to my mistress!

JULIE: Bravo!——Now kiss my shoe, to finish it properly. (*Jean hesitates, then boldly seizes her foot and kisses it lightly.*) Perfect! You should have been an actor.

100   **JEAN:** (*Rising*) That's enough now, Miss Julie! Someone might come in and see us.

JULIE: What of it?

JEAN: People talk, that's what! If you knew how their tongues were wagging just now at the dance, you'd . . .

JULIE: What were they saying? Tell me!——Sit down!

JEAN: (*Sits*) I don't want to hurt you, but they were saying things—— suggestive things, that, that . . . well, you can figure it out for yourself! You're not a child. If a woman is seen drinking alone with a man—let alone a servant—at night—then . . .

105   **JULIE:** Then what? Besides, we're not alone. Kristine is here.

JEAN: Asleep!

JULIE: Then I'll wake her up. (*Rising*) Kristine! Are you asleep? (*Kristine mumbles in her sleep.*)

JULIE: Kristine!——She certainly can sleep!

KRISTINE: (*In her sleep*) The Count's boots are brushed—put the coffee on—right away, right away—uh, huh—oh!

110   **JULIE:** (*Grabbing Kristine's nose*) Will you wake up!

JEAN: (*Severely*) Leave her alone—let her sleep!

JULIE: (*Sharply*) What?

JEAN: Someone who's been standing over a stove all day has a right to be tired by now. Sleep should be respected . . .

JULIE: (*Changing her tone*) What a considerate thought—it does you credit—thank you! (*Offering her hand*) Come outside and pick some lilacs for me! (*During the following, Kristine awakens and shambles sleepily off right to bed.*)

115   **JEAN:** Go with you?

JULIE: With me!

JEAN: We couldn't do that! Absolutely not!

JULIE: I don't understand. Surely you don't imagine . . .

JEAN: No, I don't, but the others might.

120   **JULIE:** What? That I've fallen in love with a servant?

JEAN: I'm not a conceited man, but such things happen—and for these people, nothing is sacred.

JULIE: I do believe you're an aristocrat!

JEAN: Yes, I am.

JULIE: And I'm stepping down . . .

125 JEAN: Don't step down, Miss Julie, take my advice. No one'll believe you stepped down voluntarily. People will always say you fell.

JULIE: I have a higher opinion of people than you. Come and see!——Come! (*She stares at him broodingly.*)

JEAN: You're very strange, do you know that?

JULIE: Perhaps! But so are you!——For that matter, everything is strange. Life, people, everything. Like floating scum, drifting on and on across the water, until it sinks down and down! That reminds me of a dream I have now and then. I've climbed up on top of a pillar. I sit there and see no way of getting down. I get dizzy when I look down, and I must get down, but I don't have the courage to jump. I can't hold on firmly, and I long to be able to fall, but I don't fall. And yet I'll have no peace until I get down, no rest unless I get down, down on the ground! And if I did get down to the ground, I'd want to be under the earth . . . Have you ever felt anything like that?

JEAN: No. I dream that I'm lying under a high tree in a dark forest. I want to get up, up on top, and look out over the bright landscape, where the sum is shining, and plunder the bird's nest up there, where the golden eggs lie. And I climb and climb, but the trunk's so thick and smooth, and it's so far to the first branch. But I know if I just reached that first branch, I'd go right to the top, like up a ladder. I haven't reached it yet, but I will, even if it's only in a dream!

130 JULIE: Here I am chattering with you about dreams. Come, let's go out! Just into the park! (*She offers him her arm, and they start to leave.*)

JEAN: We'll have to sleep on nine midsummer flowers, Miss Julie, to make our dreams come true! (*They turn at the door. Jean puts his hand to his eye.*)

JULIE: Did you get something in your eye?

JEAN: It's nothing—just a speck—it'll be gone in a minute.

JULIE: My sleeve must have brushed against you. Sit down and let me help you. (*She takes him by the arm and seats him. She tilts his head back and with the tip of a handkerchief tries to remove the speck.*) Sit still, absolutely still (*She slaps his hand.*) Didn't you hear me?——Why, you're trembling; the big, strong man is trembling! (*Feels his biceps*) What muscles you have!

135 JEAN: (*Warning*) Miss Julie!

JULIE: Yes, *monsieur* Jean.

JEAN: *Attention! Je ne suis qu'un homme!*

JULIE: Will you sit still!——There! Now it's gone! Kiss my hand and thank me.

JEAN: (*Rising*) Miss Julie, listen to me!——Kristine has gone to bed!——Will you listen to me!

140 JULIE: Kiss my hand first!

JEAN: Listen to me!

JULIE: Kiss my hand first!

JEAN: All right, but you've only yourself to blame!

JULIE: For what?

145 JEAN: For what? Are you still a child at twenty-five? Don't you know that it's dangerous to play with fire?

JULIE: Not for me. I'm insured.

JEAN: (*Boldly*) No, you're not! But even if you were, there's combustible material close by.

JULIE: Meaning you?

JEAN: Yes! Not because it's me, but because I'm young——

150 JULIE: And handsome—what incredible conceit! A Don Juan perhaps! Or a Joseph! Yes, that's it, I do believe you're a Joseph!

JEAN: Do you?

JULIE: I'm almost afraid so. (*Jean boldly tries to put his arm around her waist and kiss her. She slaps his face.*) How dare you?

JEAN: Are you serious or joking?

JULIE: Serious.

155 JEAN: The so was what just happened. You play games too seriously, and that's dangerous. Well, I'm tired of games. You'll excuse me if I get back to work. I haven't done the Count's boots yet and it's long past midnight.

JULIE: Put the boots down!

JEAN: No! It's the work I have to do. I never agreed to be your playmate, and never will. It's beneath me.

JULIE: You're proud.

JEAN: In certain ways, but not in others.

160 JULIE: Have you ever been in love?

JEAN: We don't use that word, but I've been fond of many girls, and once I was sick because I couldn't have the one I wanted. That's right, sick, like those princes in the Arabian Nights— who couldn't eat or drink because of love.

JULIE: Who was she? (*Jean is silent.*) Who was she?

JEAN: You can't force me to tell you that.

JULIE: But if I ask you as an equal, as a—friend! Who was she?

JEAN: You!

JULIE: (*Sits*) How amusing . . .

JEAN: Yes, if you like! It was ridiculous!——You see, that was the story I didn't want to tell you earlier. Maybe I will now. Do you know how the world looks from down below?——Of course you don't. Neither do hawks and falcons, whose backs we can't see because they're usually soaring up there above us. I grew up in a shack with seven brothers and sisters and a pig, in the middle of a wasteland, where there wasn't a single tree. But from our window I could see the tops of apple trees above the wall of your father's garden. That was the Garden of Eden, guarded by angry angels with flaming swords. All the same, the other boys and I managed to find our way to the Tree of Life.——Now you think I'm contemptible, I suppose.

JULIE: Oh, all boys steal apples.

JEAN: You say that, but you think I'm contemptible anyway. Oh well! One day I went into the Garden of Eden with my mother, to weed the onion beds. Near the vegetable garden was a small Turkish pavilion in the shadow of jasmine bushes and overgrown with honeysuckle. I had no idea what it was used for, but I'd never seen such a beautiful building. People went in and came out again, and one day the door was left open. I sneaked close and saw walls covered with pictures of kings and emperors, and red curtains with fringes at the win- dows—now you know the place I mean. I——(*Breaks off a sprig of lilac and holds it in front of Miss Julie's nose*)——I'd never been inside the manor house, never seen anything except the church—but this was more beautiful. From then on, no matter where my thoughts wandered, they returned—there. And gradually I got a longing to experience, just once, the full pleasure of—*enfin,* I sneaked in, saw, and marveled! But then I heard someone coming! There was only one exit for ladies and gentlemen, but for me there was another, and I had no choice but to take it! (*Miss Julie, who has taken the lilac sprig, lets it fall on the table.*) Afterwards, I started running. I crashed through a raspberry bush, flew over a strawberry patch, and came up onto the rose terrace. There I caught sight of a pink dress and a pair of white stockings—it was you. I crawled under a pile of weeds and I mean under—under thistles that pricked me and wet dirt that stank. And I looked at you as you walked among the roses, and I thought; if it's true that a thief can enter heaven and be with the angels, then why can't a farmhand's son here on God's earth enter the manor house garden and play with the Count's daughter?

170 JULIE: (*Romantically*) Do you think all poor children would have felt the way you did?

JEAN: (*At first hesitant, then with conviction*) If *all* poor—yes—of course. Of course!

JULIE: It must be terrible to be poor!

JEAN: (*With exaggerated suffering*) Oh, Miss Julie! Oh!——A dog can lie on the Countess's sofa, a horse can have his nose patted by a young lady's hand, but a servant——(*Changing his tone*)——oh, I know—now and then you find one with enough stuff in him to get ahead in the world, but how often?——Anyhow, do you know what I did then?——I jumped in the millstream with my clothes on, was pulled out, and got a beating. But the following Sunday, when my father and all the others went to my grandmother's, I arranged to stay home. I scrubbed myself with soap and water, put on my best clothes, and went to church just to see you! I saw you and returned home, determined to die. But I wanted to die beautifully and pleasantly, without pain. And then I remembered that it was dangerous to sleep under an elder bush. We had a big one, and it was in full flower. I plundered its treasures and bedded down under them in the oat bin. Have you ever noticed how smooth oats are?—and soft to the touch, like human skin . . .! Well, I shut the lid and closed my eyes. I fell asleep and woke up feeling very sick. But I didn't die, as you can see. What was I after?—— I don't know. There was no hope of winning you, of course.——You were a symbol of the hopelessness of ever rising out of the class in which I was born.

JULIE: You're a charming storyteller. Did you ever go to school?

175 JEAN: A bit, but I've read lots of novels and been to the theatre often. And then I've listened to people like you talk—that's where I learned most.

JULIE: Do you listen to what we say?

JEAN: Naturally! And I've heard plenty, too, driving the carriage or rowing the boat. Once I heard you and a friend . . .

JULIE: Oh?——What did you hear?

JEAN: I'd better not say. But I was surprised a little. I couldn't imagine where you learned such words. Maybe at bottom there isn't such a great difference between people as we think.

180 JULIE: Shame on you! We don't act like you when we're engaged.

JEAN: (*Staring at her*) Is that true?——You don't have play innocent with me, Miss . . .

JULIE: The man I gave my love to was a swine.

JEAN: That's what you all say—afterwards.

JULIE: All?

185 JEAN: I think so. I know I've heard that phrase before, on similar occasions.

JULIE: What occasions?

JEAN: Like the one I'm talking about. The last time . . .

JULIE: (*Rising*) Quiet! I don't want to hear any more!

JEAN: That's interesting—that's what *she* said, too. Well, if you'll excuse me, I'm going to bed.

190 JULIE: (*Gently*) To bed? On midsummer eve?

JEAN: Yes! Dancing with the rabble out there doesn't amuse me much.

JULIE: Get the key to the boat and row me out on the lake. I want to see the sun come up.

JEAN: Is that wise?

JULIE: Are you worried about your reputation?

195 JEAN: Why not? Why should I risk looking ridiculous and getting fired without a reference, just when I'm trying to establish myself. Besides, I think I owe something to Kristine.

JULIE: So, now it's Kristine . . .

JEAN: Yes, but you, too.——Take my advice, go up and go to bed!

JULIE: Am I to obey you?

JEAN: Just this once—for your own good! Please! It's very late. Drowsiness makes people giddy and liable to lose their heads! Go to bed! Besides—unless I'm mistaken—I hear the others coming to look for me. And if they find us together, you'll be lost! (*The Chorus approaches, singing:*)

> The swineherd found his true love
> a pretty girl so fair,
> The swineherd found his true love
> but let the girl beware.
>
> For then he saw the princess
> the princess on the golden hill,
> but then saw the princess,
> so much fairer still.
>
> So the swineherd and the princess
> they danced the whole night through,
> and he forgot his first love,
> to her he was untrue.
>
> And when the long night ended,
> and in the light of day, of day,
> the dancing too was ended,
> and the princess could not stay.
>
> Then the swineherd lost his true love,
> and the princess grieves him still,
> and never more she'll wander
> from atop the golden hill.

200 JULIE: I know all these people and I love them, just as they love me. Let them come in and you'll see.

JEAN: No, Miss Julie, they don't love you. They take your food, but they spit on it! Believe me! Listen to them, listen to what they're singing!——No, don't listen to them!

JULIE: (*Listening*) What are they singing?

JEAN: It's a dirty song! About you and me!

JULIE: Disgusting! Oh! How deceitful!——

205 JEAN: The rabble is always cowardly! And in a battle like this, you don't fight; you can only run away!

JULIE: Run away? But where? We can't go out—or into Kristine's room.

JEAN: True. But there's my room. Necessity knows no rules. Besides, you can trust me. I'm your friend and I respect you.

JULIE: But suppose—suppose they look for you in there?

JEAN: I'll bolt the door, and if anyone tries to break in, I'll shoot!——Come! (*On his knees*) Come!

210 JULIE: (*Urgently*) Promise me . . .?

JEAN: I swear! (*Miss Julie runs off right. Jean hastens after her.*)

(*BALLET: Led by a fiddler, the servants and farm people enter, dressed festively, with flowers in their hats. On the table they place a small barrel of beer and a keg of schnapps, both garlanded. Glasses are brought out, and the drinking starts. A dance circle is formed and "The Swineherd and the Princess" is sung. When the dance is finished, everyone leaves, singing.*)

(*Miss Julie enters a alone. She notices the mess in the kitchen, wrings her hands, then takes out her powder puff and powders her nose.*)

JEAN: (*Enters agitated*) There, you see? And you heard them. We can't possibly stay here now, you know that.

JULIE: Yes, I know, But what can we do?

JEAN: Leave, travel, far away from here.

215 JULIE: Travel? Yes, but where?

JEAN: To Switzerland, to the Italian lakes. Have you ever been there?

JULIE: No. Is it beautiful?

JEAN: Oh, an eternal summer—oranges growing everywhere, laurel trees, always green . . .

JULIE: But what'll we do there?

220 JEAN: I'll open a hotel—with first-class service for first-class people.

JULIE: Hotel?

JEAN: That's the life, you know. Always new faces, new languages. No time to worry or be nervous. No hunting for something to do—there's always work to be done: bells ringing night and day, train whistles blowing, carriages coming and going, and all the while gold rolling into the till! That's the life!

JULIE: Yes, it sounds wonderful. But what'll I do?

JEAN: You'll be mistress of the house: the jewels in our crown! With your looks . . . and your manner—oh—success is guaranteed! It'll be wonderful! You'll sit in your office like a queen and push an electric button to set your slaves in motion. The guests will file past your throne and timidly lay their treasures before you.—— You have no idea how people tremble when they get their bill.—— I'll salt the bills and you'll sweeten them with your prettiest smile.——Let's get away from here——(*Takes a timetable out of his pocket*)——Right away, on the next train!——We'll be in Malmö six-thirty tomorrow morning, Hamburg at eight-forty; from Frankfort to Basel will take a day, then on to Como by way of the St. Gotthard Tunnel, in, let's see, three days. Three days!

225 JULIE: That's all very well! But Jean—you must give me courage!——Tell me you love me! Put your arms around me!

JEAN: (*Hesitating*) I want to—but I don't dare. Not in this house, not again. I love you—never doubt that—you don't doubt it, do you, Miss Julie?

JULIE: (*Shy; very feminine*) "Miss!"——Call me Julie! There are no barriers between us any more. Call me Julie!

JEAN: (*Tormented*) I can't! There'll always be barriers between us as long as we stay in this house.——There's the past and there's the Count. I've never met anyone I had such respect for.—— When I see his gloves lying on a chair, I feel small.——When I hear that bell up there ring, I jump like a skittish horse.—— And when I look at his boots standing there so stiff and proud, I feel like bowing! (*Kicking the boots*) Superstitions and prejudices we learned as children—but they can easily be forgotten. If I can just get to another country, a republic, people will bow and scrape when they see my livery—they'll bow and scrape, you hear, not me! I wasn't born to cringe. I've got stuff in me, I've got character, and if I can only grab on to that first branch, you watch me climb! I'm a servant today, but next year I'll own my own hotel. In ten years I'll have enough to retire. Then I'll go to Rumania and be decorated. I could—mind you I said *could*—end up a count!

JULIE: Wonderful, wonderful!

230 JEAN: Ah, in Rumania you just buy your title, and so you'll be countess after all. My countess!

JULIE: But I don't care about that—that's what I'm putting behind me! Show me you love me, otherwise—otherwise, what am I?

JEAN: I'll show you a thousand times—afterwards! Not here! And whatever you do, no emotional outbursts, or we'll both be lost! We must think this through coolly, like sensible people. (*He takes out a cigar, snips the end and lights it.*) You sit there, and I'll sit here. We'll talk as if nothing happened.

JULIE: (*Desperately*) Oh, my God! Have you no feelings?

JEAN: Me? No one has more feelings than I do, but I know how to control them.

235 JULIE: A little while ago you could kiss my shoe—and now!

JEAN: (*Harshly*) Yes, but that was before. Now we have other things to think about.

JULIE: Don't speak harshly to me!

JEAN: I'm not—just sensibly! We've already done one foolish thing, let's not have any more. The Count could return any minute, and by then we've got to decide what to do with our lives. What do you think of my plans for the future? Do you approve?

JULIE: They sound reasonable enough. I have only one question: for such a big undertaking you need capital—do you have it?

240 JEAN: (*Chewing on the cigar*) Me? Certainly! I have my professional expertise, my wide experience, and my knowledge of languages. That's capital enough, I should think!

JULIE: But all that won't even buy a train ticket.

JEAN: That's true. That's why I'm looking for a partner to advance me the money.

JULIE: Where will you find one quickly enough?

JEAN: That's up to you, if you want to come with me.

245 JULIE: But I can't; I have no money of my own. (*Pause*)

JEAN: Then it's all off . . .

JULIE: And . . .

JEAN: Things stay as they are.

JULIE: Do you think I'm going to stay in this house as your lover? With all the servants pointing their fingers at me? Do you imagine I can face my father after this? No! Take me away from here, away from shame and dishonor——Oh, what have I done! My God, my God! (*She cries.*)

250 JEAN: Now, don't start that old song!——What have you done? The same as many others before you.

JULIE: (*Screaming convulsively*) And now you think I'm contemptible!——I'm falling, I'm falling!

JEAN: Fall down to my level and I'll lift you up again.

JULIE: What terrible power drew me to you? The attraction of the weak to the strong? The falling to the rising? Or was it love? Was this love? Do you know what love is?

JEAN: Me? What do you take me for? You don't think this was my first time, do you?

255 JULIE: The things you say, the thoughts you think!

JEAN: That's the way I was taught, and that's the way I am! Now don't get excited and don't play the grand lady, because we're in the same boat now! ——Come on, Julie, I'll pour you a glass of something special! (*He opens a drawer in the table, takes out a wine bottle, and fills two glasses already used.*)

JULIE: Where did you get that wine?

JEAN: From the cellar.

JULIE: My father's burgundy!

260 JEAN: That'll do for his son-in-law, won't it?

JULIE: And I drink beer! Beer!

JEAN: That only shows I have better taste.

JULIE: Thief!

JEAN: Planning to tell?

265 JULIE: Oh, oh! Accomplice of a common thief! Was I drunk? Have I been walking in a dream the whole evening? Midsummer eve! A time of innocent fun!

JEAN: Innocent, eh!

JULIE: (*Pacing back and forth*) Is there anyone on earth more miserable than I am at this moment?

JEAN: Why should you be? After such a conquest? Think of Kristine in there. Don't you think she has feelings, too?

JULIE: I thought so awhile ago, but not any more. No, a servant is a servant . . .

270 JEAN: And a whore is a whore!

JULIE: (*On her knees, her hands clasped*) Oh, God in Heaven, end my wretched life! Take me away from the filth I'm sinking into! Save me! Save me!

JEAN: I can't deny I feel sorry for you. When I lay in that onion bed and saw you in the rose garden, well . . . I'll be frank . . . I had the same dirty thoughts all boys have.

JULIE: And you wanted to die for me!

JEAN: In the oat bin? That was just talk.

275 JULIE: A lie, in other words!

JEAN: (*Beginning to feel sleepy*) More or less! I got the idea from a newspaper story about a chimney sweep who curled up in a firewood bin full of lilacs because he got a summons for not supporting his illegitimate child . . .

JULIE: So, that's what you're like . . .

JEAN: I had to think of something. And that's the kind of story women always go for.

JULIE: Swine!

280 JEAN: *Merde!*

JULIE: And now you've seen the hawk's back . . .

JEAN: Not exactly its *back* . . .

JULIE: And I was to be the first branch . . .

JEAN: But the branch was rotten . . .

285 JULIE: I was to be the sign on the hotel . . .

JEAN: And I the hotel . . .

JULIE: Sit at your desk, entice your customers, pad their bills . . .

JEAN: That I'd do myself . . .

JULIE: How can anyone be so thoroughly filthy?

290 JEAN: Better clean up then!

JULIE: You lackey, you menial, stand up, when I speak to you!

JEAN: Menial's strumpet, lackey's whore, shut up and get out of here! Who are you to lecture me on coarseness? None of my kind is ever as coarse as you were tonight. Do you think one of your maids would throw herself at a man the way you did? Have you ever seen any girl of my class offer herself like that? I've only seen it among animals and streetwalkers.

JULIE: (*Crushed*) You're right. Hit me, trample on me. I don't deserve any better. I'm worthless. But help me! If you see any way out of this, help me, Jean, please!

JEAN: (*More gently*) I'd be lying if I didn't admit to a sense of tri- umph in all this, but do you think that a person like me would have dared even to look at someone like you if you hadn't invited it? I'm still amazed . . .

295 JULIE: And proud . . .

JEAN: Why not? Though I must say it was too easy to be really exciting.

JULIE: Go on, hit me, hit me harder!

JEAN: (*Rising*) No! Forgive me for what I've said! I don't hit a man when he's down, let alone a woman. I can't deny though, that I'm pleased to find out that what looked so dazzling to us from below was only tinsel, that the hawk's back was only gray, after all, that the lovely complexion was only powder, that those pol- ished fingernails had black edges, and that a dirty handkerchief is still dirty, even if it smells of perfume . . .! On the other hand, it hurts me to find out that what I was striving for wasn't finer, more substantial. It hurts me to see you sunk so low that you're inferior to your own cook. It hurts like watching flowers beaten down by autumn rains and turned into mud.

JULIE: You talk as if you were already above me.

300 JEAN: I am. You see, I could make you a countess, but you could never make me a count.

JULIE: But I'm the child of a count—something you could never be!

JEAN: That's true. But I could be the father of counts—if . . .

JULIE: But you're a thief. I'm not.

JEAN: There are worse things than being a thief! Besides, when I'm working in a house, I consider myself sort of a member of the family, like one of the children. And you don't call it stealing when a child snatches a berry off a full bush. (*His passion is aroused again.*) Miss Julie, you're a glorious woman, much too good for someone like me! You were drinking and you lost your head. Now you want to cover up your mistake by telling yourself that you love me! You don't. Maybe there was a physical attraction—but then your love is no better than mine.——I could never be satisfied to be no more than an animal to you, and I could never arouse real love in you.

305 JULIE: Are you sure of that?

JEAN: You're suggesting it's possible——Oh, I could fall in love with you, no doubt about it. You're beautiful, you're refined——(*Approaching and taking her hand*)——cultured, lovable when you want to be, and once you start a fire in a man, it never goes out. (*Putting his arm around her waist*) You're like hot, spicy wine, and one kiss from you . . . (*He tries to lead her out, but she slowly frees herself.*)

JULIE: Let me go!?——You'll never win me like that.

JEAN: *How* then?——Not like that? Not with caresses and pretty speeches. Not with plans about the future or rescue from disgrace! *How* then?

JULIE: How? How? I don't know!——I have no idea!——I detest you as I detest rats, but I can't escape from you.

310 JEAN: Escape with me!

JULIE: (*Pulling herself together*) Escape? Yes, we must escape!——But I'm so tired. Give me a glass of wine? (*Jean pours the wine. She looks at her watch.*) But we must talk first. We still have a little time. (*She drains the glass, then holds it out for more.*)

JEAN: Don't drink so fast. It'll go to your head.

JULIE: What does it matter?

JEAN: What does it matter? It's vulgar to get drunk! What did you want to tell me?

315 JULIE: We must escape! But first we must talk, I mean I must talk. You've done all the talking up to now. You told about your life, now I want to tell about mine, so we'll know all about each other before we go off together.

JEAN: Just a minute! Forgive me! If you don't want to regret it afterwards, you'd better think twice before revealing any secrets about yourself.

JULIE: Aren't you my friend?

JEAN: Yes, sometimes! But don't rely on me.

JULIE: You're only saying that.——Besides, everyone already knows my secrets.——You see, my mother was a commoner— very humble background. She was brought up believing in social equality, women's rights, and all that. The idea of marriage repelled her. So, when my father proposed, she replied that she would never become his wife, but he could be her lover. He insisted that he didn't want the woman he loved to be less respected than he. But his passion ruled him, and when she explained that the world's respect meant nothing to her, he accepted her conditions.

But now his friends avoided him and his life was restricted to taking care of the estate, which couldn't satisfy him. I came into the world—against my mother's wishes, as far as I can understand. She wanted to bring me up as a child of nature, and, what's more, to learn everything a boy had to learn, so that I might be an example of how a woman can be as good as a man. I had to wear boy's clothes and learn to take care of horses, but I was never allowed in the cowshed. I had to groom and harness the horses and go hunting—and even had to watch them slaughter animals—that was disgusting! On the estate men were put on women's jobs and women on men's jobs— with the result that the property became run down and we became the laughing stock of the district. Finally, my father must have awakened from his trance because he rebelled and changed everything his way. My parents were then married quietly. Mother became ill—I don't know what illness it was— but she often had convulsions, hid in the attic and in the garden, and sometimes stayed out all night. Then came the great fire, which you've heard about. The house, the stables, and the cowshed all burned down, under very curious circumstances, suggesting arson, because the accident happened the day after the insurance had expired. The quarterly premium my father sent in was delayed because of a messenger's carelessness and didn't arrive in time. (*She fills her glass and drinks.*)

320 JEAN: Don't drink any more!

JULIE: Oh, what does it matter.——We were left penniless and had to sleep in the carriages. My father had no idea where to find money to rebuild the house because he had so slighted his old friends that they had forgotten him. Then my mother suggested that he borrow from a childhood friend of hers, a brick manufacturer who lived nearby. Father got the loan without having to pay interest, which surprised him. And that's how the estate was rebuilt.——(*Drinks again*) Do you know who started the fire?

JEAN: The Countess, your mother.

JULIE: Do you know who the brick manufacturer was?

JEAN: Your mother's lover?

325 JULIE: Do you know whose money it was?

JEAN: Wait a minute—no, I don't.

JULIE: It was my mother's.

JEAN: You mean the Count's, unless they didn't sign an agreement when they were married.

JULIE: They didn't.——My mother had a small inheritance which she didn't want under my father's control, so she entrusted it to her—friend.

330 JEAN: Who stole it!

JULIE: Exactly! He kept it.——All this my father found out, but he couldn't bring it to court, couldn't repay his wife's lover, couldn't prove it was his wife's money! It was my mother's revenge for being forced into marriage against her will. It nearly drove him to suicide—there was a rumor that he tried with a pistol, but failed. So, he managed to live through it and my mother had to suffer for what she'd done. You can imagine that those were a terrible five years for me. I loved my father, but I sided with my mother because I didn't know the circumstances. I learned from her to hate men—you've heard how she hated the whole male sex—and I swore to her I'd never be a slave to any man.

JEAN: But you got engaged to that lawyer.

JULIE: In order to make him my slave.

JEAN: And he wasn't willing?

335 JULIE: He was willing, all right, but I wouldn't let him. I got tired of him.

JEAN: I saw it—out near the stable.

JULIE: What did you see?

JEAN: I saw—how he broke off the engagement.

JULIE: That's a lie! I was the one who broke it off. Has he said that he did? That swine . . .

340 JEAN: He was no swine, I'm sure. So, you hate men, Miss Julie?

JULIE: Yes!——Most of the time! But sometimes—when the weakness comes, when passion burns! Oh, God, will the fire never die out?

JEAN: Do you hate me, too?

JULIE: Immeasurably! I'd like to have you put to death, like an animal . . .

JEAN: I see—the penalty for bestiality—the woman gets two years at hard labor and the animal is put to death. Right?

345 JULIE: Exactly!

JEAN: But there's no prosecutor here—and no animal. So, what'll we do?

JULIE: Go away!

JEAN: To torment each other to death?

JULIE: No! To be happy for—two days, a week, as long as we can be happy, and then—die . . .

350 JEAN: Die? That's stupid! It's better to open a hotel!

JULIE: (Without listening)——on the shore of Lake Como, where the sun always shines, where the laurels are green at Christmas and the oranges glow.

JEAN: Lake Como is a rainy hole, and I never saw any oranges outside the stores. But tourists are attracted there because there are plenty of villas to be rented out to lovers, and that's a profitable business.——Do you know why? Because they sign a lease for six months—and then leave after three weeks!

JULIE: (Naively) Why after three weeks?

JEAN: They quarrel, of course! But they still have to pay the rent in full! And so you rent the villas out again. And that's the way it goes, time after time. There's never a shortage of love—even if it doesn't last long!

355 JULIE: You don't want to die with me?

JEAN: I don't want to die at all! For one thing, I like living, and for another, I think suicide is a crime against the Providence which gave us life.

JULIE: You believe in God? You?

JEAN: Of course I do. And I go to church every other Sunday.—— To be honest, I'm tired of all this, and I'm going to bed.

JULIE: Are you? And do you think I can let it go at that? A man owes something to the woman he's shamed.

360 JEAN: (Taking out his purse and throwing a silver coin on the table) Here! I don't like owing anything to anybody.

JULIE: (Pretending not to notice the insult) Do you know what the law states . . .

JEAN: Unfortunately the law doesn't state any punishment for the woman who seduces a man!

JULIE: (*As before*) Do you see any way out but to leave, get married, and then separate?

JEAN: Suppose I refuse such a *mésalliance?*

365 JULIE: *Mésalliance* . . .

JEAN: Yes, for me! You see, I come from better stock than you. There's no arsonist in my family.

JULIE: How do you know?

JEAN: You can't prove otherwise. We don't keep charts on our ancestors—there's just the police records! But I've read about your family. Do you know who the founder was? He was a miller who let the king sleep with his wife one night during the Danish War. I don't have any noble ancestors like that. I don't have any noble ancestors at all, but I could become one myself.

JULIE: This is what I get for opening my heart to someone unworthy, for giving my family's honor . . .

370 JEAN: Dishonor!——Well, I told you so: when people drink, they talk, and talk is dangerous!

JULIE: Oh, how I regret it!——How I regret it!——If you at least loved me.

JEAN: For the last time—what do you want? Shall I cry; shall I jump over your riding crop! Shall I kiss you and lure you off to Lake Como for three weeks, and then God knows what . . .? What shall I do? What do you want? This is getting painfully embarrassing! But that's what happens when you stick your nose in women's business. Miss Julie! I see that you're unhappy. I know you're suffering, but I can't understand you. We don't have such romantic ideas; there's not this kind of hate between us. Love is a game we play when we get time off from work, but we don't have all day and night, like you. I think you're sick, really sick. Your mother was crazy, and her ideas have poisoned your life.

JULIE: Be kind to me. At least now you're talking like a human being.

JEAN: Be human yourself, then. You spit on me, and you won't let me wipe myself off—

375 JULIE: Help me! Help Me! Just tell me what to do, where to go!

JEAN: In God's name, if I only knew myself.

JULIE: I've been crazy, out of my mind, but isn't there any way out?

JEAN: Stay here and keep calm! No one knows anything!

JULIE: Impossible! The others know and Kristine knows.

380　JEAN: No they don't, and they'd never believe a thing like that!

JULIE: (*Hesitantly*) But—it could happen again!

JEAN: That's true!

JULIE: And then?

JEAN: (*Frightened*) Then?——Why didn't I think about that? Yes, there is only one thing to do—get away from here! Right away! I can't come with you, then we'd be finished, so you'll have to go alone—away—anywhere!

390　JULIE: Alone?——Where?——I can't do that!

JEAN: You must! And before the Count gets back! If you stay, we both know what'll happen. Once you make a mistake like this, you want to continue because the damage has already been done . . . Then you get bolder and bolder—until finally you're caught! So leave! Later you can write to the Count and confess everything—except that it was me! He'll never guess who it was, and he's not going to be eager to find out, anyway.

JULIE: I'll go if you come with me.

JEAN: Are you out of your head? Miss Julie runs away with her servant! In two days it would be in the newspapers, and that's something your father would never live through.

JULIE: I can't go and I can't stay! Help me! I'm so tired, so terribly tired.——Order me! Set me in motion—I can't think or act on my own . . .

395　JEAN: What miserable creatures you people are! You strut around with your noses in the air as if you were the lords of creation! All right, I'll order you. Go upstairs and get dressed! Get some money for the trip, and then come back down!

JULIE: (*In a half-whisper*) Come up with me!

JEAN: To your room?——Now you're crazy again! (*Hesitates for a moment*) No! Go, at once! (*Takes her hand to lead her out*)

JULIE: (*As she leaves*) Speak kindly to me, Jean!

JEAN: An order always sounds unkind—now you know how it feels. (*Jean, alone, sighs with relief. He sits at the table, takes out a notebook and pencil, and begins adding up figures, counting aloud as he works. He continues in dumb show until Kristine enters, dressed for church. She is carrying a white tie and shirt front.)*

400   KRISTINE: Lord Jesus, what a mess! What have you been up to?

JEAN: Oh, Miss Julie dragged everybody in here. You mean you didn't hear anything? You must have been sleeping soundly.

KRISTINE: Like a log.

JEAN: And dressed for church already?

KRISTINE: Of course! You remember you promised to come with me to Communion today!

405   JEAN: Oh, yes, that's right.——And you brought my things. Come on, then! (*He sits down. Kristine starts to put on his shirt front and tie. Pause. Jean begins sleepily*) What's the gospel text for today?

KRISTINE: On St. John's Day?—the beheading of John the Baptist, I should think!

JEAN: Ah, that'll be a long one, for sure.——Hey, you're choking me!——Oh, I'm sleepy, so sleepy!

KRISTINE: Yes, what have you been doing, up all night? Your face is absolutely green.

JEAN: I've been sitting here gabbing with Miss Julie.

410   KRISTINE: She has no idea what's proper, that one! (*Pause*)

JEAN: You know, Kristine . . .

KRISTINE: What?

JEAN: It's really strange when you think about it.——Her!

KRISTINE: What's so strange?

415   JEAN: Everything! (*Pause*)

KRISTINE: (*Looking at the half-empty glasses standing on the table*) Have you been drinking together, too?

JEAN: Yes.

KRISTINE: Shame on you!——Look me in the eye!

JEAN: Well?

420   KRISTINE: Is it possible? Is it possible?

JEAN: (*Thinking it over for a moment*) Yes, it is.

KRISTINE: Ugh! I never would have believed it! No, shame on you, shame!

JEAN: You're not jealous of her, are you?

KRISTINE: No, not of her! If it had been Clara or Sofie I'd have scratched your eyes out!——I don't know why, but that's the way I feel.——Oh, it's disgusting!

425 JEAN: Are you angry at her, then?

KRISTINE: No, at you! That was an awful thing to do, awful! Poor girl!——No, I don't care who knows it—I won't stay in a house where we can't respect the people we work for.

JEAN: Why should we respect them?

KRISTINE: You're so clever, you tell me! Do you want to wait on people who can't behave decently? Do you? You disgrace yourself that way, if you ask me.

JEAN: But it's a comfort to know they aren't any better than us.

430 KRISTINE: Not for me. If they're no better, what do we have to strive for to better ourselves.——And think of the Count! Think of him! As if he hasn't had enough misery in his life! Lord Jesus! No, I won't stay in this house any longer!——And it had to be with someone like you! If it had been that lawyer, if it had been a real gentleman . . .

JEAN: What do you mean?

KRISTINE: Oh, you're all right for what you are, but there are men and gentlemen, after all!——No, this business with Miss Julie I can never forget. She was so proud, so arrogant with men, you wouldn't have believed she could just go and give herself—and to someone like you! And she was going to have poor Diana shot for running after the gatekeeper's mutt!—— Yes, I'm giving my notice, I mean it—I won't stay here any longer. On the twenty-fourth of October, I leave!

JEAN: And then?

KRISTINE: Well, since the subject has come up, it's about time you looked around for something since we're going to get married, in any case.

435 JEAN: Where am I going to look? I couldn't find a job like this if I was married.

KRISTINE: No, that's true. But you can find work as a porter or as a caretaker in some government office. The state doesn't pay much, I know, but it's secure, and there's a pension for the wife and children . . .

JEAN: (*Grimacing*) That's all very well, but it's a bit early for me to think about dying for a wife and children. My ambitions are a little higher than that.

KRISTINE: Your ambitions, yes! Well, you have obligations, too! Think about them!

JEAN: Don't start nagging me about obligations, I know what I have to do! (*Listening for something outside*) Besides, this is something we have plenty of time to think over. Go and get ready for church.

440 KRISTINE: Who's that walking around up there?

JEAN: I don't know, unless it's Clara.

KRISTINE: (*Going*) You don't suppose it's the Count, who came home without us hearing him?

JEAN: (*Frightened*) The Count? No, I don't think so. He'd have rung.

KRISTINE: (*Going*) Well, God help us! I've never seen anything like this before. (*The sun has risen and shines through the treetops in the park. The light shifts gradually until it slants in through the windows. Jean goes to the door and signals. Miss Julie enters, dressed in travel clothes and carrying a small birdcage, covered with a cloth, which she places on a chair.*)

445 JULIE: I'm ready now.

JEAN: Shh! Kristine is awake.

JULIE: (*Very nervous during the following*) Does she suspect something?

JEAN: She doesn't know anything. But my God, you look awful!

JULIE: Why? How do I look?

450 JEAN: You're pale as a ghost and—excuse me, but your face is dirty.

JULIE: Let me wash up then.——(*She goes to the basin and washes her hands and face.*) Give me a towel! ——Oh—the sun's coming up.

JEAN: Then the goblins will disappear.

JULIE: Yes, there must have been goblins out last night! ——Jean, listen, come with me! I have some money now.

JEAN: (*Hesitantly*) Enough?

455 JULIE: Enough to start with. Come with me! I just can't travel alone on a day like this—midsummer day on a stuffy train— jammed in among crowds of people staring at me. Eternal

delays at every station, while I'd wish I had wings. No, I can't, I can't! And then there'll be memories, memories of midsummer days when I was little. The church—decorated with birch leaves and lilacs; dinner at the big table with relatives and friends; the afternoons in the park, dancing, music, flowers, and games. Oh, no matter how far we travel, the memories will follow in the baggage car, with remorse and guilt!

JEAN: I'll go with you——but right away, before it's too late. Right this minute!

JULIE: Get dressed, then! (*Picking up the birdcage*)

JEAN: But no baggage! It would give us away!

JULIE: No, nothing! Only what we can have in the compartment with us.

460 JEAN: (*Has taken his hat*) What've you got there? What is it?

JULIE: It's only my greenfinch. I couldn't leave her behind.

JEAN: What? Bring a birdcage with us? You're out of your head! Put it down!

JULIE: It's the only thing I'm taking from my home—the only living being that loves me, since Diana was unfaithful. Don't be cruel! Let me take her!

JEAN: Put the cage down, I said!——And don't talk so loudly— Kristine will hear us!

465 JULIE: No, I won't leave her in the hands of strangers! I'd rather you killed her.

JEAN: Bring the thing here, then, I'll cut its head off!

JULIE: Oh! But don't hurt her! Don't . . . no, I can't.

JEAN: Bring it here! I can!

JULIE: (*Taking the bird out of the cage and kissing it*) Oh, my little Serena, must you die and leave your mistress?

470 JEAN: Please don't make a scene! Your whole future is at stake! Hurry up! (*He snatches the bird from her, carries it over to the chopping block, and picks up a meat cleaver. Miss Julie turns away.*) You should have learned how to slaughter chickens instead of how to fire pistols. (*He chops off the bird's head.*) Then you wouldn't feel faint at the sight of blood.

JULIE: (*Screaming*) Kill me, too! Kill me! You, who can slaughter an innocent animal without blinking an eye! Oh, how I hate, how I detest you! There's blood between us now!

I curse the moment I set eyes on you! I curse the moment I was conceived in my mother's womb!

JEAN: What good does cursing do? Let's go!

JULIE: (*Approaching the chopping block, as if drawn against her will*) No, I don't want to go yet. I can't . . . until I see . . . Shh! I hear a carriage——(*She listens, but her eyes never leave the cleaver and the chopping block.*) Do you think I can't stand the sight of blood? You think I'm so weak . . . Oh—I'd like to see your blood and your brains on a chopping block!——I'd like to see your whole sex swimming in a sea of blood, like my little bird . . . I think I could drink from your skull! I'd like to bathe my feet in your open chest and eat your heart roasted whole!——You think I'm weak. You think I love you because my womb craved your seed. You think I want to carry your spawn under my heart and nourish it with my blood—bear your child and take your name! By the way, what is your family name? I've never heard it. ——Do you have one! I was to be Mrs. Bootblack—or Madame Pigsty. ——You dog, who wears my collar, you lackey, who bears my coat of arms on your buttons—do I have to share you with my cook, compete with my own servant? Oh! Oh! Oh!——You think I'm a coward who wants to run away! No, now I'm staying—and let the storm break! My father will come home . . . to find his desk broken open . . . and his money gone! Then he'll ring—that bell . . . twice for his valet—and then he'll send for the police . . . and then I'll tell everything! Everything! Oh, what a relief it'll be to have it all end—if only it will end!—And then he'll have a stroke and die . . . That'll be the end of all of us—and there'll be peace . . . quiet . . . eternal rest! ——And then our coat of arms will be broken against his coffin—the family title extinct—but the valet's line will go on in an orphange . . . win laurels in the gutter, and end in jail!

JEAN: There's the blue blood talking! Very good, Miss Julie! Just don't let that miller out of the closet! (*Kristine enters, dressed for church, with a psalmbook in her hand.*)

475   JULIE: (*Rushing to Kristine and falling into her arms, as if seeking protection*) Help me, Kristine! Help me against this man!

KRISTINE: (*Unmoved and cold*) What a fine way to behave on a Sunday morning! (*See the chopping block*) And look at this

186 | August Strindberg

mess!——What does all this mean? Why all this screaming
and carrying on?

JULIE: Kristine! You're a woman and my friend! Beware of this
swine!

JEAN: (*Uncomfortable*) While you ladies discuss this, I'll go in and
shave. (*Slips off right*)

JULIE: You must listen to me so you'll understand!

480   **KRISTINE:** No, I could never understand such disgusting behav-
ior! Where are you off to in your traveling clothes?——And
he had his hat on.——Well?——Well?——

JULIE: Listen to me, Kristine! Listen, and I'll tell you everything——

KRISTINE: I don't want to hear it . . .

JULIE: But you must listen to me . . .

KRISTINE: What about? If it's about this silliness with Jean, I'm
not interested, because it's none of my business. But if
you're thinking of tricking him into running out, we'll soon
put a stop to that!

485   **JULIE:** (*Extremely nervous*) Try to be calm now, Kristine, and listen
to me! I can't stay here, and neither can Jean—so we must go
away . . .

KRISTINE: Hm, hm!

JULIE: (*Brightening*) You see, I just had an idea.——What if all three
of us go—abroad—to Switzerland and start a hotel
together?——I have money, you see—and Jean and I could run
it—and I thought you, you could take care of the kitchen . . .
Wouldn't that be wonderful?——Say yes! And come with us,
and then everything will be settled!——Oh, do say yes!
(*Embracing Kristine and patting her warmly*)

KRISTINE: (*Coolly, thoughtfully*) Hm, hm!

JULIE: (*Presto tempo*) You've never traveled, Kristine.——You must get
out and see the world. You can't imagine how much fun it is to
travel by train—always new faces—new countries.——And when
we get to Hamburg, we'll stop off at the zoo—you'll like that.——
And then we'll go to the theatre and the opera—and when we
get to Munich, dear, there we have museums, with Rubens and
Raphael, the great painters, as you know.——You've heard
of Munich, where King Ludwig lived—the king who went
mad.——And then we'll see his castles—they're still there and
they're like castles in fairy tales.——And from there it isn't far to

Switzerland—and the Alps.——Imagine—the Alps have snow on them even in the middle of summer!——And oranges grow there and laurel trees that are green all year round——

(*Jean can be seen in the wings right, sharpening his razor on a strop which he holds with his teeth and his left hand. He listens to the conversation with satisfaction, nodding now and then in approval. Miss Julie continues tempo prestissimo.*) And then we'll start a hotel—and I'll be at the desk, while Jean greets the guests . . . does the shopping . . . writes letters.——You have no idea what a life it'll be—the train whistles blowing and the carriages arriving and the bells ringing in the rooms and down in the restaurant.——And I'll make out the bills—and I know how to salt them! . . . You'll never believe how timid travelers are when they have to pay their bills!—— And you—you'll be in charge of the kitchen.——Naturally, you won't have to stand over the stove yourself.——And since you're going to be seen by people, you'll have to wear beautiful clothes.——And you, with your looks—no, I'm not flattering you—one fine day you'll grab yourself a husband!——You'll see!——A rich Englishman—they're so easy to——(*Slowing down*) ——catch—and then we'll get rich—and build ourselves a villa on lake Como.——It's true it rains there a little now and then, but——(*Dully*)——the sun has to shine sometimes— although it looks dark—and then . . . of course we could always come back home again——(*Pause*)——here—or somewhere else——

490 **KRISTINE:** Listen, Miss Julie, do you believe all this?

JULIE: (*Crushed*) Do I believe it?

KRISTINE: Yes!

JULIE: (*Wearily*) I don't know. I don't believe in anything any more. (*She sinks down on the bench and cradles her head in her arms on the table.*) Nothing! Nothing at all!

KRISTINE: (*Turning right to where Jean is standing*) So, you thought you'd run out!

495 **JEAN:** (*Embarrassed; puts the razor on the table*) Run out? That's no way to put it. You heard Miss Julie's plan, and even if she is tired after being up all night, it's still a practical plan.

KRISTINE: Now you listen to me! Did you think I'd work as a cook for that . . .

JEAN: (*Sharply*) You watch what you say in front of your mistress! Do you understand?

KRISTINE: Mistress!

JEAN: Yes!

500 KRISTINE: Listen to him! Listen to him!

JEAN: Yes, you listen! It'd do you good to listen more and talk less! Miss Julie is your mistress. If you despise her, you have to despise yourself for the same reason!

KRISTINE: I've always had enough self-respect——

JEAN: ——to be able to despise other people!

KRISTINE: ——to stop me from doing anything that's beneath me. You can't say that the Count's cook has been up to something with the groom or the swineherd! Can you?

505 JEAN: No, you were lucky enough to get hold of a gentleman!

KRISTINE: Yes, a gentleman who sells the Count's oats from the stable.

JEAN: You should talk—taking a commission from the grocer and bribes from the butcher.

KRISTINE: What?

JEAN: And you say you can't respect your employers any longer. You, you, you!

510 KRISTINE: Are you coming to church with me, now? You could use a good sermon after your fine deed!

JEAN: No, I'm not going to church today. You'll have to go alone and confess what you've been up to.

KRISTINE: Yes, I'll do that, and I'll bring back enough forgiveness for you, too. The Savior suffered and died on the Cross for all our sins, and if we go to Him with faith and a penitent heart, He takes all our sins on Himself.

JEAN: Even grocery sins?

JULIE: And do you believe that, Kristine?

515 KRISTINE: It's my living faith, as sure as I stand here. It's the faith I learned as child, Miss Julie, and kept ever since. "Where sin abounded, grace did much more abound!"

JULIE: Oh, if I only had your faith. If only . . .

KRISTINE: Well, you see, we can't have it without God's special grace, and that isn't given to everyone——

JULIE: Who is it given to then?

KRISTINE: That's the great secret of the workings of grace, Miss Julie, and God is no respecter of persons, for the last shall be the first . . .

520   JULIE: Then He does respect the last.

       KRISTINE: (*Continuing*) . . . and it is easier for a camel to go through the eye of a needle, than for a rich man to enter the Kingdom of God. That's how it is, Miss Julie! Anyhow, I'm going now—alone, and on the way I'm gong to tell the groom not to let any horses out, in case anyone wants to leave before the Count gets back!——Goodbye! (*Leaves*)

       JEAN: What a witch!——And all this because of a greenfinch!——

       JULIE: (*Dully*) Never mind the greenfinch!——Can you see any way out of this? Any end to it?

       JEAN: (*Thinking*) No!

525   JULIE: What would you do in my place?

       JEAN: In your place? Let's see—as a person of position, as a woman who had—fallen. I don't know—wait, now I know.

       JULIE: (*Taking the razor and making a gesture*) You mean like this?

       JEAN: Yes! But—understand—*I* wouldn't do it! That's the difference between us!

       JULIE: Because you're a man and I'm a woman? What difference does that make?

530   JEAN: The usual difference—between a man and a woman.

       JULIE: (*With the razor in her hand*) I want to, but I can't——My father couldn't either, the time he should have done it.

       JEAN: No, he shouldn't have! He had to revenge himself first.

       JULIE: And now my mother is revenged again, through me.

       JEAN: Didn't you ever love your father, Miss Julie?

535   JULIE: Oh yes, deeply, but I've hated him, too. I must have done so without realizing it! It was he who brought me up to despise my own sex, making me half woman, half man. Whose fault is what's happened? My father's, my mother's, my own? My own? I don't have anything that's my own. I don't have a single thought that I didn't get from my father, not an emotion that I didn't get from my mother, and this last idea—that all people are equal—I got that from my fiancé.——That's why I called him a swine! How can it be my fault? Shall I let Jesus take on the blame, the way Kristine does?——No, I'm too proud to do that and too sensible—thanks to my father's teachings.——And as for someone rich not going to heaven, that's a lie. But Kristine won't get in—how will she explain the

money she has in the savings bank? Whose fault is it?——What does it matter whose fault it is? I'm still the one who has to bear the blame, face the consequences . . .

JEAN: Yes, but . . . (*The bell rings sharply twice. Miss Julie jumps up. Jean changes his coat.*) The Count is back! Do you suppose Kristine— (*He goes to the speaking tube, taps the lid, and listens.*)

JULIE: He's been to his desk!

JEAN: It's Jean, sir! (*Listening; the audience cannot hear the Count's voice.*) Yes, sir! (*Listening*) Yes, sir! Right away! (*Listening*) At once, sir! (*Listening*) I see, in half an hour!

JULIE: (*Desperately frightened*) What did he say? Dear Lord, what did he say?

540 JEAN: He wants his boots and his coffee in half an hour.

JULIE: So, in half an hour! Oh, I'm so tired. I'm not able to do anything. I can't repent, can't run away, can't stay, can't live—can't die! Help me! Order me, and I'll obey like a dog! Do me this last service, save my honor, save his name! You know what I *should* do, but don't have the will to . . . You will it, you order me to do it!

JEAN: I don't know why——but now I can't either——I don't understand.——It's as if this coat made it impossible for me to order you to do anything.——And now, since the Count spoke to me—I—I can't really explain it—but—ah, it's the damn lackey in me!——I think if the Count came down here now—and ordered me to cut my throat, I'd do it on the spot.

JULIE: Then pretend you're he, and I'm you!——You gave such a good performance before when you knelt at my feet.——You were a real nobleman.——Or—have you ever seen a hypnotist in the theatre? (*Jean nods.*) He says to his subject: "Take the broom," and he takes it. He says: "Sweep," and he sweeps——

545 JEAN: But the subject has to be asleep.

JULIE: (*Ecstatically*) I'm already asleep.——The whole room is like smoke around me . . . and you look like an iron stove . . . shaped like a man in black, with a tall hat—and your eyes glow like coals when the fire is dying—and your face is a white pitch, like ashes——(*The sunlight has reached the floor and now shines on Jean.*)——it's so warm and good——(*She rubs her hands as if warming them before a fire.*)——and bright—and so peaceful!

JEAN: (*Taking the razor and putting it in her hand*) Here's the broom! The sun's almost up. Go now—out to the barn—and . . . (*Whispers in her ear*)

JULIE: (*Awake*) Thank you. I'm going now to rest! But just tell me—that those who are first can also receive the gift of grace. Say it, even if you don't believe it.

JEAN: The first? No, I can't!——But wait—Miss Julie—now I know! You're no longer among the first—you're now among—the last!

JULIE: That's true.——I'm among the very last. I'm the last of all! Oh!——But now I can't go!——Tell me once more to go!

550 JEAN: No, now I can't either! I can't!

JULIE: And the first shall be the last!

JEAN: Don't think, don't think! You're taking all my strength, making me a coward.——What was that? I thought the bell moved!——No! Shall we stuff paper in it?——To be so afraid of a bell!——But it isn't just a bell.——There's someone behind it—a hand sets it in motion—and something else sets the hand in motion.——Maybe if you cover yours ears—cover your ears! But then it rings even louder! rings until someone answers.—— And then it's too late! And then the police come—and—then—— (*The bell rings twice loudly. Jean flinches, then straightens up.*) It's horrible! But there's no other way!——Go! (*Miss Julie walks firmly out through the door.*)

Anton Chekhov, 1860–1904

The Cherry Orchard *1903*

A Comedy in Four Acts
Translated by Carol Rocamora

CHARACTERS[1]

Ranevskaya, Lyubov Andreevna, *a landowner*
Anya, *her daughter, aged seventeen*
Varya, *her adopted daughter, aged twenty-four*
Gaev, Leonid Andreevich, *Ranevskaya's brother*
Lopakhin, Yermolai Alekseevich, *a merchant*
Trofimov, Pyotr Sergeevich, *a student*
Simeonov-Pishchik, Boris Borisovich,
  a landowner
Charlotta Ivanovna, *a governess*
Yepikhodov, Semyon Panteleevich, *a clerk*
Dunyasha, *a maid*
Firs, *a servant, an old man of eighty-seven*
Yasha, *a young servant*
A Passerby
A Stationmaster
A Post Office Clerk
Guests, Servants

---

1 *Cast of Characters:* The pronunciations given here approximate the sounds of the original
Russian. Accented syllables are indicated in all capitals:
Lyubov Andreevna Ranevskaya (Ly-oo-BOF Ahn-DRAY-ev-na Rah-NYEF-sky-a)

The action takes place on the estate of Lyubov Andreevna Ranevskaya.

ACT ONE

A room which is still called the nursery. One of the doors leads to Anya's room. It is dawn, just before sunrise. It is already May, the cherry trees are all in bloom, but outside it is still cold; there is an early morning frost in the orchard. The windows in the room are closed.

    Enter Dunyasha, carrying a candle, and Lopakhin with a book in his hand.

LOPAKHIN: The train's arrived, thank God. What time is it?

DUNYASHA: Almost two. (*Puts out the candle.*) It's already getting light out.

LOPAKHIN: So how late is the train, then? A couple of hours, at least. (*Yawns and stretches.*) Well, I've made a fool of myself, then, haven't I! Hm? Came all the way out here, just to meet the train, and fell fast asleep . . . Sat here waiting and dozed right off. Annoying, isn't it . . . You should have woken me up.

DUNYASHA: I thought you'd already gone. (*Listens.*) Listen, I think they're here.

5 **LOPAKHIN:** (*Listens.*) No . . . They've got to get their baggage first, you know, that sort of thing . . .

(*Pause.*)

Lyubov Andreevna, she's been living abroad for five years, I don't know, I can't even imagine what's become of her now . . . She's a fine person, you know . . . a warm, kind

---

Anya (AHN-ya)
Varya (VAR-ya)
Leonid Andreevich Gaev (Lee-o-NEED Ahn-DRAY-e-veech GA-yef)
Yermolai Alekseevich Lopakhin (Yer-mo-LIE Ah-lek-SAY-e veech Lo-PA-keen)
Pyotr Sergeevich Trofimov (PYO-tir Sehr-GAY-e-veech Tro-FEE-mof)
Boris Borisovich Simeonov-Pishchik (Bo-FEES Bo-REE-so-veech Si-MEE-o-nof-PEESH-cheek)
Charlotta Ivanovna (Shr-LO-ta Ee-VAN-ov-na)
Semyon Panteleevich Yepikhodov (Sem-YON Pahn-te-LAY-veech Yep-ee-KOH-dof)
Dunyasha (Doon-YAH-sha)
Firs (Feers)
Yasha (YAH-sha)

person. I remember, once, when I was a boy, oh, about fifteen years old, say, and my father—he had a shop here in the village then—my father, he hit me in the face with his fist, blood was pouring from my nose . . . We'd come out into the courtyard together, somehow, and he was drunk. And there was Lyubov Andreevna, I remember her so vividly, so young then, so graceful, so slender, she took me by the hand, brought me over to the washstand, right into this very room, into the nursery. "Don't cry, little peasant," she said, "it will heal before your wedding day . . . "

(*Pause.*)

Little peasant . . . yes, my father was a peasant, it's true enough and here I am in a three-piece suit and fancy shoes. A silk purse from a sow's ear, or something like that, isn't that how the expression goes . . . Yes . . . The only difference is, now I'm rich, I've got a lot of money, but don't look too closely, once a peasant . . . (*Leafs through the book.*) Look at me, I read through this entire book and didn't understand a word of it. Read it and dozed right off.

(*Pause.*)

DUNYASHA: The dogs didn't sleep at all last night, they can sense their masters are coming home.

LOPAKHIN: What's wrong with you, Dunyasha . . .

DUNYASHA: My hands are trembling. I'm going to faint, I know I am.

LOPAKHIN: You're much too high-strung, Dunyasha. And look at you, all dressed up like a young lady, hair done up, too. You mustn't do that. Remember who you are.

(*Enter Yepikhodov with a bouquet; he is wearing a jacket and highly polished boots, which squeak loudly; upon entering, he drops the bouquet.*)

10 YEPIKHODOV: (*Picks up the bouquet.*) Look what the gardener sent. Put them on the dining room table. That's what he said. (*Gives the bouquet to Dunyasha.*)

LOPAKHIN: Bring me some kvass, will you?

DUNYASHA: Yes, sir. (*Leaves.*)

YEPIKHODOV: We have an early morning frost, we have three degrees below zero, and we have the cherry blossoms all in bloom. I don't approve of our climate. (*Sighs.*) Really, I don't. Our climate doesn't work, it just doesn't work. It's not conducive. And would you like to hear more, Yermolai Alekseich, well, then you will, because the day before yesterday, I bought these boots, and, trust me, they squeak so much, that they are beyond hope. Now how can I oil them? Tell me? How?

LOPAKHIN: Enough. You're getting on my nerves.

15 YEPIKHODOV: Every day some new disaster befalls me. A new day, a new disaster. But do I grumble, do I complain, no, I don't, I accept it, look, I'm smiling, even.

(*Dunyasha enters, gives Lopakhin some kvass.*)

I'm going now. (*Stumbles against a chair which falls down.*) There . . . (*As if vindicated.*) You see? I mean, that's the situation, and excuse me for saying so . . . Remarkable, even . . . isn't it! (*Exits.*)

DUNYASHA: Yermolai Alekseich, I have something to tell you . . . Yepikhodo has proposed to me.

LOPAKHIN: Ah!

DUNYASHA: But I don't know, really . . . He's a nice enough fellow, you know, quiet and all, it's just that whenever he starts to talk, I can't understand a word he's saying. I mean, it all sounds so sweet and sincere, only it just doesn't make any sense. I like him, I mean, I think I like him. And he? He adores me. But he's such an unfortunate fellow, you know, really, every day it's something else. They even have a name for him, do you know what they call him: "Mister Disaster" . . .

LOPAKHIN: (*Listens.*) I think they're coming . . .

20 DUNYASHA: They're coming! What's happening to me . . . I'm freezing, look, I'm shivering all over.

LOPAKHIN: They're really coming! Let's go meet them. Will she recognize me? We haven't seen each other in five years.

DUNYASHA: (*Agitated.*) I'm going to faint, I know I am . . . Look, I'm fainting!

(*Two carriages are heard pulling up to the house. Lopkhin and Dunyasha exit quickly. The stage is empty. Then there is noise in the adjacent rooms. Firs hurries*) *across the stage to meet Lyubov Andreevna; he is leaning on a cane, and is dressed in old-fashioned livery and a high hat; he mutters something to himself, but it is impossible to make out a single word. The offstage noise crescendos. A voice calls out: "Let's go this way, through here . . ." Enter Lyubov Andreevna, Anya, and Charlotta Ivanovna with a little dog on a leash; they are all dressed in traveling clothes. Enter Varya, wearing a coat and a shawl, Gaev, Simeonov-Pishchik, Lopakhin, Dunyasha carrying a bundle and an umbrella, Servants carrying luggage—they all come through the room.)*

ANYA: This way! Mama, do you remember what room this is?

LYUBOV ANDREEVNA: *(Ecstatic, in tears.)* The nursery!

25 VARYA: How cold it is, my hands are numb. *(To Lyubov Andreevna.)* Look, Mamochka, your rooms, violet and white, just as you left them.

LYUBOV ANDREEVNA: My nursery, my darling nursery, my beautiful room . . . I slept here, when I was a child . . . *(Weeps.)* And now, I'm a child again . . . *(Kisses her brother, Varya, and her brother again.)* And Varya looks the same as ever, just like a little nun. And Dunyasha I recognize, of course . . . *(Kisses Dunyasha.)*

GAEV: The train was two hours late. How do you like that? How's that for efficiency!

CHARLOTTA: *(To Pishchik.)* My dog eats walnuts, too.

PISHCHIK: *(Amazed.)* Imagine that!

(They all exit, except for Anya and Dunyasha.)

30 DUNYASHA: We've been waiting forever . . . *(Takes Anya's coat and hat.)*

ANYA: I didn't sleep one moment the whole journey long, four whole nights . . . and now I'm absolutely frozen!

DUNYASHA: You left during Lent, we had snow then, and frost, and now! My darling! *(Bursts out laughing, kisses her.)* I've waited forever for you, my precious, my joy . . . And I've got something to tell you, I can't wait one minute longer . . .

ANYA: *(Listlessly.)* Now what . . .

DUNYASHA: Yepikhodov, the clerk, proposed to me just after Easter.

35 ANYA: Not again . . . *(Adjusts her hair.)* I've lost all my hairpins . . . *(She is exhausted; she almost sways on her feet.)*

DUNYASHA: No, really, I don't know what to think any more. He adores me, God, how he adores me!

ANYA: (*Gazes at the door to her room, tenderly.*) My very own room, my windows, it's as if I never left. I'm home! And tomorrow I'll wake up, and I'll run out into the orchard . . . Oh, if only I could rest! I'm so exhausted—I didn't sleep one moment the whole way, I was so worried.

DUNYASHA: Pyotr Sergeich arrived the day before yesterday.

ANYA: (*Overjoyed.*) Petya!

40 DUNYASHA: He's out in the bathhouse, asleep, that's where he's staying. "I'm afraid of being in the way," he said. (*Glances at her pocket watch.*) We ought to wake him up, but Varvara Mikhailovna gave us strict orders not to. "Don't you dare wake him up," she said.

(*Enter Varya, a bunch of keys hanging from her belt.*)

VARYA: Dunyasha, go, quickly, bring the coffee . . . Mamochka wants coffee.

DUNYASHA: Right away. (*Exits.*)

VARYA: So, thank God, you're here. You're home at last! (*Embracing her.*) My darling's home! My angel is home.

ANYA: I've been through so much.

45 VARYA: I can imagine.

ANYA: I left during Holy Week, it was so cold then, remember? And Charlotta Ivanovna talked the whole way, talked and played card tricks. How could you have stuck me with Charlotta! . . .

VARYA: You can't travel alone, darling. At seventeen!

ANYA: When we arrived in Paris, it was cold there, too, and snowing. My French is terrible. Mama lived on the fifth floor, and when I finally got there, the flat was filled with all sorts of French people, ladies, and old Catholic priest with a little book, and, oh, it was so uncomfortable there, so stuffy, the room was filled with smoke. And suddenly I felt sorry for Mama, so very sorry, I threw my arms around her neck, I held her so tight, I couldn't let go. And Mama kept clinging to me, and weeping . . .

VARYA: (*In tears.*) Enough, enough . . .

50 ANYA: She had already sold the dacha near Menton, she had nothing left, nothing at all. And neither did I, not a single kopek, we hardly had enough money to get home. And Mama just doesn't understand it, still! There we are, sitting in the station

restaurant, and she orders the most expensive thing on the menu, she gives the waiter a ruble tip for tea. Charlotta, too. And Yasha orders a complete dinner, it's simply terrible. Yasha is Mama's butler, you know. We brought him with us . . .

VARYA: I've seen him, the devil . . .

ANYA: So, tell me! Have we paid the interest yet?

VARYA: With what?

ANYA: Dear God, dear God . . .

55 VARYA: And in August, the estate will be sold . . .

ANYA: Dear God . . .

LOPHAKHIN: (*Peeks through the door and makes a "bleating" sound.*) Ba-a-a . . . (*Exits.*)

VARYA: (*In tears.*) I'd like to give him such a . . . (*Makes a threatening gesture with her fist.*)

ANYA: (*Embraces Varya, softly.*) Varya, has he proposed yet? (*Varya shakes her head "no."*) But he loves you, he does . . . Why don't you talk about it, what are you two waiting for?

60 VARYA: I know nothing will ever come of it, nothing. He's so busy, he has no time for me, really . . . he pays no attention to me at all. Well, God bless him, but it's too painful for me even to look at him . . . Everyone talks about our wedding, everyone congratulates us, but the fact is, there's absolutely nothing to it, it's all a dream . . . (*Changes tone.*) Your brooch looks just like a little bee.

ANYA: (*Sadly.*) Mama bought it. (*She goes to her room, speaking in a gay, childlike voice.*) And in Paris, I went up in a hot air balloon!

VARYA: My darling's home! My angel is home!

(*Dunyasha has already returned with the coffee pot and prepares the coffee.*)

(*Stands by the doorway.*) All day long, darling, I go about my business, I run the household, I do my chores, but all the time I'm thinking, dreaming. If only we could marry you off to a rich man, then I'd find peace, I'd go to a cloister, and then on a pilgrimage to Kiev, to Moscow, and on and on, from one holy place to the next . . . on and on. A blessing!

ANYA: The birds are singing in the orchard. What time is it?

VARYA: After two, it must be . . . Time for you to sleep, darling. (*Goes into Anya's room.*) Yes, a blessing!

(Yasha enters with a rug, and a traveling bag.)

65 **YASHA:** *(Crosses the stage, discreetly.)* May I?

DUNYASHA: I wouldn't have recognized you, Yasha. How you've changed, since you've been abroad.

YASHA: Hm . . . And who are you?

DUNYASHA: When you left, I was about "so" high . . . *(Indicates.)* Dunyasha, Fyodor Kozoedov's daughter. Don't you remember!

YASHA: Hm . . . Ripe as a cucumber! *(Glances around, and then grabs her and embraces her; she screams and drops a saucer. Yasha exits quickly.)*

70 **VARYA:** *(In the doorway, displeased.)* What's going on here?

DUNYASHA: *(In tears.)* I broke a saucer . . .

VARYA: That means good luck.

ANYA: *(Coming out of her room.)* We'd better warn Mama: Petya's here . . .

VARYA: I gave strict orders not to wake him up.

75 **ANYA:** *(Deep in thought.)* Father died six years ago, and one month later my little brother Grisha drowned in the river, a lovely little seven-year-old boy. Mama couldn't endure it, she ran away, she ran away without once looking back . . . *(Shudders.)* How well I understand her, if only she knew! And Petya Trofimov was Grisha's tutor, he might remind her of it all . . .

(Enter Firs, in a jacket and white waistcoat.)

FIRS: *(Goes to the coffee pot, anxiously.)* The mistress will take her coffee here . . . *(Puts on white gloves.)* Is the coffee ready? *(Sternly, to Dunyasha.)* You! Where is the cream?

DUNYASHA: Oh, my God! *(Rushes out.)*

FIRS: *(Fusses with the coffee pot.)* Pathetic fool. . . . *(Mutters to himself under his breath.)* They've just returned from Paris . . . Now in the old days, the master used to go to Paris, too . . . by horse and carriage . . . *(Bursts out laughing.)*

VARYA: What is it, Firs?

80 **FIRS:** Yes, and what may I do for you? *(Overjoyed.)* My mistress has come home! I've waited for so long! Now I can die . . . *(Weeps with joy.)*

(Enter Lyubov Andreevna, Gaev, Lopakhin, and Simeonov-Pishchik; Simeonov-Pishchik wears a lightweight coat, fitted at the waist, and wide trousers. As he walks, Gaev gestures, as if he were playing a game of billiards.)

LYUBOV ANDREEVNA: How does it go? Wait—don't tell me, let me think . . . "Yellow into the corner pocket! Double into the middle!"

GAEV: "Gut shot into the corner!" Once upon a time, sister dearest, we slept in this very room, you and I, and now I'm fifty-one years old, strange, isn't it? . . .

LOPAKHIN: Yes, time flies.

GAEV: Beg pardon?

85   **LOPAKHIN:** As I was saying, time flies.

GAEV: It smells of patchouli in here.

ANYA: I'm going to bed. Good night, Mama. (*Kisses her mother.*)

LYUBOV ANDREEVNA: My beloved child. (*Kisses her hands.*) Are you glad you're home? I simply can't get hold of myself.

ANYA: Good night, Uncle.

90   **GAEV:** (*Kisses her face, hands.*) God bless you. You are the image of your mother! (*To his sister.*) Lyuba, you looked exactly like this at her age.

(*Anya gives her hand to Lopakhin and Pishchik; she exits, and closes the door behind her.*)

LYUBOV ANDREEVNA: She's exhausted, really.

PISHCHIK: A tiring journey, no doubt.

VARYA: (*To Lopakhin and Pishchik.*) So, gentlemen? It's almost three o'clock in the morning, let's not overstay our welcome.

LYUBOV ANDREEVNA: (*Laughs.*) You're the same as ever, Varya. (*Draws her close and kisses her.*) First I'll have my coffee, then we'll all go, yes?

(*Firs places a cushion under her feet.*)

Thank you, dearest. I've gotten so used to coffee. I drink it day and night. Thank you, my darling old man. (*Kisses Firs.*)

95   **VARYA:** I'll go see if they've brought everything in . . . (*Exits.*)

LYUBOV ANDREEVNA: Am I really sitting here? (*Bursts out laughing.*) I feel like jumping up and down, and waving my arms in the air! (*Covers her face with her hands.*) No, really, I must be dreaming! God knows, I love my country , I love it passionately, I couldn't even see out of the train window, I wept the whole way. (*In tears.*) Never mind, we must have our coffee. Thank you, Firs, thank you, my darling old man. I'm so glad you're still alive.

FIRS: The day before yesterday.

GAEV: He's hard of hearing.

LOPAKHIN: I'd better be going; I leave for Kharkov at five this morning. What a nuisance! I only wanted to see you, that's all, to talk to you a little . . . You're as lovely as ever . . .

PISHCHIK: (*Sighs heavily.*) Even lovelier . . . All dressed up, Parisian style . . . I'm head-over-heels, as they say!

LOPAKHIN: People like Leonid Andreich here, they say all sorts of things about me, call me a boor, a kulak, but really, it doesn't matter; I couldn't care less. Let them say whatever they like. I only want you to believe in me, as you always did, to look at me with those beautiful, soulful eyes, as you used to, once. Merciful God! My father was a serf, he belonged to your grandfather and then to your father, but it was you, yes, you, who did so much for me once, so much, and I've forgotten everything now, I love you like my own flesh and blood . . . more, even than my own flesh and blood.

LYUBOV ANDREEVNA: I can't sit still, I'm in such a state . . . (*Jumps up and walks around the room, agitated.*) I simply can't bear all this joy . . . Go ahead, laugh at me, I'm being foolish, I know it . . . My dear little bookcase . . . (*Kisses the bookcase.*) My own little table.

GAEV: Nanny died while you were gone.

LYUBOV ANDREEVNA: (*Sits and drinks coffee.*) Yes, God rest her soul. They wrote me.

GAEV: Anastasy died, too. And cross-eyed Petrushka—you remember him—he ran away, he lives in town now, at the district superintendent's. (*Takes a box of fruit drops out of his pocket, pops one into his mouth.*)

PISHCHIK: My daughter, Dashenka. . . . she sends her regards . . .

LOPAKHIN: I'd like to tell you some good news, if I may, some cheerful news, all right? (*Looks at his watch.*) I've got to go, there's no time to talk. . . . so, very briefly, then. As you already know, your cherry orchard is being sold to pay off the debts, the auction date has been set for the twenty-second of August, but don't you worry, my dear, you don't have to lose any sleep over this, rest assured, there is a way out. . . . Here's my plan. Your attention, please! Your estate is located only thirteen miles from town, roughly, a railroad runs nearby, so if the cherry orchard and the land along the river are divided up into plots and then leased for summer homes, why then you'll receive at least 25,000 in yearly income.

GAEV: Forgive me, but what nonsense!

LYUBOV ANDREEVNA: I don't quite understand you, Yermolai Alekseich.

110 LOPAKHIN: You'll receive at least twenty-five rubles a year per three acre plot from the summer tenants, and if you advertise right away, I'll guarantee you, by autumn, there won't be a single plot left, they'll all be bought up. In a word, congratulations, you're saved. The site is marvelous, the river is deep. Only, of course, you'll have to clear it out, get rid of some things . . . for example, let us say, tear down all the old buildings, and this house, too, which isn't much good for anything any more, cut down the old cherry orchard. . .

LYUBOV ANDREEVNA: Cut it down? Forgive me, my darling, but you have no idea what you're talking about. If there is one thing in the entire province that's of interest, that's remarkable, even, why it's our own cherry orchard.

LOPAKHIN: The only thing remarkable about this orchard is that it's so big. There's a cherry crop once every two years, and yes, there are a lot of them, but what good are they, nobody buys them.

GAEV: There is reference to this cherry orchard in the Encyclopaedia.

LOPAKHIN: (Looks at his watch.) Unless we come up with a plan, unless we reach a decision, then on the twenty-second of August the cherry orchard and the entire estate will be auctioned off. Make up your minds, will you, please! There is no other way, I swear to you. None. Absolutely none.

115 FIRS: Once upon a time, forty—fifty years ago, they used to dry the cherries, soak them, marinate them, preserve them, and often . . .

GAEV: Hush, Firs.

FIRS: And often, they would send cart loads of dried cherries to Moscow and Kharkov. Brought in heaps of money! And those dried cherries, oh, how soft they were, soft, sweet, plump, juicy, fragrant . . . They knew the recipe in those days . . .

LYUBOV ANDREEVNA: Yes, where is that recipe now?

FIRS: Forgotten. No one remembers it any more.

120 **PISHCHIK:** (*To Lyubov Andreevna.*) Tell us! What is it like in Paris? Did you eat frogs' legs?

LYUBOV ANDREEVNA: I ate crocodile.

PISHCHIK: Imagine that . . .

LOPAKHIN: Up until now, we've only had landowners and peasants living in our countryside, but now, the summer people are starting to appear among us. All the towns, even the smallest ones, are surrounded by summer homes now. And, it's possible to predict that, in twenty years or so, the summer population will multiply beyond our wildest dreams. Now they're just sitting out on their balconies, drinking their tea, but just wait, soon it will come to pass, you'll see, they'll start cultivating their little plots of land, and your cherry orchard will bloom again with wealth, prosperity, happiness . . .

GAEV: (*Indignant.*) What nonsense!

(*Enter Varya and Yasha.*)

125 **VARYA:** Two telegrams came for you, Mamochka. (*Takes keys and unlocks the antique bookcase; the keys make a clinking sound.*) Here they are.

LYUBOV ANDREEVNA: From Paris. (*Rips them up, without reading them.*) I'm through with Paris.

GAEV: And do you know, Lyuba, how old this bookcase is? Only one week ago, I pull out the bottom drawer, I look, and what do I see—a mark burned into it, a number. This bookcase was built exactly one hundred years ago. How do you like that? Eh? We may now celebrate the jubilee anniversary of this bookcase, ladies and gentlemen. Yes, it's an inanimate object, of course, but nevertheless, it is still a *book* case.

PISHCHIK: (*Amazed.*) One hundred years old. Imagine that . . . !

GAEV: Yes. . . a work of art . . . (*Touching the bookcase.*) O venerable bookcase! I salute thy existence. For over a century, thou hast sought the pure ideals of truth and justice; thy silent exhortation for fruitful labor has not yet faltered these one hundred years, inspiring courage and I hope for the brightest future (*In tears.*) in generation after generation of our kin, and fostering in us the noble ideals of charity and good.

(*Pause.*)

130   **LOPAKHIN**: Yes . . .

LYUBOV ANDREEVNA: You haven't changed a bit, Lyonya.

GAEV: (*A bit embarrassed.*) "Off the ball . . . right-hand corner! Cut shot into the middle."

LOPAKHIN: (*Glances at his watch.*) Time for me to go.

YASHA: (*Gives Lyubov Andreevna medicine.*) Perhaps you'll take your pills now. . .

135   **PISHCHIK**: Why bother taking medicine, lovely lady . . . doesn't do any harm, doesn't do any good either . . . Do let me have them. . . dearest lady. (*Takes the pills, pours them into the palm of his hand, blows on them, puts them in his mouth, and washes them down with kvass.*) There!

LYUBOV ANDREEVNA: (*Frightened.*) You've gone mad!

PISHCHIK: Took them all.

LOPAKHIN: There's an appetite.

(*Everyone laughs.*)

FIRS: When he was here during Holy Week, he ate half a bucket of cucumbers . . . (*Mutters to himself.*)

140   **LYUBOV ANDREEVNA**: What is he saying?

VARYA: He's been muttering like that for three years now. We're used to it.

YASHA: Old age.

(*Enter Charlotta Ivanovna wearing a white dress; she is very thin and tightly laced, with a lorgnette on her belt; she crosses the stage.*)

LOPAKHIN: Forgive me, Charlotta Ivanovna, I didn't have the chance to greet you. (*Goes to kiss her hand.*)

CHARLOTTA IVANOVNA: (*Takes her hand away.*) If I let you kiss my hand, next you'll want to kiss my elbow, then my shoulder. . .

145   **LOPAKHIN**: Not my lucky day.

(*Everyone laughs.*)

So, Charlotta Ivanovna, show us a trick!

LYUBOV ANDREEVNA: Yes, Charlotta, show us a trick!

CHARLOTTA: I don't want to. I wish to sleep. (*Exits.*)

LOPAKHIN: We'll see each other again in three weeks. (*Kisses Lyubov Andreevna's hand.*) Farewell for now. Time to go. (*To Gaev.*) A very goodbye to you. (*Kisses Pishchik.*) And to you. (*Shakes hands with Varya, then with Firs and Yasha.*) I don't feel like going. (*To Lyubov Andreevna.*) If you make up your mind about the summer homes, if you decide to proceed, just let me know, I'll lend you 50,000. Think about it, seriously.

VARYA: (*Angrily.*) So go, then!

150 **LOPAKHIN:** I'm going, I'm going. . . . (*Exits.*)

GAEV: What a boor. Oh, wait, "pardon" . . . Our Varya's going to marry him. That's our Varya's fiancé.

VARYA: Don't talk so much, Uncle.

LYUBOV ANDREEVNA: Why not, Varya, I'd be so pleased. He's a good man.

PISHCHIK: And a most worthy man, as they say, truth be told . . . Now my Dashenka . . . she also says, that . . . well, she says a variety of things. (*Snores, then suddenly awakes with a start.*) Nevertheless, dearest lady, oblige me, would you, please . . . lend me two hundred and forty rubles . . . tomorrow I must pay off the interest on my mortgage.

155 **VARYA:** (*Startled.*) We have no money! None!

LYUBOV ANDREEVNA: As a matter of fact, I don't, I have nothing, really.

PISHCHIK: Some will turn up, you'll see! (*Bursts out laughing.*) I never lose hope. There, I say to myself, all is lost, all is ruined, and then suddenly, what do you know—they build a railroad right through my land, and . . . they pay me for it! So just wait and see, something will happen, if not today, then tomorrow. My Dashenka is going to win 200,000 . . . she has a lottery ticket.

LYUBOV ANDREEVNA: The coffee's finished, now we can go to bed.

FIRS: (*Brushes Gaev's clothes, scolding him.*) And you've gone and put on the wrong trousers again. What am I going to do with you?

160 **VARYA:** (*Softly.*) Anya's sleeping. (*Quietly opens the window.*) The sun is up now, it isn't cold any more. Look, Mamochka: what glorious trees! My God, the air! And the starlings are singing!

GAEV: (*Opens another window.*) The orchard is all in white. You haven't forgotten, Lyuba, have you? Look—that long row of trees stretching on and on, like a silver cord, on and on, do you remember, how it gleams on moonlit nights? You haven't forgotten, have you?

LYUBOV ANDREEVNA: (*Looks out the window onto the orchard.*) O, my childhood, my innocence! Once I slept in this very nursery. I'd look out on the orchard, right from here, and happiness would awaken with me, every morning, every morning, and look, it's all the same, nothing has changed. (*Laughs with joy.*) White, all white! O, my orchard! After the dark, dreary autumn, the cold winter, you're young again, blooming with joy, the heavenly angels have not forsaken you . . . If only this terrible weight could be lifted form my soul, if only I could forget my past!

GAEV: Yes, and the orchard will be sold to pay off our debts, strange, isn't it . . .

LYUBOV ANDREEVNA: Look, there's my mother, walking through the orchard . . . all in white! (*Laughs with joy.*) There she is.

165 GAEV: Where?

VARYA: God bless you, Mamochka.

LYUBOV ANDREEVNA: There's no one there, I only dreamed it . . . Look, to the right, on the way to the summer-house, a white sapling, bowing low, I thought it was a woman . . .

(*Trofimov enters, wearing a shabby, threadbare student's uniform, and spectacles.*)

What an astonishing orchard! Masses of white blossoms, radiant blue sky . . .

TROFIMOV: Lyubov Andreevna!

(*She turns and looks at him.*)

I only came to pay my respects. I'll go, right away. (*Kisses her hand passionately.*) They told me I had to wait till morning, but I couldn't bear it any longer . . .

(*Lyubov Andreevna looks at him with bewilderment.*)

VARYA: (*In tears.*) It's Petya Trofimov . . .

170 TROFIMOV: Petya Trofimov, former tutor to your Grisha . . . Have I really changed that much?

(*Lyubov Andreevna embraces him and weeps softly.*)

GAEV: (*Embarrassed.*) Now, now Lyuba.

VARYA: (*Weeps.*) You see, Petya, didn't I tell you to wait till tomorrow.

LYUBOV ANDREEVNA: My Grisha . . . my little boy . . . Grisha . . . son . . .

VARYA: But what can we do, Mamochka. It's God's will.

175 TROFIMOV: (*Gently, in tears.*) There, there . . .

LYUBOV ANDREEVNA: (*Weeps softly.*) My little boy . . . lost . . . drowned . . . Why? Why, my friend? (*Softer.*) Anya's sleeping, and here I am, raising my voice . . . carrying on . . . So, now, Petya, tell me! Why have you grown so ugly? And so old, too!

TROFIMOV: There was an old peasant woman on the train once, she called me "a shabby-looking gentleman."

LYUBOV ANDREEVNA: You were just a boy then, a sweet, young student, and now look at you, you're hair's gotten thin, you wear glasses . . . Don't tell me you're still a student? (*Goes to the door.*)

TROFIMOV: And I shall be an eternal student, so it seems.

180 LYUBOV ANDREEVNA: (*Kisses her brother, then Varya.*) Better go to bed now . . . You've gotten old, too, Leonid.

PISHCHIK: (*Follows her.*) Yes, time for bed . . . Ach, this gout of mine . . . I'll stay the night with you . . . Lyubov Andreevna, lovely lady, tomorrow morning, if only you would . . . two hundred and forty rubles . . .

GAEV: He never gives up.

PISHCHIK: Two hundred and forty rubles . . . to pay the interest on the mortgage.

LYUBOV ANDREEVNA: But I don't have any money, really, my sweet, I don't.

185 PISHCHIK: I'll pay you back, charming lady . . . Such a small amount . . .

LYUBOV ANDREEVNA: Oh, all right, Leonid will give it to you . . . Give it to him, Leonid.

GAEV: I should give it to him? Don't hold your pockets open.

LYUBOV ANDREEVNA: Give it to him, what else can we do . . . He needs it . . . He'll pay it back.

(*Exeunt Lyubov Andreevna, Torfimov, Pishchik, and Firs. Gaev, Varya, and Yasha remain.*)

GAEV: My sister just can't seem to hold on to her money. (*To Yasha.*) Move away, good fellow, you smell like a chicken coop.

190 YASHA: (*With a grin.*) And you, Leonid Andreich, you haven't changed a bit.

GAEV: Beg pardon? (*To Varya.*) What did he say?

VARYA: (*To Yasha.*) Your mother's come from the village to see you, she's been waiting since yesterday in the servants' quarters . . .

YASHA: Good for her!

VARYA: Shame on you!

195 YASHA: Who needs her? She could have waited till tomorrow to come. (*Exits.*)

VARYA: Mamochka's the same as she's always been, she hasn't changed at all. If she could, she'd give away everything.

GAVE: Yes . . .

(*Pause.*)

If there are many remedies offered for a disease, then that means the disease is incurable. Now, I've been thinking, wracking my brain, and I've got lots of remedies, oh yes, lots and lots of remedies, and you know what that means, don't you, in essence, that means I don't have any. Wouldn't it be nice, for example, if we received a large inheritance from somebody or other, wouldn't it be nice to marry our Anya off to a very rich fellow, wouldn't it be nice to go to Yaroslavl and try and get some money from our aunt, the countess. Our aunty's very very rich, you know.

VARYA: (*Weeps.*) If only God would help us.

GAEV: Stop weeping. The old lady's very rich, it's true, but the fact is, she doesn't like us. For one thing, my dear sister went off and married a lawyer, and not a gentleman . . .

(*Anya appears in the doorway.*)

She didn't marry a gentleman, and you can't really say she's led a particularly conventional life. I mean, she's a good, kind person, a splendid person, and I love her very very much, of course, but, whatever the extenuating circumstances may have been, let's face it, she hasn't exactly been the model of virtue. Why, you can sense it in everything about her, her slightest gesture, her movements.

200 **VARYA:** (*In a whisper.*) Anya's standing in the doorway.

GAEV: Beg pardon?

(*Pause.*)

> Amazing, there's something in my right eye . . . I can't see a
> thing. And on Thursday, when I was at the district court . . .

(*Anya enters.*)

VARYA: Why aren't you in bed, Anya?

ANYA: I can't fall asleep. I just can't.

GAEV: My little one. (*Kisses Anya's face, hands.*) My child . . . (*In tears.*)
You're not my niece, you're my angel, you're everything to
me. Believe me, believe me . . .

205 **ANYA:** I believe you, Uncle, I do. Everyone loves you, everyone
reveres you . . . but, darling Uncle, you must try to be quiet,
really, just be quiet. What were you saying just now about my
Mama, about your own sister? Why would you say such a thing?

GAEV: Yes, yes . . . (*Covers his face with her hand.*) As a matter of fact,
it's terrible! My God! My God, save me! And today, I made
a speech before a bookcase . . . how foolish of me! And it was
only after I'd finished, that I realized how foolish it was.

VARYA: It's true, Uncle dear, you should try to be quiet. Just be
very quiet, that's all.

ANYA: And if you're quiet, you'll feel much better, really.

GAEV: I'll be quiet. (*Kisses Anya's and Varya's hands.*) I'll be quiet. Just
one small matter. On Thursday I was as the circuit court, and,
well, some people got together and started talking, you know,
about this, that, the other thing, and so on and so on, and one
thing led to another, and so it seems that a loan might be
arranged, to pay off the interest to the bank.

210 **VARYA:** God willing!

GAEV: And, on Tuesday, I'm going to have another little talk with
them again. (*To Varya.*) Stop weeping. (*To Anya.*) Your mama will
have a word with Lopakhin; he won't refuse her, of course . . .
As for you, as soon as you've had your rest, off you'll go to
Yaroslavl to see the countess, your great-aunt. So that way,
we'll mount a three-pronged attack—and presto! it's in the
bag. We'll pay off that interest, I'm sure of it . . . (*Pops a fruit drop*

into his mouth.) On my honor, I swear to you, if you like, this estate will not be sold! (*Excited.*) I swear on my happiness! I give you my hand, call me a worthless good-for-nothing, a dishonorable fellow, if I allow it to go up for auction! I swear on my entire being!

ANYA: (*She regains her composure; she is happy.*) How good you are, Uncle, how wise! (*Embraces her uncle.*) Now I'm content! I'm content! I'm happy, now!

(*Enter Firs.*)

FIRS: (*Reproachfully.*) Leonid Andreich, have you no fear of God in you? When are you going to bed?

GAEV: In a minute, in a minute. Go on, Firs. Yes, it's all right, I'm quite capable of undressing myself. So, children dear, night-night . . . Details tomorrow, but now, it's time for bed. (*Kisses Anya and Varya.*) I am a man of the eighties . . . These are not laudable times, but nevertheless, I can say that I've suffered greatly for my convictions in this life. It's not without reason that the peasants love me. One must give the peasant his due! Give him his due, for . . .

215 ANYA: You're off again, Uncle!

VARYA: Uncle, be quiet!

FIRS: (*Angrily.*) Leonid Andreich!

GAEV: I'm coming, I'm coming . . . And so, to bed. "Off two cushions into the middle. Pocket the white . . . clean shot." (*Exits, with Firs shuffling behind him.*)

ANYA: Now, I'm content. I don't want to go to Yaroslavl, not really, I don't like my great-aunt that much, but, all the same, I'm content. Thanks to Uncle. (*Sits.*)

220 VARYA: We must get to bed. I know I'm going to . . . Oh, an awful thing happened here while you were gone. You remember the old servants' quarters, well, only the old ones live there now: you know, Yefimyushka, Polya, Yevstigney, oh, and don't forget Karp . . . Anyway, they started letting some homeless folks stay the night with them—I didn't say anything at first. But then, I hear, they're spreading this rumor, that I'd been giving orders to feed them nothing but dried peas. Because I was being stingy, you see . . . And all this coming

from Yevstigney . . . So I say to myself, fine. If that's the way you want it, I say, just you wait and see. So I call for Yevstigney . . . (*Yawns.*) And he comes in . . . And I say to him, how dare you, Yevstigney . . . you're such a fool . . . (*Looks at Anya.*) Anyechka!

(*Pause.*)

She's asleep! (*Takes Anya by the arm.*) Come to bed . . . Come! . . . (*Leads her.*) My darling's sleeping! Come . . .

(*They go.*)

(*Far beyond the orchard, a shepherd plays on a pipe. Trofimov enters, crosses the stage, and, seeing Varya and Anya, stops.*)

VARYA: Shh . . . she's asleep . . . fast asleep . . . Come, my precious.
ANYA: (*Softly, half-asleep.*) I'm so tried . . . do you hear the bells . . . Dearest Uncle . . . Mama and Uncle . . .
VARYA: Come, my precious, come . . . (*Exits into Anya's room.*)
TROFIMOV: (*Tenderly.*) My sunlight! My springtime!

(*Curtain.*)

ACT TWO

A field. There is a small, dilapidated old chapel, long deserted, and beside it, a well, an old bench, and several large stones, once apparently gravestones. The road to Gaev's country estate is visible. To the side, towering poplar trees loom darkly, where the cherry orchard begins. In the distance, there is a row of telegraph poles, and far beyond that, on the horizon, is the indistinct outline of a large town, visible only in very clear, fine weather. Soon, it will be sunset. Charlotta, Yasha, and Dunyasha sit on the bench; Yepikhodov stands nearby and plays the guitar; all are lost in thought. Charlotta is wearing an old, peaked military cap; she removes the rifle from her shoulder and adjusts the buckle on the rifle sling.

CHARLOTTA: (*Deep in thought.*) I have no passport, no real one . . . no one ever told me how old I was, not really . . . but I always have this feeling that I'm still very young. When I was a little girl, Papa and Mama traveled in a circus, they were acrobats, good ones. And I performed the "salto-mortale," the dive of death, and all kinds of tricks. And when Papa and Mama died, a German lady took me in, she raised me, gave me lessons. "Gut." I grew up, I became a governess. But where I am from, and who I am—I don't know . . . Who were my parents, were they ever married . . . I don't know. (*Takes a cucumber out of her pocket and eats it.*) I don't know anything.

(*Pause.*)

So now I feel like talking, but to whom . . . I have no one to talk to.

YEPIKHODOV: (*Plays guitar and sings.*) "What care I for worldly woe, / What care I for friend and foe . . ." How pleasant it is to play upon the mandolin!

DUNYASHA: That's a guitar, not a mandolin. (*Looks in a little mirror and powders her nose.*)

YEPIKHODOV: For the man, who is mad with love, it's a mandolin. (*Sings.*) "If my true love were requited, / It would set my heart aglow . . ."

(*Yasha joins in, harmonizing.*)

5   CHARLOTTA: These people sing terribly . . . Phooey! Like jackals.

DUNYASHA: (*To Yasha.*) How blissful, to have been abroad.

YASHA: Well, of course. I'm not going to disagree with you on that one. (*Yawns, then lights a cigar.*)

YEPIKHODOV: But we know that already. Everything abroad is very well organized, and has been so for a long long time.

YASHA: Right.

10   YEPIKHODOV: I am a man of the world. I am. I read many many remarkable books. But, speaking for myself, personally, I have no clue, no clue as to what direction I, personally, want my life to take, I mean: Do I want to live, or do I want to shoot myself, in the head . . . So just in case, I always carry a revolver around with me. Here it is . . . (*Shows them a revolver.*)

CHARLOTTA: I'm finished. And now, I'm leaving. (*Puts on the rifle.*) You, Yepikhodov, you are a very intelligent man and also a very dangerous one; women must be mad for you. Brrr! (*Starts to leave.*) These clever people, they're all such fools, no one for me to talk to . . . Alone, all alone, I have no one . . . and who I am, why I am on this earth, no one knows . . . (*Exits, without hurrying.*)

YEPIKHODOV: Now. Speaking for myself, personally, again, putting all else aside, that is, if I may, when it comes to me, I mean, personally, again, I ask myself: Does fate care? No, fate doesn't care, very much as a terrible storm doesn't care about a tiny boat upon the sea. Now. Let us assume I am wrong in this regard, so then, tell me, would you, please, why is it that this morning, yes, this morning, I wake up, just to give you an example, I look up, and there, sitting right on my chest, is this huge and terrifying spider . . . About "so" big. (*Indicates with both hands.*) And then, to give you yet another example, I go to pick up a glass of kvass, you know, to drink it, I look inside it, and what do I see? Possibly the most offensive species on the face of this earth—like a cockroach.

(*Pause.*)

Have you ever read Buckle?[1]

(*Pause.*)

May I trouble you, Avdotya Fyodorovna, for a word or two.

DUNYASHA: Speak.

YEPIKHODOV: It would be far more desirable to speak to you in private . . . (*Sighs.*)

15   DUNYASHA: (*Embarrassed.*) Oh, all right . . . only first, bring me my cloak . . . I left it near the cupboard . . . it's a bit chilly out . . .

YEPIKHODOV: Of course . . . Right away . . . Of course. Now I know what to do with my revolver . . . (*Takes the guitar and exits, strumming.*)

YASHA: Mister Disaster! He's hopeless, just between you and me. (*Yawns.*)

DUNYASHA: God forbid he should shoot himself.

(*Pause.*)

I'm so nervous, I worry all the time. I was just a girl when they took me in, you know, I'm not used to the simple life any more, look at my hands, how lily-white they are, like a young lady's. Can't you see, I've become so delicate, so fragile,

---

[1] *Buckle:* Thomas Henry Buckle (1821–1862), an English radical historian and economist.

so ... so sensitive, every little thing upsets me ... It's just awful. And if you deceive me, Yasha, I just don't know what will happen to my nerves.

YASHA: (*Kisses her.*) My little cucumber! Of course, a girl should know how to behave, I can't stand a girl who doesn't know how to behave.

20 DUNYASHA: I've fallen madly in love with you, you are so refined, you can talk about anything.

(*Pause.*)

YASHA: (*Yawns.*) Right! ... Now, in my opinion, if a girl falls in love, that means she's immoral.

(*Pause.*)

Nice, isn't it, to smoke a cigar in the fresh, open air ... (*Listens.*) Someone's coming ... It's the ladies and gentlemen ...

(*Dunyasha embraces him impetuously.*)

Go home, pretend you've gone for a swim in the river, take that path there, or else they'll run into you and think I arranged this little rendezvous. I can't have that.

DUNYASHA: (*Coughs quietly.*) I've got a headache from all this cigar smoke ... (*Exits.*)

(*Yasha remains; he sits by the chapel. Enter Lyubov Andreevna, Gaev, and Lopakhin.*)

LOPAKHIN: You must decide, once and for all—time waits for no one. The question's simple, you know. Will you or won't you agree to lease your land for conversion into summer homes? Answer in one word: yes or no? One word, that's all!

LYUBOV ANDREEVNA: Who has been smoking those disgusting cigars here ... (*Sits.*)

25 GAEV: Since they've built the railroad, it's all become so convenient. (*Sits down.*) We took a little ride into town, we had our lunch ... "yellow into the middle pocket!" Now, if only I'd gone home first and played one little game ...

LYUBOV ANDREEVNA: You'll have plenty of time.

LOPAKHIN: One word, that's all! (*Entreating.*) Give me your answer!

GAEV: (*Yawns.*) Beg pardon?

LYUBOV ANDREEVNA: (*Looks in her purse.*) Yesterday I had so much money, and today I have hardly any at all. My poor, thrifty Varya feeds everyone milk soup, the old folks in the kitchen get nothing but dried peas to eat, and I manage to let money slip right through my fingers. (*Drops her purse, gold coins scatter.*) There, you see, now I've gone and spilled it . . . (*She is annoyed.*)

30   **YASHA:** I'll get them, allow me. (*Collects the coins.*)

LYUBOV ANDREEVNA: Please do, Yasha. And why on earth did I go out to lunch . . . That ridiculous restaurant of yours with the music, and the tablecloths that smell of soap . . . And why drink so much, Lyonya? Why eat so much? Why talk so much? Today in the restaurant you went on and on again, on and on . . . About the seventies, about the decadents. And to whom? Talking to the waiters about the decadents!

LOPAKHIN: Yes.

GAEV: (*Waves his hand.*) I'm incorrigible, it's obvious . . . (*Irritably, to Yasha.*) What is it with you, you're always disturbing my line of vision . . .

YASHA: (*Laughs.*) I can't hear the sound of your voice without laughing.

35   **GAEV:** (*To his sister.*) It's either him or me . . .

LYUBOV ANDREEVNA: Go away, Yasha, go on . . .

YASHA: (*Gives Lyubov Andreevna her purse.*) Right away. (*Barely contains his laughter.*) At once . . . (*Exits.*)

LOPAKHIN: Your estate is going to be bought by that millionaire, Deriganov. He's coming to the auction himself, they say, in person.

LYUBOV ANDREEVNA: And where did you hear that?

40   **LOPAKHIN:** They were talking about it in town.

GAEV: Our aunty from Yaroslavl promised to send us something, but when and how much she will send, who knows . . .

LOPAKHIN: How much is she sending? One hundred thousand? Two hundred thousand?

LYUBOV ANDREEVNA: Oh, well, . . . ten–fifteen thousand, at most, and that much we can be thankful for . . .

LOPAKHIN: Forgive me, but such frivolous people as you, my friends, such strange, impractical people, I have never before met in my entire life. I'm speaking to you in the Russian language, I'm telling you that your estate is about to be sold, and you simply don't understand.

45 LYUBOV ANDREEVNA: But what on earth are we to do? Tell us, what?

LOPAKHIN: Every day I've been telling you. Every day I've been repeating the same thing, over and over again. The cherry orchard and the land must be leased for summer homes, it must be done immediately, as soon as possible—the auction is imminent! Do you understand! As soon as you decide, once and for all, about the summer homes, you'll have as much money as you'll ever want, and then you will be saved.

LYUBOV ANDREEVNA: Summer homes, summer people—forgive me, please, it all sounds so vulgar.

GAEV: I agree with you, absolutely.

LOPAKHIN: Either I'm going to burst out sobbing, or screaming, or else I'm going to fall on the ground, right here in front of you. I can't stand it any more! You're driving me mad! (*To Gaev.*) And you, you act like an old woman!

50 GAEV: Beg pardon?

LOPAKHIN: An old woman! (*Wants to leave.*)

LYUBOV ANDREEVNA: (*Frightened.*) No, don't go, please, stay, dearest. I beg of you. Who knows, perhaps we'll think of something!

LOPAKHIN: What's there to think of!

LYUBOV ANDREEVNA: Don't go, I beg of you. It's so much more cheerful when you're here . . .

(*Pause.*)

I keep waiting for something to happen, as if the house were going to tumble down on top of us.

55 GAEV: (*Deep in thought.*) "Double into the corner pocket . . . Croisé into the middle . . ."

LYUBOV ANDREEVNA: How we have sinned . . .

LOPAKHIN: What are you talking about, what sins . . .

GAEV: (*Pops a fruit drop in his mouth.*) They say I've squandered an entire fortune on fruit drops . . . (*Laughs.*)

LYUBOV ANDREEVNA: O my sins, my sins . . . I've always thrown money around, uncontrollably, like a madwoman, and

I married a man, who did nothing but keep us in debt. My husband died from too much champagne—he drank himself to death,—then, for my next misfortune, I fell in love with another man, I began living with him . . . and just at that time, there came my first great punishment, and what a blow it dealt me—right here in this river . . . my little boy drowned, and so I fled, abroad, I simply fled, never to return, never to see this river again . . . I closed my eyes and I ran, not knowing where I was going, what I was doing, and *he* following after . . . ruthlessly, relentlessly. I bought a dacha near Menton, *he* had fallen ill there, and for three years I knew no rest, neither day nor night; his illness exhausted me, wasted me, my soul withered away. And then last year, when the dacha was sold to pay off the debts, I fled again, to Paris, and there he robbed me, he left me for another woman, I tried to poison myself . . . How stupid, how shameful . . . And suddenly I felt drawn again to Russia, to my homeland, to my daughter . . . (*Wipes away her tears.*) Dear God, dear God, be merciful, forgive me my sins! Don't punish me any longer! (*Pulls a telegram from her pocket.*) Today, I received this from Paris . . . He begs my forgiveness, beseeches me to return . . . (*Rips up the telegram.*) There's music playing, somewhere. (*Listens.*)

60 GAEV: It's our celebrated Jewish orchestra. Don't you remember, four violins, flute, and contrabass.

LYUBOV ANDREEVNA: Does it still exist? We ought to invite them sometime, plan a little soirée.

LOPAKHIN: (*Listens.*) I don't hear anything. (*Hums softly.*)

"An enterprising man, the Prussian,

He'll make a Frenchman from a Russian!"

(*Laughs.*) What a play I saw at the theatre last night, it was very funny, really.

LYUBOV ANDREEVNA: There probably wasn't anything funny about it. Why go to the theatre to see a play! Better to see yourselves more often. How grey your lives are, how endlessly you talk.

LOPAKHIN: It's the truth. And the truth must be told, our lives are foolish . . .

(*Pause.*)

My papa was a peasant, an ignorant fool, he understood nothing, taught me nothing, he only beat me when he was drunk,
and always with a stick. And the fact of the matter is, I'm the
same kind of ignorant fool that he was. I never learned anything, I'm ashamed of my own handwriting, it's not even
human, it's more like a hoof-mark than a signature.

65 LYUBOV ANDREEVNA: You ought to get married, my friend.

LOPAKHIN: Yes . . . It's the truth.

LYUBOV ANDREEVNA: Why not to our Varya? She's a good girl.

LOPAKHIN: Yes.

LYUBOV ANDREEVNA: She's of simple origin, she works all day
long, but the important thing is, she loves you. And you've
been fond of her for a long time now.

70 LOPAKHIN: Well . . . I have nothing against it . . . She's a good girl.

(*Pause.*)

GAEV: They've offered me a job at the bank. 6,000 a year . . .
Have you heard?

LYUBOV ANDREEVNA: You, in a bank! Stay where you are . . .

(*Firs enters; he is carrying a coat.*)

FIRS: (*To Gaev.*) Please, sir, better put this on . . . it's chilly out.

GAEV: (*Puts on the coat.*) You get on my nerves, old man.

75 FIRS: Now, there's no need for that . . . You went out this morning, without telling anyone. (*Looks him over.*)

LYUBOV ANDREEVNA: How old you've grown, Firs!

FIRS: Yes, what may I do for you?

LOPAKHIN: She said: How old you've grown!

FIRS: Well, I've lived a long time. They were marrying me off, and
your papa wasn't even in this world yet . . . (*Laughs.*) Then,
when the emancipation came, I was already head valet . . .
I didn't want my freedom, so I stayed with my masters . . .

(*Pause.*)

I remember how glad everyone was, but what they were glad
about, they didn't even know themselves.

80   **LOPAKHIN**: Ah yes, the good old days. At least there was flogging.

FIRS: (*Not hearing.*) I'll say. The servants belonged to the masters, the masters belonged to the servants, but now everything's all mixed up, you can't tell one from the other.

GAEV: Hush, Firs. Tomorrow I've got to go to town. They've promised to introduce me to some general, he might give us a loan on a promissory note.

LOPAKHIN: Nothing will come of it. And you won't pay off the interest, rest assured.

LYUBOV ANDREEVNA: He's delirious. There are no generals, they don't exist.

(*Enter Trofimov, Anya, and Varya.*)

85   **GAEV**: Ah, here they come.

ANYA: Here's Mama.

LYUBOV ANDREEVNA: (*Tenderly.*) Come, come . . . My darling children . . . (*Embraces Anya and Varya.*) If you only knew how much I love you both. Sit here, right next to me.

(*They all get settled.*)

LOPAKHIN: Our eternal student is always in the company of the young ladies.

TROFIMOV: Mind your own business.

90   **LOPAKHIN**: And when he's fifty, he'll still be a student.

TROFIMOV: Stop your foolish joking.

LOPAKHIN: You're such a peculiar fellow! Why are you so angry with me, anyway?

TROFIMOV: Because you won't stop bothering me.

LOPAKHIN: (*Laughs.*) Permit me to ask you, if I may, what do you think of me?

95   **TROFIMOV**: Here is what I think of you, Yermolai Alekseich: You are a rich man, soon you'll be a millionaire. So, in the general scheme of things, that is, according to the laws of nature, we need you, we need predatory beasts, who devour everything which stands in their path, so in that sense you are a necessary evil.

(*All laugh.*)

VARYA: Petya, you do better when you talk about astronomy.

LYUBOV ANDREEVNA: No, let's continue yesterday's conversation.

TROFIMOV: What about?

GAEV: About pride. Pride in man.

100 TROFIMOV: That. We talked about that forever, but we did not come to any conclusion. According to your way of thinking, there is something mystical about the proud man, an aura, almost. Perhaps you are correct in your beliefs, but if you analyze the issue clearly, without complicating things, then why does this pride even exist, what reason can there be for pride, if a man is not physically distinguished, if the vast majority of mankind is coarse, stupid, or profoundly miserable. There is no time for the admiration of self. There is only time for work.

GAEV: We're all going to die, anyway, so what difference does it make?

TROFIMOV: Who knows? And what does it really mean—to die? For all we know, man is endowed with a hundred sensibilities, and when he dies, only the five known to us perish along with him, while the other ninety-five remain alive.

LYUBOV ANDREEVNA: How intelligent you are, Petya! . . .

LOPAKHIN: (*Ironically.*) Yes, terribly!

105 TROFIMOV: Mankind marches onward, ever onward, strengthening his skills, his capacities. All that has up until now been beyond his reach may one day be attainable, only he must work, indeed, he must do everything in his power to help those who seek the truth. In Russia, however, very few people actually do work. The vast majority of the intelligentsia, as I know them, do nothing, purse nothing, and, meanwhile, have no predisposition whatsoever to work, they're completely incapable of it. They call themselves "the intelligentsia," and yet they address their servants with disrespect, they treat the peasants as if they were animals, they're dismal students, they're poorly educated, they never read serious literature, they're absolutely idle, they don't do a thing except sit around talking about science and art, about which they know nothing at all. And they're all so grim looking, they have tense, taut faces, they only talk

222 | Anton Chekhov

about "important things," they spend all their time philosophizing, and meanwhile, right before their very eyes, the workers live atrociously, eat abominably, sleep without bedding, thirty—forty to a room, together with bedbugs, stench, dankness, depravity . . . And so it seems that all this lofty talk is simply meant to conceal the truth from themselves and others. Show me, please, where are the day nurseries, about which they speak so much and so often, where are the public reading rooms? They only write about them in novels, they never become a reality, never. There is only filth, vulgarity, barbarism . . . I dread their serious countenances, their serious conversations, I despise them. Better to be silent!

LOPAKHIN: You know, I get up before five every morning, I work from dawn until night, I deal with money, constantly, mine and others, and yes, I see how people really are. You only have to try to get something done to realize how few honest, decent people there are in this world. Sometimes, when I can't fall asleep, I lie there thinking: "Dear Lord, you have given us the vast forests, the boundless plains, the endless horizons, and we who live here on this earth, we should be true giants . . ."

LYUBOV ANDREEVNA: What good are giants . . . They're very nice in fairy tales, you know, but in true life, they're terrifying.

(*Yepikhodov crosses upstage, playing the guitar.*)

(*Pensively.*) There goes Yepikhodov.

ANYA: (*Pensively.*) There goes Yepikhodov.

GAEV: The sun has set, ladies and gentlemen.

110   TROFIMOV: Yes.

GAEV: (*Softly, as if reciting.*) O nature, wondrous nature, you shine on, radiant and eternal, beauteous and indifferent, you whom we call mother, you embody birth and death, you create and you destroy, you . . .

VARYA: (*Imploring.*) Uncle, dear!

ANYA: Not again, Uncle!

TROFIMOV: You're better off "pocketing the yellow . . ."

115   GAEV: I'll be quiet, I'll be quiet.

(*All sit, deep in thought. Silence. Only Firs's muttering can be heard. Suddenly from far, far away, a sound is heard, as if coming from the sky, the sound of a breaking string, dying away in the distance, a mournful sound.*)

LYUBOV ANDREEVNA: What was that?

LOPAKHIN: Don't know. Somewhere far away, deep in the mines, a bucket broke loose and fell . . . But somewhere very far away.

GAEV: Or a bird of some kind . . . a heron, perhaps.

TROFIMOV: Or an owl . . .

120 LYUBOV ANDREEVNA: (*Shudders.*) Disturbing, somehow.

(*Pause.*)

FIRS: Right before the time of trouble, it was the same thing: The owl screeched, and the samovar hissed, it never stopped.

GAEV: What time of trouble?

FIRS: Why, before the emancipation of the serfs.

(*Pause.*)

LYUBOV ANDREEVNA: Let's go, dear friends, shall we, it's getting dark. (*To Anya.*) You've got tears in your eyes . . . What is it, my pet? (*Embraces her.*)

125 ANYA: I'm fine, Mama. It's nothing

TROFIMOV: Someone's coming.

(*A passerby appears in a shabby, white cap and a coat; he is slightly drunk.*)

PASSERBY: Permit me to inquire, may I pass through here to get to the train station?

GAEV: You may. Go down that road.

PASSERBY: I'm deeply grateful. (*Coughs.*) What superb weather we're having . . . (*Recites.*) "My brother, my suffering brother . . . Come down to the Volga, whose moan . . ." (*To Varya.*) Mademoiselle, please, give a poor starving Russian thirty kopeks . . .

(*Varya cries out in fear.*)

130 LOPAKHIN: (*Angrily.*) This has gone too far!

LYUBOV ANDREEVNA: (*Stunned.*) Here . . . take this . . . (*Searches in her purse.*) I have no silver . . . Never mind, here's a gold piece . . .

PASSERBY: I'm deeply grateful! (*Exits.*)

(*Laughter.*)

VARYA: (*Frightened.*) I'm leaving . . . I'm leaving . . . Oh, Mamochka, the servants at home have nothing to eat, and you gave him a gold piece.

LYUBOC ANSREEVNA: What are you going to do with me, I'm such a silly fool! I'll give you everything I have. Yermolai Alekseich, please, lend me some more money! . . .

135   **LOPAKHIN:** Yes, madam.

LYUBOV ANDREEVNA: Come, ladies and gentlemen, time to go. Oh, yes, Varya, we've just made a match for you. Congratulations.

VARYA: (*In tears.*) Mama, you mustn't joke about that.

LOPAKHIN: "Oh-phel-i-a, get thee to a nunnery . . ."

GAEV: It's been so long since I've played a game of billiards, my hands are shaking.

140   **LOPAKHIN:** "Oh-phel-i-a, o nymph, remember me in thy prayers!"

LYUBOV ANREEVNA: Come, ladies and gentlemen. It's almost suppertime.

VARYA: How he frightened me. My heart is pounding.

LOPAKHIN: May I remind you, ladies and gentlemen: On the twenty-second of August, the cherry orchard will be sold. Think about it! Think! . . .

(*They all leave, except Trofimov and Anya.*)

ANYA: (*Laughing.*) The stranger frightened Varya off, thank goodness, now we're alone.

145   **TROFIMOV:** Varya's afraid we'll fall madly in love, she hasn't let us out of her sight for days. She's so narrow-minded, she can't understand we're above love. To overcome all obstacles, real and imagined, which stand in the path of freedom and happiness,—that is our quest in life. Onward! We set forth, undaunted, toward that star, burning bright in the distance! Onward! Don't fall behind, my friends!

ANYA: (*Clasps her hands.*) How beautifully you talk!

(*Pause.*)

It's glorious here today!

TROFIMOV: Yes, the weather is amazing.

ANYA: What have you done to me, Petya, why don't I love the cherry orchard, as I did, once? I loved it so tenderly, I couldn't imagine any other place on earth more lovely than our orchard.

TROFIMOV: All Russia is our orchard. The land is vast and beautiful, there are many marvelous places on it.

(*Pause.*)

Just think, Anya: Your grandfather, your great-grandfather, and his forefathers before him, all were serf-owners, they all owned living souls, so isn't it possible, then, that in every blossom, every leaf, every tree trunk in the orchard, a human soul now gazes down upon us, can't you hear their voices ... To own human souls—can't you see how this has transformed each and every one of us, those who have lived before and those who live today, so that you, your mother, your uncle, all of you, are no longer aware that you are alive at the expense of others, at the expense of those whom you would not even permit beyond your front hall ... We have fallen behind, by two hundred years or so, at least, we have nothing left, absolutely nothing, no clear understanding of the past, we only philosophize, complain about our boredom, or drink vodka. And it's all so clear, can't you see, that to begin a new life, to live in the present, we must first redeem our past, put an end to it, and redeem it we shall, but only with suffering, only with extraordinary, everlasting toil and suffering. You must understand this, Anya.

150 ANYA: The house, in which we live, is no longer our house, and I shall leave it, I give you my word.

TROFIMOV: If you have the key, throw it in the well and run, run far, far away. Be free, like the wind.

ANYA: (*Ecstatic.*) How wonderfully you say it!

TROFIMOV: Believe me, Anya, believe me! I'm not even thirty yet, I'm young, I'm still a student, and yet, I've endured so much! Come winter, I'm hungry, sick, anxiety-ridden, poverty-stricken, like a beggar, and wherever fate carries me, there I shall be! And yet, all the while, every waking moment, day and night, my soul is filled with an indescribable premonition, a vision. A vision of happiness, Anya, I can see it now . . .

ANYA: (*Pensively.*) The moon is rising.

(*Yepikhodov is heard playing the guitar, the same melancholy song as before. The moon is rising. Somewhere near the poplars, Varya is looking for Anya and calling: "Anya! Where are you?"*)

155 TROFIMOV: Yes, the moon is rising.

(*Pause.*)

Here comes happiness, here it comes, closer and closer, I can already hear its footsteps. And if we don't see it, if we don't recognize it, then what does it matter? Others will!

(*Varya's voice: "Anya! Where are you?"*)

Varya, again! (*Angrily.*) It's disgraceful!

ANYA: I know! Let's go down to the river. It's lovely there.

TROFIMOV: Let's go.

(*They go.*)

(*Varya's voice: "Anya! Anya!"*)

(*Curtain.*)

ACT THREE

The drawing room, separated from the ballroom by an archway. A chandelier burns brightly. A Jewish orchestra, the same one referred to in Act Two, is heard playing in the entrance hall. It is evening. In the ballroom, the crowd is dancing the "grand-rond." The voice of Simeonov-Pishchik is heard: "Promenade à une paire!"[1] The couples dance through the drawing room, as follows: first Pishchik and Charlotta Ivanovna; then Trofimov and Lyubov Andreevna; then Anya and the Post Office Clerk; then Varya and the Stationmaster, and so on. Varya is weeping quietly and

---

[1]*"Promenade à une paire!"*: Instructions in the dance: "Walk in a pair!" (French).

wipes away her tears as she dances. Dunyasha is in the last couple. They dance around the drawing room. Pishchik calls out: "Grand-rond, balancez!" and "Les cavaliers à genoux et remerciez vos dames!" [2]

Firs, wearing a tailcoat, carries a tray with seltzer water. Pishchik and Trofimov enter the drawing room.

PISHCHIK: I have high blood pressure, I've had two strokes already, it's difficult for me to dance, but, you know what they say: "If you run in a pack, whether you bark or not, you'd better wag your tail." Never you mind, I'm as healthy as a horse. My dear departed father, joker that he was, God rest his soul, always used to say, on the subject of our ancestry, that the Simeonov-Pishchiks are descended from the same horse that Caligula[3] appointed to the Senate . . . (*Sits.*) The only trouble is: We don't have any money! And you know what they say: "A hungry dog believes only in meat . . ." (*Snores and suddenly wakes up.*) And that's my problem . . . all I ever dream about is money . . .

TROFIMOV: As a matter of fact, you do bear some resemblance to a horse.

PISHCHIK: And why not . . . a horse is a good animal . . . you can get a very good price for a horse, you know . . .

In the next room, the sound of a billiard game is heard. Varya appears in the archway to the hall.

TROFIMOV: (*Teasing.*) Madame Lopakhina! Madame Lopakhina! . . .

5 VARYA: (*Angrily.*) The shabby-looking gentleman!

TROFIMOV: Yes, I'm a shabby-looking gentleman, and proud of it!

VARYA: (*Bitterly.*) We've gone and hired the musicians, now how are we going to pay for them? (*Exits.*)

TROFIMOV: (*To Pishchik.*) Think about it: The energy you've wasted your whole life through in search of money to pay off the interest on your debts, if only you'd spent that energy elsewhere, then, no doubt, you could have changed the world.

---

[2]*Grand-rond . . . dames!":* "Large circle!." And "Gentlemen, kneel down and thank your ladies!" (French).

[3]*Caligula:* Flamboyant and controversial Roman emperor (A.D. 37–41).

PISHCHIK: Nietzsche ... the philosopher ... the supreme, the exalted ... a man of the greatest genius, this man once said, in his own writings, that it's all right to forge banknotes.

10 TROFIMOV: Have you ever read Nietzsche?

PISHCHIK: Well ... Dashenka told me that one. And anyway, given my situation, even if I could forge banknotes ... Day after tomorrow, I owe a payment of three hundred and ten rubles ... I've already scraped up one hundred and thirty so far ... (*Searches in his pockets, anxiously.*) My money's gone! I've lost my money! (*In tears.*) Where is my money? (*Overjoyed.*) Here it is, in the lining ... Look, I even broke into a sweat ...

(*Enter Lyubov Andreevna and Charlotta Ivanovna.*)

LYUBOV ANDREEVNA: (*Humming the "lezginka."*)[4] Why has Leonid been gone so long? What is he doing in town? (*To Dunyasha.*) Dunyasha, offer the musicians some tea ...

TROFIMOV: The auction didn't take place, in all probability.

LYUBOV ANDREEVNA: And of all times to invite the musicians and give a ball ... Oh well, never mind ... (*Sits and hums softly.*)

15 CHARLOTTA: (*Gives Pishchik a deck of cards.*) Here is a deck of cards, think of a card, any card.

PISHCHIK: I've got one.

CHARLOTTA: Now shuffle the deck. Give it to me, oh my dear Mr. Pishchik, Eins, zwei, drei![5] Now go look, it's in your side pocket ...

PISHCHIK: (*Takes a card from his side pocket.*) The eight of spades, you're absolutely right! (*Amazed.*) Imagine that!

CHARLOTTA: (*Holds out the deck of cards in her palm to Trofimov.*) Tell me, quickly, which card is the top card?

20 TROFIMOV: What? Oh, the queen of spades.

CHARLOTTA: Right! (*To Pishchik*) So? Which card is the top card?

PISHCHIK: The ace of hearts.

CHARLOTTA: Right! (*Claps her hands, and the deck of cards disappears.*) My, what lovely weather we're having today.

---

[4]*lezginka:* Russian dance tune.

[5]*Eins, zwei, drei!:* "One, two, three!" (German).

(*A mysterious female voice answers her as if coming from underneath the floor:* "Oh yes, the weather is splendid, dear lady.")

You are the image of perfection . . .

(*Voice:* "And you I like very much too, dear lady.")

STATIONMASTER: (*Applauds.*) Madame Ventriloquist, bravo!

25 **PISHCHIK:** (*Amazed.*) Imagine that! Most enchanting Charlotta Ivanovna . . . I'm head-over-heels in love . . .

CHARLOTTA: In love? (*Shrugs her shoulders.*) How could you possibly be in love? "Guter Mensch, aber schlechter Musikant."[6]

TROFIMOV: (*Claps Pishchik on the shoulder.*) Well done, old horse . . .

CHARLOTTA: Your attention please, for one more trick. (*Gets a lap robe from a chair.*) Here's very lovely lap robe, I wish to sell it . . . (*Shakes it.*) Doesn't anyone wish to buy it?

PISHCHIK: (*Amazed.*) Imagine that!

30 **CHARLOTTA:** Eins, zwei, drei! (*Quickly lifts the lap robe.*)

(*Anya appears behind the lap robe; she curtsies, runs to her mother, embraces her, and runs out into the ballroom, amidst general delight.*)

LYUBOV ANDREEVNA: (*Applauds.*) Bravo, bravo! . . .

CHARLOTTA: Once more. Eins, zwei, drei! (*Lifts the lap robe.*)

(*Varya appears behind the lap robe; she bows.*)

PISHCHIK: (*Amazed.*) Imagine that!

CHARLOTTA: The end! (*Throws the lap robe over Pishchik, curtsies, and runs out into the ballroom.*)

35 **PISHCHIK:** (*Hurries after her.*) Sorceress . . . how did you do it? How? (*Exits.*)

LYUBOV ANDREEVNA: And Leonid is still not back. What can he be doing in town this long, I don't understand it! Surely everything is over by now, either the estate has been sold or else the auction never took place, one or the other, so why must we be kept in the dark forever!

VARYA: (*Attempting to console her.*) Uncle has bought it, I'm sure of it.

TROFIMOV: (*Sarcastically.*) Yes.

---

[6] *"Guter Mensch, aber schlechter Musikant"*: "A good man, but a poor musician" (German).

VARYA: Great-aunt sent him power of attorney to buy the estate in her name and transfer the mortgage to her. She did it for Anya. And Uncle will buy it, with God's help, I'm sure of it.

40 LYUBOV ANDREEVNA: Great-aunt in Yaroslavl sent 50,000 to buy the estate in her name because she doesn't trust us,—and that wasn't even enough to pay the interest. (*Covers her face with her hands.*) Today my destiny will be decided, my destiny . . .

TROFIMOV: (*Teasing Varya.*) Madame Lopakhina!

VARYA: (*Angrily.*) The eternal student! Twice you've been expelled from the university.

LYUBOV ANDREEVNA: Why are you so angry, Varya? He's teasing you about Lopakhin, but what does it matter? If you want to—marry Lopakhin he's a fine man, a fascinating man. And if you don't want to—don't; no one is forcing you to, darling . . .

VARYA: I take this matter very seriously, Mamochka, I must tell you. He is a good man, I like him, I do.

45 LYUBOV ANDREEVNA: Then marry him. What are you waiting for, I don't understand.

VARYA: But Mamochka, I can't propose to him myself. For two years now everyone's been talking to me about him, everyone, and either he says nothing, or else he jokes about it. I understand. He's busy getting rich, he's preoccupied with his affairs, he has no time for me. Oh, if only I had money, only a little, a hundred rubles even, I'd give up everything, I'd run away as far as I could. I'd enter a convent.

TROFIMOV: Blessings on you!

VARYA: (*To Trofimov.*) A student's supposed to be intelligent! (*Gently, in tears.*) How ugly you've grown, Petya, and how old, too! (*To Lyubov Andreevna, no longer crying.*) I simply can't live without work, Mamochka. I must be doing something, every minute.

(*Enter Yasha.*)

YASHA: (*Hardly able to contain his laughter.*) Yepikhodov has broken a billiard cue! . . . (*Exits.*)

50 VARYA: Why is Yepikhodov here? Who allowed him to play billiards? I don't understand these people . . . (*Exits.*)

LYUBOV ANDREEVNA: Don't tease her, Petya, can't you see how miserable she is.

TROFIMOV: She's overbearing, that's what she is . . . always poking her nose into other people's business. She hasn't given Anya and me a moment's peace all summer, she's afraid we might fall in love. What business is it of hers, anyway? And how could she even think that of me, I'm far beyond such vulgarity. We are above love!

LYUBOV ANDREEVNA: And I suppose that means I must be beneath love. (*Tremendously agitated.*) Why isn't Leonid back yet? I only want to know: Is the estate sold or isn't it? This terrible business has gone too far, I don't know what to think any more, I'm at my wits' end . . . I might scream any minute . . . I might do something foolish. Save me, Petya. Say something, anything . . .

TROFIMOV: Whether the estate is sold today or not—does it really matter? It's over, it's been so for a long time, there's no turning back again, that path is long overgrown. Face it, dear friend. You mustn't delude yourself any longer, for once in your life you must look the truth straight in the eye.

55 LYUBOV ANDREEVNA: What truth? Oh, yes, of course, you see what is true and what is not true, while I have lost my vision, I see nothing. You boldly solve all the problems of the world, don't you, but tell me, my darling, isn't that because you're still so young, because you haven't even suffered through one of life's problems yet, not even one? You boldly look to the future, but isn't that because you see nothing so terrible lying ahead, because life is still safely hidden from your young eyes? You have more courage, more character, more honesty than any of us, so then why not have compassion, find it, somewhere in a corner of your heart, have mercy on me. I was born here, my mother and father lived here, my grandfather, too, I love this house, I can't comprehend a life without the cherry orchard, and if it must be sold, then sell me with it . . . (*Embraces Trofimov, kisses him on the forehead.*) My son drowned here . . . (*Weeps.*) Have pity on me, my good, kind fellow.

TROFIMOV: You know I do, with all my heart.

LYUBOV ANDREEVNA: Yes, but there must be another way to say it, another way . . . (*Takes out a handkerchief, a telegram falls on the floor.*) My soul is so heavy today, you can't possibly imagine. There is such a din here, I'm trembling with each and every sound, trembling all over, but I can't be alone, the silence would be terrifying. Don't judge me, Petya . . . I love you, as if you were my own child. And I'd gladly let you marry Anya, I would, I swear to you, only first you must finish your education, darling, get your degree. You don't do a thing, you just let fate carry you from place to place, and that's such a strange way to live . . . Isn't it? Well? And you simply must do something about that beard, to make it grow, somehow . . . (*Bursts out laughing.*) How funny-looking you are!

TROFIMOV: (*Picks up the telegram.*) I don't wish to be handsome.

LYUBOV ANDREEVNA: It's telegram from Paris. Every day I receive one. Yesterday, and today, too. That terrible man is ill again, he's in trouble again . . . He begs my forgiveness, he beseeches me to return to him, I really ought to be going to Paris, to be near him. You should see your face now, Petya, so severe, so judgmental, but, really, what am I to do, darling, tell me, what can I do, he's ill, he's alone, unhappy, and who will take care of him, who will keep him from harm, who will nurse him through his illness? Oh, why hide it, why keep silent, I love him, it's the truth. I love him, I love him . . . He is the stone around my neck, and I shall sink with him to the bottom, and how I love this stone, I can't live without it! (*Presses Trofimov's hand.*) Don't think ill of me, Petya, and don't speak, please, not a word . . .

60   TROFIMOV: (*In tears.*) Forgive me for saying it, but for God's sake: This man robbed you, he cleaned you out!

LYUBOV ANDREEVNA: No, no, no, you mustn't talk like that . . . (*Covers her ears.*)

TROFIMOV: He's an absolute scoundrel, and you're the only one who doesn't know it! A petty thief, a good-for-nothing . . .

LYUBOV ANDREEVNA: (*With controlled anger.*) And you're twenty-six or twenty-seven years old, and still a schoolboy!

TROFIMOV: So be it!

65 **LYUBOV ANDREEVNA:** You're supposed to be a man, at your age you're supposed to understand how lovers behave. Why don't you know this by now . . . why haven't you fallen in love yourself? (*Angrily.*) Yes, yes! You and all your talk about purity . . . why, you're nothing but a prude, that's what you are, an eccentric, a freak . . .

TROFIMOV: (*Horrified.*) What is she saying!

LYUBOV ANDREEVNA: "I am above love!" You're not above love, no, as Firs says, you're pathetic! At your age, not to have a lover! . . .

TROFIMOV: (*Horrified.*) This is terrible! What is she saying?! (*Rushes out into the ballroom, holding his head.*) This is terrible . . . I can't bear it, I'm leaving . . . (*Exits, but returns again immediately.*) It's all over between us! (*Exits, into the front hall.*)

LYUBOV ANDREEVNA: (*Calls after him.*) Petya, wait! Don't be silly, I was only joking! Petya!

(*In the front hall, someone is heard dashing down the stairs, and suddenly falling the rest of the way with a crash. Anya and Varya cry out, but then, almost immediately, laughter is heard.*)

What happened?

(*Anya runs in.*)

70 **ANYA:** (*Laughing.*) Petya fell down the stairs! (*Runs out.*)

LYUBOV ANDREEVNA: What a peculiar fellow that Petya is . . .

(*The Stationmaster stands in the middle of the ballroom, and starts to recite a poem: "The Fallen Woman" by Alexey Knostantinovich Tolstoy. Everyone stops to listen, but after a few lines, the strains of a waltz are heard coming from the front hall, and the recitation is interrupted. Everyone dances. Trofimov, Anya, Varya, and Lyubov Andreevna pass through from the entrance hall.*)

Petya . . . my pure Petya . . . I beg your forgiveness . . . Come, dance with me . . . (*Dances with him.*)

(*Anya and Varya dance together. Firs enters, and places his cane near the side door. Yasha also enters, and watches the dancing.*)

YASHA: So, what's new, grandpa?

FIRS: I don't feel very well. In the old days, we used to have generals, barons, admirals dancing at our balls; nowadays we have to send for the postal clerk and the stationmaster, and even they come reluctantly. And I'm getting weaker, somehow. In the old days, when anyone of us fell ill, my old master—that would be their grandfather—he would treat us all with sealing wax. I've taken a dose of sealing wax every day for twenty years now, even more, who knows; perhaps that's why I'm still alive.

YASHA: You get on my nerves, grandpa. (*Yawns.*) Maybe it's time for you to kick the bucket.

75   FIRS: And you're a pathetic fool, that's what you are. (*Mumbles.*)

(*Trofimov and Lyubov Andreevna dance in the ballroom, and then in the drawing room.*)

LYUBOV ANDREEVNA: "Merci." Let me sit down ... (*Sits.*) I'm exhausted.

(*Enter Anya.*)

ANYA: (*Agitated.*) There's a man out in the kitchen, he was just saying that the cherry orchard was sold today.

LYUBOV ANDREEVNA: To whom?

ANYA: He didn't say. He left. (*Dances with Trofimov.*)

(*Both exit into the ballroom.*)

80   YASHA: Some old fellow jabbering, that's all. A stranger.

FIRS: And Leonid Andreich is still not here, he's still not back yet. All he has on is a lightweight overcoat, one for in-between seasons, he's bound to catch cold. Oh, these young people nowadays!

LYUBOV ANDREEVNA: I think I'm going to die. Go, Yasha, hurry, find out to whom it was sold.

YASHA: Oh, he left a long time ago, that old fellow. (*Laughs.*)

LYUBOV ANDREEVNA: (*Slightly annoyed.*) And what are you laughing about? What's so funny?

85   YASHA: That Yepikhodov, he's a clown. The man is pitiful. "Mister Disaster."

LYUBOV ANDREEVNA: Firs, if the estate is sold, where will you go?

FIRS: Wherever you tell me, that's where I'll go.

LYUBOV ANDREEVNA: Why do you look like that? Are you ill? You should be in bed, you know . . .

FIRS: Yes . . . (*With a grin.*) I'll go to bed, and who will serve, who will manage everything? Hm? One servant for the whole household.

90 YASHA: (*To Lyubov Andreevna.*) Lyubov Andreevna! One small request, allow me, please! If you go to Paris again, take me with you, I beg of you. I can't stay here any more, it's absolutely impossible. (*Looks around, in a low voice.*) What can I say, you see for yourself, this is an ignorant country, the people are immoral, and anyway, life here is boring, the food they give you in the kitchen is disgusting, and you have Firs wandering around everywhere, muttering all kinds of nonsense. Take me with you, I beg of you!

(*Enter Pishchik.*)

PISHCHIK: May I have the pleasure . . . a little waltz, most charming lady . . .

(*Lyubov Andreevna joins him.*)

But, don't forget, one hundred eighty rubles, enchanting lady . . . That, I'll take . . . (*They dance.*) Once hundred and eighty sweet little rubles . . .

(*They cross into the ballroom.*)

YASHA: (*Sings softly.*) "O, do you know how my heart is yearning . . ."

(*In the ballroom, a figure in a grey top hat and checkered trousers waves her hands and jumps up and down; there are cries of: "Bravo, Charlotta Ivanovna!"*)

DUNYASHA: (*Stops to powder her face.*) The mistress told me to dance—too many gentlemen, too few ladies,—but now my head is spinning from too much waltzing, my heart is pounding, and, do you know what else, Firs Nikolaevich, the postmaster just told me something that took my breath away.

(*The music dies down.*)

FIRS: What did he say?

95 DUNYASHA: "You," he said, "are like a little flower."

YASHA: (*Yawns.*) What ignorance . . . (*Exits.*)

DUNYASHA: "A little flower" . . . I'm such a sensitive young woman, you know, I adore a few tender words.

FIRS: You'll get yourself into a lot of trouble.

(*Enter Yepikhodov.*)

YEPIKHODOV: Avdotya Fyodorovna, you keep avoiding me . . . what am I, some sort of insect? (*Sighs.*) Ach, life!

100 DUNYASHA: Yes, what may I do for you?

YEPIKHODOV: And no doubt, probably, you're right. Of course. (*Sighs.*) Who can blame you. And yet, look at if from my point, of view, I mean, if I may say so myself, and I shall, so excuse me, but you have reduced me to a complete state of mind. Now I know my destiny in life, every day some new disaster befalls me, and have I accepted this?—yes, I have, I look upon my fate with a smile. You have given me your word, and though . . .

DUNYASHA: Can we have our little talk later, please? Leave me alone now. I'm in a fantasy. (*Plays with her fan.*)

YEPIKHODOV: A new day, a new disaster, and excuse me, I just keep smiling, I even laugh, sometimes.

(*Enter Varya from the ballroom.*)

VARYA: You still haven't left yet, Semyon? Who do you think you are, really. (*To Dunyasha.*) Get out of here, Dunyasha. (*To Yepikhodov.*) First you play billiards and you break a cue, then you parade around the drawing room like a guest.

105 YEPIKHODOV: You should not reprimand me. Excuse me.

VARYA: I'm not reprimanding you, I'm telling you. All you do is float from one place to the next, you don't do a blessed bit of work. Why we keep you as clerk, God only knows.

YEPIKHODOV: (*Offended.*) Whether I work, or float, or eat, or play billiards, for that matter, excuse me, but that's a subject of discussion only for our elders.

VARYA: How dare you speak to me like that! (*Enraged.*) How dare you? Do you mean to tell me I don't know what I'm doing? Get out of here! This minute!

YEPIKHODOV: (*Cowering.*) Excuse me, may I ask that you express yourself in a more delicate fashion?

110   **VARYA:** (*Beside herself.*) Get out, this minute! Out!

(*He goes to the door, she follows him.*)

"Mister Disaster!" Never set foot in here again, do you hear! I never want to lay eyes on you!

(*Yepikhodov has exited; from behind the door, his voice is heard: "I am going to file a complaint against you."*)

So, you think you're coming back, eh? (*Grabs the cane, which Firs has left by the door.*) Come on . . . come on . . . come on, I'll show you . . . So, are you coming back? Are you? This is for you, then . . . (*Swings the cane.*)

(*Just at this moment Lopakhin enters.*)

LOPAKHIN: I humbly thank you.

VARYA: (*Angrily and sarcastically.*) Sorry!

LOPAKHIN: Please, it's nothing. I'm most grateful for the warm reception.

VARYA: Don't mention it. (*She turns to go, then looks around and asks, meekly.*) I didn't hurt you, did I?

115   **LOPAKHIN:** No, of course not, it's nothing. Just a bump, an enormous one, that's all.

(*Voices in the ballroom: "Lopakhin has returned! Yermolai Alekseich!"*)

PISHCHIK: Well, well, well, and speaking of the devil! . . . (*Kisses Lopakhin.*) I smell a touch of brandy, my dear, good fellow, yes, I do! And we've been celebrating here, too!

(*Enter Lyubov Andreevna.*)

LYUBOV ANDREEVNA: Yermolai Alekseich, you're back. Why did it take you so long? Where is Leonid?

LOPAKHIN: Leonid Andreich returned with me, he's coming . . .

LYUBOV ANDREEVNA: (*Upset.*) So? Was there an auction? Tell me!

120   **LOPAKHIN:** (*Disconcerted, afraid to reveal his excitement.*) The auction was over at four o'clock . . . We missed the train, we had to wait till nine-thirty. (*Sighs heavily.*) Oh! My head is spinning . . .

(*Enter Gaev. In his right hand he carries some packages; he wipes away the tears with his left hand.*)

LYUBOV ANDREEVNA: Lyonya, what is it? Lyonya? (*Impatiently, in tears.*) Tell me, quickly, for God's sake . . .

GAEV: (*Doesn't answer her, simply waves his hands; weeping, to Firs.*) Here, take it . . . anchovies, and some kerch herring . . . I haven't had a thing to eat all day . . . What I have lived through!

(*The door of the billiard room is open; the clicking of billiard balls is heard and Yasha's voice: "Seven and eighteen!" Gaev's expression changes; he is no longer crying.*)

I'm terribly tired. Help me change my clothes, Firs. (*Exits through the ballroom to his room, Firs follows behind.*)

PISHCHIK: What happened at the auction? Tell us! Please!

LYUBOV ANDREEVNA: Is the cherry orchard sold?

125 **LOPAKHIN:** It is sold.

LYUBOV ANDREEVNA: Who bought it?

LOPAKHIN: I bought it.

(*Pause. Lyubov Andreevna is stunned; she might have fallen, were she not standing near an armchair and table. Varya takes the keys off her belt, throws them on the floor in the middle of the drawing room, and exits.*)

I bought it! Wait, ladies and gentlemen, bear with me, please, my head is spinning, I can't speak . . . (*Laughs.*) We arrived at the auction, and Deriganov was already there. Leonid Andreich only had 15,000, so right away Deriganov bid 30,000 over and above the debt on the mortgage. I saw how it was going, so I decided to take him on, I bid forty. And he bid forty-five. Then I bid fifty-five. You see—he'd raise it by five, I'd raise it by ten . . . And then, it was all over. I bid ninety over and above the debt, and that was it, it went to me. And now, the cherry orchard is mine! Mine! (*Roars with laughter.*) My God, ladies and gentlemen, the cherry orchard is mine! Tell me that I'm drunk, that I'm out of my mind, that I've made it all up . . . (*Stamps his feet.*) Don't you laugh at me! If only my father and my grandfather could get up from their graves and witness all these events, how their Yermolai, their ignorant little Yermolai, the one who was beaten, the one who ran barefoot in the bitter winter, how this same little Yermolai bought the estate, the most beautiful estate in the world. I bought the estate, where my grandfather and my father were slaves, where they were forbidden to set foot in the kitchen. No, I'm dreaming, I'm hallucinating, it's only an illusion . . . a figment of the imagination, shrouded in a cloak of mystery . . . (*Picks up the keys, smiles tenderly.*) She threw down the keys, she's saying she's not the mistress of the house any more . . . (*Jingles the keys.*) Ah, well, what does it matter.

(*The orchestra can be heard tuning up.*)

Eh, musicians, play, I want to hear you play! Everyone, come and see, how Yermolai Lopakhin will take an axe out into the cherry orchard, and all the trees will come crashing to the ground! And we'll build summer homes, and our grand-children and great grandchildren will see a new life . . . Let's have music, play!

(*The music plays. Lyubov Andreevna lowers herself into a chair and weeps bitterly.*)

(*Reproachfully.*) Why, why didn't you listen to me? My, poor, dear friend, you'll never get it back now, never. (*In tears.*) Oh, the sooner all this is behind us, the sooner we can change our chaotic lives, our absurd, unhappy lives.

PISHCHIK: (*Takes him by the hand, in a low voice.*) She is weeping. Come into the ballroom, let's leave her alone . . . Come . . . (*Takes him by the hand and leads him into the ballroom.*)

LOPAKHIN: What's going on here? Let there be music? Loud, the way I want it! Let everything be the way I want it! (*With irony.*) Here comes the new master, the owner of the cherry orchard! (*Accidentally shoves against a table, almost turning over a cande-labra.*) I can pay for it all, for everything! (*Exits with Pishchik.*)

(*There is no one left in the ballroom or the drawing room, except Lyubov Andreevna, who is sitting, huddled over, weeping bitterly. The music plays softly. Anya and Trofimov rush in. Anya goes to her mother and kneels before her. Trofimov stays at the entrance to the ballroom.*)

130 ANYA: Mama! . . . Mama, are you crying? My dear, good, kind Mama, my beautiful Mama, I love you . . . I bless you. The cherry orchard is sold, it's gone, it's true, it's true, but don't cry, Mama, you still have your whole life before you to live, and your pure and beautiful soul . . . Come with me, come,

my darling, away from here, come! . . . We'll plant a new orchard, more glorious than this one, you'll see, you'll understand, and joy, a deep, peaceful, gentle joy will settle into your soul, like the warm, evening sun, and you will smile, Mama! Come, darling! Come! . . .

(*Curtain.*)

ACT FOUR

The same setting as Act One. There are no curtains on the windows, no pictures on the walls; only a few pieces of furniture remain, stacked in a corner, as if for sale. There is a feeling of emptiness. There are suitcases, travel bags, etc., piled high upstage by the door leading to the outside. The door to stage left is open, from which the voices of Varya and Anya can be heard. Lopakhin stands there, waiting. Yasha holds a tray of glasses, filled with champagne. In the entrance hall, Yepikhodov is packing a case. Offstage, voices are heard—the peasants have come to say good-bye. Gaev's voice is heard: "Thank you, my friends, I thank you."

YASHA: The peasants have come to say good-bye. Now here's my opinion on that subject, Yermolai Alekseich: The people are good, but what do *they* know.

(*The noise dies down. Lyubov Andreevna and Gaev enter through the entrance hall; she is no longer crying, but she is very pale: she is trembling, and it is difficult for her to speak.*)

GAEV: You gave them everything in your purse, Lyuba. No! You mustn't do that!

LYUBOV ANDREEVNA: I couldn't help it! I couldn't help it!

(*Both exit.*)

LOPAKHIN: (*At the door, following after them.*) Please, I humbly beg you! A farewell toast! I didn't think to bring any from town . . . and I could only find one bottle at the station. Please!

(*Pause.*)

So, my friends! You don't want any? (*Steps away from the door.*) If I'd known, I wouldn't have bought it. Never mind, I won't have any, either.

(*Yasha carefully places the tray on the table.*)

Drink up, Yasha, why don't you.

5 YASHA: To those who are leaving! And to those who are staying behind! (*Drinks.*) This isn't real champagne, that much I can tell you.

LOPAKHIN: Eight rubles a bottle.

(*Pause.*)

Wickedly cold in here, isn't it.

YASHA: They didn't stoke up the stoves today, what's the point, everybody's leaving. (*Laughs.*)

LOPAKHIN: What are you laughing about?

YASHA: I'm happy.

10 LOPAKHIN: It's October, but outside it's sunny and mild, like summertime. Good weather for construction. (*Looks at his watch, at the door.*) Ladies and gentlemen, bear in mind, only forty-six minutes left until the train departs! That means we have to leave for the station in twenty minutes. Hurry, everyone!

(*Trofimov enters from the outside, wearing a coat.*)

TROFIMOV: I think it's time to go now. They've already brought the horses around. Where are my galoshes, damn it! They've disappeared. (*At the door.*) Anya, my galoshes aren't here! I can't find them!

LOPAKHIN: And I've got to get to Kharkov. I'll go with you as far as the station. I'm going to spend the winter in Kharkov. Yes. Here I am, standing around, talking to you, I'm lost when I'm not working. I can't live without work, I don't know what to do with my hands; isn't it strange, look, they're hanging there, as if they belonged to someone else.

TROFIMOV: We'll be leaving momentarily, and you'll return to all your worthy enterprises.

LOPAKHIN: Have a glass with me.

15 TROFIMOV: I can't.

LOPAKHIN: So, it's off to Moscow, then?

TROFIMOV: Yes, that's right, I'll go with them into town, and tomorrow, it's off to Moscow.

LOPAKHIN: Yes . . . Well, the professors haven't started their lectures yet, no doubt they're all waiting for you!

TROFIMOV: That's none of your business.

20 **LOPAKHIN:** How many years is it, then, since you've been at the university?

TROFIMOV: Think up something new, why don't you? That's a stale and feeble joke, it's not funny any more. (*Searches for his galoshes.*) It's very likely we may never see each other again, you know, so allow me, please, to give you some parting advice. Don't wave your arms around so much! Try to get out of the habit of waving your arms when you talk, if you can. All this planning of yours, you know, building summer houses, creating a new generation of independent landowners, and so on and so forth,—why, that's just another form of waving your arms . . . Oh, well, never mind, all things considered, I like you . . . I do. You have delicate, sensitive fingers, the fingers of an artist . . . you have a delicate, sensitive soul . . .

LOPAKHIN: (*Embraces him.*) Good-bye, my friend. Thanks for everything. Just in case, here, take some money for the journey.

TROFIMOV: Why should I? I don't need it.

LOPAKHIN: But you don't have any!

25 **TROFIMOV:** Yes, I do, thank you very much. I've just received some money for a translation. Here it is, right here, in my pocket. (*Anxiously.*) Now where are my galoshes!

VARYA: (*From the other room.*) Here, take the filthy things! (*Tosses a pair of rubber galoshes on the stage.*)

TROFIMOV: Why are you so angry, Varya? Hm . . . These are not my galoshes!

LOPAKHIN: This spring I planted almost 3,000 acres of poppies, and made a clean profit of 40,000. And when my poppies bloomed, now what a sight that was! So, here's what I'm saying, I've just made 40,000 rubles, and I'm offering you a loan because I can afford to. Why do you look down your nose at me? I'm a peasant . . . what do you expect?

TROFIMOV: Your father was a peasant, mine was a chemist, none of it means a thing.

(*Lopakhin takes out his wallet.*)

> Stop that, stop . . . Even if you were to give me 200,000, I
> wouldn't take it. I am a free man. And everything that is so
> sacred and dear to all of you, rich and poor alike, hasn't the
> slightest significance to me, it's all dust, adrift in the wind.
> I can survive without you, I can even surpass you, I am proud
> and strong. Mankind is on a quest to seek the highest truth,
> the greatest happiness possible on this earth, and I am in the
> front ranks!

30   **LOPAKHIN:** And will you reach your destination?

  TROFIMOV: Yes, I shall.

(*Pause.*)

> I shall, or else I'll show others the way.

(*In the distance, the sound is heard of an axe falling on a tree.*)

LOPAKHIN: So, good-bye, my friend. Time to go. Here we
are, looking down our noses at one another, and all the
while, life goes on, in spite of any of us. When I work, for
days on end, without any rest, that's when my thoughts
come most clearly, that's when I know why I am on this
earth, why I exist. And how many of us are there in Russia,
my friend, who still don't know why they exist. Ah well,
what does it matter, that's not the point, is it. They say that
Leonid Andreich has taken a position at a bank, 6,000
a year . . . He won't be able to keep it, though, he's too
lazy . . .

ANYA: (*At the door.*) Mama asks you not to cut down the orchard
till after she's gone.

TROFIMOV: Isn't it possible to show some tact . . . (*Exits through the
entrance hall.*)

35   **LOPAKHIN:** Yes, yes, right away . . . Really.

  ANYA: Have they sent Firs to the hospital yet?

  YASHA: I told them about it this morning. I'm sure they did.

  ANYA: (*To Yepikhodov, who is walking through the hall.*) Semyon
Panteleich, please, go find out, would you, if they've taken
Firs to the hospital yet.

YASHA: (*Offended.*) I told Yegor this morning. Why ask the same question over and over!

40 YEPIKHODOV: The ancient Firs, in my final opinion, is beyond repair; he should return to his forefathers. And I can only envy him. (*Places the suitcase on a hat box, and crushes it.*) Oh, well, of course. I knew it. (*Exits.*)

YASHA: (*Mocking.*) "Mister Disaster" . . .

VARYA: (*From behind the door.*) Have they taken Firs to the hospital?

ANYA: Yes, they have.

VARYA: Why didn't they bring the letter to the doctor?

45 ANYA: We'll just have to send it along . . . (*Exits.*)

VARYA: (*From the adjacent room.*) Where's Yasha? Tell him his mother's here, she wants to say good-bye to him.

YASHA: (*Waves his hand.*) I'm losing my patience.

(*During this, Dunyasha has been busying herself with the luggage; now that Yasha is alone, she goes up to him.*)

DUNYASHA: Just one last look, Yasha. You're leaving . . . you're abandoning me . . . (*Weeps and throws her arms around his neck.*)

YASHA: What's there to cry about? (*Drinks champagne.*) In six days, I'll be in Paris again. Tomorrow we'll board an express train, and off we'll go, that's the last you'll ever see of us. I just can't believe it. "Vive la France!" . . . This place is not for me, I can't live here . . . and that's all there is to it. I've seen a lot of ignorance—and I've had enough. (*Drinks champagne.*) What's there to cry about? Behave yourself properly, then you won't cry so much.

50 DUNYASHA: (*Powders her face, looks at herself in the mirror.*) Send me a letter from Paris. You know how much I have loved you, Yasha, I have loved you very, very much! I'm a sensitive creature, Yasha!

YASHA: They're coming. (*Busies himself with the luggage, hums softly.*)

(*Enter Lyubov Andreevna, Gaev, Anya, and Charlotta Ivanovna.*)

GAEV: We really ought to be going. There's hardly any time left. (*Looks at Yasha.*) Who smells of herring in here?

LYUBOV ANDREEVNA: In ten minutes time we'll be getting into the carriages . . . (*Glances around the room.*) Good-bye, beloved home, home of my forefathers. Winter will pass, spring will come, and you'll no longer be here, they will have destroyed you. How much these walls have seen! (*Kisses her daughter passionately.*) My treasure, you're radiant, your eyes are sparkling, like two diamonds. Are you happy? Very happy?

ANYA: Very! We're starting a new life, Mama!

55 GAEV: (*Cheerfully.*) Everything's turned out quite well, as a matter of fact, yes, indeed. Before the cherry orchard was sold, we were all upset, we suffered a great deal, but then, when everything was settled, once and for all, finally and irrevocably, we all calmed down, we were even glad . . . And now I'm a bank official, a financier . . . "yellow into the middle pocket," and you, Lyuba, for all that we've been through, you're looking better than ever, no doubt about it.

LYUBOV ANDREEVNA: Yes, I'm calmer, it's true.

(*She is given her hat and coat.*)

I can sleep better now. Take my things out, Yasha. It's time. (*To Anya.*) My darling child, we shall see each other again, soon . . . I am going to Paris, I shall live there on the money your great-aunt from Yaroslavl sent to buy the estate—God bless great-aunt! — but that money won't last very long.

ANYA: You'll come home soon, Mama, soon . . . won't you? And I'll study, take my examinations, and then I'll work, I'll take care of you. And we'll read all sorts of marvelous books together, Mama . . . Won't we? (*Kisses her mother's hands.*) We'll read through the long autumn evenings, we'll read so many books, and a wonderful new world will open before us . . . (*Dreaming.*) Come home, Mama . . .

LYUBOV ANDREEVNA: I'll come, my jewel. (*Embraces her daughter.*)

(*Enter Lopakhin, and Charlotta, who is softly humming a tune.*)

GAEV: Charlotta is happy: she's singing!

60 CHARLOTTA: (*Picks up a bundle, resembling an infant in swaddling clothes.*) "My sweet little baby, 'bye, 'bye . . ."

(*The child's cry: "Wa, Wa! . . ." can be heard.*)

"Hushabye, baby, my sweet little boy."

246 | Anton Chekhov

(The child's cry: "Wa! . . . wa! . . .")

Poor baby! I feel so sorry for you! *(Throws the bundle down.)* Now, please, find me another job. I can't go on like this.

LOPAKHIN: We shall, Charlotta Ivanovna, don't worry.

GAEV: We're all being cast out, Varya's going away . . . suddenly no one needs us any more.

CHARLOTTA: There's nowhere for me to live in town. I must go away . . . *(Hums.)* It doesn't matter . . .

(Enter Pishchik.)

LOPAKHIN: One of nature's wonders! . . .

65   PISHCHIK: *(Out of breath.)* Oy, let me catch my breath . . . I'm all worn out . . . Most honorable friends . . . Give me some water . . .

GAEV: Looking for money, by any chance? I remain your humble servant, but, forgive me, I really must avoid the temptation . . . *(Exits.)*

PISHCHIK: I haven't been here in such a long, long, time . . . loveliest lady . . . *(To Lopakhin.)* And you are here, too . . . so good to see you . . . a man of the highest intelligence . . . here, take it . . . it's yours . . . *(Gives Lopakhin some money.)* Four hundred rubles . . . I still owe you eight hundred and forty . . .

LOPAKHIN: *(Shrugs his shoulders in amazement.)*: I must be dreaming . . . Where on earth did you get this?

PISHCHIK: Wait . . . So hot . . . Most extraordinary circumstances. Some Englishmen came to visit my estate, and what do you know, they found white clay in the earth . . . whatever that is . . . *(To Lyubov Andreevna.)* And here's four hundred for you . . . elegant, exquisite lady . . . *(Gives her some money.)* The rest will come later. *(Drinks the water.)* Just now, a young man on the train was telling us about this great philosopher . . . how he's advising everyone to jump off the roof . . . "Jump!"—he says, and that will solve everything. *(Amazed.)* Imagine that! Water! . . .

70   LOPAKHIN: What Englishmen are you talking about?

PISHCHIK: I leased them a plot of the land with the white clay for twenty-four years . . . But now, forgive me, please, I've run out of time . . . a long ride ahead . . . I'm going to the

Znoykovs . . . to the Kardamonovs . . . I owe everybody . . . (*Drinks.*) Good day to you all . . . I'll drop by again on Thursday . . .

LYUBOV ANDREEVNA: We're just moving into town now, and tomorrow I'm going abroad . . .

PISHCHIK: What? (*Anxiously.*) Why to town? What's this I see . . . furniture . . . suitcases . . . Well, never mind . . . (*In tears.*) Never mind . . . Very very smart people, these Englishmen . . . people of the highest intelligence . . . Never mind . . . I wish you happiness . . . God will watch over you . . . Never mind . . . Everything on this earth must come to an end . . . (*Kisses Lyubov Andreevna's hand.*) And when you hear the news that my own end has come, remember this good old horse, won't you, and say: "Once upon a time there lived an old so-and-so . . . Simeonov-Pishchik . . . God rest his soul" . . . Magnificent weather we're having . . . Yes . . . (*Exits in great confusion, and immediately returns and speaks from the doorway.*) Dashenka sends her regards. (*Exits.*)

LYUBOV ANDREEVNA: And now we can go. But I'm leaving with two worries. The first is Firs—he's ill. (*Looks at her watch.*) We still have five minutes . . .

75 ANYA: Mama, they've already sent Firs to the hospital. Yasha sent him this morning.

LYUBOV ANDREEVNA: My second sorrow is Varya. She's used to getting up early and working, and now, without work, she's like a fish out of water. She's grown thin and pale, she weeps all the time, poor thing . . .

(*Pause.*)

You know very well, Yermolai Alekseich, I have dreamed . . . that one day she would marry you, in fact, it was obvious to everyone that you would be married. (*She whispers to Anya, who motions to Charlotta, and both exit.*) She loves you, you seem to be fond of her, and I don't know why, I simply don't know why it is that you go out of your way to avoid one another. I don't understand it!

LOPAKHIN: I don't understand it myself, to tell the truth. It's all so strange, somehow . . . if there's still time, then I'm ready to do it now . . . Basta![1] Let's settle it once and for all; without you here, I don't think I could possibly propose to her.

LYUBOV ANDREEVNA: Excellent! It only takes a minute, you know. I'll call her in right away . . .

LOPAKHIN: Oh yes, and there's champagne, too. (*Looks at glasses.*) It's empty, someone drank it all up.

(*Yasha coughs.*)

Or, should I say, lapped it all up . . .

80 LYUBOV ANDREEVNA: (*Excited.*) Splendid. We're leaving . . . Yasha, "allez!"[2] I'll call her . . . (*At the door.*) Varya, stop what you're doing, and come here, Come! (*Exits with Yasha.*)

LOPAKHIN: (*Looks at his watch.*): Yes . . .

(*Pause.*)

(*Muffled laughter and whispering is heard from behind the door; finally, Varya enter.*)

VARYA: (*In a lengthy search for something.*) That's strange, I can't find it anywhere . . .

LOPAKHIN: What are you looking for?

VARYA: I put it away myself, I can't remember where.

(*Pause.*)

85 LOPAKHIN: So where will you go now, Varvara Mikhailovna?

VARYA: Me? To the Ragulins' . . . I've agreed to work for them . . . you know . . . as a housekeeper.

LOPAKHIN: Aren't they in Yashnevo? That's about forty-five miles from here.

(*Pause.*)

And so, life has come to an end in this house . . .

VARYA: (*Searching among the things.*) Where can it be . . . Perhaps I put it in the trunk . . . Yes, life has come to an end in this house . . . and will be no more . . .

---

[1]*Basta!*: "Enough!" (Italian).
[2]*"allez!"*: "Go!" (French).

LOPAKHIN: And I'm off to Kharkov now . . . on the same train. I've got a lot of business there. But I'm leaving Yepikhodov here to look after things . . . I've hired him, you know.

90   VARYA: Really!

LOPAKHIN: Last year at this time it was already snowing, if you remember, and now it's so sunny and calm. Only it's quite cold . . . Three degrees of frost, almost.

VARYA: I hadn't noticed.

(*Pause.*)

Anyway, our thermometer's broken . . .

(*Pause.*)

(*A voice is heard calling from outside: "Yermolai Alekseich! . . ."*)

LOPAKHIN: (*As if he'd long been waiting for this call.*) Coming! (*He hurries out.*)

(*Varya sits on the floor, puts her head on a bundle of clothing, and sobs quietly. The door opens, and Lyubov Andreevna enters cautiously.*)

LYUBOV ANDREEVNA: So?

(*Pause.*)

We'd better go.

95   VARYA: (*No longer weeping, wipes her eyes.*) Yes, Mamochka, it's time. If I don't miss the train. I might even get to the Ragulins' today . . .

LYUBOV ANDREEVNA: (*At the door.*) Anya, put your coat on!

(*Enter Anya, then Gaev, Charlotta Ivanovna. Gaev is wearing a warm coat with a hood. The servants and carriage drivers assemble. Yepikhodov is busy with the luggage.*)

Now, we can be on our way.

ANYA: (*Overjoyed.*) We're on our way!

GAEV: My friends, my dear, kind friends! Upon leaving this house forever, how can I be silent, how can I refrain, upon this our departure, from expressing those feelings, which now fill my very being . . .

ANYA: (*Imploring.*) Uncle!

100   **VARYA:** Uncle, must you!

    GAEV: (*Dejected.*) "Double the yellow into the middle . . ." I'll be quiet . . .

(*Enter Trofimov, then Lopakhin.*)

TROFIMOV: All right, ladies and gentlemen, time to depart.

LOPAKHIN: Yepikhodov, my coat!

LYUBOV ANDREEVNA: I want to sit for just one minute longer. I never really noticed before, what walls this house has, what ceilings, and now I look at them with such longing, with such tender love . . .

105   **GAEV:** I remember, when I was six, on Trinity Sunday, I sat at this window and watched my father walking to church . . .

    LYUBOV ANDREEVNA: Have they taken everything out?

    LOPAKHIN: I think so. (*To Yepikhodov, who is putting on his coat.*) Yepikhodov, see to it that everything's been taken care of.

    YEPIKHODOV: (*Speaking in a hoarse voice.*) Don't you worry, Yermolai Alekseich.

    LOPAKHIN: What's the matter with your voice?

110   **YEPIKHODOV:** I just drank some water, and I must have swallowed something.

    YASHA: (*Contemptuously.*) What ignorance . . .

    LYUBOV ANDREEVNA: We're leaving—and not a soul will be left here . . .

    LOPAKHIN: Until springtime.

    VARYA: (*Pulls and umbrella out of a bundle—it appears as if she were about to strike someone; Lopakhin pretends to be frightened.*) What's wrong with you? . . . I wouldn't think of it . . .

115   **TROFIMOV:** Ladies and gentlemen, please, let's get into the carriages now . . . It's time to go! The train will arrive any minute!

    VARYA: Petya, here they are, your galoshes, beside the suitcase. (*In tears.*) Look how old and muddy they are . . .

    TROFIMOV: (*Putting on his galoshes.*) We're off, ladies and gentlemen!

    GAEV: (*Very confused, afraid of bursting into tears.*) Train . . . station . . . "Croisé into the middle pocket, Double the white into the corner . . ."

    LYUBOV ANDREEVNA: We're off!

120 **LOPAKHIN:** Is everyone here? No one left behind? (*Locks the side door stage left.*) There are some things stored in here, better lock up. We're off!

ANYA: Good-bye, house! Good-bye, old life!

TROFIMOV: Hello, new life! . . . (*Exits with Anya.*)

Varya glances around the room and exits without hurrying. Exit Yasha, and Charlotta, with the little dog,

LOPAKHIN: And so, until springtime. Come now, ladies and gentlemen, we'd better be going . . . Once more, a very good-bye!! . . . (*Exits.*)

Lyubov Andreevna and Gaev are left alone together. It is as if they have been waiting for this moment; they throw themselves into each other's arms and sob quietly, with restraint, fearing they might be heard.

GAEV: (*In despair.*) My sister, my sister . . .

125 **LYUBOV ANDREEVNA:** O my precious orchard, my sweet, lovely orchard! . . . My life, my youth, my happiness, farewell! . . . Farewell! . . .

(*Anya's voice calls out, merrily: "Mama! . . ."*)

(*Trofimov's voice calls out, gaily, excitedly: "A-oo! . . ."*)

LYUBOV ANDREEVNA: For the last time, let me look at these walls, these windows . . . how my mother loved to walk about this room . . .

GAEV: My sister, my sister! . . .

(*Anya's voice: "Mamma! . . ."*)

(*Trofimov's voice: "A-oo . . ."*)

LYUBOV ANDREEVNA: We're off! . . .

(*They exit.*)

(*The stage is empty. There is the sound of all the doors being locked, and then of the carriages pulling away. It grows very still. Through the stillness comes the remote sound of the axe falling on a tree, a lonely, melancholy sound. Footsteps are heard. Firs appears at the door, stage right. He is dressed, as always, in a jacket and a white waistcoat, with slippers on his feet. He is ill.*)

FIRS: (*Goes to the door, tries the handle.*) Locked! They've gone . . . (*Sits on the sofa.*) They've forgotten about me . . . Never mind . . . I'll sit here for just a bit . . . And Leonid Andreich, most likely, didn't put his fur coat on, went off wearing his light one . . . (*Sighs, anxiously.*) Just slipped my notice . . . These young people nowadays! (*Mutters something incomprehensible.*) And life has passed by, somehow, as if I never lived it at all. (*Lies down.*) I'll lie down for just a bit . . . Don't have too much strength left, now, do you, no, not much, not much at all . . . You pathetic old fool, you! . . . (*Lies there, immobile.*)

(*A distant sound is heard, as if coming from the sky, the sound of a breaking string, dying away, a mournful sound. Silence falls, and all that is heard, far off in the orchard, is the sound of the axe falling on a tree.*)

(*Curtain.*)

Edward Albee, 1928–

The Sandbox *1960*

CHARACTERS

The Young Man, *twenty-five, a good-looking, well-built boy in a bathing suit.*

Mommy, *fifty-five, a well-dressed, imposing woman.*

Daddy, *sixty, a small man; gray, thin.*

Grandma, *eighty-six, a tiny, wizened woman with bright eyes.*

The Musician, *no particular age, but young would be nice.*

NOTE:

When, in the course of the play, Mommy and Daddy call each other by these names, there should be no suggestion of regionalism. These names are of empty affection and point up the pre-senility and vacuity of their characters.

THE SCENE:

A bare stage, with only the following: near the footlights, far stage-right, two simple chairs set side by side, facing the audience; near the footlights, far stage-left, a chair facing stage-right with a music stand before it; farther back, and stage-center, slightly elevated and raked, a large child's sandbox with a toy pail and shovel; the background is the sky, which alters from brightest day to deepest night.

At the beginning, it is brightest day; the Young Man is alone on stage, to the rear of the sandbox, and to one side. He is doing calisthenics; he does calisthenics until quite at the very end of the play. These calisthenics, employing the arms only, should suggest the beating and fluttering of wings. The Young Man is, after all, the Angel of Death.

Mommy and Daddy enter from stage-left, Mommy first.

MOMMY: (*Motioning to Daddy*) Well, here we are; this is the beach.

DADDY: (*Whining*) I'm cold.

MOMMY: (*Dismissing him with a little laugh*) Don't be silly; it's as warm as toast. Look at that nice young man over there: he doesn't think it's cold. (*Waves to the Young Man.*) Hello.

YOUNG MAN: (*With an endearing smile*) Hi!

5   **MOMMY:** (*Looking about*) This will do perfectly . . . don't you think so, Daddy? There's sand there . . . and the water beyond. What do you think, Daddy?

DADDY: (*Vaguely*) Whatever you say, Mommy.

MOMMY: (*With the same little laugh*) Well, of course . . . whatever I say. Then, it's settled, is it?

DADDY: (*Shrugs*) She's *your* mother, not mine.

MOMMY: *I* know she's my mother. What do you take me for? (*A pause.*) All right, now; let's get on with it. (*She shouts into the wings, stage-left.*) You! Out there! You can come in now.

(*The Musician enters, seats himself in the chair, stage-left, places music on the music stand, is ready to play. Mommy nods approvingly.*)

10   **MOMMY:** Very nice; very nice. Are you ready, Daddy? Let's go get Grandma.

DADDY: Whatever you say, Mommy.

MOMMY: (*Leading the way out, stage-left*) Of course, Whatever I say. (*To the Musician.*) You can begin now.

(*The Musician begins playing; Mommy and Daddy exit; the Musician, all the while playing, nods to the Young Man.*)

YOUNG MAN: (*With the same endearing smile*) Hi!

(*After a moment, Mommy and Daddy re-enter, carrying Grandma. She is borne in by their hands under her armpits; she is quite rigid; her legs are brawn up; her feet do not touch the ground; the expression on her ancient face is that of puzzlement and fear.*)

DADDY: Where do we put her?

15 **MOMMY:** (*The same little laugh*) Wherever I say, of course. Let me see . . . well . . . all right, over there . . . in the sandbox. (*Pause.*) Well, what are you waiting for, Daddy? . . . The sandbox!

(*Together they carry Grandma over to the sandbox and more or less dump her in.*)

GRANDMA: (*Righting herself to a sitting position; her voice a cross between a baby's laugh and cry*) Ahhhhhh! Graaaaa!

DADDY: (*Dusting himself*) What do we do now?

MOMMY: (*To the Musician*) You can stop now.

(*The Musician stops.*)

(*Back to Daddy.*) What do you mean, what do we do now? We go over there and sit down, of course. (*To the Young Man.*) Hello there.

YOUNG MAN: (*Again smiling*) Hi!

(*Mommy and Daddy move to the chairs, stage-right, and sit down. A pause.*)

20 **GRANDMA:** (*Same as before*) Ahhhhhh! Ah-haaaaaa! Graaaaaa!

DADDY: Do you think . . . do you think she's . . . comfortable?

MOMMY: (*Impatiently*) How would I know?

DADDY: (*Pause*) What do we do now?

MOMMY: (*As if remembering*) We . . . wait. We . . . sit here . . . and we wait that's what we do.

25 **DADDY:** (*After a pause*) Shall we talk to each other?

MOMMY: (*With that little laugh; picking something off her dress*) Well, you can talk, if you want to . . . if you can think of anything to *say* . . . if you can think of anything *new*.

DADDY: (*Thinks*) No . . . I suppose not.

MOMMY: (*With a triumphant laugh*) Of course not!

GRANDMA: (*Banging the toy shovel against the pail*) Haaaaaa! Ah-haaaaaa!

30 **MOMMY:** (*Out over the audience*) Be quiet, Grandma . . . just be quiet, and wait.

(*Grandma throws a shovelful of sand at Mommy.*)

MOMMY: (*Still out over the audience*) She's throwing sand at me! You stop that, Grandma; you stop throwing sand at Mommy! (*To Daddy.*) She's throwing sand at me.

(*Daddy looks around at Grandma, who screams at him.*)

GRANDMA: GRAAAAAA!

MOMMY: Don't look at her. Just . . . sit here . . . be very still . . . and wait. (*To the Musician.*) You . . . uh . . . you go ahead and do whatever it is you do.

(*The Musician plays.*)

(*Mommy and Daddy are fixed, staring out beyond the audience. Grandma looks at them, looks at the Musician, looks at the sandbox, throws down the shovel.*)

GRANDMA: Ah-haaaaaa! Graaaaaa! (*Looks for reaction; gets none. Now . . . directly to the audience.*) Honestly! What a way to treat an old woman! Drag her out of the house . . . stick her in a car . . . bring her out here from the city . . . dump her in a pile of sand . . . and leave her here to set. I'm eighty-six years old! I was married when I was seventeen. To a farmer. He died when I was thirty. (*To the Musician.*) Will you stop that, please?

(*The Musician stops playing.*)

I'm a feeble old woman . . . how do you expect anybody to hear me over that peep! peep! peep! (*To herself.*) There's no respect around here. (*To the Young Man.*) There's no respect around here!

35 YOUNG MAN: (*Same smile*) Hi!

GRANDMA: (*After a pause, a mild double-take, continues, to the audience*) My husband died when I was thirty (*Indicates Mommy*), and I had to raise that big cow over there all by my lonesome. You can imagine what *that* was like. Lordy! (*To the Young Man.*) Where'd they get *you*?

YOUNG MAN: Oh . . . I've been around for a while.

GRANDMA: I'll bet you have! Heh, heh, heh. Will you look at you!

YOUNG MAN: (*Flexing his muscles*) Isn't that something? (*Continues his calisthenics.*)

40 GRANDMA: Boy, oh boy; I'll say. Pretty good.

YOUNG MAN: (*Sweetly*) I'll say.

GRANDMA: Where ya from?

YOUNG MAN: Southern California.

GRANDMA: (*Nodding*) Figgers; figgers. What's your name, honey?

45   **YOUNG MAN:** I don't know. . . .

    GRANDMA: (*To the audience*) Bright, too!

    YOUNG MAN: I mean . . . I mean, they haven't given me one yet . . . the studio . . .

    GRANDMA: (*Giving him the once-over*) You don't say . . . you don't say. Well . . . uh, I've got to talk some more . . . don't you go 'way.

    YOUNG MAN: Oh, no.

50   **GRANDMA:** (*Turning her attention back to the audience*) Fine; fine. (*Then, once more, back to the Young Man.*) You're . . . you're an actor, hunh?

    YOUNG MAN: (*Beaming*) Yes. I am.

    GRANDMA: (*To the audience again; shrugs*) I'm smart that way. *Anyhow,* I had to raise . . . *that* over there all by my lonesome; and what's next to her there . . . that's what she married. Rich? I tell you . . . money, money, money. They took me off the *farm* . . . which was real decent of them . . . and they moved me into the big town house with *them* . . . fixed a nice place for me under the stove . . . gave me an army blanket . . . and my own dish . . . my very own dish! So, what have I got to complain about? Nothing, of course. I'm not complaining. (*She looks up at the sky, shouts to someone off stage.*) Shouldn't it be getting dark now, dear?

(*The lights dim; night comes on. The Musician begins to play; it becomes deepest night. There are spots on all the players, including the Young Man, who is, of course, continuing his calisthenics.*)

    DADDY: (*Stirring*) It's nighttime.

    MOMMY: Shhhh. Be still . . . wait.

55   **DADDY:** (*Whining*) It's so hot.

    MOMMY: Shhhhhh. Be still . . . wait.

    GRANDMA: (*To herself*) That's better. Night. (*To the Musician.*) Honey, do you play all through this part?

(*The Musician nods.*)

Well, keep it nice and soft; that's a good boy.

(*The Musician nods again; plays softly.*)

That's nice.

(*There is an off-stage rumble.*)

    DADDY: (*Starting*) What was that?

MOMMY: (*Beginning to weep*) It was nothing.

60 **DADDY:** It was ... it was ... thunder ... or a wave breaking ... or something.

MOMMY: (*Whispering, through her tears*) It was an off-stage rumble ... and you know what *that* means ...

DADDY: I forget. . . .

MOMMY: (*Barely able to talk*) It means the time has come for poor Grandma ... and I can't bear it!

DADDY: (*Vacantly*) I ... I suppose you've got to be brave.

65 **GRANDMA:** (*Mocking*) That's right, kid; be brave. You'll bear up; you'll get over it.

(*Another off-stage rumble ... louder.*)

MOMMY: Ohhhhhhhhhh ... poor Grandma ... poor Grandma. . . .

GRANDMA: (*To Mommy*) I'm fine! I'm all right! It hasn't happened yet!

(*A violent off-stage rumble. All the lights go out, save the spot on the Young Man; the Musician stops playing.*)

MOMMY: Ohhhhhhhhhh. . . . Ohhhhhhhhhh. . . .

(*Silence.*)

GRANDMA: Don't put the lights up yet ... I'm not ready; I'm not quite ready. (*Silence.*) All right, dear ... I'm about done.

(*The lights come up again, to brightest day; the Musician begins to play. Grandma is discovered, still in the sandbox, lying on her side, propped up on an elbow, half covered, busily shoveling sand over herself.*)

70 **GRANDMA:** (*Muttering*) I don't know how I'm supposed to do any-thing with this goddam toy shovel. . . .

DADDY: Mommy! It's daylight!

MOMMY: (*Brightly*) So it is! Well! Our long night is over. We must put away our tears, take off our mourning ... and face the future. It's our duty.

GRANDMA: (*Still shoveling; mimicking*) ... take off our mourning ... face the future. . . . Lordy!

(*Mommy and Daddy rise, stretch. Mommy waves to the Young Man.*)

YOUNG MAN: (*With that smile*) Hi!

(Grandma plays dead. (!) Mommy and Daddy go over to look at her; she is a lit-tle more than half buried in the sand; the toy shovel is in her hands, which are crossed on her breast.)

75 **MOMMY**: *(Before the sandbox; shaking her head)* Lovely! It's . . . it's hard to be sad . . . she looks . . . so happy. *(With pride and conviction.)* It pays to do things well. *(To the Musician.)* All right, you can stop now, if you want to. I mean, stay around for a swim, or some-thing; it's all right with us. *(She sighs heavily.)* Well, Daddy . . . off we go.

DADDY: Brave Mommy!

MOMMY: Brave Daddy!

(They exit, stage-left.)

GRANDMA: *(After they leave; lying quite still)* It pays to do things well. . . . Boy, oh boy! *(She tries to sit up.)* . . . well, kids . . . *(But she finds she can't)* . . . I . . . I can't get up. I . . . I can't move. . . .

(The Young Man stops his calisthenics, nods to the Musician, walks over to Grandma, kneels down by the sandbox.)

GRANDMA: I . . . can't move. . . .

80 **YOUNG MAN**: Shhhhh . . . be very still. . . .

GRANDMA: I . . . I can't move. . . .

YOUNG MAN: Uh . . . ma'am; I . . . I have a line here.

GRANDMA: Oh, I'm sorry, sweetie; you go right ahead.

YOUNG MAN: I am . . . uh . . .

85 **GRANDMA**: Take your time, dear.

YOUNG MAN: *(Prepares; delivers the line like a real amateur)* I am the Angel of Death. I am . . . uh . . . I am come for you.

GRANDMA: What . . . wha . . . *(Then, with resignation.)* . . . ohhhh . . . ohhhh, I see.

(The Young Man bends over, kisses Grandma gently on the forehead.)

GRANDMA: *(Her eyes closed, her hands folded on her breast again, the shovel between her hands, a sweet smile on her face)* Well . . . that was very nice, dear. . . .

YOUNG MAN: *(Still kneeling)* Shhhhhh . . . be still. . . .

90 **GRANDMA**: What I meant was . . . you did that very well, dear. . . .

YOUNG MAN: *(Blushing)* . . . oh . . .

GRANDMA: No; I mean it. You've got that . . . you've got a quality.

YOUNG MAN: (*With his endearing smile*) Oh . . . thank you; thank you very much . . . ma'am.

GRANDMA: (*Slowly; softly — as the young Man puts his hands on top of Grandma's*) You're . . . you're welcome . . . dear.

(*Tableau. The Musician continues to play as the curtain slowly comes down.*)
(*Curtain*)

Sam Shepard, 1943–

True West *1980*

CHARACTERS

Austin, *early thirties, light blue sports shirt, light tan*
cardigan sweater, clean blue jeans, white tennis shoes

Lee, *his older brother, early forties, filthy white t-shirt,*
tattered brown overcoat covered with dust, dark blue
baggy suit pants from the Salvation Army, pink suede
belt, pointed black forties dress shoes scuffed up, holes in
the soles, no socks, no hat, long pronounced sideburns,
"Gene Vincent" hairdo, two days' growth of beard,
bad teeth.

Saul Kimmer, *late forties, Hollywood producer, pink*
and white flower print sports shirt, white sports coat with
matching polyester slacks, black and white loafers

Mom, *early sixties, mother of the brothers, small woman,*
conservative white skirt and matching jacket, red shoulder
bag, two pieces of matching red luggage.

SCENE.

All nine scenes take place on the same set; a kitchen and adjoining alcove of an older home in a Southern California suburb, about 40 miles east of Los Angeles. The kitchen takes up most of the playing area to stage left. The kitchen consists of a sink, upstage center, surrounded by counter space, a wall telephone, cupboards, and a small window just above it bordered by neat yellow curtains. Stage left of sink is a stove. Stage right, a refrigerator. The alcove adjoins the kitchen to stage right. There is no wall division or door to the alcove. It is open and easily accessible from the kitchen and defined only by the objects in it: a small round glass breakfast table mounted on white iron legs, two matching white iron chairs set across from each other. The two exterior walls of the alcove which prescribe a corner in the upstage right are composed of many small windows, beginning from a solid wall about three feet high and extending to the ceiling. The windows look out to bushes and citrus trees. The alcove is filled with all sorts of house plants in various pots, mostly Boston ferns hanging in planters at different levels. The floor of the alcove is composed of green synthetic grass.

All entrances and exits are made stage left from the kitchen. There is no door. The actors simply go off and come onto the playing area.

NOTE ON SET AND COSTUME.

The set should be constructed realistically with no attempt to distort its dimensions, shapes, objects, or colors. No objects should be introduced which might draw special attention to themselves other than the props demanded by the script. If a stylistic "concept" is grafted onto the set design it will only serve to confuse the evolution of the characters' situation, which is the most important focus of the play.

Likewise, the costumes should be exactly representative of who the characters are and not added onto for the sake of making a point to the audience.

NOTE ON SOUND.

The Coyote of Southern California has a district yapping, dog-like bark, similar to a Hyena. This yapping grows more intense and maniacal as the pack grows in numbers, which is usually the case when they lure and kill pets from suburban yards. The sense of growing frenzy in the pack should be felt in the background, particularly in Scenes 7 and 8. In any case, these Coyotes never make the long, mournful, solitary howl of the Hollywood stereotype.

The sound of Crickets can speak for itself.

These sounds should also be treated realistically even though they sometimes grow in volume and numbers.

ACT I

SCENE I

Night. Sound of cricket in dark. Candlelight appears in alcove, illuminating Austin, seated at glass table hunched over a writing notebook, pen in hand, cigarette burning in ashtray, cup of coffee, typewriter on table, stacks of paper, candle burning on table.

Soft moonlight fills kitchen illuminating Lee, beer in hand, six-pack on counter behind him. He's leaning against the sink, mildly drunk; takes a slug of beer.

LEE: So, Mom took off for Alaska, huh?

AUSTIN: Yeah.

LEE: Sorta' left you in charge.

AUSTIN: Well, she knew I was coming down here so she offered me the place.

5   LEE: You keepin' the plants watered?

AUSTIN: Yeah.

LEE: Keepin' the sink clean? She don't like even a single tea leaf in the sink ya' know.

AUSTIN: *(Trying to concentrate on writing)* Yeah, I know.

(Pause)

LEE: She gonna' be up there a long time?

10   AUSTIN: I don't know.

LEE: Kinda' nice for you, huh? Whole place to yourself.

AUSTIN: Yeah, it's great.

LEE: Ya' got crickets anyway. Tons a' crickets out there. *(Looks around kitchen)* Ya' got groceries? Coffee?

AUSTIN: *(Looking up from writing)* What?

15   LEE: You got coffee?

AUSTIN: Yeah.

LEE: At's good. *(Short pause)* Real coffee? From the bean?

AUSTIN: Yeah. You want some?

LEE: Naw. I brought some uh—*(Motions to beer)*

20   AUSTIN: Help yourself to whatever's—*(Motions to refrigerator)*

LEE: I will. Don't worry about me. I'm not the one to worry about. I mean I can uh—*(Pause)* You always work by candlelight?

AUSTIN: No—uh—not always.

LEE: Just sometimes?

AUSTIN: (*Puts pen down, rubs his eyes*) Yeah. Sometimes it's soothing.

25 LEE: Isn't that what the old guys did?

AUSTIN: What old guys?

LEE: The Forefathers. You know.

AUSTIN: Forefathers?

LEE: Isn't that what they did? Candlelight burning into the night? Cabins in the wilderness.

30 AUSTIN: (*Rubs hand through his hair*) I suppose.

LEE: I'm not botherin' you am I? I mean I don't wanna break into yer uh—concentration or nothin'.

AUSTIN: No, it's all right.

LEE: That's good. I mean I realize that yer line a' work demands a lota' concentration.

AUSTIN: It's okay.

35 LEE: You probably think that I'm not fully able to comprehend somethin' like that, huh?

AUSTIN: Like what?

LEE: That stuff yer doin'. That art. You know. Whatever you call it.

AUSTIN: It's just a little research.

LEE: You may not know it but I did a little art myself once.

40 AUSTIN: You did?

LEE: Yeah! I did some a' that. I fooled around with it. No future in it.

AUSTIN: What'd you do?

LEE: Never mind what I did! Just never mind about that. (*Pause*) It was ahead of its time.

(*Pause*)

AUSTIN: So, you went out to see the old man, huh?

45 LEE: Yeah, I seen him.

AUSTIN: How's he doing?

LEE: Same. He's doin' just about the same.

AUSTIN: I was down there too, you know.

LEE: What d'ya' want, an award? You want some kinda' medal? You were down there. He told me all about you.

50 AUSTIN: What'd he say?

LEE: He told me. Don't worry.

(*Pause*)

AUSTIN: Well—

LEE: You don't have to say nothin'.

AUSTIN: I wasn't.

55 LEE: Yeah, you were gonna' make somethin' up. Somethin' brilliant.

(*Pause*)

AUSTIN: You going to be down here very long, Lee?

LEE: Might be. Depends on a few things.

AUSTIN: You got some friends down here?

LEE: (*Laughs*) I know a few people. Yeah.

60 AUSTIN: Well, you can stay here as long as I'm here.

LEE: I don't need your permission do I?

AUSTIN: No.

LEE: I mean she's my mother too, right?

AUSTIN: Right.

65 LEE: She might've just as easily asked me to take care of her places as you.

AUSTIN: That's right.

LEE: I mean I know how to water plants.

(*Long pause*)

AUSTIN: So you don't know how long you'll be staying then?

LEE: Depends mostly on houses, ya' know.

70 AUSTIN: Houses?

LEE: Yeah. Houses. Electric devices. Stuff like that. I gotta' make a little tour first.

(*Short pause*)

AUSTIN: Lee, why don't you just try another neighborhood, all right?

LEE: (*Laughs*) What'sa' matter with this neighborhood? This is a great neighborhood. Lush. Good class a' people. Not many dogs.

AUSTIN: Well, our uh—Our mother just happens to live here. That's all.

75   LEE: Nobody's gonna' know. All they know is somethin's missing. That's all. She'll never even hear about it. Nobody's
gonna' know.

  AUSTIN: You're going to get picked up if you start walking
around here at night.

  LEE: Me? I'm gonna' git picked up? What about you? You stick out
like a sore thumb. Look at you. You think yer regular lookin'?

  AUSTIN: I've got too much to deal with here to be worrying about—

  LEE: Yer not gonna' have to worry about me! I've been doin' all
right without you. I haven't been anywhere near you for five
years! Now isn't that true?

80   AUSTIN: Yeah.

  LEE: So you don't have to worry about me. I'm a free agent.

  AUSTIN: All right.

  LEE: Now all I wanna' do is borrow yer car.

  AUSTIN: No!

85   LEE: Just fer a day. One day.

  AUSTIN: No!

  LEE: I won't take it outside a twenty mile radius. I promise ya'.
You can check the speedometer.

  AUSTIN: You're not borrowing my car! That's all there is to it.

(Pause)

  LEE: Then I'll just take the damn thing.

90   AUSTIN: Lee, look—I don't want any trouble, all right?

  LEE: That's dumb line. That is a dumb fuckin' line. You git paid
fer dreamin' up a line like that?

  AUSTIN: Look, I can give you some money if you need money.

*(Lee suddenly lunges at Austin, grabs him violently by the shirt and shakes him with
tremendous power)*

  LEE: Don't you say that to me! Don't you ever say that to me! (*Just
as suddenly he turns him loose, pushes him away and backs off*) You may be
able to git away with that with the Old Man. Git him tanked up
for a week! Buy him off with yer Hollywood blood money, but
not me! I can git my own money my own way. Big money!

  AUSTIN: I was just making an offer.

95   LEE: Yeah, well keep it to yourself!

(*Long pause*)

Those are the most monotonous fuckin' crickets I ever heard in my life.

AUSTIN: I kinda' like the sound.

LEE: Yeah. Supposed to be able to tell the temperature by the number a' pulses. You believe that?

AUSTIN: The temperature?

LEE: Yeah. The air. How hot it is.

100   AUSTIN: How do you do that?

LEE: I don't know. Some woman told me that. She was a botanist. So I believed her.

AUSTIN: Where'd you meet her?

LEE: What?

AUSTIN: The woman botanist?

105   LEE: I met her on the desert. I been spendin' a lota' time on the desert.

AUSTIN: What were you doing out there?

LEE: (*Pause, stares in space*) I forgit. Had me a pit bull there for a while but I lost him.

AUSTIN: Pit bull?

LEE: Fightin' dog. Damn I made some good money off that little dog. Real good money.

(*Pause*)

110   AUSTIN: You could come up north with me, you know.

LEE: What's up there?

AUSTIN: My family.

LEE: Oh, that's right, you got the wife and kiddies now don't ya'. The house, the car, the whole slam. That's right.

AUSTIN: You could spend a couple days. See how you like it. I've got an extra room.

115   LEE: Too cold up there.

(*Pause*)

AUSTIN: You want to sleep for a while?

LEE: (*Pause, stares at Austin*) I don't sleep.

(*Lights to black*)

SCENE 2

Morning. Austin is watering plants with a vaporizer, Lee sits at glass table in alcove drinking beer.

LEE: I never realized the old lady was so security-minded.

AUSTIN: How do you mean?

LEE: Made a little tour this morning. She's got locks on everything. Locks and double-locks and chain locks and—What's she got that's so valuable?

AUSTIN: Antiques I guess. I don't know.

5 LEE: Antiques? Brought everything with her from the old place, huh. Just the same crap we always had around. Plates and spoons.

AUSTIN: I guess they have personal value to her.

LEE: Personal value. Yeah. Just a lota' junk. Most of it's phony anyway. Idaho decals. Now who in the hell wants to eat offa' plate with the State of Idaho starin' ya' in the face. Every time ya' take a bite ya' get to see a little bit more.

AUSTIN: Well it must mean something to her or she wouldn't save it.

LEE: Yeah, well personally I don't wann' be invaded by Idaho when I'm eatin'. When I'm eatin' I'm home. Ya' know what I'm sayin'? I'm not driftin', I'm home. I don't need my thoughts swept off to Idaho. I don't need that!

(Pause)

10 AUSTIN: Did you go out last night?

LEE: Why?

AUSTIN: I thought I heard you go out.

LEE: Yeah, I went out. What about it?

AUSTIN: Just wondered.

15 LEE: Damn coyotes kept me awake.

AUSTIN: Oh yeah, I heard them. They must've killed somebody's dog or something.

LEE: Yappin' their fool heads off. They don't yap like that on the desert. They howl! These are city coyotes here.

AUSTIN: Well, you don't sleep anyway do you?

(Pause, Lee stares at him)

LEE: You're pretty smart aren't ya?

20 AUSTIN: How do you mean?

LEE: I mean you never had any more on the ball than I did. But here you are gettin' invited into prominent people's houses. Sittin' around talkin' like you know somethin'.

AUSTIN: They're not so prominent.

LEE: They're a helluva' lot more prominent than the houses I get invited into.

AUSTIN: Well you invite yourself.

25 LEE: That's right. I do. In fact I probably got a wider range a' choices than you do, come to think of it.

AUSTIN: I wouldn't doubt it.

LEE: In fact I been inside some pretty classy places in my time. And I never even went to an Ivy League school either.

AUSTIN: You want some breakfast or something?

LEE: Breakfast?

30 AUSTIN: Yeah. Don't you eat breakfast?

LEE: Look, don't worry about me pal. I can take care a' myself. You just go ahead as though I wasn't even here, all right?

(*Austin goes into kitchen, makes coffee*)

AUSTIN: Where'd you walk to last night?

(*Pause*)

LEE: I went up in the foothills there. Up in the San Gabriels. Heat was driven' me crazy.

AUSTIN: Well, wasn't it hot out on the desert?

35 LEE: Different kinda' heat. Out there it's clean. Cools off at night. There's a nice little breeze.

AUSTIN: Where were you, the Mojave?

LEE: Yeah. The Mojave. That's right.

AUSTIN: I haven't been out there in years.

LEE: Out past Needles there.

40 AUSTIN: Oh yeah.

LEE: Up here it's different. This country's real different.

AUSTIN: Well, it's been built up.

LEE: Built up? Wiped out is more like it. I don't even hardly recognize it.

AUSTIN: Yeah. Foothills are the same though, aren't they?

45   LEE: Pretty much. It's funny goin' up in there. The smells and everything. Used to catch snakes up there, remember?

AUSTIN: You caught snakes.

LEE: Yeah. And you'd pretend you were Geronimo or some damn thing. You used to go right out to lunch.

AUSTIN: I enjoyed my imagination.

LEE: That what you call it. Looks like yer still enjoyin' it.

50   AUSTIN: So you just wandered around up there, huh?

LEE: Yeah. With a purpose.

AUSTIN: See any houses?

(*Pause*)

LEE: Couple. Couple a' real nice ones. One of 'em didn't even have a dog. Walked right up and stuck my head in the window. Not a peep. Just a sweet kinda' surburban silence.

AUSTIN: What kind of a place was it?

55   LEE: Like a paradise. Kinda' place that sorta' kills ya' inside. Warm yellow lights. Mexican tile all around. Copper pots hangin' over the stove. Ya' know like they got in the magazines. Blonde people movin' in and outa' the rooms, talkin' to each other. (*Pause*) Kinda' place you wish you sorta' grew up in, ya know.

AUSTIN: That's the kind of place you wish you'd grown up in?

LEE: Yeah, why not?

AUSTIN: In thought you hated that kind of stuff.

LEE: Yeah, well you never knew too much about me did ya'?

(*Pause*)

60   AUSTIN: Why'd you go out to the desert in the first place?

LEE: I was on my way to see the old man.

AUSTIN: You mean you just passed through there?

LEE: Yeah. That's right. Three months of passin' through.

AUSTIN: Three months?

65   LEE: Somethin' like that. Maybe more. Why?

AUSTIN: You lived on the Mojave for three months?

LEE: Yeah. What'sa' matter with that?

AUSTIN: By yourself?

LEE: Mostly. Had a couple a' visitors. Had that dog for a while.
70 AUSTIN: Didn't you miss people?
LEE: (*Laughs*) People?
AUSTIN: Yeah. I mean I go crazy if I have to spend three nights in a motel by myself.
LEE: Yer not in a motel now.
AUSTIN: No, I know. But sometimes I have to stay in motels.
75 LEE: Well, they got people in motels don't they?
AUSTIN: Strangers
LEE: Yer friendly aren't ya'? Aren't you the friendly type?

(*Pause*)

AUSTIN: I'm going to have somebody coming by here later, Lee.
LEE: Ah! Lady friend?
80 AUSTIN: No, a producer.
LEE: Aha! What's he produce?
AUSTIN: Film. Movies. You know.
LEE: Oh, movies. Motion Pictures! A big wig huh?
AUSTIN: Yeah.
85 LEE: What's he comin' by here for?
AUSTIN: We have to talk about a project.
LEE: Whadya' mean, "a project"? What's "a project"?
AUSTIN: A script.
LEE: Oh. That's what yer doin' with all these papers?
90 AUSTIN: Yeah.
LEE: Well, what's the project about?
AUSTIN: We're uh—it's a period piece.
LEE: What's a "period piece"?
AUSTIN: Look, it doesn't matter. The main thing is we need to discuss this alone. I mean—
95 LEE: Oh, I get it. You want me outa' the picture.
AUSTIN: Not exactly. I just need to be alone with him for a couple of hours. So we can talk.
LEE: Yer afraid I'll embarrass ya' huh?
AUSTIN: I'm not afraid you'll embarrass me!
LEE: Well, I tell ya' what—Why don't you just gimme the keys to yer car and I'll be back here around six o'clock or so. That give ya' enough time?

100   **AUSTIN:** I'm not loaning you my car, Lee.

     LEE: You want me to just git lost huh? Take a hike? Is that it? Pound the pavement for a few hours while you bullshit yer way into a million bucks.

     AUSTIN: Look, it's going to be hard enough for me to face this character on my own without—

     LEE: You don't know this guy?

     AUSTIN: No I don't know—He's a producer. I mean I've been meeting with him for months but you never get to know a producer.

105   **LEE:** Yer tryin' to hustle him? Is that it?

     AUSTIN: I'm not trying to hustle him! I'm trying to work out a deal! It's not easy.

     LEE: What kinda' deal?

     AUSTIN: Convince him it's a worthwhile story.

     LEE: He's not convinced? How come he's comin' over here if he's not convinced? I'll convince him for ya'.

110   **AUSTIN:** You don't understand the way things work down here.

     LEE: How do things work down here?

(Pause)

     AUSTIN: Look, if I loan you my car will you have it back here by six?

     LEE: On the button. With a full tank a' gas.

     AUSTIN: *(Digging in his pocket for keys)* Forget about the gas.

115   **LEE:** Hey, these days gas is gold, old buddy.

(Austin hands the keys to Lee)

     You remember that car I used to loan you?

     AUSTIN: Yeah.

     LEE: Forty Ford. Flathead.

     AUSTIN: Yeah.

     LEE: Sucker hauled ass didn't it?

120   **AUSTIN:** Lee, it's not that I don't want to loan you my car—

     LEE: You are loanin' me yer car.

(Lee gives Austin a pat on the shoulder, pause)

     AUSTIN: I know. I just wish—

     LEE: What? You wish what?

AUSTIN: I don't know. I wish I wasn't—I wish I didn't have to be doing business down here. I'd like to just spend some time with you.

125 LEE: I thought it was "Art" you were doin'.

(*Lee moves across kitchen toward exit, tosses keys in his hand*)

AUSTIN: Try to get it back here by six, okay?

LEE: No sweat. Hey, ya' know, if that uh—story of yours doesn't go over with the guy—tell him I got a couple a' "projects" he might be interested in. Real commercial. Full a' suspense. True-to-life stuff.

(*Lee exits, Austin stares after Lee then turns, goes to papers at table, leafs through pages, lights fade to black*)

SCENE 3

Afternoon. Alcove, Saul Kimmer and Austin seated across from each other at table.

SAUL: Well, to tell you the truth Austin, I have never felt so confident about a project in quite a long time.

AUSTIN: Well, that's good to hear, Saul.

SAUL: I am absolutely convinced we can get this thing off the ground. I mean we'll have to make a sale to television and that means getting a major star. Somebody bankable. But I think we can do it. I really do.

AUSTIN: Don't you think we need a first draft before we approach a star?

5 SAUL: No, no, not at all. I don't think it's necessary. Maybe a brief synopsis. I don't want you to touch the typewriter until we have some seed money.

AUSTIN: That's fine with me.

SAUL: I mean it's a great story. Just the story alone. You've really managed to capture something this time.

AUSTIN: I'm glad you like it, Saul.

(*Lee enters abruptly into kitchen carrying a stolen television set, short pause*)

LEE: Aw shit, I'm sorry about that. I am really sorry Austin.

10 AUSTIN: (*Standing*) That's all right.

LEE: (*Moving toward them*) I mean I thought it was way past six already. You said to have it back here by six.

AUSTIN: We were just finishing up. (*To Saul*) This is my, uh—brother Lee.

SAUL: (*Standing*) Oh, I'm very happy to meet you.

(*Lee sets T.V. on sink counter, shakes hands with Saul*)

LEE: I can't tell ya' how happy I am to meet you sir.

15 SAUL: Saul Kimmer.

LEE: Mr. Kipper.

SAUL: Kimmer.

AUSTIN: Lee's been living out on the desert and he just uh—

SAUL: Oh, that's terrific! (*To Lee*) Palm Springs?

20 LEE: Yeah. Yeah, right. Right around in that area. Near uh—Bob Hope Drive there.

SAUL: Oh I love it out there. I just love it. The air is wonderful.

LEE: Yeah. Sure is. Healthy.

SAUL: And the golf. I don't know if you play golf, but the golf is just about the best.

LEE: I play a lota' golf.

25 SAUL: Is that right?

LEE: Yeah. In fact I was hoping I'd run into somebody out here who played a little golf. I've been lookin' for a partner.

SAUL: Well, I uh—

AUSTIN: Lee's just down for a visit while our mother's in Alaska.

SAUL: Oh, your mother's in Alaska?

30 AUSTIN: Yes She went up there on a little vacation. This is her place.

SAUL: I see. Well isn't that something. Alaska.

LEE: What kinda' handicap do ya' have, Mr. Kimmer?

SAUL: Oh I'm just a Sunday duffer really. You know.

LEE: That's good 'cause I haven't swung a club in months.

35 SAUL: Well we ought to get together sometime and have a little game. Austin, do you play?

(*Saul mimes a Johnny Carson golf swing for Austin*)

AUSTIN: No. I don't uh—I've watched it on T.V.

LEE: (*To Saul*) How 'bout tomorrow morning? Bright and early. We could get out there and put in eighteen holes before breakfast.

SAUL: Well, I've got uh—I have several appointments—

LEE: No, I mean real early. Crack a' dawn. While the dew's still thick on the fairway.

40 SAUL: Sounds really great.

LEE: Austin could be our caddie.

SAUL: Now that's an idea. (*Laughs*)

AUSTIN: I don't know the first thing about golf.

LEE: There's nothin' to it. Isn't that right, Saul? He'd pick it up in fifteen minutes.

45 SAUL: Sure. Doesn't take long. 'Course you have to play for years to find your true form. (*Chuckles*)

LEE: (*To Austin*) We'll give ya' a quick run-down on the club faces. The irons, the woods. Show ya' a couple pointers on the basic swing. Might even let ya' hit the ball a couple times. Whatya' think, Saul?

SAUL: Why not. I think it'd be great. I haven't had any exercise in weeks.

LEE: 'At's the spirit! We'll have a little orange juice right afterwards.

(*Pause*)

SAUL: Orange juice?

50 LEE: Yeah! Vitamin C! Nothin' like a shot a' orange juice after a round a' golf. Hot shower. Snappin' towels at each others' privates. Real sense a' fraternity.

SAUL: (*Smiles at Austin*) Well, you make it sound very inviting, I must say. It really does sound great.

LEE: Then it's a date.

SAUL: Well, I'll call the country club and see if I can arrange something.

LEE: Great! Boy, I sure am sorry that I busted in on ya' all in the middle of yer meeting.

55 SAUL: Oh that's quite all right. We were just about finished anyway.

LEE: I can wait out in the other room if you want.

SAUL: No really—

LEE: Just got Austin's color T.V. back from the shop. I can watch a little amateur boxing now.

(*Lee and Austin exchange looks*)

SAUL: Oh—Yes.

60 LEE: You don't fool around in television, do you Saul?

SAUL: Uh—I have in the past. Produced some T.V. Specials. Network stuff. But it's mainly features now.

LEE: That's where the big money is, huh?

SAUL: Yes. That's right.

AUSTIN: Why don't I call you tomorrow, Saul and we'll get together. We can have lunch or something.

65 SAUL: That'd be terrific.

LEE: Right after the golf.

(*Pause*)

SAUL: What?

LEE: You can have lunch right after the golf.

SAUL: Oh, right.

70 LEE: Austin was tellin' me that yer interested in stories.

SAUL: Well, we develop certain projects that we feel have commercial potential.

LEE: What kinda' stuff do ya' go in for?

SAUL: Oh, the usual. You know. Good love interest. Lots of action. (*Chuckles at Austin*)

LEE: Westerns?

75 SAUL: Sometimes.

AUSTIN: I'll give you a ring, Saul.

(*Austin tries to move Saul across the kitchen but Lee blocks their way*)

LEE: I got a Western that'd knock yer lights out.

SAUL: Oh really?

LEE: Yeah. Contemporary Western. Based on a true story. 'Course I'm not a writer like my brother here. I'm not a man of the pen.

80 SAUL: Well—

LEE: I mean I can tell ya' a story off the tongue but I can't put it down on paper. That don't make any difference though does it?

SAUL: No, not really.

LEE: I mean plenty a' guys have stories don't they? True-life stories. Musta' been a lota' movies made from real life.

SAUL: Yes. I suppose so.

85 LEE: I haven't seen a good Western since "Lonely Are the Brave."
You remember that movie?

SAUL: No, I'm afraid I—

LEE: Kirk Douglas. Helluva' movie. You remember that movie,
Austin?

AUSTIN: Yes.

LEE: (*To Saul*) The man dies for the love of a horse.

90 SAUL: Is that right.

LEE: Yeah. Ya' hear the horse screamin' at the end of it. Rain's
comin' down. Horse is screamin'. Then there's a shot.
BLAM! Just a single shot like that. Then nothin' but the
sound of rain. And Kirk Douglas is ridin' in the ambulance.
Ridin' away from the scene of the accident. And when he
hears that shot he knows that his horse has died. He knows.
And you see his eyes. And his eyes die. Right inside his
face. And then his eyes close. And you know that he's died
too. You know that Kirk Douglas has died from the death of
his horse.

SAUL: (*Eyes Austin nervously*) Well, it sounds like a great movie. I'm
sorry I missed it.

LEE: Yeah, you shouldn't a' missed that one.

SAUL: I'll have to try to catch it some time. Arrange a screening
or something. Well, Austin, I'll have to hit the freeway
before rush hour.

95 AUSTIN: (*Ushers him toward exit*) It's good seeing you, Saul.

(*Austin and Saul shake hands*)

LEE: So ya' think there's room for a real Western these days?
A true-to-life Western?

SAUL: Well, I don't see why not. Why don't you uh—tell the story
to Austin and have him write a little outline.

LEE: You'd take a look at it then?

SAUL: Yes. Sure. I'll give it a read-through. Always eager for new
material. (*Smiles at Austin*)

100 LEE: That's great! You'd really read it then huh?

SAUL: It would just be my opinion of course.

LEE: That's all I want. Just an opinion. I happen to think it has lota' possibilities.

SAUL: Well, it was great meeting you and I'll—

(*Saul and Lee shake*)

LEE: I'll call you tomorrow about the golf.

105 SAUL: Oh. Yes, right.

LEE: Austin's got your number, right?

SAUL: Yes.

LEE: So long Saul. (*Gives Saul a pat on the back*)

(*Saul exits, Austin turns to Lee, looks at T.V. then back to Lee*)

AUSTIN: Give me the keys.

(*Austin extends his hand toward Lee, Lee doesn't move, just stares at Austin, smiles, lights to black*)

SCENE 4

Night. Coyotes in distance, fade, sound of typewriter in dark, crickets, candlelight in alcove, dim light in kitchen, lights reveal Austin at glass table typing, Lee sits aross from him, foot on table, drinking beer and whiskey, the T.V. is still on sink counter, Austin types for a while, then stops.

LEE: All right, now read it back to me.

AUSTIN: I'm not reading it back to you, Lee. You can read it when we're finished. I can't spend all night on this.

LEE: You got better things to do?

AUSTIN: Let's just go ahead. Now what happens when he leaves Texas?

5 LEE: Is he ready to leave Texas yet? I didn't know we were that far along. He's not ready to leave Texas.

AUSTIN: He's right at the border.

LEE: (*Sitting up*) No, see this is one a' the crucial parts. Right here. (*Taps paper with beer can*) We can't rush through this. He's not right at the border. He's a good fifty miles from the border. A lot can happen in fifty miles.

AUSTIN: It's only an outline. We're not writing an entire script now.

LEE: Well ya' can't leave things out even if it is an outline. It's one a' the most important parts. Ya' can't go leavin' it out.

10 AUSTIN: Okay, okay. Let's just—get it done.

LEE: All right. Now. He's in the truck and he's got his horse trailer and his horse.

AUSTIN: We've already established that.

LEE: And he sees this other guy comin' up behind him in another truck. And that truck is pullin' a gooseneck.

AUSTIN: What's a gooseneck?

15 LEE: Cattle trailer. You know the kind with a gooseneck, goes right down in the bed a' the pick-up.

AUSTIN: Oh. All right. (*Types*)

LEE: It's important.

AUSTIN: Okay. I got it.

LEE: All these details are important.

(*Austin types as they talk*)

20 AUSTIN: I've got it.

LEE: An this other guy's got his horse all saddled up in the back a' the gooseneck.

AUSTIN: Right.

LEE: So both these guys have got their horse right along with 'em, see.

AUSTIN: I understand.

25 LEE: Then this first guy suddenly realizes two things.

AUSTIN: The guy in front?

LEE: Right. The guy in front realizes two things almost at the same time. Simultaneous.

AUSTIN: What were the two things?

LEE: Number one, the realizes that the guy behind him is the husband of the woman he's been—

(*Lee makes gesture of screwing by pumping his arm*)

30 AUSTIN: (*Sees Lee's gesture*) Oh. Yeah.

LEE: And number two, he realizes he's in the middle of Tornado Country.

AUSTIN: What's "Tornado Country"?

LEE: Panhandle.

AUSTIN: Panhandle?

35   LEE: Sweetwater. Around in that area. Nothin'. Nowhere. And number three—

AUSTIN: I thought there was only two.

LEE: There's three. There's a third unforseen realization.

AUSTIN: And what's that?

LEE: That he's runnin' outa' gas.

40   AUSTIN: (*Stops typing*) Come on, Lee.

(*Austin gets up, moves to kitchen, gets a glass of water*)

LEE: Whadya' mean, "come on"? That's what it is. Write it down! He's runnin' outa' gas.

AUSTIN: It's too—

LEE: What? It's too what? It's too real! That's what ya' mean isn't it? It's too much like real life!

AUSTIN: It's not like real life! It's not enough like real life. Things don't happen like that.

45   LEE: What! Men don't fuck other men's women?

AUSTIN: Yes. But they don't end up chasing each other across the Panhandle. Through "Tornado Country."

LEE: They do in this movie!

AUSTIN: And they don't have horses conveniently along with them when they run out of gas! And they don't run out of gas either!

LEE: These guys run outa' gas! This is my story and one a' these guys runs outa' gas!

50   AUSTIN: It's just a dumb excuse to get them into a chase scene. It's contrived.

LEE: It is a chase scene! It's already a chase scene. They been chasin' each other fer days.

AUSTIN: So now they're supposed to abandon their trucks, climb on their horses and chase each other into the mountains?

LEE: (*Standing suddenly*) There aren't any mountains in the Panhandle! It's flat!

(*Lee turns violently toward windows in alcove and throws beer can at them*)

LEE: Goddam these crickets! (*Yells at crickets*) Shut up out there! (*Pause, turns back towards table*) This place is like a fuckin' rest home here. How're you supposed to think!

55 AUSTIN: You wanna' take a break?

LEE: No, I don't wanna' take a break? I wanna' get this done! This is my last chance to get this done.

AUSTIN: (*Moves back into alcove*) All right. Take it easy.

LEE: I'm gonna' be leavin' this area. I don't have time to mess around here.

AUSTIN: Where are you going?

60 LEE: Never mind where I'm goin'! That's got nothin' to do with you. I just gotta' get this done. I'm not like you. Hangin' around bein' a parasite offa' other fools. I gotta' do this thing and get out.

(*Pause*)

AUSTIN: A parasite? Me?

LEE: Yeah, you!

AUSTIN: After you break into people's houses and take their televisions?

LEE: They don't need their television! I'm doin' them a service.

65 AUSTIN: Give me back my keys, Lee.

LEE: Not until you write this thing! You're gonna' write this outline thing for me or that car's gonna' wind up in Arizona with a different paint job.

AUSTIN: You think you can force me to write this? I was doing you a favor.

LEE: Git off yer high horse will ya'! Favor! Big favor. Handin' down favors from the mountain top.

AUSTIN: Let's just write it, okay? Let's sit down and not get upset and see if we can just get through this.

(*Austin sits at typewriter*)

(*Long pause*)

70 LEE: Yer not gonna' even show it to him, are ya'?

AUSTIN: What?

LEE: This outline. You got no intention of showin' it to him. Yer just doin' this 'cause yer afraid a' me.

AUSTIN: You can show it to him yourself.

LEE: I will, boy! I'm gonna' read it to him on the golf course.

75 AUSTIN: And I'm not afraid of you either.

LEE: Then how come yer doin' it?

AUSTIN: (Pause) So I can get my keys back.

(Pause as Lee takes keys out of his pocket slowly and throws them on table, long pause, Austin stares at keys)

LEE: There. Now you got yer keys back.

(Austin looks up at Lee but doesn't take keys)

LEE: Go ahead. There's yer keys.

(Austin slowly takes keys off table and puts them back in his own pocket)

Now what're you gonna' do? Kick me out?

80 AUSTIN: I'm not going to kick you out, Lee.

LEE: You couldn't kick me out, boy.

AUSTIN: I know.

LEE: So you can't even consider that one. (Pause) You could call the police. That'd be the obvious thing.

AUSTIN: You're my brother.

85 LEE: That don't mean a thing. You go down to the L.A. Police Department there and ask them what kinda' people kill each other the most. What do you think they'd say?

AUSTIN: Who said anything about killing?

LEE: Family people. Brothers. Brothers-in-law. Cousins. Real American-type people. They kill each other in the heat mostly. In the Smog-Alerts. In the Brush Fire Season. Right about this time a' year.

AUSTIN: This isn't the same.

LEE: Oh no? What makes it different?

90 AUSTIN: We're not insane. We're not driven to acts of violence like that. Not over a dumb movie script. Now sit down.

(Long pause, Lee considers which way to go with it)

LEE: Maybe not. (*He sits back down at table across from Austin*) Maybe you're right. Maybe we're too intelligent, huh? (*Pause*) We got our heads on our shoulders. One of us has even got a Ivy League diploma. Now that mean somethin' don't it? Doesn't that mean somethin'?

AUSTIN: Look, I'll write this thing for you, Lee. I don't mind writing it. I just don't want to get all worked up about it. It's not worth it. Now, come on. Let's just get through it, okay?

LEE: Nah. I think there's easier money. Lotsa' places I could pick up thousands. Maybe millions. I don't need this shit. I could go up to Sacramento Valley and steal me a diesel. Ten thousand a week dismantling one a' those suckers. Ten thousand a week!

(*Lee opens another beer, puts his foot back up on table*)

AUSTIN: No, really, look, I'll write it out for you. I think it's a great idea.

95 LEE: Nah, you got yer own work to do. I don't wanna' interfere with yer life.

AUSTIN: I mean it'd be really fantastic if you could sell this. Turn it into a movie. I mean it.

(*Pause*)

LEE: Ya' think so huh?

AUSTIN: Absolutely. You could really turn your life around, you know. Change things.

LEE: I could get me a house maybe.

100 AUSTIN: Sure you could get a house. You could get a whole ranch if you wanted to.

LEE: (*Laughs*) A ranch? I could get a ranch?

AUSTIN: Course you could. You know what a screenplay sells for these days?

LEE: No. What's it sell for?

AUSTIN: A lot. A whole lot of money.

105 LEE: Thousands?

AUSTIN: Yeah. Thousands.

LEE: Millions?

AUSTIN: Well—

LEE: We could get the old man outa' hock then.

110 AUSTIN: Maybe.

LEE: Maybe? Whadya' mean, maybe?

AUSTIN: I mean it might take more than money.

LEE: You were just tellin' me it'd change my whole life around. Why wouldn't it change his?

AUSTIN: He's different.

115 LEE: Oh, he's of a different ilk huh?

AUSTIN: He's not gonna' change. Let's leave the old man out of it.

LEE: That's right. He's not gonna' change but I will. I'll just turn myself right inside out. I could be just like you then, huh? Sittin' around dreamin' stuff up. Gettin' paid to dream. Ridin' back and forth on the freeway just dreamin' my fool head off.

AUSTIN: It's not all that easy.

LEE: It's not huh?

120 AUSTIN: No. There's lot of work involved.

LEE: What's the toughest part? Deciding whether to jog or play tennis?

(Long pause)

AUSTIN: Well, look. You can stay here—do whatever you want to. Borrow the car. Come in and out. Doesn't matter to me. It's not my house. I'll help you write this thing or—not. Just let me know what you want. You tell me.

LEE: Oh. So now suddenly you're at my service. Is that it?

AUSTIN: What do you want to do Lee?

(Long pause, Lee stares at him then turns and dreams at windows)

125 LEE: I tell ya' what I'd do if I still had that dog. Ya' wanna' know what I'd do?

AUSTIN: What?

LEE: Head out to Ventura. Cook up a little match. God that little dog could bear down. Lota' money in dog fightin'. Big money.

(Pause)

AUSTIN: Why don't we try to see this through, Lee. Just for the hell of it. Maybe you've really got something here. What do you think?

(*Pause, Lee considers*)

LEE: Maybe so. No harm in tryin' I guess. You think it's such a hot idea. Besides, I always wondered what'd be like to be you.

130 AUSTIN: You did?

LEE: Yeah, sure. I used to picture you walkin' around some campus with yer arms fulla' books. Blondes chasin' after ya'.

AUSTIN: Blondes? That's funny.

LEE: What's funny about it?

AUSTIN: Because I always used to picture you somewhere.

135 LEE: Where'd you picture me?

AUSTIN: Oh, I don't know. Different places. Adventures. You were always on some adventure.

LEE: Yeah.

AUSTIN: And I used to say to myself, "Lee's got the right idea. He's out there in the world and here I am. What am I doing?"

LEE: Well you were settin' yourself up for somethin'.

140 AUSTIN: I guess.

LEE: We better get started on this thing then.

AUSTIN: Okay.

(*Austin sits up at typewriter, puts new paper in*)

LEE: Oh. Can I get the keys back before I forget?

(*Austin hesitates*)

You said I could borrow the car if I wanted, right? Isn't that what you said?

AUSTIN: Yeah. Right.

(*Austin takes keys out of his pocket, sets them on table, Lee takes keys slowly, plays with them in his hand*)

145 LEE: I could get a ranch, huh?

AUSTIN: Yeah. We have to write it first though.

LEE: Okay. Let's write it.

(*Lights start dimming slowly to end of scene as Austin types, Lee speaks*)

So they take off after each other straight into an endless black prairie. The sun is just comin' down and they can feel the night on their backs. What they don't know is that each one of 'em is afraid, see. Each one separately thinks that he's the only one that's afraid. And they keep ridin' like that straight into the night. Not knowing. And the one who's chasin' doesn't know where the other one is taking him. And the one who's being chased doesn't know where he's going.

(*Lights to black, typing stops in the dark, crickets fade*)

ACT II

SCENE 5

Morning. Lee at the table in alcove with a set of golf clubs in a fancy leather bag, Austin at sink washing a few dishes.

AUSTIN: He really liked it, huh?

LEE: He wouldn't a' gave me these clubs if he didn't like it.

AUSTIN: He gave you the clubs?

LEE: Yeah. I told ya' he gave me the clubs. The bag too.

5   AUSTIN: I though he just loaned them to you.

LEE: He said it was part a' the advance. A little gift like. Gesture of his good faith.

AUSTIN: He's giving you an advance?

LEE: Now what's so amazing about that? I told ya' it was a good story. You even said it was a good story.

AUSTIN: Well that is really incredible Lee. You know how many guys spend their whole lives down here trying to break into this business? Just trying to get in the door?

10   LEE: (*Pulling clubs out of bag, testing them*) I got no idea. How many?

(*Pause*)

AUSTIN: How much of an advance is he giving you?

LEE: Plenty. We were talkin' big money out there. Ninth hole is where I sealed the deal.

AUSTIN: He made a firm commitment?

LEE: Absolutely.

15   AUSTIN: Well. I know Saul and he doesn't fool around when he says he like something.

LEE: I thought you said you didn't know him.

AUSTIN: Well, I'm familiar with his tastes.

LEE: I let him get two up on me goin' into the back nine. He was sure he had me cold. You shoulda' seen his face when I pulled out the old pitching wedge and plopped it pin-high, two feet from the cup. He 'bout shit his pants. "Where'd a guy like you ever learn how to play golf like that?" he says.

(*Lee laughs, Austin stares at him*)

AUSTIN: 'Course there's no contract yet. Nothing's final until it's on paper.

20   LEE: It's final, all right. There's no way he's gonna' back out of it now. We gambled for it.

AUSTIN: Saul, gambled?

LEE: Yeah, sure. I mean he liked the outline already so he wasn't risking that much. I just guaranteed it with my short game.

(*Pause*)

AUSTIN: Well, we should celebrate or something. I think Mom left a bottle of champagne in the refrigerator. We should have a little toast.

(*Austin gets glasses from cupboard, goes to refrigerator, pulls out bottle of champagne*)

LEE: You shouldn't oughta' take her champagne, Austin, She's gonna' miss that.

25   AUSTIN: Oh, she's not going to mind. She'd be glad we put it to good use. I'll get her another bottle. Besides, it's perfect for the occasion.

(*Pause*)

LEE: Yer gonna' get a nice fee fer writin' the script a' course. Straight fee.

(*Austin stops, stares at Lee, puts glasses and bottle on table, pause*)

AUSTIN: I'm writing the script?

LEE: That's what he said. Said we couldn't hire a better screen-writer in the whole town.

AUSTIN: But I'm already working on a script. I've got my own project. I don't have time to write two scripts.

30 LEE: No, he said he was gonna' drop that other one.

(*Pause*)

AUSTIN: What? You mean mine? He's going to drop mine and do yours instead?

LEE: (*Smiles*) Now look, Austin, it's jest beginner's luck ya' know. I mean I sank a fifty foot putt for this deal. No hard feelings.

(*Austin goes to phone on wall, grabs it, starts dialing*)

He's not gonna' be in, Austin. Told me he wouldn't be in 'till late this afternoon.

AUSTIN: (*Stays on phone, dialing, listens*) I can't believe this. I just can't believe it. Are you sure he said that? Why would he drop mine?

LEE: That's what he told me?

35 AUSTIN: He can't do that without telling me first. Without talking to me at least. He wouldn't just make a decision like that without talking to me!

LEE: Well I was kinda' surprised myself. But he was real enthusiastic about my story.

(*Austin hangs up phone violently, paces*)

AUSTIN: What'd he say! Tell me everything he said!

LEE: I been tellin' ya'! He said he liked the story a whole lot. It was the first authentic Western to come along in a decade.

AUSTIN: He liked that story! Your story?

40 LEE: Yeah! What's so surprisin' about that?

AUSTIN: It's stupid! It's the dumbest story I ever heard in my life.

LEE: Hey, hold on! That's my story yer talkin' about!

AUSTIN: It's a bullshit story! It's idiotic. Two lamebrains chasing each other across Texas! Are you kidding? Who do you think's going to go see a film like that?

LEE: It's not a film! It's a movie. There's a big difference. That's somethin' Saul told me.

45 AUSTIN: Oh he did, huh?

LEE: Yeah, he said, "In this business we make movies, American movies. Leave the films to the French."

AUSTIN: So you got real intimate with old Saul huh? He started pouring forth his vast knowledge of Cinema.

LEE: I think he liked me a lot, to tell ya' the truth. I think he felt I was somebody he could confide in.

AUSTIN: What'd you do, beat him up or something?

50 LEE: (*Stands fast*) Hey, I've about had it with the insults buddy! You think yer the only one in the brain department here? Yer the only one that can sit around and cook things up? There's other people got ideas too, ya' know!

AUSTIN: You must've done something. Threatened him or something. Now what'd you do Lee?

LEE: I convinced him!

(*Lee makes sudden menacing lunge toward Austin, wielding golf club above his head, stops himself, frozen moment, long pause, Lee lowers club*)

AUSTIN: Oh, Jesus. You didn't hurt him did you?

(*Long silence, Lee sits back down at table*)

Lee ! Did you hurt him?

LEE: I didn't do nothin' to him! He liked my story. Pure and simple. He said it was the best story he's come across in a long, long time.

55 AUSTIN: That's what he told me about my story! That's the same thing he said to me.

LEE: Well, he musta' been lyin'. He musta' been lyin' to one of us anyway.

AUSTIN: You can't come into this town and start pushing people around. They're gonna' put you away!

LEE: I never pushed anybody around! I beat him fair and square. (*Pause*) They can't touch me anyway. They can't put a finger on me. I'm gone. I can come in through the window and go out through the door. They never knew what hit 'em. You, yer stuck. Yer the one that's stuck. Not me. So don't be warnin' me what to do in this town.

(*Pause, Austin crosses to table, sits at typewriter, rests*)

AUSTIN: Lee, come on, level with me will you? It doesn't make any sense that suddenly he'd throw my idea out the window. I've been talking to him for months. I've got too much at stake. Everything's riding on this project.

60 LEE: What's yer idea?

AUSTIN: It's just a simple love story.

LEE: What kinda' love story?

AUSTIN: (*Stands, crosses into kitchen*) I'm not telling you!

LEE: Ha! 'Fraid I'll steal it huh? Competition's gettin' kinda' close to home isn't it?

65 AUSTIN: Where did Saul say he was going?

LEE: He was gonna' take my story to a couple studios.

AUSTIN: That's *my* outline you know! I wrote that outline! You've got no right to be peddling it around.

LEE: You weren't ready to take credit for it last night.

AUSTIN: Give me my keys!

70 LEE: What?

AUSTIN: The keys! I want my keys back!

LEE: Where you goin'?

AUSTIN: Just give me my keys! I gotta' take a drive. I gotta' get out of here for a while.

LEE: Where you gonna' go, Austin?

75 AUSTIN: (*Pause*) I might just drive out to the desert for a while. I gotta' think.

LEE: You can think here just as good. This is the perfect setup for thinkin'. We got some writin' to do here, boy. Now let's just have us a little toast. Relax. We're partners now.

(*Lee pops the cork of the champagne bottle, pours two drinks as the lights fade to black*)

SCENE 6

Afternoon. Lee and Saul in kitchen, Austin in alcove

LEE: Now you tell him. You tell him, Mr. Kipper.

SAUL: Kimmer.

LEE: Kimmer. You tell him what you told me. He don't believe me.

AUSTIN: I don't want to hear it.

5 SAUL: It's really not a big issue, Austin. I was simply amazed by your brother's story and—

AUSTIN: Amazed? You lost a bet! You gambled with my material!

SAUL: That's really beside the point, Austin. I'm ready to go all the way with your brother's story. I think it has a great deal of merit.

AUSTIN: I don't want to hear about it, okay? Go tell it to the executives! Tell it to somebody who's going to turn it into a package deal or something. A T.V. series. Don't tell it to me.

SAUL: But I want to continue with your project too, Austin. It's not as though we can't do both. We're big enough for that aren't we?

10 AUSTIN: "We"? *I* can't do both! I don't know about "we."

LEE: (*To Saul*) See, what'd I tell ya'. He's totally unsympathetic.

SAUL: Austin, there's no point in our going to another screenwriter for this. It just doesn't make sense. You're brothers. You know each other. There's a familiarity with the material that just wouldn't be possible otherwise.

AUSTIN: There's no familiarity with the material! None! I don't know what "Tornado Country" is. I don't know what a "gooseneck" is. And I don't want to know! (*Pointing to Lee*) He's a hustler! He's bigger hustler than you are! If you can't see that, then—

LEE: (*To Austin*) Hey, now hold on. I didn't have to bring this bone back to you, boy. I persuaded Saul here that you were the right man for the job. You don't have to go throwin' up favors in my face.

15 AUSTIN: Favors! I'm the one who wrote the fuckin' outline! You can't even spell.

SAUL: (*To Austin*) Your brother told me about the situation with your father.

(*Pause*)

AUSTIN: What? (*Looks at Lee*)

SAUL: That's right. Now we have a clear-cut deal here, Austin. We have big studio money standing behind this thing. Just on the basis of your outline.

AUSTIN: (*To Saul*) What'd he tell you about my father?

20 SAUL: Well—that he's destitute. He needs money.

LEE: That's right. He does.

(*Austin shakes his head, stares at them both*)

AUSTIN: (*To Lee*) And this little assignment is supposed to go toward the old man? A charity project? Is that what this is? Did you cook this up on the ninth green too?

SAUL: It's a big slice, Austin.

AUSTIN: (*To Lee*) I gave him money! I already gave him money. You know that. He drank it all up!

25 LEE: This is a different deal here.

SAUL: We can set up a trust for your father. A large sum of money. It can be doled out to him in paracels so he can't misuse it.

AUSTIN: Yeah, and who's doing the doling?

SAUL: Your brother volunteered.

(*Austin laughs*)

LEE: That's right. I'll make sure he uses it for groceries.

30 AUSTIN: (*To Saul*) I'm not doing this script! I'm not writing this crap for you or anybody else. You can't blackmail me into it. You can't threaten me into it. There's no way I'm doing it. So just give it up. Both of you.

(*Long pause*)

SAUL: Well, that's it then. I mean this is an easy three hundred grand. Just for a first draft. It's incredible, Austin. We've got three different studios all trying to cut each other's throats to get this material. In one morning. That's how hot it is.

AUSTIN: Yeah, well you can afford to give me a percentage on the outline then. And you better get the genius here an agent before he gets burned.

LEE: Saul's gonna' be my agent. Isn't that right, Saul?

SAUL: That's right. (*To Austin*) Your brother has really got something, Austin. I've been around too long not to recognize it. Raw talent.

35 AUSTIN: He's got a lota' balls is what he's got. He's taking you right down the river.

SAUL: Three hundred thousand, Austin. Just for a first draft. Now you've never been offered that kind of money before.

AUSTIN: I'm not writing it.

(*Pause*)

SAUL: I see. Well—

LEE: We'll just go to another writer then. Right, Saul? Just hire us somebody with some enthusiasm. Somebody who can recognize the value of a good story.

40 SAUL: I'm sorry about this, Austin.

AUSTIN: Yeah.

SAUL: I mean I was hoping we could continue both things but now I don't see how it's possible.

AUSTIN: So you're dropping my idea altogether. Is that it? Just trade horses in midstream? After all these months of meetings.

SAUL: I wish there was another way.

45 AUSTIN: I've got everything riding on this, Saul. You know that. It's my only shot. If this falls through—

SAUL: I have to go with what my instincts tell me—

AUSTIN: Your instincts!

SAUL: My gut reaction.

AUSTIN: You lost! That's your gut reaction. You lost a gamble. Now you're trying to tell me you like his story? How could you possibly fall for that story? It's as phony as Hoppalong Cassidy. What do you see in it? I'm curious.

50 SAUL: It has the ring of truth, Austin.

AUSTIN: (*Laughs*) Truth?

LEE: It is true.

SAUL: Something about the real West.

AUSTIN: Why? Because it's got horses? Because it's got grown men acting like little boys?

55 SAUL: Something about the land. Your brother is speaking from experience.

AUSTIN: So am I!

SAUL: But nobody's interested in love these days, Austin. Let's face it.

LEE: That's right.

AUSTIN: (*To Saul*) He's been camped out on the desert for three months. Talking to cactus. What's he know about what people wanna' see on the screen! I drive on the freeway every day. I swallow the smog. I watch the news in color. I shop in the Safeway. I'm the one who's in touch! Not him!

60 SAUL: I have to go now, Austin.

(*Saul starts to leave*)

AUSTIN: There's no such thing as the West anymore! It's a dead issue! It's dried up, Saul, and so are you.

(*Saul stops and turns to Austin*)

SAUL: Maybe you're right. But I have to take the gamble, don't I?

AUSTIN: You're a fool to do this, Saul.

SAUL: I've always gone on my hunches. Always. And I've never been wrong. (*To Lee*) I'll talk to you tomorrow, Lee.

65 LEE: All right, Mr. Kimmer.

SAUL: Maybe we could have some lunch.

LEE: Fine with me. (*Smiles at Austin*)

SAUL: I'll give you a ring.

(*Saul exits, lights to black as brothers look at each other from a distance*)

SCENE 7

Night. Coyotes, crickets, sound of typewriter in dark, candlelight up on Lee at typewriter struggling to type with one finger system, Austin sits sprawled out on kitchen floor with whiskey bottle, drunk.

AUSTIN: (*Singing, from floor*)
"Red sails in the sunset

Way out on the blue
Please carry my loved one
Home safely to me
Red sails in the sunset—"

LEE: (*Slams fist on table*) Hey! Knock it off will ya'! I'm tryin' to concentrate here.

AUSTIN: (*Laughs*) You're tryin' to concentrate?

LEE: Yeah. That's right.

5 AUSTIN: Now you're tryin' to concentrate.

LEE: Between you, the coyotes and the crickets a thought don't have much of a chance.

AUSTIN: "Between me, the coyotes and the crickets." What a great title.

LEE: I don't need a title! I need a thought.

AUSTIN: (*Laughs*) A thought! Here's a thought for ya'—

10 LEE: I'm not askin' fer yer thoughts! I got my own. I can do this thing on my own.

AUSTIN: You're going to write an entire script on you own?

LEE: That's right.

(*Pause*)

AUSTIN: Here's a thought. Saul Kimmer—

LEE: Shut up will ya'!

15 AUSTIN: He thinks we're the same person.

LEE: Don't get cute.

AUSTIN: He does! He's lost his mind. Poor old Saul. (*Giggles*) Thinks we're one and the same.

LEE: Why don't you ease up on that champagne.

AUSTIN: (*Holding up bottle*) This isn't champagne anymore. We went through the champagne a long time ago. This is serious stuff. The days of champagne are long gone.

20 LEE: Well, go and drink it.

AUSTIN: I'm enjoying your company, Lee. For the first time since your arrival I am finally enjoying your company. And now you want me to go outside and drink alone?

LEE: That's right.

(*Lee reads through paper in typewriter, makes an erasure*)

AUSTIN: You think you'll make more progress if you're alone?
You might drive yourself crazy.

LEE: I could have this thing done in a night if I had a little silence.

25 AUSTIN: Well you'd still have the crickets to contend with. The
coyotes. The sounds of the police helicopters prowling
above the neighborhood. Slashing their searchlights down
through the streets. Hunting for the likes of you.

LEE: I'm a screenwriter now! I'm legitimate.

AUSTIN: (Laughing) A screenwriter!

LEE: That's right. I'm on salary. That's more'n I can say for you.
I got an advance coming.

AUSTIN: This is true. This is very true. An advance. (Pause) Well,
maybe I oughta' go out and try my hand at your trade. Since
you're doing so good at mine.

30 LEE: Ha!

(Lee attempts to type some more but gets the ribbon tangled up, starts trying to re-thread it as they continue talking)

AUSTIN: Well why not? You don't think I've got what it takes to
sneak into people's houses and steal their T.V.s?

LEE: You couldn't steal a toaster without losin' yer lunch.

(Austin stands with a struggle, supports himself by the sink)

AUSTIN: You don't think I could sneak into somebody's house
and steal a toaster?

LEE: Go take a shower or somethin' will ya!

(Lee gets more tangled up with the typewriter ribbon, pulling it out of the machine as though it was fishing line)

35 AUSTIN: You really don't think I could steal a crumby toaster?
How much you wanna' bet I can't steal a toaster! How much?
Go ahead! You're a gambler aren't you? Tell me how much yer
willing to put on the line. Some part of your big advance? Oh,
you haven't got that yet have you. I forgot.

LEE: All right. I'll bet you your car that you can't steal a toaster
without gettin' busted.

AUSTIN: You already got my car!

LEE: Okay, your house then.

AUSTIN: What're you gonna' give me! I'm not talkin' about my house and my car, I'm talkin' about what are you gonna' give me. You don't have nothin' to give me.

40 LEE: I'll give you—shared screen credit. How 'bout that? I'll have it put in the contract that this was written by the both of us.

AUSTIN: I don't want my name on that piece of shit! I want something of value. You got anything of value? You got any tidbits from the desert? Any Rattlesnake bones? I'm not a greedy man. Any little personal treasure will suffice.

LEE: I'm gonna' just kick yer ass out in a minute.

AUSTIN: Oh, so now you're gonna' kick me out! Now I'm the intruder. I'm the one who's invading your precious privacy.

LEE: I'm trying to do some screenwriting here!!

(*Lee stands, picks up typewriter, slams it down hard on table, pause, silence except for crickets*)

45 AUSTIN: Well, you got everything you need. You got plenty a' coffee? Groceries. You got a car. A contract. (*Pause*) Might need a new typewriter ribbon but other than that you're pretty well fixed. I'll just leave ya' alone for a while.

(*Austin tries to steady himself to leave, Lee makes a move toward him*)

LEE: Where you goin'?

AUSTIN: Don't worry about me. I'm not the one to worry about.

(*Austin weaves toward exit, stops*)

LEE: What're you gonna' do? Just go wander out into the night?

AUSTIN: I'm gonna' make a little tour.

50 LEE: Why don't ya' just go to bed for Christ's sake. Yer makin' me sick.

AUSTIN: I can take care a' myself. Don't worry about me.

(*Austin weaves badly in another attempt to exit, he crashes to the floor, Lee goes to him but remains standing*)

LEE: You want me to call your wife for ya' or something?

AUSTIN: (*From floor*) My wife?

LEE: Yeah. I mean maybe she can help ya' out. Talk to ya' or somethin'.

55 AUSTIN: (*Struggles to stand again*) She's five hundred miles away. North. North of here. Up in the North country where things are calm. I don't need any help. I'm gonna' go outside and I'm gonna' steal a toaster. I'm gonna' steal some other stuff too. I might even commit bigger crimes. Bigger than you ever dreamed of. Crimes beyond the imagination!

(*Austin manages to get himself vertical, tries to head for exit again*)

LEE: Just hang on a minute, Austin.

AUSTIN: Why? What for? You don't need my help, right? You got a handle on the project. Besides, I'm lookin' forward to the smell of the night. The bushes. Orange blossoms. Dust in the driveways. Rain bird sprinklers. Lights in people's houses. You're right about the lights, Lee. Everybody else is livin' the life. Indoors. Safe. This is a Paradise down here. You know that? We're livin' in a Paradise. We've forgotten about that.

LEE: You sound just like the old man now.

AUSTIN: Yeah, well we all sound alike when we're sloshed. We just sorta' echo each other.

60 LEE: Maybe if we could work on this together we could bring him back out here. Get him settled down some place.

(*Austin turns violently toward Lee, takes a swing at him, misses and crashes to the floor again, Lee stays standing*)

AUSTIN: I don't want him out here! I've had it with him! I went all the way out there! I went out of my way. I gave him money and all he did was play Al Jolson records and spit at me! I gave him money!

(*Pause*)

LEE: Just help me a little with the characters, all right? You know how to do it, Austin.

AUSTIN: (*On floor, laughs*) The characters!

LEE: Yeah. You know. The way they talk and stuff. I can hear it in my head but I can't get it down on paper.

65 AUSTIN: What characters?

LEE: The guys. The guys in the story.

AUSTIN: Those aren't characters.

LEE: Whatever you call 'em then. I need to write somethin' out.

AUSTIN: Those are illusions of characters.

70 LEE: I don't give a damn what ya' call 'em! You know what I'm talkin' about!

AUSTIN: Those are fantasies of a long lost boyhood.

LEE: I gotta' write somethin' out on paper!!

(*Pause*)

AUSTIN: What for? Saul's gonna' get you a fancy screenwriter isn't he?

LEE: I wanna' do it myself!

75 AUSTIN: Then do it! Yer on your own now, old buddy. You bull-dogged yer way into contention. Now you gotta' carry it through.

LEE: I will but I need some advice. Just a couple a' things. Come on, Austin. Just help me get 'em talkin' right. It won't take much.

AUSTIN: Oh, now you're having a little doubt huh? What happened? The pressure's on, boy. This is it. You gotta' come up with it now. You don't come up with a winner on your first time out they just cut your head off. They don't give you a second chance ya' know.

LEE: I got a good story! I know it's a good story. I just need a little help is all.

AUSTIN: Not from me. Not from yer little old brother. I'm retired.

80 LEE: You could save this thing for me, Austin. I'd give ya' half the money. I would. I only need half anyway. With this kinda' money I could be a long time down the road. I'd never brother ya' again. I promise. You'd never even see me again.

AUSTIN: (*Still on floor*) You'd disappear?

LEE: I would for sure.

AUSTIN: Where would you disappear to?

LEE: That don't matter. I got plenty a' places.

85 AUSTIN: Nobody can disappear. The old man tried that. Look where it got him. He lost his teeth.

LEE: He never had any money.

AUSTIN: I don't mean that. I mean his teeth! His real teeth. First he lost his real teeth, then he lost his false teeth. You never knew that did ya'? He never confided in you.

LEE: Nah, I never knew that.

AUSTIN: You wanna' drink?

(*Austin offers bottle to Lee, Lee takes it, sits down on kitchen floor with Austin, they share the bottle*)

Yeah, he lost his real teeth one at a time. Woke up every morning with another tooth lying on the mattress. Finally, he decides he's gotta' get 'em all pulled out but he doesn't have any money. Middle of Arizona with no money and no insurance and every morning another tooth is lying on the mattress. (*Takes a drink*) So what does he do?

90 LEE: I dunno'. I never knew about that.

AUSTIN: He begs the government. G.I. Bill or some damn thing. Some pension plan he remembers in the back of his head. And they send him out the money.

LEE: They did?

(*They keep trading he bottle between them, taking drinks*)

AUSTIN: Yeah. They send him the money but it's not enough money. Costs a lot to have all yer teeth yanked. They charge by the individual tooth, ya' know. I mean one tooth isn't equal to another tooth. Some are more expensive. Like the big ones in the back—

LEE: So what happened?

95 AUSTIN: So he locates a Mexican dentist in Juarez who'll do the whole thing for a song. And he takes off hitchhiking to the border?

LEE: Hitchhiking?

AUSTIN: Yeah. So how long you think it takes him to get to the border? A man his age.

LEE: I dunno.

AUSTIN: Eight days it takes him. Eight days in the rain and the sun and every day he's droppin' teeth on the blacktop and nobody'll pick him up 'cause his mouth's full a' blood.

(*Pause, they drink*)

So finally he stumbles into the dentist. Dentist takes all his money and all his teeth. And there he is, in Mexico, with his gums sewed up and his pockets empty.

(Long silence, Austin drinks)

100   LEE: That's it?

AUSTIN: Then I go out to see him, see. I go out there and I take him out for a nice Chinese dinner. But he doesn't eat. All he wants to do is drink Martinis outa' plastic cups. And he takes his teeth out and lay 'em on the table 'cause he can't stand the feel of 'em. And we ask the waitress for one a' those doggie bags to take the Chop Suey home in. So he drops his teeth in the doggie bag along with the Chop Suey. And then we go out to hit all the bars up and down the highway. Says he wants to introduce me to all his buddies. And in one a' those bars, in one a' those bars up and down the highway, he left that doggie bag with his teeth laying in the Chop Suey.

LEE: You never found it?

AUSTIN: We went back but we never did find it. *(Pause)* Now that's a true story. True to life.

(They drink as lights fade to black)

SCENE 8

Very early morning, between night and day. No crickets, coyotes yapping feverishly in distance before light comes up, a small fire blazes up in the dark from alcove area, sound of Lee smashing typewriter with a golf club, lights coming up, Lee seen smashing typewriter methodically then dropping pages of his script into a burning bowl set on the floor of alcove, flames leap up, Austin has a whole bunch of stolen toasters lined up on the sink counter along with Lee's stolen T.V., the toasters are of a wide variety of models, mostly chrome, Austin goes up and down the line of toasters, breathing on them and polishing them with a dish towel, both men are drunk, empty whiskey bottles and beer cans litter floor of kitchen, they share a half empty bottle on one of the chairs in the alcove, Lee keeps periodically taking deliberate axchops at the typewriter using a nine-iron as Austin speaks, all of their mother's house plants are dead and drooping.

AUSTIN: *(Polishing toasters)* There's gonna' be a general lack of toast in the neighborhood this morning. Many, many unhappy, bewildered breakfast faces. I guess it's best not to

302 | Sam Shepard

even think of the victims. Not to even entertain it. Is that the
right psychology?

LEE: (*Pause*) What?

AUSTIN: Is that the correct criminal psychology? Not to think of
the victims?

LEE: What victims?

(*Lee takes another swipe at typewriter with nine-iron, adds pages to the fire*)

5   AUSTIN: The victims of crime. Of breaking and entering. I mean
is it a prerequisite for a criminal not to have a conscience?

LEE: Ask a criminal.

(*Pause, Lee stares at Austin*)

What're you gonna' do with all those toasters? That's the
dumbest thing I ever saw in my life.

AUSTIN: I've got hundreds of dollars worth of household appli-
ances here. You may not realize that.

LEE: Yeah, and how many hundreds of dollars did you walk right
past?

AUSTIN: It was toasters you challenged me to. Only toasters. I
ignored every other temptation.

10 LEE: I never challenged you! That's no challenge. Anybody can
steal a toaster.

(*Lee smashes typewriter again*)

AUSTIN: You don't have to take it out on my typewriter ya' know.
It's not the machine's fault that you can't write. It's a sin to
do that to a good machine.

LEE: A sin?

AUSTIN: When you consider all the writers who never even had a
machine. Who would have given an eyeball for a good typewriter. Any typewriter.

(*Lee smashes typewriter again*)

AUSTIN: (*Polishing toasters*) All the ones who wrote on matchbook
covers. Paper bags. Toilet paper. Who had their writing
destroyed by their jailers. Who persisted beyond all odds.
Those writers would find it hard to understand your actions.

(Lee comes down on typewriter with one final crushing blow of the nine-iron then collapses in one of the chairs, takes a drink from bottle, pause)

15 AUSTIN: *(After pause)* Not to mention demolishing a perfectly good golf club. What about all the struggling golfers? What about Lee Trevino? What do you think he would've said when he was batting balls around with broomsticks at the age of nine. Impoverished.

(Pause)

LEE: What time is it anyway?
AUSTIN: No idea. Time stands still when you're havin' fun.
LEE: Is it too late to call a woman? You know any women?
AUSTIN: I'm a married man.
20 LEE: I mean a local woman.

(Austin looks out at light through window above sink)

AUSTIN: It's either too late or too early. You're the nature enthusiast. Can't you tell the time by the light in the sky? Orient yourself around the North Star or something?
LEE: I can't tell anything.
AUSTIN: Maybe you need a little breakfast. Some toast! How 'bout some toast?

(Austin goes to cupboard, pulls out loaf of bread and starts dropping slices into every toaster, Lee stays sitting, drinks, watches Austin)

LEE: I don't need toast. I need a woman.
25 AUSTIN: A woman isn't the answer. Never was.
LEE: I'm not talkin' about permanent. I'm talking' about temporary.
AUSTIN: *(Putting toast in toasters)* We'll just test the merits of these little demons. See which brands have a tendency to burn. See which one can produce a perfectly golden piece of fluffy toast.
LEE: How much gas you got in yer car?
AUSTIN: I haven't driven my car for days now. So I haven't had an opportunity to look at the gas gauge.
30 LEE: Take a guess. You think there's enough to get me to Bakersfield?

AUSTIN: Bakersfield? What's in Bakersfield?

LEE: Just never mind what's in Bakersfield! You think there's enough goddamn gas in the car!

AUSTIN: Sure.

LEE: Sure. You could care less, right. Let me run outa' gas on the Grapevine. You could give a shit.

35 **AUSTIN**: I'd say there was enough gas to get you just about anywhere, Lee. With your determination and guts.

LEE: What the hell time is it anyway?

(*Lee pulls out his wallet, starts going through dozens of small pieces of paper with phone numbers written on them, drops some on the floor, drops others in the fire*).

AUSTIN: Very early. This is the time of morning when the coyotes kill people's cocker spaniels. Did you hear them? That's what they were doing out there. Luring innocent pets away from their homes.

LEE: (*Searching through his papers*) What's the area code for Bakersfield? You know?

AUSTIN: You could always call the operator.

40 **LEE**: I can't stand that voice they give ya'.

AUSTIN: What voice?

LEE: That voice that warns you that if you'd only tried harder to find the number in the phone book you wouldn't have to be calling the operator to begin with.

(*Lee gets up, holding a slip of paper form his wallet, stumbles toward phone on wall, yanks receiver, starts dialing*)

AUSTIN: Well I don't understand why you'd want to talk to anybody else anyway. I mean you can talk to me. I'm your brother.

LEE: (*Dialing*) I wanna' talk to a woman. I haven't heard a woman's voice in a long time.

45 **AUSTIN**: Not since the Botanist?

LEE: What?

AUSTIN: Nothing. (*Starts singing as he tends toast*)
"Red sails in the sunset
Way out on the blue
Please carry my loved one
Home safely to me"

LEE: Hey, knock if off will ya'! This is long distance here.

AUSTIN: Bakersfield.

50 LEE: Yeah, Bakersfield. It's Kern County.

AUSTIN: Well, what County are *we* in?

LEE: You better get yourself a 7-Up, boy.

AUSTIN: One County's as good as another.

(*Austin hums "Red Sails" softly as Lee talks on phone*)

LEE: (*To phone*) Yeah, operator look—first off I wanna' know the area code for Bakersfield. Right. Bakersfield! Okay. Good. Now I wanna' know if you can help me track somebody down. (*Pause*) No, no I mean a phone number. Just a phone number. Okay. (*Holds a piece of paper up and reads it*) Okay, the name is Melly Ferguson. Melly. (*Pause*) I dunno'. Melly. Maybe. Yeah. Maybe Melanie. Yeah. Melanie Ferguson. Okay. (*Pause*) What? I can't hear ya' so good. Sounds like yer under the ocean. (*Pause*) You got ten Melanie Fergusons? How could that be? Ten Melanie Fergusons in Bakersfield? Well gimme all of 'em then. (*Pause*) What d'ya' mean? Gimme all ten Melanie Fergusons! That's right. Just a second. (*To Austin*) Gimme a pen.

55 AUSTIN: I don't have a pen.

LEE: Gimme a pencil then!

AUSTIN: I don't have a pencil.

LEE: (*To phone*) Just a second, operator. (*To Austin*) Yer a writer and ya' don't have a pen or a pencil!

AUSTIN: I'm not a writer. You're a writer.

60 LEE: I'm on the phone here! Get me a pen or a pencil.

AUSTIN: I gotta' watch the toast.

LEE: (*To phone*) Hang on a second, operator.

(*Lee lets the phone drop then starts pulling all the drawers in the kitchen out on the floor and dumping the contents, searching for a pencil, Austin watches him casually*)

LEE: (*Crashing through drawers, throwing contents around kitchen*) This is the last time I try to live with people, boy! I can't believe it. Here I am! Here I am again in a desperate situation! This would never happen out on the desert. I would never be in this kinda' situation out on the desert. Isn't there a pen or a pencil in this house! Who lives in this house anyway!

AUSTIN: Out mother.

65 LEE: How come she don't have a pen or a pencil! She's a social person isn't she? Doesn't she have to make shopping lists? She's gotta' have a pencil. (*Finds a pencil*) Aaha! (*He rushes back to phone, picks up receiver*) All right operator. Operator! Hey! Operator! Goddamnit!

(*Lee rips the phone off the wall and throws it down, goes back to chair and falls into it, drinks, long pause*)

AUSTIN: She hung up?

LEE: Yeah, she hung up. I knew she was gonna' hang up. I could hear it in her voice.

(*Lee starts going through his slips of paper again*)

AUSTIN: Well, you're probably better off staying here with me anyway. I'll take care of you.

LEE: I don't need takin' care of! Not by you anyway.

70 AUSTIN: Toast is almost ready.

(*Austin starts buttering all the toast as is pops up*)

LEE: I don't want any toast!

(*Long pause*)

AUSTIN: You gotta' eat something. Can't just drink. How long have we been drinking, anyway?

LEE: (*Looking through slips of paper*) Maybe it was Fresno. What's the area code for Fresno? How could I have lost that number! She was beautiful.

(*Pause*)

AUSTIN: Why don't you just forget about that, Lee. Forget about the woman.

75 LEE: She had green eyes. You know what green eyes do to me?

AUSTIN: I know but you're not gonna' get it on with her now anyway. It's dawn already. She's in Bakersfield for Christ's sake.

(*Long pause, Lee considers the situation*)

LEE: Yeah. (*Looks at windows*) It's dawn?

AUSTIN: Let's just have some toast and—

LEE: What is this bullshit with the toast anyway! You make it sound like salvation or something. I don't want any god-damn toast! How many times I gotta' tell ya'! (*Lee gets up, crosses upstage to windows in alcove, looks out, Austin butters toast*)

80 AUSTIN: Well it is like salvation sort of. I mean the smell. I love the smell of toast. And the sun's coming up. It make me feel like anything's possible. Ya' know?

LEE: (*Back to Austin, facing windows upstage*) So go to church why don't ya'.

AUSTIN: Like a beginning. I love beginnings.

LEE: Oh yeah. I've always been kinda' partial to endings myself.

AUSTIN: What if I come with you, Lee?

85 LEE: (*Pause as Lee turns toward Austin*) What?

AUSTIN: What if I come with you out to the desert?

LEE: Are you kiddin'?

AUSTIN: No. I'd just like to see what it's like.

LEE: You wouldn't last a day out there pal.

90 AUSTIN: That's what you said about the toasters. You said I couldn't steal a toaster either.

LEE: A toaster's got nothin' to do with the desert.

AUSTIN: I could make it, Lee. I'm not that helpless. I can cook.

LEE: Cook?

AUSTIN: I can.

95 LEE: So what! You can cook. Toast.

AUSTIN: I can make fires. I know how to get fresh water from condensation.

(*Austin stacks buttered toast up in a tall stack on plate*)

(*Lee slams table*)

LEE: It's not somethin' you learn out of a Boy Scout handbook!

AUSTIN: Well how do you learn it then! How're you supposed to learn it!

(*Pause*)

LEE: Ya' just learn it, that's all. Ya' learn it 'cause ya' have to learn it. You don't *have* to learn it.

100 AUSTIN: You could teach me.

LEE: (*Stands*) What're you, crazy or somethin'? You went to college. Here, you are down here, rollin' in bucks. Floatin' up and down in elevators. And you wanna' learn how to live on the desert!

AUSTIN: I do, Lee. I really do. There's nothin' down here for me. There never was. When we were kids here it was different. There was a life here then. But now—I keep comin' down here thinkin' it's the fifties or somethin'. I keep finding myself getting off the freeway at familiar landmarks that turn out to be unfamiliar. On the way to appointments. Wandering down streets I thought I recognized that turn out to be replicas of streets I remember. Streets I misremember. Streets I can't tell if I lived on or saw in a postcard. Fields that don't even exist anymore.

LEE: There's no point cryin' about that now.

AUSTIN: There's nothin' real down here, Lee! Least of all me!

105 LEE: Well I can't save you from that!

AUSTIN: You can let me come with you.

LEE: No dice, pal.

AUSTIN: You could let me come with you, Lee!

LEE: Hey, do you actually think I chose to live out in the middle a' nowhere? Do ya'? Ya' think it's some kinda' philosophical decision I took or somethin'? I'm livin' out there 'cause I can't make it here! And yer bitchin' to me about all yer success!

110 AUSTIN: I'd cash it all in in a second. That's the truth.

LEE: (*Pause, shakes his head*) I can't believe this.

AUSTIN: Let me go with you.

LEE: Stop sayin' that will ya'! Yer worse than a dog.

(*Austin offers out the plate of neatly stacked toast to Lee*)

AUSTIN: You want some toast?

(*Lee suddenly explodes and knocks the plate out of Austin's hand, toast goes flying, long frozen moment where it appears Lee might go all the way this time when Austin breaks it by slowly lowering himself to his knees and begins gathering the scattered toast from the floor and stacking it back on the plate, Lee begins to circle Austin in a slow, predatory way, crushing pieces of toast in his wake, no words for a while, Austin keeps gathering toast, even the crushed pieces*)

115   **LEE:** Tell ya' what I'll do, little brother. I might just consider makin' you a deal. Little trade. (*Austin continues gathering toast as Lee circles him through this*) You write me up this screenplay thing just like I tell ya'. I mean you can use all yer usual tricks and stuff. Yer fancy language. Yer artistic hocus pocus. But ya' gotta' write everything like I say. Every move. Every time they run outa' gas, they run outa' gas. Every time they wanna' jump on a horse, they do just that. If they wanna' stay in Texas, by God they'll stay in Texas! (*Keeps circling*) And you finish the whole thing up for me. Top to bottom. And you put my name on it. And I own all the rights. And every dime goes in my pocket. You do that and I'll sure enough take ya' with me to the desert. (*Lee stops, pause, looks down at Austin*) How's that sound?

(*Pause as Austin stands slowly holding plate of demolished toast, their faces are very close, pause*)

AUSTIN: It's a deal.

(*Lee stares straight into Austin's eyes, then he slowly takes a piece of toast off the plate, raises it to his mouth and takes a huge crushing bite never taking his eyes off Austin's, as Lee crunches into the toast the lights black out*)

SCENCE 9

Mid-day. No sound, blazing heat, the stage is ravaged; bottles, toasters, smashed typewriter, ripped out telephone, etc. All the debris from previous scene is now starkly visible in intense yellow light, the effect should be like a desert junkyard at high noon, the coolness of the preceding scenes is totally obliterated. Austin is seated at table in alcove, shirt open, pouring with sweat, hunched over a writing notebook, scribbling notes desperately with a ballpoint pen. Lee with no shirt, beer in hand, sweat pouring down his chest, is walking a slow circle around the table, picking his way though the objects, sometimes kicking them aside.

LEE: (*As he walks*) All right, read it back to me. Read it back to me!
AUSTIN: (*Scribbling at top speed*) Just a second.
LEE: Come on, come on! Just read what ya' got.

AUSTIN: I can't keep up! It's not the same as if I had a typewriter.

5　LEE: Just read what we got so far. Forget about the rest

AUSTIN: All right. Let's see—okay—(*Wipes sweat from his face, reads as Lee circles*). Luke says uh—

LEE: Luke?

AUSTIN: Yeah.

LEE: His name's Luke? All right, all right—we can change the names later. What's he say? Come on, come on.

10　AUSTIN: He says uh—(*Reading*) "I told ya' you were a fool to follow me in here. I know this prairie like the back a' my hand."

LEE: No, no, no! That's not what I said. I never said that.

AUSTIN: That's what I wrote.

LEE: It's not what I said. I never said "like the back a' my hand." That's stupid. That's one a' those—whadya' call it? Whatya' call that?

AUSTIN: What?

15　LEE: Whadya' call it when somethin's been said a thousand times before. Whadya' call that?

AUSTIN: Um—a cliché?

LEE: Yeah. That's right. Cliché. That's what that is. A cliché. "The back a' my hand." That's stupid.

AUSTIN: That's what you said.

LEE: I never said that! And even if I did, that's where yer supposed to come in. That's where yer supposed to change it to somethin' better.

20　AUSTIN: Well how am I supposed to do that and write down what you say at the same time?

LEE: Ya' just do, that's all! You hear a stupid line you change it. That's yer job.

AUSTIN: All right. (*Makes more notes*)

LEE: What're you changin' it to?

AUSTIN: I'm not changing it. I'm just trying to catch up.

25　LEE: Well change it! We gotta' change that, we can't leave that in there like that. ". . . the back a' my hand." That's dumb.

AUSTIN: (*Stops writing, sits back*) All right.

LEE: (pacing) So what'll we change it to?

AUSTIN: Um—How 'bout—"I'm on intimate terms with this prairie."

LEE: (*To himself considering line as he walks*) "I'm on intimate terms with this prairie." Intimate terms, intimate terms. Intimate—that means like uh—sexual right?

30 AUSTIN: Well—yeah—or—

LEE: He's on sexual terms with the prairie? How dya' figure that?

AUSTIN: Well it doesn't necessarily have to mean sexual.

LEE: What's it mean then?

AUSTIN: It means uh—close—personal—

35 LEE: All right. How's it sound? Put it into the uh—the line there. Read it back. Let's see how it sounds. (*To himself*) "Intimate terms."

AUSTIN: (*Scribbles in notebook*) Okay It'd go something like this: (*Reads*) "I told ya' you were a fool to follow me in here. I'm on intimate terms with this prairie."

LEE: That's good. I like that. That's real good.

AUSTIN: You do?

LEE: Yeah. Don't you?

40 AUSTIN: Sure.

LEE: Sounds original now. "Intimate terms." That's good. Okay. Now we're cookin! That has a real ring to it.

(*Austin makes more notes, Lee walks around, pours beer on his arms and rubs it over his chest feeling good about the new progress, as he does this Mom enters unobtrusively down left with her luggage, she stops and stares at the scene still holding luggage as the two men continue, unaware of her presence, Austin absorbed in his writing, Lee cooling himself off with beer*)

LEE: (*Continues*) "He's on intimate terms with this prairie." Sounds real mysterious and kinda' threatening at the same time.

AUSTIN: (*Writing rapidly*) Good.

LEE: Now—(*Lee turns and suddenly sees Mom, he stares at her for a while, she stares back, Austin keeps writing feverishly, not noticing, Lee walks slowly over to Mom and takes a closer look, long pause*)

45 LEE: Mom?

(*Austin looks up suddenly from his writing, sees Mom, stands quickly, long pause, Mom surveys the damage*)

AUSTIN: Mom. What're you doing back?

MOM: I'm back.

LEE: Here, lemme take those for ya.

(*Lee sets beer on counter then takes both her bags but doesn't know where to set them down in the sea of junk so he just keeps holding them*)

AUSTIN: I wasn't expecting you back so soon. I thought uh—How was Alaska?

50   MOM: Fine.

LEE: See any igloos?

MOM: No. Just glaciers.

AUSTIN: Cold huh?

MOM: What?

55   AUSTIN: It must've been cold up there?

MOM: Not really.

LEE: Musta' been colder than this here. I mean we're havin' a real scorcher here.

MOM: Oh? (*She looks at damage*)

LEE: Yeah. Must be in the hundreds.

60   AUSTIN: You wanna' take your coat off, Mom?

MOM: No. (*Pause, she surveys space*) What happened in here?

AUSTIN: Oh um—Me and Lee were just sort of celebrating and uh—

MOM: Celebrating?

AUSTIN: Yeah. Uh—Lee sold a screenplay. A story, I mean.

65   MOM: Lee did?

AUSTIN: Yeah.

MOM: Not you?

AUSTIN: No. Him.

MOM: (*To Lee*) You sold a screenplay?

70   LEE: Yeah. That's right. We're just sorta' finishing it up right now. That's what we're doing here.

AUSTIN: Me and Lee are going out to the desert to live.

MOM: You and Lee?

AUSTIN: Yeah. I'm taking off with Lee.

MOM: (*She looks back and forth at each of them, pause*) You gonna go live with your father?

75   AUSTIN: No. We're going to a different desert Mom.

MOM: I see. Well, you'll probably wind up on the same desert sooner or later. What're all these toasters doing here?

AUSTIN: Well—we had kind of a contest.

MOM: Contest?

LEE: Yeah.

80 AUSTIN: Lee won.

MOM: Did you win a lot of money, Lee?

LEE: Well not yet. It's comin' in any day now.

MOM: (*To Lee*) What happened to your shirt?

LEE: Oh. I was sweatin' like a pig and I took it off.

(*Austin grabs Lee's shirt off the table and tosses it to him, Lee sets down suitcases and puts his shirt on*)

85 MOM: Well it's one hell of a mess in here isn't it?

AUSTIN: Yeah, I'll clean it up for you, Mom. I just didn't know
   you were coming back so soon.

MOM: I didn't either.

AUSTIN: What happened?

MOM: Nothing. I just started missing all my plants.

(*She notices dead plants*)

90 AUSTIN: Oh.

MOM: Oh, they're all dead aren't they. (*She crosses toward them, exam-
   ines them closely*) You didn't get a chance to water I guess.

AUSTIN: I was doing it and then Lee came and—

LEE: Yeah I just distracted him a whole lot here, Mom. It's not
   his fault.

(*Pause, as Mom stares at plants*)

MOM: Oh well, one less thing to take care of I guess. (*Turns toward
   brothers*) Oh, that reminds me— You boys will probably never
   guess who's in town. Try and guess.

(*Long pause, brothers stare at her*)

95 AUSTIN: Whadya' mean, Mom?

MOM: Take a guess. Somebody very important has come to town.
   I read it, coming down on the Greyhound.

LEE: Somebody very important?

MOM: See if you can guess. You'll never guess.

AUSTIN: Mom—we're trying to uh—(*Points to writing pad*)

100 MOM: Picasso. (*Pause*) Picasso's in town. Isn't that incredible? Right now.

(*Pause*)

AUSTIN: Picasso's dead, Mom.

MOM: No, he's not dead. He's visiting the museum. I read it on the bus. We have to go down there and see him.

AUSTIN: Mom—

MOM: This is the chance of a lifetime. Can you imagine? We could all go down and meet him. All three of us.

105 LEE: Uh—I don't think I'm really up fer meetin' anybody right now. I'm uh—What's his name?

MOM: Picasso! Picasso! You've never heard of Picasso? Austin, you've heard of Picasso.

AUSTIN: Mom, we're not going to have time.

MOM: It won't take long. We'll just hop in the car and go down there. An opportunity like this doesn't come along every day.

AUSTIN: We're gonna' be leavin' here, Mom!

(*Pause*)

110 MOM: Oh.

LEE: Yeah.

(*Pause*)

MOM: You're both leaving?

LEE: (*Looks at Austin*) Well we were thinkin' about that before but now I—

AUSTIN: No, we are! We're both leaving. We've got it all planned.

115 MOM: (*To Austin*) Well you can't leave. You have a family.

AUSTIN: I'm leaving. I'm getting out of here.

LEE: (*To Mom*) I don't really think Austin's cut out for the desert do you?

MOM: No. He's not.

AUSTIN: I'm going with you, Lee!

120 MOM: He's too thin.

LEE: Yeah, he'd just burn up out there.

AUSTIN: (*To Lee*) We just gotta' finish this screenplay and then we're gonna' take off. That's the plan. That's what you said. Come on, let's get back to work, Lee.

LEE: I can't work under these conditions here. It's too hot.

AUSTIN: Then we'll do it on the desert.

125 LEE: Don't be tellin' me what we're gonna do!

MOM: Don't shout in the house.

LEE: We're just gonna' have to postpone the whole deal.

AUSTIN: I can't postpone it! It's gone past postponing! I'm doing everything you said. I'm writing down exactly what you tell me.

LEE: Yeah, but you were right all along see. It is a dumb story. "Two lamebrains chasin' each other across Texas." That's what you said, right?

130 AUSTIN: I never said that.

(*Lee sneers in Austin's face then turns to Mom*)

LEE: I'm gonna' just borrow some a' your antiques, Mom. You don't mind do ya'? Just a few plates and things. Silverware.

(*Lee starts going through all the cupboards in kitchen pulling out plates and stacking them on counter as Mom and Austin watch*)

MOM: You don't have any utensils on the desert?

LEE: Nah, I'm fresh out.

AUSTIN: (*To Lee*) What're you doing?

135 MOM: Well some of those are very old. Bone China.

LEE: I'm tired of eatin' outa' my bare hands, ya' know. It's not civilized.

AUSTIN: (*To Lee*) What're you doing? We made a deal!

MOM: Couldn't you borrow the plastic ones instead? I have plenty of plastic ones.

LEE: (*As he stacks plates*) It's not the same. Plastic's not the same at all. What I need is somethin' authentic. Somethin' to keep me in touch. It's easy to get outa' touch out there. Don't worry I'll get 'em back to ya'.

(*Austin rushes up to Lee, grabs him by shoulders*)

140 AUSTIN: You can't just drop the whole thing, Lee!

(*Lee turns, pushes Austin in the chest knocking him backwards into the alcove, Mom watches numbly, Lee returns to collecting the plates, silverware, etc.*)

MOM: You boys shouldn't fight in the house. Go outside and fight.

LEE: I'm not fightin'. I'm leavin'.

MOM: There's been enough damage done already.

LEE: (*His back to Austin and Mom, stacking dishes on counter*) I'm clearin' outa' here once and for all. All this town does is drive a man insane. Look what it's done to Austin there. I'm not lettin' that happen to me. Sell myself down the river. No sir. I'd rather be a hundred miles from nowhere than let that happen to me.

(*During this Austin has picked up the ripped-out phone from the floor and wrapped the cord tightly around both his hands, he lunges at Lee whose back is still to him, wraps the cord around Lee's back and pulls back on the cord, tightening it, Lee chokes desperately, can't speak and can't reach Austin with his arms, Austin keeps applying pressure on Lee's back with his foot, bending him into the sink, Mom watches*)

145   **AUSTIN:** (*Tightening cord*). You're not goin' anywhere! You're not takin' anything with you. You're not takin' my car! You're not takin' the dishes! You're not takin' anything! You're stayin' right here!

MOM: You'll have to stop fighting in the house. There's plenty of room outside to fight. You've got the whole outdoors to fight in.

(*Lee tries to tear himself away, he crashes across the stage like an enraged bull dragging Austin with him, he snorts and bellows but Austin hangs on and manages to keep clear of Lee's attempts to grab him, they crash into the table, to the floor, Lee is face down thrashing wildly and choking, Austin pulls cord tighter, stands with one foot planted on Lee's back and the cord stretched taut*)

AUSTIN: (*Holding cord*) Gimme back my keys, Lee! Take the keys out! Take 'em out!

(*Lee desperately tries to dig in his pockets, searching for the car keys, Mom moves closer*)

MOM: (*Calmly to Austin*) You're not killing him are you?

AUSTIN: I don't know. I don't know if I'm killing him. I'm stopping him. That's all. I'm just stopping him.

(*Lee thrashes but Austin is relentless*)

150   **MOM:** You oughta' let him breathe a little bit.

AUSTIN: Throw the keys out, Lee!

(*Lee finally gets keys out and throws them on the floor but out of Austin's reach, Austin keeps pressure on cord, pulling Lee's neck back, Lee gets one hand to the cord but can't relieve the pressure*)

Reach me those keys would ya', Mom.

MOM: (*Not moving*) Why are you doing this to him?

AUSTIN: Reach me the keys!

MOM: Not until you stop choking him.

155   **AUSTIN:** I can't stop choking him! He'll kill me if I stop choking him!

MOM: He won't kill you. He's your brother.

AUSTIN: Just get me the keys would ya'!

(*Pause. Mom picks keys up off floor, hands them to Austin*)

AUSTIN: (*To Mom*) Thanks.

MOM: Will you let him go now?

160   **AUSTIN:** I don't know. He's not gonna' let me get outa' here.

MOM: Well you can't kill him.

AUSTIN: I can kill him! I can easily kill him. Right now. Right here. All I gotta' do is just tighten up. See? (*He tightens cord, Lee thrashes wildly, Austin releases pressure a little, maintaining control*) Ya' see that?

MOM: That's a savage thing to do.

AUSTIN: Yeah well don't tell me I can't kill him because I can. I can just twist. I can just keep twisting. (*Austin twists the cord tighter, Lee weakens, his breathing changes to a short rasp*)

165   **MOM:** Austin!

(*Austin relieves pressure, Lee breathes easier but Austin keeps him under control*)

AUSTIN: (*Eyes on Lee, holding cord*) I'm goin' to the desert. There's nothing stopping me. I'm going by myself to the desert.

(*Mom moving toward her luggage*)

MOM: Well, I'm going to go check into a motel. I can't stand this anymore.

AUSTIN: Don't go yet!

(*Mom pauses*)

MOM: I can't stay here. This is worse than being homeless.

170   **AUSTIN:** I'll get everything fixed up for you, Mom. I promise. Just stay for a while.

      MOM: (*Picking up luggage*) You're going to the desert.

      AUSTIN: Just wait!

(*Lee thrashes, Austin subdues him, Mom watches holding luggage, pause*)

      MOM: It was the worst feeling being up there. In Alaska. Staring out a window. I never felt so desperate before. That's why when I saw that article on Picasso I thought—

      AUSTIN: Stay here, Mom. This is where you live.

(*She looks around the stage*)

175   **MOM:** I don't recognize it at all.

(*She exits with luggage, Austin makes a move toward her but Lee starts to struggle and Austin subdues him again with cord, pause*)

      AUSTIN: (*Holding cord*) Lee? I'll make ya' a deal. You let me get outa' here. Just let me get to my car. All right, Lee? Gimme a little headstart and I'll turn you loose. Just gimme a little headstart. All right?

(*Lee makes no response, Austin slowly releases tension cord, still nothing from Lee*)

      AUSTIN: Lee?

(*Lee is motionless, Austin very slowly begins to stand, still keeping a tenuous hold on the cord and his eyes riveted to Lee for any sign of movement, Austin slowly drops the cord and stands, he stares down at Lee who appears to be dead*)

      AUSTIN: (*Whispers*) Lee?

(*Pause, Austin considers, looks toward exit, back to Lee, then makes a small movement as if to leave. Instantly Lee is on his feet and moves toward exit, blocking Austin's escape. They square off to each other, keeping a distance between them. Pause, a single coyote heard in distance, lights fade softly into moonlight, the figures of the brothers now appear to be caught in a vast desert-like landscape, they are very still but watchful for the next move, lights go slowly to black as the after-image of the brother pulses in the dark, coyote fades*)

Wendy Wasserstein, 1950–

Tender Offer *1983*

CHARACTERS
Lisa
Paul

A girl of around nine is alone in a dance studio. She is dressed in traditional leotards and tights. She begins singing to herself, "Nothing Could Be Finer Than to Be in Carolina." She maps out a dance routine, including parts for the chorus. She builds to a finale. A man, Paul, around thirty-five, walks in. He has a sweet, though distant demeanor. As he walks in, Lisa notices him and stops.

PAUL: You don't have to stop, sweetheart.
LISA: That's okay.
PAUL: Looked very good.
LISA: Thanks.
5   PAUL: Don't I get a kiss hello?
LISA: Sure.
PAUL: (*Embraces her*) Hi, Tiger.
LISA: Hi, Dad.
PAUL: I'm sorry I'm late.
10   LISA: That's okay.
PAUL: How'd it go?

LISA: Good.

PAUL: Just good?

LISA: Pretty good.

15 PAUL: "Pretty good." You mean you got a lot of applause or "pretty good" you could have done better.

LISA: Well, Courtney Palumbo's mother thought I was pretty good. But you know the part of the middle when everybody's supposed to freeze and the big girl comes out. Well, I think I moved a little bit.

PAUL: I thought what you were doing looked very good.

LISA: Daddy, that's not what I was doing. That was tap-dancing I made that up.

PAUL: Oh. Well it looked good. Kind of sexy.

20 LISA: Yuch!

PAUL: What do you mean "yuch"?

LISA: Just yuch!

PAUL: You don't want to be sexy?

LISA: I don't care.

25 PAUL: Let's go Tiger. I promised your mother I'd get you home in time for dinner.

LISA: I can't find my leg warmers.

PAUL: You can't find your what?

LISA: Leg warmers. I can't go home till I find my leg warmers.

PAUL: I don't see you looking for them.

30 LISA: I was waiting for you.

PAUL: Oh.

LISA: Daddy.

PAUL: What?

LISA: Nothing.

35 PAUL: Where do you think you left them?

LISA: Somewhere around here. I can't remember.

PAUL: Well, try to remember, Lisa. We don't have all night.

LISA: I told you. I think somewhere around here.

PAUL: I don't see them. Let's go home now. You'll call the dancing school tomorrow.

40 LISA: Daddy, I can't go home till I find them. Miss Judy says it's not professional to leave things.

PAUL: Who's Miss Judy?

LISA: She's my ballet teacher. She once danced the lead in *Swan Lake,* and she was a June Taylor dancer.

PAUL: Well, then, I'm sure she'll understand about the leg warmers.

LISA: Daddy, Miss Judy wanted to know why you were late today.

45 PAUL: Hmmmmmmmmm?

LISA: Why were you late?

PAUL: I was in a meeting. Business I'm sorry.

LISA: Why did you tell Mommy you'd come instead of her if you knew you had business?

PAUL: Honey, something just came up. I thought I'd be able to be here. I was looking forward to it.

50 LISA: I wish you wouldn't make appointments to see me.

PAUL: Hmmmmmmmmm?

LISA: You shouldn't make appointments to see me unless you know you're going to come.

PAUL: Of course I'm going to come.

LISA: No, you're not. Talia Robbins told me she's much happier living without her father in the house. Her father used to come home late and go to sleep early.

55 PAUL: Lisa, stop it. Let's go.

LISA: I can't find my leg warmers.

PAUL: Forget your leg warmers.

LISA: Daddy.

PAUL: What is it?

60 LISA: I saw this show on television, I think it was WPIX Channel 11. Well, the father was crying about his daughter.

PAUL: Why was he crying? Was she sick?

LISA: No. She was at school. And he was at business. And he just missed her, so he started to cry.

PAUL: What was the name of this show?

LISA: I don't know. I came in in the middle.

65 PAUL: Well, Lisa, I certainly would cry if you were sick or far away, but I know that you're well and you're home. So no reason to get maudlin.

LISA: What's maudlin?

PAUL: Sentimental, soppy. Frequently used by children who make things up to get attention.

LISA: I am sick! I am sick! I have Hodgkin's disease and a bad itch on my leg.

PAUL: What do you mean you have Hodgkin's disease? Don't say things like that.

70 LISA: Swoosie Kurtz, she had Hodgkin's disease on a TV movie last year, but she got better and now she's on *Love Sidney*.

PAUL: Who is Swoosie Kurtz?

LISA: She's an actress named after an airplane. I saw her on *Live at Five*

PAUL: You watch too much television; you should do your homework. Now put your coat on.

LISA: Daddy, I really do have a bad itch on my leg. Would you scratch it?

75 PAUL: Lisa, you're procrastinating.

LISA: Why do you use words I don't understand? I hate it. You're like Daria Feldman's mother. She always talks in Yiddish to her husband so Daria won't understand.

PAUL: Procrastinating is not Yiddish.

LISA: Well, I don't know what it is.

PAUL: Procrastinating means you don't want to go about your business.

80 LISA: I don't go to business. I go to school.

PAUL: What I mean is you want to hang around here until you and I are late for dinner and your mother's angry and it's too late for you to do your homework.

LISA: I do not.

PAUL: Well, it sure looks that way. Now put your coat on and lets go.

LISA: Daddy.

85 PAUL: Honey, I'm tired. Really, later.

LISA: Why don't you want to talk to me?

PAUL: I do want to talk to you. I promise when we get home we'll have a nice talk.

LISA: No, we won't. You'll read the paper and fall asleep in front of the news.

PAUL: Honey, we'll talk on the weekend, I promise. Aren't I taking you to the theater this weekend? Let me look. (*He takes out an appointment book.*) Yes. Sunday. *Joseph and the Amazing Technicolor Raincoat* with Lisa. Okay, Tiger?

90   LISA: Sure. It's *Dreamcoat*.

PAUL: What?

LISA: Nothing. I think I see my leg warmers. (*She goes to pick them up and an odd-looking trophy.*)

PAUL: What's that?

LISA: It's stupid. I was second best at the dance recital, so they gave me this thing. It's stupid.

95   PAUL: Lisa.

LISA: What?

PAUL: What did you want to talk about?

LISA: Nothing.

PAUL: Was it about my missing your recital? I'm really sorry, Tiger. I would have liked to have been here.

100   LISA: That's okay.

PAUL: Honest?

LISA: Daddy, you're prostrastinating.

PAUL: I'm procrastinating. Sit down. Let's talk. How's school?

LISA: Fine.

105   PAUL: You like it?

LISA: Yup.

PAUL: You looking forward to camp this summer?

LISA: Yup.

PAUL: Is Daria Feldman going back?

110   LISA: Nope.

PAUL: Why not?

LISA: I don't know. We can go home now. Honest, my foot doesn't itch anymore.

PAUL: Lisa, you know what you do in business when it seems like there's nothing left to say? That's when you really start talking. Put a bid on the table.

LISA: What's a bid?

115   PAUL: You tell me what you want and I'll tell you what I've got to offer. Like Monopoly. You want Boardwalk, but I'm only willing to give you the Railroads. Now, because you are my daughter I'd throw in Water Works and Electricity. Understand, Tiger?

LISA: No. I don't like board games. You know, Daddy, we could get Space Invaders for our home for thirty-five dollars. In fact, we could get an Osborne System for two thousand. Daria Feldman's parents . . .

PAUL: Daria Feldman's parents refuse to talk to Daria, so they bought a computer to keep Daria busy so they won't have to speak in Yiddish. Daria will probably grow up to be a homicidal maniac lesbian prostitute.

LISA: I know what the word prostitute means.

PAUL: Good. (*Pause.*) You still haven't told me about school. Do you still like your teacher?

120   LISA: She's okay.

PAUL: Lisa, if we're talking try to answer me.

LISA: I am answering you. Can we go home now, please?

PAUL: Damn it, Lisa, if you want to talk to me . . . Talk to me!

LISA: I can't wait till I'm old enough so I can make my own money and never have to see you again. Maybe I'll become a prostitute.

125   PAUL: Young lady, that's enough.

LISA: I hate you, Daddy! I hate you! (*She throws her trophy into the trash bin.*)

PAUL: What'd you do that for?

LISA: It's stupid.

PAUL: Maybe I wanted it.

130   LISA: What for?

PAUL: Maybe I wanted to put it where I keep your dinosaur and the picture you made of Mrs. Kimbel with the chicken pox.

LISA: You got mad at me when I made that picture. You told me I had to respect Mrs. Kimbel because she was my teacher.

PAUL: That's true. But she wasn't my teacher. I liked her better with the chicken pox. (*Pause.*) Lisa, I'm sorry. I was very wrong to miss your recital, and you don't have to become a prostitute. That's not the type of profession Miss Judy has in mind for you.

LISA: (*Mumbles*) No.

135   PAUL: No. (*Pause.*) So Talia Robbins is really happy her father moved out?

LISA: Talia Robbins picks open the eighth-grade lockers during gym period. But she did that before her father moved out.

PAUL: You can't always judge someone by what they do or what they don't do. Sometimes you come home from dancing school and run upstairs and shut the door, and when I finally get to talk to you, everything is "okay" or "fine." Yup or nope?

LISA: Yup.

PAUL: Sometimes, a lot of times, I come home and fall asleep in front of the television. So you and I spend a lot of time being a little scared of each other. Maybe?

140 LISA: Maybe.

PAUL: Tell you what. I'll make you a tender offer.

LISA: What?

PAUL: I'll make you a tender offer. That's when one company publishes in the newspaper that they want to buy another company. And the company that publishes is called the Black Knight because they want to gobble up the poor little company. So the poor little company needs to be rescued. And then a White Knight comes along and makes a bigger and better offer so the shareholders won't have to tender shares to the Big Black Knight. You with me?

LISA: Sort of.

145 PAUL: I'll make you a tender offer like the White Knight. But I don't want to own you. I just want to make a much better offer. Okay?

LISA: (Sort of understanding) Okay. (Pause. They sit for a moment.) Sort of, Daddy, what do you think about? I mean, like when you're quiet what do you think about?

PAUL: Oh, business usually. If I think I made a mistake or if I think I'm doing okay. Sometimes I think about what I'll be doing five years from now and if it's what I hoped it would be five years ago. Sometimes I think about what your life will be like, if Mount Saint Helen's will erupt again. What you'll become if you'll study penmanship or word processing. If you speak kindly of me to your psychiatrist when you are in graduate school. And how the hell I'll pay for your graduate school. And sometimes I try and think what it was I thought about when I was your age.

LISA: Do you ever look out your window at the clouds and try to see which kinds of shapes they are? Like one time, honest,

I saw the head of Walter Cronkite in a flower vase. Really! Like look don't those kinda look like if you turn it upside down, two big elbows or two elephant trunks dancing?

PAUL: Actually still looks like Walter Cronkite in a flower vase to me. But look up a little. See the one that's still moving? That sorts looks like a whale on a thimble.

150 LISA: Where?

PAUL: Look up to your right.

LISA: I don't see it. Where?

PAUL: The other way.

LISA: Oh, yeah! There's the head and there's the stomach. Yeah! (*Lisa picks up her trophy.*) Hey, Daddy.

155 PAUL: Hey, Lisa.

LISA: You can have this thing if you want it. But you have to put it like this, because if you put it like that it is gross.

PAUL: You know what I'd like? So I can tell people who come into my office why I have this gross stupid thing on my shelf, I'd like it if you could show me your dance recital.

LISA: Now?

PAUL: We've got time. Mother said she won't be home till late.

160 LISA: Well, Daddy, during a lot of it I freeze and the big girl in front dances.

PAUL: Well, how 'bout the number you were doing when I walked in?

LISA: Well, see, I have parts for a lot of people in that one, too.

PAUL: I'll dance the other parts.

LISA: You can't dance.

165 PAUL: Young lady, I played Yvette Mimieux in a *Hasty Pudding* Show.

LISA: Who's Yvette Mimieux?

PAUL: Watch more television. You'll find out. (*Paul stands up.*) So I'm ready. (*He begins singing.*) "Nothing could be finer than to be in Carolina."

LISA: Now I go. In the morning. And now you go. Dum-da.

PAUL: (*Obviously not a tap dancer*) Da-da-dum.

170 LISA: (*Whines*) Daddy!

PAUL: (*Mimics her*) Lisa! Nothing could be finer . . .

LISA: That looks dumb.

PAUL: Oh, yeah? You think they do this better in *The Amazing Minkcoat?* No way! Now you go — da da da dum.

LISA: Da da da dum.

175 PAUL: If I had Aladdin's lamp for only a day, I'd make a wish . . .

LISA: Daddy, that's maudlin!

PAUL: I know it's maudlin. And here's what I'd say:

LISA AND PAUL: I'd say that "nothing could be finer than to be in Carolina in the moooooooooooornin'."

Milcha Sanchez-Scott, 1955–

The Cuban
Swimmer 1984

CHARACTERS

Margarita Suárez, *the swimmer*
Eduardo Suárez, *her father, the coach*
Simón Suárez, *her brother*
Aída Suárez, *her mother*
Abuela, *her grandmother*
Voice of Mel Munson
Voice of Mary Beth White
Voice of Radio Operator

SETTING: *The Pacific Ocean between San Pedro and Catalina Island.*

TIME: *Summer.*
Live conga drums can be used to punctuate the action of the play.

SCENE I

Pacific Ocean. Midday. On the horizon, in perspective, a small boat enters upstage left crosses to upstage right, and exits. Pause. Lower on the horizon, the same boat, in larger perspective, enters upstage right, crosses and exits upstage left. Blackout.

SCENE 2

Pacific Ocean. Midday. The swimmer, Margarita Suárez, is swimming. On the boat following behind her are her father, Eduardo Suárez, holding a megaphone, and Simón her brother, sitting on top of the cabin with his shirt off, punk sunglasses on, binoculars hanging on his chest.

EDUARDO: (*Learning forward, shouting in time to Margarita's swimming*) Uno, dos, uno, dos. Y uno, dos . . keep your shoulders parallel to the water.

SIMÓN: I'm gonna take these glasses off and look straight into the sun.

EDUARDO: (*Through megaphone*) Muy bien, muy bien . . . but punch those arms in, baby.

SIMÓN: (*Looking directly at the sun through binoculars*) Come on, come on, zap me. Show me something. (*He looks behind at the shoreline and ahead at the sea.*) Stop! Stop, Papi! Stop!

(*Aída Suárez and Abuela, the swimmer's mother and grandmother, enter running from the back of the boat.*)

5   **AÍDA AND ABUELA:** Qué? Qué es?

AÍDA: Es un shark?

EDUARDO: Eh?

ABUELA: Que es un shark dicen?

(*Eduardo blows whistle. Margarita looks up at the boat.*)

SIMÓN: No, Papi, no shark, no shark. We've reached the halfway mark.

10   **ABUELA:** (*Looking into the water*) A dónde está?

AÍDA: It's not in the water.

ABUELA: Oh, no? Oh, no?

AÍDA: No! A poco do you think they're gonna have signs in the water to say you are halfway to Santa Catalina? No. It's done very scientific. A ver, hijo, explain it to your grandma.

SIMÓN: Well, you see, Abuela — (*He points behind.*) There's San Pedro. (*He points ahead.*) And there's Santa Catalina. Looks halfway to me.

(*Abuela shakes her head and is looking back and forth, trying to make the decision, when suddenly the sound of a helicopter is heard.*)

15   **ABUELA**: (*Looking up*) Virgencita de la Caridad del Cobre. *Qué es eso?*

(*Sound of helicopter gets closer. Margarita looks up.*)

MARGARITA: *Papi, Papi!*

(*A small commotion on the boat, with Everybody pointing at the helicopter above. Shadows of the helicopter fall on the boat. Simón looks up at it through binoculars.*)

Papi—qué es? What is it?

EDUARDO: (*Through megaphone*) Uh . . . uh . . . uh, *un momentico* . . . *mi hija*. . . . Your *papi's* got everything under control, understand? Uh . . . you just keep stroking. And stay . . . uh . . . close to the boat.

SIMÓN: Wow, *Papi!* We're on TV, man! Holy Christ, we're all over the fucking U.S.A.! It's Mel Munson and Mary Beth White!

AÍDA: *Por Dios!* Simón, don't swear. And put on your shirt.

(*Aída fluffs her hair, puts on her sunglasses and waves to the helicopter. Simón leans over the side of the boat and yells to Margarita.*)

20   **SIMÓN**: Yo, Margo! You're on TV, man.

EDUARDO: Leave your sister alone. Turn on the radio.

MARGARITA: *Papi! Qué está pasando?*

ABUELA: *Que es la televisión dicen?* (*She shakes her head.*) *Porque como yo no puedo ver nada sin mis espejuelos.*

(*Abuela rummages through the boat, looking for her glasses. Voices of Mel Munson and Mary Beth White are heard over the boat's radio.*)

MEL'S VOICE: As we take a closer look at the gallant crew of *La Havana* . . . and there . . . yes, there she is . . . the little Cuban swimmer from Long Beach, California, nineteen-year-old Margarita Suárez. The unknown swimmer is our Cinderella entry . . . a bundle of tenacity, battling her way through the choppy, murky waters of the cold Pacific to reach the Island of Romance . . . Santa Catalina . . . where should she be the first to arrive, two thousand dollars and a gold cup will be waiting for her.

25   **AÍDA**: Doesn't even cover our expenses.

ABUELA: *Qué dice?*

EDUARDO: Shhhh!

MARY BETH'S VOICE: This is really a family effort, Mel, and—

MEL'S VOICE: Indeed it is. Her trainer, her coach, her mentor, is her father, Eduardo Suárez. Not a swimmer himself, it says here, Mr. Suárez is head usher of the Holy Name Society and the owner-operator of Suárez Treasures of the Sea and Salvage Yard. I guess it's one of those places—

30 **MARY BETH'S VOICE:** If I might interject a fact here, Mel, assisting in this swim is Mrs. Suárez, who is a former Miss Cuba.

MEL'S VOICE: And a beautiful woman in her own right. Let's try and get a closer look.

(*Helicopter sound gets louder. Margarita, frightened, looks up again.*)

MARGARITA: *Papi!*

EDUARDO: (*Through megaphone*) *Mi hija,* don't get nervous . . . it's the press. I'm handling it.

AÍDA: I see how you're handling it.

35 **EDUARDO:** (*Through megaphone*) Do you hear? Everything is under control. Get back into your rhythm. Keep your elbows high and kick and kick and kick and kick . . .

ABUELA: (*Finds her glasses and puts them on*) *Ay sí, es la televisión* . . . (*She points to helicopter.*) *Qué lindo mira* . . . (*She fluffs her hair, gives a big wave.*) *Aló América! Viva mi Margarita, viva todo los Cubanos en los Estados Unidos!*

AÍDA: *Ay por Dios,* Cecilia, the man didn't come all this way in his helicopter to look at you jumping up and down, making a fool of yourself.

ABUELA: I don't care. I'm proud.

AÍDA: He can't understand you anyway.

40 **ABUELA:** *Viva* . . . (*She stops.*) *Simón, comóse dice viva?*

SIMÓN: Hurray.

ABUELA: Hurray for *mi Margarita y* for all the Cubans living *en* the United States, *y un abrazo* . . . *Simón, abrazo* . . .

SIMÓN: A big hug.

ABUELA: *Sí,* a big hug to all my friends in Miami, Long Beach, Union City, except for my son Carlos, who lives in New York in sin! He lives . . . (*She crosses herself.*) in Brooklyn with a Puerto Rican woman in sin! *No decente* . . .

45 SIMÓN: Decent.

ABUELA: Carlos, *no decente*. This family, *decente*.

AÍDA: Cecilia, *por Dios.*

MEL'S VOICE: Look at that enthusiasm. The whole family has turned out to cheer little Margarita on to victory! I hope they won't be too disappointed.

MARY BETH'S VOICE: She seems to be making good time, Mel.

50 MEL'S VOICE: Yes, it takes all kinds to make a race. And it's a testimonial to the all-encompassing fairness ... the greatness of this, the Wrigley Invitational Women's Swim to Catalina, where among all the professionals there is still room for the amateurs ... like these, the simple people we see below us on the ragtag *La Havana*, taking their long-shot chance to victory. *Vaya con Dios!*

(Helicopter sound fading as family, including Margarita, watch silently. Static as Simón turns radio off. Eduardo walks to bow of boat, looks out on the horizon.)

EDUARDO: *(To himself)* Amateurs.

AÍDA: Eduardo, that person insulted us. Did you hear, Eduardo? That he called us a simple people in a ragtag boat? Did you hear ...?

ABUELA: *(Clenching her fist at departing helicopter)* Mal-Rayo los parta!

SIMÓN: *(Same gesture)* Asshole!

(Aída follows Eduardo as he goes to side of boat and stares at Margarita.)

55 AÍDA: This person comes in his helicopter to insult your wife, your family, your daughter ...

MARGARITA: *(Pops her head out of the water)* Papi?

AÍDA: Do you hear me, Eduardo? I am not simple.

ABUELA: *Sí.*

AÍDA: I am complicated.

60 ABUELA: *Sí, demasiada complicada.*

AÍDA: Me and my family are not so simple.

SIMÓN: Mom, the guy's an asshole.

ABUELA: *(Shaking her fist at helicopter)* Asshole!

AÍDA: If my daughter was simple, she would not be in that water swimming.

65 MARGARITA: Simple? Papi ...?

AÍDA: *Ahora,* Eduardo, this is what I want you to do. When we get to Santa Catalina, I want you to call the TV station and demand an apology.

EDUARDO: *Cállete mujer! Aquí mando yo.* I will decide what is to be done.

MARGARITA: *Papi,* tell me what's going on.

EDUARDO: Do you understand what I am saying to you, Aída?

70　SIMÓN: (*Leaning over side of boat, to Margarita*) Yo Margo! You know that Mel Munson guy on TV? He called you a simple amateur and said you didn't have a chance.

ABUELA: (*Leaning directly behind Simón.*) *Mi hija, insultó a la familia. Desgraciado!*

AÍDA: (*Leaning in behind Abuela*) He called us peasants! And your father is not doing anything about it. He just knows how to yell at me.

EDUARDO: (*Through megaphone*) Shut up! All of you! Do you want to break her concentration. Is that what you are after? Eh?

(*Abuela and Aída, and Simón shrink back. Eduardo paces before them.*)

Swimming is rhythm and concentration. You win a race *aquí.* (*Pointing to his head.*) Now . . . (*To Simón*) you, take care of the boat, Aída *y Mama* . . . do something. Anything. Something practical.

(*Abuela and Aída get on knees and pray in Spanish.*)

Hija, give it everything, eh? . . . *por la familia. Uno . . . dos. . . .* You must win.

(*Simón goes into cabin. The prayers continue as lights change to indicate bright sunlight, later in the afternoon.*)

SCENE 3

Tableau for a couple of beats. Eduardo on bow with timer in one hand as he counts strokes per minute. Simón is in the cabin steering, wearing his sunglasses, baseball cap on backward. Abuela and Aída are at the side of the boat, heads down, hands folded, still muttering prayers in Spanish.

AÍDA AND ABUELA: (*Crossing themselves*) *En el nombre del Padre, del Hijo y del Espíritu Santo amén.*

EDUARDO: (*Through megaphone*) You're stroking seventy-two!

SIMÓN: (*Singing*) Mama's stroking, Mama's stroking seventy-two. . . .

EDUARDO: (*Through megaphone*) You comfortable with it?

5   **SIMÓN:** (*Singing*) Seventy-two, seventy-two, seventy-two for you.

AÍDA: (*Looking at the heavens*) Ay, Eduardo, *ven acá*, we should be grateful that *Nuestro Señor* gave us such a beautiful day.

ABUELA: (*Crosses herself*) *Si, gracias a Dios.*

EDUARDO: She's stroking seventy-two, with no problem. (*He throws a kiss to the sky*). It's a beautiful day to win.

AÍDA: *Qué hermoso!* So clear and bright. Not a cloud in the sky. *Mira! Mira!* Even rainbows on the water . . . a sign from God.

10   **SIMÓN:** (*Singing*) Rainbows on the water . . . you in my arms . . .

ABUELA AND EDUARDO: (*Looking the wrong way.*) *Dónde?*

AÍDA: (*Pointing toward Margarita*) There, dancing in front of Margarita, leading her on . . .

EDUARDO: Rainbows on . . . *Ay coño!* It's an oil slick! You . . . you . . . (*To Simón.*) Stop the boat. (*Runs to bow, yelling.*) Margarita! Margarita!

(*On the next stroke, Margarita comes up all covered in black oil.*)

MARGARITA: *Papi! Papi* . . . !

(*Everybody goes to the side and stares at Margarita, who stares back. Eduardo freezes.*)

15   **AÍDA:** *Apúrate*, Eduardo, move . . . what's wrong with you . . . *no me oíste*, get my daughter out of the water.

EDUARDO: (*Softly*) We can't touch her. If we touch her, she's disqualified.

AÍDA: But I'm her mother.

EDUARDO: Not even by her own mother. Especially by her own mother. . . . You always want the rules to be different for you, you always want to be the exception. (*To Simón.*) And you . . . you didn't see it, eh? You were playing again?

SIMÓN: *Papi*, I was watching . . .

20   **AÍDA:** (*Interrupting*) Pues, do something Eduardo. You are the big coach, the monitor.

SIMÓN: Mentor! Mentor!

EDUARDO: How can a person think around you? (*He walks off to bow, puts head in hands.*)

ABUELA: (*Looking over side*) *Mira como todos los* little birds are dead. (*She crosses herself.*)

AÍDA: Their little wings are glued to their sides.

25   **SIMÓN:** Christ, this is like the La Brea tar pits.

AÍDA: They can't move their little wings.

ABUELA: *Esa niña tiene que moverse.*

SIMÓN: Yeah, Margo, you gotta move, man.

(*Abuela and Simón gesture for Margarita to move. Aída gestures for her to swim.*)

ABUELA: *Anda niña, muévete.*

30   **AÍDA:** Swim, *hija,* swim or the *aceite* will stick to your wings.

MARGARITA: *Papi?*

ABUELA: (*Taking megaphone*) Your *papi* say "move it!"

(*Margarita with difficulty starts moving.*)

ABUELA, AÍDA AND SIMÓN: (*Laboriously counting*) *Uno, dos* . . . *uno, dos* . . . *anda* . . . *uno, dos.*

EDUARDO: (*Running to take megaphone from Abuela*) *Uno, dos* . . .

(*Simón races into cabin and starts the engine. Abuela, Aída and Eduardo count together.*)

35   **SIMÓN:** (*Looking ahead*) *Papi,* it's over there!

EDUARDO: Eh?

SIMÓN: (*Pointing ahead and to the right*) It's getting clearer over there.

EDUARDO: (*Through megaphone*) Now pay attention to me. Go to the right.

(*Simón, Abuela, Aída and Eduardo all lean over side. They point ahead and to the right, except Abuela, who points to the left.*)

FAMILY: (*Shouting together*) *Para yá! Para yá!*

(*Lights go down on boat. A special light on Margarita, swimming through the oil, and on Abuela, watching her.*)

40   **ABUELA:** *Sangre de mi sangre,* you will be another to save us. En Bolondron, where your great-grandmother Luz Suárez was born, they say one day it rained blood. All the people, they run into their houses. They cry, they pray, *pero* your great-grandmother Luz she had *cojones* like a man. She run outside. She look straight at the sky. She shake her fist. And she

say to the evil one, "*Mira . . . (Beating her chest) coño, Diablo, aquí estoy si me quieres.* " And she open her mouth, and she drunk the blood.

(*Blackout.*)

SCENE 4

Lights up on boat. Aída and Eduardo are on deck watching Margarita swim. We hear the gentle, rhythmic lap, lap, lap of the water, then the sound of inhaling and exhaling as Margarita's breathing becomes louder. Then Margarita's heartbeat is heard, with the lapping of the water and the breathing under it. These sounds continue beneath the dialogue to the end of the scene.

AÍDA: *Dios mío.* Look how she moves through the water. . . .

EDUARDO: You see, it's very simple. It is a matter of concentration.

AÍDA: The first time I put her in water she came to life, she grew before my eyes. She moved, she smiled, she loved it more than me. She didn't want my breast any longer. She wanted the water.

EDUARDO: And of course, the rhythm. The rhythm takes away the pain and helps the concentration.

(*Pause. Aída and Eduardo watch Margarita.*)

5   AÍDA: Is that my child or a seal. . . .

EDUARDO: Ah, a seal, the reason for that is that she's keeping her arms very close to her body. She cups her hands, and then she reaches and digs, reaches and digs.

AÍDA: To think that a daughter of mine . . .

EDUARDO: It's the training, the hours in the water. I used to tie weights around her little wrists and ankles.

AÍDA: A spirit, an ocean spirit, must have entered my body when I was carrying her.

10   EDUARDO: (*To Margarita*) Your stroke is slowing down.

(*Pause. We hear Margarita's heartbeat with the breathing under, faster now.*)

AÍDA: Eduardo, that night, the night on the boat . . .

EDUARDO: Ah, the night on the boat again . . . the moon was . . .

AÍDA: The moon was full. We were coming to America. . . . *Qué romantico.*

(*Heartbeat and breathing continue.*)

EDUARDO: We were cold, afraid, with no money, and on top of everything, you were hysterical, yelling at me, tearing at me with your nails. (*Opens his shirt, points to the base of his neck.*) Look, I still bear the scars . . . telling me that I didn't know what I was doing . . . saying that we were going to die. . . .

15 AÍDA: You took me, you stole me from my home . . . you didn't give me a chance to prepare. You just said we have to go now, now! Now, you said. You didn't let me take anything. I left everything behind. . . . I left everything behind.

EDUARDO: Saying that I wasn't good enough, that your father didn't raise you so that I could drown you in the sea.

AÍDA: You didn't let me say even a good-bye. You took me, you stole me, you tore me from my home.

EDUARDO: I took you so we could be married.

AÍDA: That was in Miami. But that night on the boat, Eduardo. . . . We were not married, that night on the boat.

20 EDUARDO: *No pasó nada!* Once and for all get it out of your head, it was cold, you hated me, and we were afraid. . . .

AÍDA: *Mentiroso!*

EDUARDO: A man can't do it when he is afraid.

AÍDA: Liar! You did it very well.

EDUARDO: I did?

25 AÍDA: *Sí.* Gentle. You were so gentle and then strong . . . my passion for you so deep. Standing next to you . . . I would ache . . . looking at your hands I would forget to breathe, you were irresistible.

EDUARDO: I was?

AÍDA: You took me into your arms, you touched my face with your fingertips . . . you kissed my eyes . . . *la esquina de la boca y* . . .

EDUARDO: *Sí, sí,* and then . . .

AÍDA: I look at your face on top of mine, and I see the lights of Havana in your eyes. That's when you seduced me.

30   **EDUARDO**: Shhh, they're gonna hear you.

(*Lights go down. Special on Aída.*)

AÍDA: That was the night. A woman doesn't forget those things . . . and later that night was the dream . . . the dream of a big country with fields of fertile land and big, giant things growing. And there by a green, slimy pond I found a giant pea pod and when I opened it, it was full of little, tiny baby frogs.

(*Aída crosses herself as she watches Margarita. We hear louder breathing and heartbeat.*)

MARGARITA: Santa Teresa. Little flower of God, pray for me. San Martín de Porres, pray for me. Santa Rosa de Lima, *Virgencita de la Caridad del Cobre,* pray for me. . . . Mother pray for me.

SCENE 5

Loud howling of wind is heard, as lights change to indicate unstable weather, fog and mist. Family on deck, braced and huddled against the wind. Simón is at the helm.

AÍDA: *Ay Dios mío, qué viento.*

EDUARDO: (*Through megaphone*) Don't drift out . . . that wind is pushing you out. (*To Simón.*) You! Slow down. Can't you see your sister is drifting out?

SIMÓN: It's the wind, *Papi.*

AÍDA: Baby, don't go so far. . . .

5   **ABUELA**: (*To heaven*) *Ay Gran Poder de Dios, quita este maldito viento.*

SIMÓN: Margo! Margo! Stay close to the boat.

EDUARDO: Dig in. Dig in hard. . . . Reach down from your guts and dig in.

ABUELA: (*To heaven*) *Ay Virgen de la Caridad del cobre, por lo más tú quieres a pararla.*

AÍDA: (*Putting her hand out, reaching for Margarita*) Baby, don't go far.

(*Abuela crosses herself. Action freezes. Lights get dimmer, special on Margarita. She keeps swimming, stops, starts, again, stops, then, finally exhausted, stops altogether. The boat stops moving.*)

10   **EDUARDO**: What's going on here? Why are we stopping?

SIMÓN: *Papi,* she's not moving! Yo Margo!

(*The family all run to the side.*)

EDUARDO: *Hija!* . . . *Hijita!* You're tired, eh?

AÍDA: *Por supuesto* she's tired. I like to see you get in the water, waving your arms and legs from San Pedro to Santa Catalina. A person isn't a machine, a person has to rest.

SIMÓN: Yo, Mama! Cool out, it ain't fucking brain surgery.

15 **EDUARDO**: (*To Simón*) Shut up, you. (*Louder to Margarita.*) I guess your mother's right for once, huh? . . . I guess you had to stop, eh? . . . Give your brother, the idiot . . . a chance to catch up with you.

SIMÓN: (*Clowning like Mortimer Snerd*) Dum dee dum dee dum ooops, ah shucks . . .

EDUARDO: I don't think he's Cuban.

SIMÓN: (*Like Ricky Ricardo*) Oye, Lucy! I'm home! Ba ba lu!

EDUARDO: (*Joins in clowning, grabbing Simón in a headlock*) What am I gonna do with this idiot, eh? I don't understand this idiot. He's not like us, Margarita. (*Laughing.*) You think if we put him into your bathing suit with a cap on his head . . . (*He laughs hysterically.*) You think anyone would know . . . huh? Do you think anyone would know? (*Laughs.*)

20 **SIMÓN**: (*Vamping*) Ay, mi amor. Anybody looking for tits would know.

(*Eduardo slaps Simón across the face, knocking him down. Aída runs to Simón's aid. Abuela holds Eduardo back.*)

MARGARITA: *Mía culpa! Mía culpa!*

ABUELA: *Qué dices hija?*

MARGARITA: *Papi,* it's my fault, it's all my fault. . . . I'm so cold, I can't move. . . . I put my face in the water . . . and I hear them whispering . . . laughing at me. . . .

AÍDA: Who is laughing at you?

25 **MARGARITA**: The fish are all biting me . . . they hate me . . . they whisper about me. She can't swim, they say. She can't glide. She has no grace. . . . Yellowtails, bonita, tuna, man-o'-war, snub-nose sharks, *los baracudas* . . . they all hate me . . . only the dolphins care . . . and sometimes I hear the whales crying . . . she is lost, she is dead. I'm so numb, I can't feel. *Papi! Papi!* Am I dead?

EDUARDO: *Vamos*, baby, punch those arms in. Come on . . . do you hear me?

MARGARITA: *Papi* . . . *Papi* . . . forgive me. . . .

(*All is silent on the boat. Eduardo drops his megaphone, his head bent down in dejection. Abuela, Aída, Simón, all leaning over the side of the boat. Simón slowly walks away.*)

AÍDA: *Mi hija, qué tienes?*

SIMÓN: Oh, Christ, don't make her say it. Please don't make her say it.

30 ABUELA: Say what? *Qué cosa?*

SIMÓN: She wants to quit, can't you see she's had enough?

ABUELA: *Mira, para eso. Esta niña* is turning blue.

AÍDA: *Oyeme, mi hija.* Do you want to come out of the water?

MARGARITA: *Papi?*

35 SIMÓN: (*To Eduardo*) She won't come out until *you* tell her.

AÍDA: Eduardo . . . answer your daughter.

EDUARDO: *Le dije* to concentrate . . . concentrate on your rhythm. Then the rhythm would carry her . . . ay, it's beautiful thing, Aída. It's like yoga, like meditation, the mind over matter . . . the mind controlling the body . . . that's how the great things in the world have been done. I wish you . . . I wish my wife could understand.

MARGARITA: *Papi?*

SIMÓN: (*To Margarita*) Forget him.

40 AÍDA: (*Imploring*) Eduardo, *por favor.*

EDUARDO: (*Walking in circles*) Why didn't you let her concentrate? Don't you understand, the concentration, the rhythm is everything. But no, you wouldn't listen. (*Screaming to the ocean.*) Goddamn Cubans, why, God, why do you make us go everywhere with our families? (*He goes to back of boat.*)

AÍDA: (*Opening her arms*) Mi hija, ven, come to Mami. (*Rocking.*) Your *mami* knows.

(*Abuela has taken the training bottle, puts it in a net. She and Simón lower it to Margarita.*)

SIMÓN: Take this. Drink it. (*As Margarita drinks, Abuela crosses herself.*)

ABUELA: *Sangre de mi sangre.*

(*Music comes up softly. Margarita drinks, gives the bottle back, stretches out her arms, as if on a cross. Floats on her back. She beings a graceful backstroke. Lights fade on boat as special lights come up on Margarita. She stops. Slowly turns over and starts to swim, gradually picking up speed. Suddenly as if in pain she stops, tries again, then stops in pain again. She becomes disoriented and falls to the bottom of the sea. Special on Margarita at the bottom of the sea.*)

45 **MARGARITA:** *Ya no puedo* . . . I can't. . . . A person isn't a machine . . . *es mi culpa* . . . Father forgive me . . . *Papi! Papi!* One, two. *Uno, dos.* (*Pause.*) *Papi! A dónde estás?* (*Pause.*) One, two, one, two. *Papi! Ay, Papi!* Where are you . . .? Don't leave me. . . . Why don't you answer me? (*Pause. She starts to swim, slowly.*) *Uno, dos, uno, dos.* Dig in, dig in. (*Stops swimming.*) *Por favor, Papi!* (*Starts to swim again.*) One, two, one, two. Kick from your hip, kick from your hip. (*Stops swimming. Starts to cry.*) Oh God, please. . . . (*Pause.*) Hail Mary, full of grace . . . dig in, dig in. . . . the Lord is with thee. . . . (*She swims to the rhythms of her Hail Mary.*) Hail Mary, full of grace . . . dig in, dig in . . . the Lord is with thee . . . dig in, dig in. . . . Blessed art thou among women. . . . *Mami,* it hurts. You let go of my hand. I'm lost. . . . And blessed is the fruit of thy womb, now and at the hour of our death. Amen. I don't want to die, I don't want to die.

(*Margarita is still swimming. Blackout. She is gone.*)

SCENE 6

Lights up on boat, we hear radio static. There is a heavy mist. On deck we see only black outline of Abuela with shawl over her head. We hear the voices of Eduardo, Aída, and Radio Operator.

EDUARDO'S VOICE: *La Havana!* Coming from San Pedro. Over.

RADIO OPERATOR'S VOICE: Right, DT6-6, you say you've lost a swimmer.

AÍDA'S VOICE: Our child, our only daughter . . . listen to me. Her name is Margarita Inez Suárez, she is wearing a black one-piece bathing suit cut high in the legs with a white racing stripe down the sides, a white bathing cap with goggles and her whole body covered with a . . . with a . . .

EDUARDO'S VOICE: With lanolin and paraffin.

5 AÍDA'S VOICE: *Sí . . . con lanolin and paraffin.*

(*More radio static. Special on Simón, on the edge of the boat.*)

SIMÓN: Margo! Yo Margo! (*Pause.*) Man don't do this. (*Pause.*) Come on. . . . Come on. . . . (*Pause.*) God, why does everything have to be so hard? (*Pause.*) Stupid. You know you're not supposed to die for this. Stupid. It's his dream and he can't even swim. (*Pause.*) Punch those arms in. Come home. Come home. I'm your little brother. Don't forget what Mama said. You're not supposed to leave me behind. *Vamos,* Margarita, take your little brother, hold his hand tight when you cross the street. He's so little. (*Pause.*) Oh, Christ, give us a sign. . . . I know! I know! Margo, I'll send you a message . . . like mental telepathy, I'll hold my breath, close my eyes, and I'll bring you home. (*He takes a deep breath; a few beats.*) This time I'll beep . . . I'll send out sonar signals like a dolphin. (*He imitates dolphin sounds.*)

(*The sound of real dolphins takes over from Simón, then fades into sound of Abuela saying the Hail Mary in Spanish, as full lights come up slowly.*)

SCENE 7

Eduardo coming out of cabin, sobbing, Aída holding him. Simón anxiously scanning the horizon. Abuela looking calmly ahead.

EDUARDO: *Es mi culpa, sí, es mi culpa.* (*He hits his chest.*)

AÍDA: *Ya, ya viejo* . . . it was my sin . . . I left my home.

EDUARDO: Forgive me, forgive me. I've lost our daughter, our sister, our granddaughter, *mi carne, mi sangre, mis ilusiones.* (*To heaven.*) *Dios mío,* take me . . . take me, I say . . . Goddammit, take me!

SIMÓN: I'm going in.

5 AÍDA AND EDUARDO: No!

EDUARDO: (*Grabbing and holding Simón, speaking to heaven*) God, take me, not my children. They are my dreams, my illusions . . . and not this one, this one is my mystery . . . he has my secret dreams. In him are the parts of me I cannot see.

(*Eduardo embraces Simón. Radio static becomes louder.*)

AÍDA: I . . . I think I see her.

SIMÓN: No, it's just a seal.

ABUELA: (*Looking out with binoculars*) Mi nietacita, dónde estás? (*She feels her heart.*) I don't feel the knife in my heart . . . my little fish is not lost.

(*Radio crackles with static. As lights dim on boat, Voices of Mel and Mary Beth are heard over the radio.*)

10   **MEL'S VOICE:** Tragedy has marred the face of the Wrigley Invitational Women's Race to Catalina. The Cuban swimmer, little Margarita Suárez, has reportedly been lost at sea. Coast Guard and divers are looking for her as we speak. Yet in spite of this tragedy the race must go on because . . .

MARY BETH'S VOICE: (*Interrupting loudly*) Mel!

MEL'S VOICE: (*Startled*) What!

MARY BETH'S VOICE: Ah . . . excuse me, Mel . . . we have a winner. We've just received word from Catalina that one of the swimmers is just fifty yards from the breakers . . . it's, oh, it's . . . Margarita Suárez!

(*Special on family in cabin listening to radio.*)

MEL'S VOICE: What? I thought she died!

(*Special on Margarita, taking off bathing cap, trophy in hand, walking on the water.*)

15   **MARY BETH'S VOICE:** Ahh . . . unless . . . unless this is a tragic . . . No . . . there she is, Mel. Margarita Suárez! The only one in the race wearing a black bathing suit cut high in the legs with a racing stripe down the side.

(*Family cheering, embracing.*)

SIMÓN: (*Screaming*) Way to go, Margo!

MEL'S VOICE: This is indeed a miracle! It's a resurrection! Margarita Suárez, with a flotilla of boats to meet her, is now walking on the waters, through the breakers ... onto the beach, with crowds of people cheering her on. What a jubilation! This is a miracle!

(*Sound of crowds cheering. Lights and cheering sounds fade.*)

(*Blackout*)

Jane Martin

Beauty 2000

CHARACTERS
Carla
Bethany

An apartment. Minimalist set. A young woman, Carla, on the phone.

CARLA: In love with me? You're in love with me? Could you describe yourself again? Uh-huh. Uh-huh. And you spoke to me? (*A knock at the door.*) Listen, I always hate to interrupt a marriage proposal, but . . . could you possibly hold that thought? (*Puts phone down and goes to door. Bethany, the same age as Carla, and a friend is there. She carries the sort of Mideastern lamp we know of from Aladdin.*)

BETHANY: Thank God you were home. I mean, you're not going to believe this!

CARLA: Somebody on the phone. (*Goes back to it.*)

BETHANY: I mean, I just had a beach urge, so I told them at work my uncle was dying . . .

5   **CARLA:** (*Motions to Bethany for quiet*) And you were the one in the leather jacket with the tattoo? What was the tattoo? (*Carla again asks Bethany, who is gesturing wildly that she should hang up, to cool it.*) Look, a screaming eagle from shoulder to shoulder, maybe. There were a lot of people in the bar.

BETHANY: (*Gesturing and mouthing*) I have to get back to work.

CARLA: (*On phone*) See, the thing is, I'm probably not going to marry someone. I can't remember . . . particularly when I don't drink. Sorry. Sorry. Sorry. (*She hangs up.*) Madness.

BETHANY: So I ran out to the beach . . .

CARLA: This was some guy I never met who apparently offered me a beer . . .

10   **BETHANY:** . . . low tide and this . . . (*The lamp.*) . . . was just sitting there, lying there . . .

CARLA: . . . and he tracks me down . . .

BETHANY: . . . on the beach, and I lift this lid thing . . .

CARLA: . . . and seriously proposes marriage.

BETHANY: . . . and a genie comes out.

15   **CARLA:** I mean, that's twice in a . . . what?

BETHANY: A genie comes out of this thing.

CARLA: A genie?

BETHANY: I'm not kidding, the whole Disney kind of thing, swirling smoke, and then this twenty-foot-high, see-through guy in like an Arabian outfit.

CARLA: Very funny.

20   **BETHANY:** Yes, funny, but twenty feet high! I look up and down the beach, I'm alone. I don't have my pepper spray or my hand alarm. You know me, when I'm petrified I joke. I say his voice is too high for Robin Williams, and he says he's a castrati. Naturally. Who else would I meet?

CARLA: What's a castrati?

BETHANY: You know . . .

(*The appropriate gesture.*)

CARLA: Bethany, dear one, I have three modeling calls. I am meeting Ralph Lauren!

BETHANY: Okay, good. Ralph Lauren. Look, I am not kidding!

25   **CARLA:** You're not kidding what?!

BETHANY: There is a genie in this thingamajig.

CARLA: Uh-huh. I'll be back around eight.

BETHANY: And he offered me *wishes!*

CARLA: Is this some elaborate practical joke because it's my birthday?

30   **BETHANY:** No, happy birthday, but I'm like crazed because I'm on this deserted beach with a twenty-foot-high, see-through genie, so like sarcastically . . . you know how I need a new car . . . I said fine, gimme 25,000 dollars . . .

CARLA: On the beach with the genie?

BETHANY: Yeah, right, exactly, and it rains down out of the sky.

CARLA: Oh sure.

BETHANY: (*Pulling a wad out of her purse*) Count it, those are thousands. I lost one in the surf.

(*Carla sees the top bill. Looks at Bethany, who nods encouragement. Carla thumbs through them.*)

35   **CARLA:** These look real.

BETHANY: Yeah.

CARLA: And they rained down out of the sky?

BETHANY: Yeah.

CARLA: You've been really strange lately, are you dealing?

40   **BETHANY:** Dealing what, I've even given up chocolate.

CARLA: Let me see the genie.

BETHANY: Wait, wait.

CARLA: Bethany, I don't have time to screw around. Let me see the genie or let me go on my appointments.

BETHANY: Wait! So I pick up the money . . . see, there's sand on the money . . . and I'm like nuts so I say, you know, "Okay, look, ummm, big guy, my uncle is in the hospital" . . . because as you know when I said to the people at work my uncle was dying, I was on one level telling the truth although it had nothing to do with the beach, but he was in Intensive Care after the accident, and that's on my mind, so I say, okay, Genie, heal my uncle . . . which is like impossible given he was hit by two trucks, and the genie says, "Yes, Master" . . . like they're supposed to say, and he goes into this like kind of whirlwind, kicking up sand and stuff, and I'm like, "Oh my God" and the air clears, and he bows, you know, and says, "It is done, Master," and I say, "Okay, whatever-you-are, I'm calling on my cell phone," and I get it out and I get this doctor who is like dumbstruck who says my uncle came to, walked out of Intensive Care and left the hospital! I'm not kidding, Carla.

45 CARLA: On your mother's grave?

BETHANY: On my mother's grave.

(*They look at each other.*)

CARLA: Let me see the genie.

BETHANY: No, no look, that's the whole thing . . . I was just, like, reacting, you know, responding, and that's already two wishes . . . although I'm really pleased about my uncle, the $25,000 thing, I could have asked for $10 million, and there is only one wish left.

CARLA: So ask for $10 million.

50 BETHANY: I don't think so. I don't think so. I mean, I gotta focus in here. Do you have a sparkling water?

CARLA: No. Bethany, I'm missing Ralph Lauren now. Very possibly my one chance to go from catalogue model to the very, very big time, so, if you are joking, stop joking.

BETHANY: Not joking. See, see, the thing is, I know what I want. In my guts. Yes. Underneath my entire bitch of a life is this unspoken, ferocious, all-consuming urge . . .

CARLA: (*Trying to get her to move this along*) Ferocious, all-consuming urge . . .

BETHANY: I want to be like you.

55 CARLA: Me?

BETHANY: Yes.

CARLA: Half the time you don't even like me.

BETHANY: Jealous. The ogre of jealousy.

CARLA: You're the one with the $40,000 job straight out of school. You're the one who has published short stories. I'm the one hanging on by her fingernails in modeling. The one who has creeps calling her on the phone. The one who had to have a nose job.

60 BETHANY: I want to be beautiful.

CARLA: You are beautiful.

BETHANY: Carla, I'm not beautiful.

CARLA: You have charm. You have personality. You know perfectly well you're pretty.

BETHANY: "Pretty," see, that's it. Pretty is the minor leagues of beautiful. Pretty is what people discover about you after they know you. Beautiful is what knocks them out across the room. Pretty, you get called a couple of times a year; *beautiful* is twenty-four hours a day.

65 CARLA: Yeah? So?

BETHANY: So?! We're talking *beauty* here. Don't say "So?" Beauty is the real deal. You are the center of any moment of your life. People stare. Men flock. I've seen you get offered discounts on makeup for no reason. Parents treat beautiful children better. Studies show your income goes up. You can have sex anytime you want it. Men have to know me. That takes up to a year. I'm continually horny.

CARLA: Bethany, I don't even like sex. I can't have a conversation without men coming on to me. I have no privacy. I get hassled on the street. They start pressuring me from the beginning. Half the time, it never occurs to them to start with a conversation. Smart guys like you. You've had three long-term relationships, and you're only twenty-three. I haven't had one. The good guys, the smart guys are scared to death of me. I'm surrounded by male bimbos who think a preposition is when you go to school away from home. I have no woman friends except you. I don't even want to talk about this!

BETHANY: I knew you'd say something like this. See, you're "in the club" so you can say this. It's the way beauty functions as an elite. You're trying to keep it all for yourself.

CARLA: I'm trying to tell you it's no picnic.

70 BETHANY: But it's what everybody wants. It's the nasty secret at large in the world. It's the unspoken tidal desire in every room and on every street. It's the unspoken, the soundless whisper . . . millions upon millions of people longing hopelessly and forever to stop being whatever they are and be beautiful, but the difference between those ardent multitudes and me is that I have a goddamn genie and one more wish!

CARLA: Well, it's not what I want. This is me, Carla. I have never read a whole book. Page six, I can't remember page four. The last thing I read was *The Complete Idiot's Guide to WordPerfect*. I leave dinner parties right after the dessert because I'm out of conversation. You know the dumb blond joke about the application where it says, "Sign here," she put Sagittarius? I've done that. Only beautiful guys approach me, and that's because they want to borrow my eye shadow. I barely exist outside a mirror! You don't want to *be me.*

BETHANY: None of you tell the truth. That's why you have no friends. We can all see you're just trying to make us feel better because we aren't in your league. This only proves to me it should be my third wish. Money can only buy things. Beauty makes you the center of the universe.

(*Bethany picks up the lamp.*)

CARLA: Don't do it. Bethany, don't wish it! I am telling you you'll regret it.

(*Bethany lifts the lid. There is a tremendous crash, and the lights go out. Then they flicker and come back up, revealing Bethany and Carla on the floor where they have been thrown by the explosion. We don't realize it at first, but they have exchanged places.*)

CARLA/BETHANY: Oh God.

75 BETHANY/CARLA: Oh God.

CARLA/BETHANY: Am I bleeding? Am I dying?

BETHANY/CARLA: I'm so dizzy. You're not bleeding.

CARLA/BETHANY: Neither are you.

BETHANY/CARLA: I feel so weird.

80 CARLA/BETHANY: Me too. I feel . . . (*Looking at her hands.*) Oh, my God, I'm wearing your jewelry. I'm wearing your nail polish.

BETHANY/CARLA: I know I'm over here, but I can see myself over there.

CARLA/BETHANY: I'm wearing your dress. I have your legs!!

BETHANY/CARLA: These aren't my shoes. I can't meet Ralph Lauren wearing these shoes!

CARLA/BETHANY: I wanted to be beautiful, but I didn't want to be you.

85 BETHANY/CARLA: Thanks a lot!!

CARLA/BETHANY: I've got to go. I want to pick someone out and get laid.

BETHANY/CARLA: You can't just walk out of here in my body!

CARLA/BETHANY: Wait a minute. Wait a minute. What's eleven eighteenths of 1,726?

BETHANY/CARLA: Why?

90   CARLA/BETHANY: I'm a public accountant. I want to know if you have my brain.

BETHANY/CARLA: One hundred thirty-two and a half.

CARLA/BETHANY: You have my brain.

BETHANY/CARLA: What shade of Rubenstein lipstick does Cindy Crawford wear with teal blue?

CARLA/BETHANY: Raging Storm.

95   BETHANY/CARLA: You have my brain. You poor bastard.

CARLA/BETHANY: I don't care. Don't you see?

BETHANY/CARLA: See what?

CARLA/BETHANY: We both have the one thing, the one and only thing everybody wants.

BETHANY/CARLA: What is that?

CARLA/BETHANY: It's better than beauty for me; it's better than

100   brains for you.

BETHANY/CARLA: What? What?!

CARLA/BETHANY: Different problems.

Blackout.

Credits

Resetting.

ANTON CHEKHOV, "The Cherry Orchard" by Anton Chekhov, from *Chekhov Volume I: Four Plays*, translated by Carol Rocamora. Reprinted by permission of Smith and Kraus Inc.

JANE MARTIN, "Beauty" by Jane Martin. Copyright © 2001 by Alexander Speer, Trustee. Reprinted with permission. All rights reserved. All inquiries concerning rights should be addressed to Alexander Speer, Actors Theatre of Louisville, 316 West Main Street, Louisville, KY 40202.

MILCHA SANCHEZ-SCOTT, "The Cuban Swimmer" by Milcha Sanchez-Scott. Copyright © 1984, 1988 by Milcha Sanchez-Scott. Reprinted by permission of William Morris Agency, Inc. on behalf of the Author. CAUTION: Professionals and amateurs are hereby warned that "The Cuban Swimmer" is subject to a royalty. It is fully protected under the copyright laws of the United States of America and of all countries covered by the International Copyright Union (including the Dominion of Canada and the rest of the British Commonwealth), the Berne Convention, the Pan-American Copyright Convention and the Universal Copyright Convention as well as all countries with which the United States has reciprocal copyright relations. All rights, including professional/amateur stage rights, motion picture, recitation, lecturing, public reading, radio broadcasting, television, video or sound recording, all other forms of mechanical or electronic reproduction, such as CD-ROM, CD-I, information storage and retrieval systems and photocopying, and the rights of translation into foreign languages, are strictly reserved. Particular emphasis is laid upon the matter of readings, permission for which must be secured from the Author's agent in writing. Inquiries concerning rights should be addressed to: William Morris Agency, Inc., 1325 Avenue of the Americas, New York, NY 10019, Attn: Catherine Bennett.

William Shakespeare, Footnotes and Commentary from *The Tragedy of Othello* by William Shakespeare, edited by Alvin Kernan, copyright © 1963 by Alvin Kernan. Used by permission of Dutton Signet, a division of Penguin Group (USA) Inc.

SAM SHEPARD, "True West" from *Seven Plays* by Sam Shepard. Used by permission of Bantam Books, a division of Random House, Inc.